T5-ARJ-825

BUSINESS TRAVELLER'S HANDBOOK

A Guide To
THE MIDDLE EAST

Other areas covered by books in the BUSINESS TRAVELLER'S HANDBOOK series:

Latin America
Europe
Africa
Asia, Australia and the Pacific
The United States and Canada

BUSINESS TRAVELLER'S HANDBOOK

A Guide To THE MIDDLE EAST

Editor: Jane Walker
Associate Editor: Mark Ambrose

Facts On File, Inc.
460 Park Avenue South
New York, N.Y. 10016

BUSINESS TRAVELLER'S HANDBOOK
A Guide To
THE MIDDLE EAST

Library of Congress Cataloging in Publication Data
Main entry under title:

Business Traveller's Handbook, the Middle East.

Includes index.
1. Near East—Description and travel—Guide-books.
2. Near East—Commerce—Handbooks, manuals, etc.
I. Walker, Jane, 1956– II. Ambrose, Mark, 1955–
DS43.B87 915.6′044 80-39527
ISBN 0-87196-343-4
ISBN 0-87196-323-X (pbk.)

Printed in the United States of America

10 9 8 7 6 5 4 3 2 1

Acknowledgements

For their help and cooperation in the compilation of this handbook, the publishers wish to acknowledge: Aeroflot; Air Canada; Air France; Air India; Algerian Embassy, London; ALIA, Royal Jordanian Airlines; Alitalia; American Express; Arab-British Joint Chamber of Commerce, London; Arab League Office, London; Avis Rent a Car; Embassy of the State of Bahrain, London; Bank of America NT & SA; Bank of Nova Scotia; Barclays Bank International Ltd; British Airways; British Bank of the Middle East; British Caledonian; British Overseas Trade Board, Export Services & Promotions Division; Central Information Services, The Thomas Cook Group Ltd; Chase Manhattan Bank NA; Citibank NA; Committee for Middle East Trade, London; Cyprus High Commission, London; Diners Club; Embassy of the Arab Republic of Egypt, London; Egypt Air; Financial Times Ltd; Gulf Air; Hertz Rent a Car; Hilton International Hotels; Holiday Inns (UK) Ltd; Institute for International Research; Iranian Embassy, London; Iraqi Embassy, London; Embassy of Israel, London; Israel Information, London; Japan Airlines (JAL); Embassy of the Hashemite Kingdom of Jordan, London; KLM, Royal Dutch Airlines; Embassy of the State of Kuwait, London; Lebanese Embassy, London; Embassy of the Libyan Arab Republic, London; Lloyds Bank International; Lufthansa; Middle East Airlines; Middle East Association, London; Midland Bank International; Moroccan Embassy, London; National Westminster Bank; Pakistan International Airlines; Pan Am; Qantas Airways; Qatar Embassy, London; Royal Bank of Canada; Royal Embassy of Saudi Arabia, London; Saudi Arabian Airlines; Scandinavian Airlines System (SAS); Sheraton Hotels & Motor Inns; Sudan Embassy, London; Swissair; Embassy of the Syrian Arab Republic, London; Trans World Airlines (TWA); Tunisian Embassy, London; Turkish Embassy, London; Embassy of the United Arab Emirates, London; United Nations London Information Centre; Embassy of the United States of America, London; Embassy of the Yemen Arab Republic, London.

Special thanks are also due to Edmund Swinglehurst and Len Crockford of the Thomas Cook Group Ltd and to Steve Warshal of the Institute for International Research.

CONTENTS

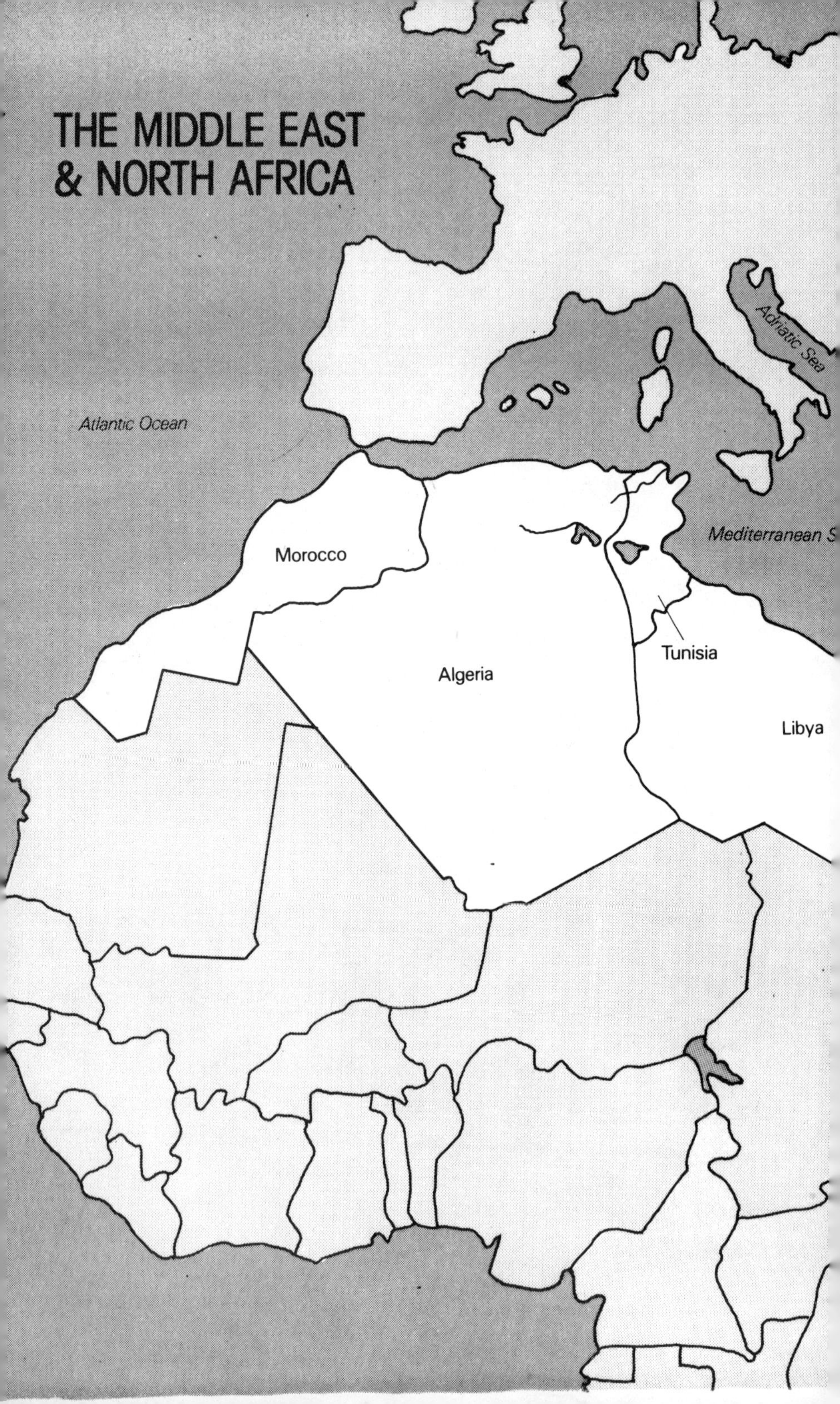
THE MIDDLE EAST
& NORTH AFRICA
Atlantic Ocean
Adriatic Sea
Mediterranean S
Morocco
Algeria
Tunisia
Libya

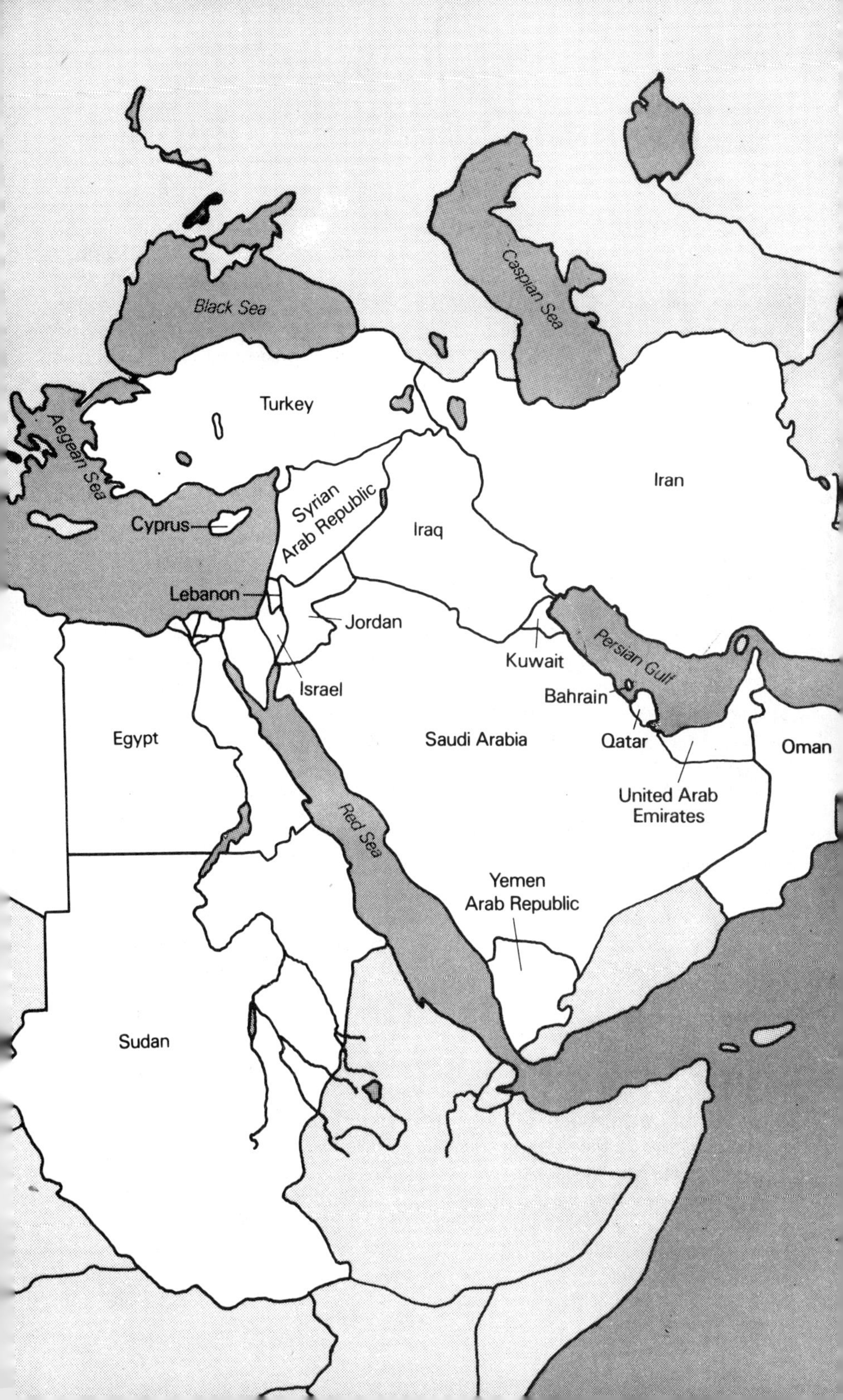
Black Sea
Caspian Sea
Aegean Sea
Turkey
Iran
Syrian Arab Republic
Iraq
Cyprus
Lebanon
Jordan
Kuwait
Persian Gulf
Israel
Bahrain
Egypt
Saudi Arabia
Qatar
Oman
United Arab Emirates
Red Sea
Yemen Arab Republic
Sudan

INTRODUCTION

The Business Traveller's Handbook: The Middle East is one of a series of travel guides designed especially for today's business traveller. Each handbook in the series covers one of the world's regions, country by country, giving detailed information as well as practical advice and useful suggestions. The needs of the business traveller, so different from those of the tourist, have been thoroughly researched and considered. The result is a handbook which is not merely a handy travel guide but, more importantly, an invaluable reference book for use by any traveller at home or abroad.

Today, business travellers are visiting the Middle East in increasing numbers and the importance of this region in the modern world cannot be overstated. The enormous wealth of the Middle East and its emergence as the world's foremost producer of oil have made it of vital importance to every industrial nation. The Middle East is, in fact, one of the most frequently visited areas by business travellers the world over.

Yet to many people the Middle East remains a region of unknown dimensions with a way of life in sharp contrast to that of the Western world. Business customs and practices, traditions and habits are quite different, making the need for information about the countries in this region even greater. The information contained in this handbook will dispel the fears and apprehensions of the first-time visitor and provides valuable, up-to-date facts and figures about an area of the world which has undergone dramatic change in the past two decades.

This handbook contains extensive chapters on twenty-one countries of the Middle East and includes those North African countries which, together with Cyprus and Turkey, are generally considered to be part of the Middle East by virtue of their geographical location and historical development. Each chapter is arranged in a similar manner to facilitate the reader's quest for information, and reference material, important statistics and useful addresses are clearly distinguished from the informative descriptions of the economy, geography, business climate and places of historical interest of each country. A detailed map can be found at the beginning of each chapter, showing the country's main cities and towns, major roads, railways and airports.

General information about the individual country is given at the beginning of every chapter – basic facts about the size and population, religion, language and government followed by descriptions of the geography, climate and agriculture of the country. The subsequent section on the economy will be of considerable use to all business travellers, providing valuable information about the general economic climate within the country. Basic economic data are combined with concise details of foreign trade, major industries, development programmes, inflation, balance of payments and much more.

A most useful feature in every chapter is entitled 'How To Get There' and covers the various means of travel available to the country from Europe, North America and others parts of the world, together with information about visas and other entry requirements, health regulations, customs formalities, regulations governing the import of commercial samples and duty-free allowances – in short, everything which the business visitor needs to know when planning a trip abroad. Prior knowledge of such details can save both time and trouble on arrival.

'Practical Information for the Visitor' deals with all those details and useful hints which make any stay in a foreign country more comfortable and enjoyable. The information given in this section ranges from the addresses of major domestic and foreign commercial banks, details of the electricity supply and system of weights and measures used, names of the principal newspapers and trade publications, use of commercial advertising on radio and television, to advice about medical care, details of telephone and telex services, public holidays, internal flights, car hire and tipping. A list of useful addresses includes those of foreign embassies and consulates, cultural organisations, local tourist information centres and major international travel agents.

'Business Information' is an invaluable part of each chapter, outlining general business conditions with an analysis of the trade opportunities for foreign suppliers and manufacturers. The list of companies and organisations dealing with advertising, shipping, insurance and translation are useful for reference both at home and while travelling abroad, and chambers of commerce, major government ministries, trade and professional associations are also included.

Although business visitors have little time for sightseeing and recreational activities, a visit to some of the more beautiful and unusual attractions within a country can be both profitable and relaxing. A brief resumé of the principal historical sights and attractions of the major cities and towns in each of the twenty-one countries is given, as are suggestions for short trips and excursions.

A selection of the better hotels in each city includes details of location in relation to the city centre and airport, and of the facilities and services offered by each hotel. Particular attention has been paid to those which are of use to the business visitor, such as secretarial and translation services, public telex facilities, availability of audio-visual equipment and the capacity of conference and banquet rooms. Restaurants and nightclubs are listed, together with sports and social clubs, cultural attractions and local sporting events. A selection of the best buys available in local shops and markets will make the task of gift-buying much easier.

A special chapter on 'Muslim Social Customs' is essential reading for anyone visiting the Middle East, particularly for the first time. A general explanation of the Islamic faith and its effect on the Muslim's way of life, together with practical information about general etiquette and practices, goes a long way towards helping the non-Muslim visitor adapt to conditions in the Middle East. Those customs and mores which are peculiar to an individual country are dealt with separately within each chapter. Another important feature of the handbook is 'Health Information', which looks at the problems and health risks most visitors are likely to encounter in a tropical climate, and offers advice and suggestions on how to remain in good health.

The appendices to this book include an international cost of living index, and two useful tax charts giving details of personal and corporate tax rates of more than 50 countries throughout the world. Other handy reference material includes metric and imperial conversion tables, a centigrade/fahrenheit chart and a map of the world time zones. An index to places mentioned in the text can be found at the end of the handbook.

No aspect of a business visit has been overlooked in the compilation of the information included in this handbook, and the presentation and arrangement of the various sections within each chapter make this a readable guide as well as a source of information for quick and easy reference purposes.

Much of the information contained in this guide is subject to constant change and it is widely accepted that the regulations governing visa and health requirements are frequently altered and revised. Whilst every effort has been made to ensure that the information given is both accurate and up-to-date, the publishers are unable to assume any responsibility in this connection. If in any doubt, visitors are advised to contact the nearest diplomatic mission or tourist office of the country they intend to visit.

MUSLIM SOCIAL CUSTOMS

It is essential for any business visitor to the Middle East to have some knowledge of the social customs and mores which are particular to that part of the world. The majority of countries dealt with in this handbook are either Muslim states or have a large Muslim population, and an understanding of the Muslim way of life is of fundamental importance to anyone intending to visit the Middle East, particularly for the first time. Many of the customs and practices encountered by travellers to Arab countries seem strange and often contrary to their own beliefs, and visitors often find themselves in an embarrassing situation where they have offended their hosts quite innocently and unwittingly. Such a situation could easily be avoided if the visitor had some previous knowledge of the Muslim traditions and practices which play such an important role in all aspects of life in the Middle East.

The information given here is intended primarily as a guide to visitors to the Middle East, and may also serve to clear up many of the misunderstandings and queries which occur time and time again in the mind of the non-Muslim. We have dealt with the most common beliefs and practices which, in general, apply to all Muslim countries, but it is important to remember that every country also has its own particular customs and mores which may differ from those stated here. These have been dealt with separately in a section on social customs under the individual country headings in the handbook.

Muslims, or Muhammadans, belong to the Islamic faith and observe, to varying degrees, the following basic tenets of Islam: profession of the faith; prayer (five times a day); almsgiving; fasting; and pilgrimage or *Hajj*. Faith and the ritual accompanying such faith are extremely important to the Muslim believer. It is from the teachings of Islam that most of the Arab customs and practices are derived, and the non-Muslim may find these easier to understand when seen in the light of their traditional significance.

The month of *Ramadan* is perhaps the best known of all the Muslim religious festivals – this is the major event of the Muslim calendar and is a time of fasting for all Muslims. Strict Muslims must refrain from eating, drinking and smoking during daylight hours and non-Muslims are also expected to respect this tradition and refrain from such practices, at least while in public places. (In some countries meals are served during the daytime to non-Muslims in their hotel rooms.) It is important not to infringe the laws of *Ramadan* as this would cause considerable offence to many Muslims and may be punishable in some of the stricter Muslim countries.

Business visitors will find that the month of *Ramadan* is best avoided in most parts of the Middle East as business comes to a virtual standstill in many cities, particularly during the 3–4 day festival of *Eid-el-Fitr* at the end of the month, and it is difficult to accomplish much work during this period.

The subject of 'alcohol' is extremely important in relation to the Middle East although the mention of the actual word is virtually taboo in some countries in the area. This is a matter where visitors should be certain to observe the laws and practices of the individual country, even if this requires a great amount of effort and strong will. Infringement of the laws relating to alcohol is certainly a punishable offence in most Muslim states, and quite frankly it is not worth the risk and could easily jeopardise a valuable business relationship.

Generally speaking, Muslims consider that alcohol damages personal health and efficiency and diminishes the emotional control of the individual – for this reason alcohol is prohibited under Islamic law. Alcohol is readily available in few Muslim countries although it can be purchased and consumed by foreigners in hotels and restaurants in the more liberal countries. Visitors should acquaint themselves with the alcohol laws of a particular country before commencing their visit, and it is best to avoid the temptation of smuggling alcohol past the customs authorities on arrival. More detailed information can be found within the individual chapters in the handbook.

The Arabs are noted for their generous hospitality but non-Muslims are often intimidated by the rituals of receiving and entertaining guests within the Muslim world. There is no reason to feel ill at ease with these practices if the following basic points of general etiquette are observed.

Handshaking is mandatory on arrival and departure and an Arab may often keep hold of your hand while engaging you in conversation. The most common greeting used in the Middle East is '*Salaam Alaykum*', meaning 'Peace be with you' – to which the reply is '*Wa Alaykum As-Salaam*', meaning 'And on you be peace'. The correct form of address when speaking to a male is '*Sayyid*' and to a female '*Sayida*' or '*Sitt*'. In Egypt and the eastern Arab states, an alternative form of address is '*Abu*' (father of) or '*Umm*' (mother of) followed by the name of the eldest son. In some areas it has become common practice to use the name of the eldest daughter if she is the firstborn.

When calling upon a Muslim, never make the sole of your foot plainly visible as this is considered rude. When offered anything receive it in the right hand, and always give with the right hand. If coffee is offered it should be accepted, and the cup should be taken and given back with the right hand. It is preferable to drink at least two cups – if no further coffee is required simply shake the cup when returning it to your host or hostess and this will signify your refusal. When returning hospitality to an Arab, remember that the consumption of alcohol and pig meat is forbidden by Muslim law and neither of these should be offered.

Arabs place great importance on punctuality and expect visitors to be on time for an appointment. However, do not expect to be seen immediately as few business people work to a tight schedule and you may have to wait some time.

Female business visitors to the Middle East will encounter more difficulty in adapting to the Muslim way of life than their male counterparts. Women are viewed in a special way in the Arab world and the Western visitor will notice a definite discrimination against women, although this is less severe in countries such as Egypt and Jordan.

Women should dress soberly and avoid clothes which might be considered in any way revealing. In Saudi Arabia this is particularly important and it is advisable to adopt a form of dress similar to that of Saudi women themselves. This may seem burdensome and even unfair, but will avoid any instances of embarrassment or offence and, in fact, this is the coolest way to dress in very hot climates. In the more conservative countries women may find themselves excluded from certain business and social functions and, although this often seems unreasonable, there is nothing one can do other than accept this practice. In general Arab men do not talk about their womenfolk and would not expect, for example, to be asked about the health of their wife. However, despite certain disadvantages and discriminatory practices, women can and do function perfectly well in the Middle East.

The various social customs and practices outlined here are not intended as a definitive summary of the Muslim code of behaviour. We have tried to highlight the more important points of etiquette and law which are most likely to affect the non-Muslim visitor. Observance of these few rules should ensure an enjoyable and trouble-free visit and, more importantly, should enable the development of lasting and profitable relationships with Arab business contacts who, for their part, will take note of and appreciate the respect shown for their way of life.

HEALTH INFORMATION

Any traveller visiting one of the world's tropical regions will be exposed to health risks which are rarely found to exist in the more temperate areas of Europe and North America. These risks may take the form of epidemic diseases, many of which have now been eradicated or brought under control through a wide-scale vaccination programme and against which a number of vaccinations are readily available. Yet, more commonly, these risks are the minor complaints caused by a drastic change of climate, general insanitary conditions, a change of diet or the lack of immunity against local diseases and infections.

Whilst good health can never be totally guaranteed in a different climate and environment, there are many steps which you can take personally to ensure that you remain in good health and enjoy a visit abroad which is free from illness and health problems. Precautions such as vaccinations are the more obvious ones, and indeed entry regulations into many tropical countries require that the visitor be in possession of certain international certificates of vaccination. General caution about food and drink, the water supply and the type of clothing suitable for a hot climate is not so obvious, and it is these small points which the traveller often forgets about and suffers from in the long run.

The advice and recommendations listed here apply in general to most tropical regions. Where a more uncommon disease is endemic in a particular country, travellers should seek additional advice from their doctor or should contact the nearest diplomatic mission of that country or the World Health Organisation (WHO). Travellers suffering from a chronic illness or with a personal medical history of illness may need to take extra precautions and, once again, the advice of a doctor should be sought. The information given here is aimed at the traveller who already enjoys good health and who should, if the advice given here is needed, remain that way.

Vaccination Schedule

The schedules listed below are intended for international travel. Schedule I is designed for those travellers who have sufficient time to complete the course – it provides the maximum immunity but can be modified according to individual requirements and circumstances. Schedule II gives a lesser degree of immunity but provides adequate protection for those who have to arrange a long-distance trip at short notice.

International Certificates of Vaccination are issued for smallpox, yellow fever and cholera only.

Schedule I

Week 1 Yellow fever vaccination. Available at special centres only. A certificate will only become valid ten days after the inoculation and the period of immunity is ten years.

4 Smallpox vaccination (primary or re-vaccination). Certificates become valid eight days after a primary vaccination or from the day of a re-vaccination for a period of three years.
5 Reading of smallpox vaccination.
7 TAB or T (typhoid) (1) and tetanus toxoid (1).
10 Polio (oral) vaccination (1).
13 TAB or T (typhoid) (2) and tetanus toxoid (2).
16 Polio (oral) vaccination (2).
22 Polio (oral) vaccination (3).
39 TAB or T (typhoid) (3) and tetanus toxoid (3).

Schedule II

Day 1 Yellow fever, cholera (1) and polio (oral) (1).
5 Smallpox, TAB or T (typhoid) (1) and tetanus toxoid (1).
11 Cholera (2).
13 Reading of smallpox vaccination.
28 Polio (oral) (2), TAB or T (typhoid) (2) and tetanus toxoid (2).

Malaria

Although malaria has been eradicated from many parts of the world and brought under control in others, it is still the main cause of illness and death among people living in the tropics and is the principal health hazard to visitors from malaria-free countries who have not acquired immunity from the disease. The risk of malaria varies according to altitude and temperature and does not usually occur when the mean annual temperature is less than 15.6°C/60°F.

In all there are four types of malaria bug which affect humans, and common to all of them is the fact that they are transmitted only by the female anopheline mosquito. When the mosquito bites, the malaria parasites are inserted into the bloodstream from where they spread to other parts of the body.

Preventative measures:

The anopheline mosquito usually bites only after dark and therefore you should keep well covered during this period – long sleeves and long trousers or skirts should be worn. The use of an effective insect repellent such as Flypel or Skeet-o-Stick or any other preparation containing DET (diethyl toluamide) on the exposed areas of the body, combined with protective clothing as suggested above, will considerably reduce the risk of malaria. Mosquito nets should always be used at night in unscreened bedrooms and an insecticidal spray is also useful in the bedroom.

However, the most successful and effective means of prevention is the anti-malarial tablet or prophylactic. Most of these are taken on a daily basis throughout the stay in the malarial area, for one week prior to the visit and for at least 28 days after departure from the risk area. Some tablets need only be taken once or twice a week but it is generally easier to remember to take a daily tablet, and the consequences of forgetting one daily tablet are less serious than if the weekly tablet is forgotten. (The drugs mentioned below are manufactured under a variety of names, some of which are listed in brackets.)

Proguanil (Paludrine or Chlorguanide) is among the most effective tablets and is taken daily as described above. Weekly tablets include Pyrimethamine (Daraprim), Chloroquine (Aralen, Avlocor, Nivaquine, Resochin) and Amodiaquine (Camoquin, Flavoquine). In their recommended doses Proguanil, Pyrimethamine and Chloroquine are considered safe during pregnancy. However, those prophylactics which contain sulphonamides should be avoided during pregnancy.

The main symptoms of malaria are fever, enlargement of the spleen and progressive anaemia caused by the destruction of the red blood cells. If, despite taking anti-malarial tablets, you develop any of these symptoms you should consult a doctor immediately. The incubation period of the disease is 10–14 days and it is essential that prophylactics are taken for at least 28 days after leaving a malaria area. If you should fall ill a few weeks after returning home you should visit your doctor immediately and explain exactly where you have been.

Infectious Hepatitis

This is endemic throughout South America and in many parts of Africa and Asia, and is often caught by travellers to these areas. The best means of prevention is to eat only well-prepared food, avoid drinking water which you suspect may be contaminated and pay careful attention to personal hygiene. An injection of human immuno-globulin (gammaglobulin) will give added protection lasting for between 4 and 6 months. No preventative vaccine for infectious hepatitis is yet available.

Intestinal Upsets

Few travellers escape stomach upsets of one kind or another when visiting hot, tropical areas and although the result is usually an attack of diarrhoea lasting a few days, this can be very unpleasant and can prevent any business traveller from carrying out a planned schedule of meetings and visits.

Intestinal upsets are largely the result of unhygienic food preparation and general insanitary conditions, and the chances of suffering from this complaint can be reduced if the following precautions are taken:

- avoid eating uncooked vegetables, unpeeled fruit and salads.
- keep away from fly-infested restaurants and those which have a grubby appearance. Do not buy food from street vendors.
- particular care should be taken with shellfish and it is best to see them alive and make sure the cooked product is the same that you have chosen.
- tap water is safe to drink in most large cities and towns but, if in any doubt, drink only filtered or boiled water. Bottled water is usually available in those places where the water supply is considered unsafe – alternatively,

water-sterilising tablets can be used. Milk should also be boiled unless you are sure that it has been properly pasteurised. (Further information about the water supply in individual countries is given in the Medical Care section of each chapter.)

The most effective drugs against diarrhoea are Diphenoxylate with Atropine (e.g., Lomotil), Kaolin and Morphine, Paregoric and Codeine Phosphate. Travellers affected by vomiting in addition to diarrhoea should take Metoclopramide (Maxolon, Primperan, Berk) in tablet or injection form. Streptotriad tablets have proven relatively effective as an anti-diarrhoea tablet.

If you suffer a more serious outbreak of diarrhoea, accompanied by severe abdominal pain, fever and passing of blood, it is likely that you are suffering from dysentery and medical advice should be sought immediately.

Heat

Acclimatisation to high temperatures usually takes at least two weeks and most visitors, unused to working in extreme heat conditions, feel tired and apathetic. This is even more noticeable where the relative humidity is high. Drink plenty of liquids and take extra salt with your food – alternatively, additional salt can be taken in tablet or solution form but this is less effective.

It is most important to encourage perspiration by wearing clothes that will absorb sweat and therefore encourage you to sweat more. Cotton is the ideal fabric for hot climates and man-made fibres should be avoided wherever possible as they do not absorb sweat, leaving the skin permanently moist and susceptible to 'prickly heat'.

Although you may be tempted in excessive heat to take a quick dip in a freshwater lake or river, avoid doing this as the water is more than likely contaminated and there is a high risk of schistosomiasis or bilharzia.

Altitude

Visitors to high altitude areas (in general those over 3,000m/9,840ft) may be susceptible to *soroche* or mountain sickness. This can be avoided if you rest for a few hours on arrival and avoid the consumption of alcohol and greasy food. Heavy smokers should try and cut down on cigarettes while in high altitude areas.

A gentle process of acclimatisation is essential, so avoid rushing about and over-exertion of any kind – a good lesson in how to move around can be learnt from the local people. You may feel breathless and suffer from heart pounding together with insomnia, but these are general conditions mainly caused by the lack of oxygen and do not give cause for alarm.

The symptoms of *soroche* are headache, dizziness, nausea, flatulence and vomiting – pain-killers (avoid aspirin-based ones) can be taken for such headaches and anti-emetics for the vomiting. A useful form of relief which is available in most South American countries is *mate de coca*, a tea made from coca leaves.

Air Travel

Despite the comfort and ease of modern air travel, even the most experienced traveller can fall victim to a number of disorders ranging from sickness and general discomfort to the common complaint of jet-lag. There are no hard and fast rules for avoiding these problems, but the following hints and suggestions may go a long way to overcoming them and ensuring trouble-free air travel.

Air sickness is usually caused by a bumpy flight combined with excitement, worry or any form of mental strain which the traveller may be experiencing at that time. Turbulence can affect the inner ear and thus the balance mechanism of the individual, resulting in sickness. Try and avoid all greasy and fatty foods served on the aircraft and drink and smoke in moderation. Try and keep your head as still as possible.

Dehydration may occur on long flights due to the rather dry atmosphere within the aircraft cabin. Drink plenty of fluids, but avoid alcohol as this will increase dehydration rather than reduce it.

Pressurisation within an aircraft cabin differs from that at ground level and this difference can cause bodily discomfort as the gases in the body, and particularly in the intestines, expand. Avoid overeating and fizzy drinks as these will only cause the body gases to expand further. It is advisable to wear loose clothing and loose-fitting shoes or the socks provided on long-distance flights by some airlines (this will also help those who suffer from swollen feet and ankles).

The change of pressure during take-off and landing can cause a popping sensation in the ears or ear-ache and sometimes partial deafness. Repeated yawning or swallowing will overcome this. Sinus trouble is often aggravated when flying and the use of nose drops helps to alleviate this. Smokers are particularly affected by cabin pressure and the decrease in oxygen often causes headaches and dizziness. The obvious remedy is to reduce smoking and, if possible, cut it out altogether during a flight.

Jet-lag will affect any traveller on a journey involving a change of time zone whether from east to west or vice versa. The body is programmed to a 24-hour clock and cannot immediately adjust to change where, for example, bedtime occurs several hours later or earlier than usual. Sleeping and eating habits are usually affected and travellers may also suffer from constipation. Your general alertness and reactions will be much slower, in general for a period of two to three days. It is interesting to note that the effects of jet-lag appear to be greater on west–east flights than on westbound flights as it is far more difficult to adjust to a daily routine several hours *ahead* of your habitual one.

General medical advice on the question of jet-lag is to allow a 24-hour rest period after a five-hour time change; similarly 48 hours are recommended for a ten-hour time change. On arrival try and get to bed as close as possible to your normal bedtime. Do not arrange to attend any important meetings or business functions immediately after your arrival and avoid having to make important decisions until you feel fully recovered and acclimatised to the time change.

The traveller who is continually flying all over the world is most likely to suffer from jet-lag. This, in effect, really means the business traveller and it is vital that you should give yourself time to recover from a long journey before embarking on a series of business meetings and visits.

(For detailed information regarding time changes, refer to the time zones map in the Appendices to this book.)

KEY TO SYMBOLS

Hotels

- Air conditioning in rooms
- Central heating in rooms
- Direct dial telephones in rooms
- Credit cards accepted
- FC Foreign currency exchanged
- TC Travellers' cheques exchanged
- Laundry and valet service available
- Radio in rooms
- Television in rooms
- Room service available
- 24-hour room service available
- S Secretarial services available
- Translation services available

Maps

- National boundaries
- Cease-fire lines
- Major roads
- Major railways
- △ Oilfields
- International airports

The Middle East

ALGERIA

Democratic and Popular Republic of Algeria

Size: 2,381,741 sq.km/919,594 sq. miles.

Population: 17.91 million (1977).

Distribution: 30% in urban areas.

Density: 7 persons per sq.km/20 per sq.mile.

Population Growth Rate: 3.3% p.a.

Ethnic Composition: The population of Algeria is largely of Arabo-Berber stock and includes some 70,000 Europeans, mainly French and Spanish.

Capital: Algiers Pop. 2 million (1978).

Major Cities: Oran Pop. 700,000; Constantine Pop. 600,000; Annaba Pop. 500,000.

Language: Arabic is the official language, but French is widely used in government and business circles.

Religion: Islam is the official religion and the majority of Algerians are Muslims. The European population is mainly Roman Catholic, with Protestant and Jewish minorities.

Government: Algeria gained independence from France in 1962. The country is governed by a National Revolutionary Council, presided over by the President who also heads the Cabinet of Ministers. Legislative power is held by the Assemblée Nationale Populaire. The Front de Libération Nationale (FLN) is the only recognised political party.

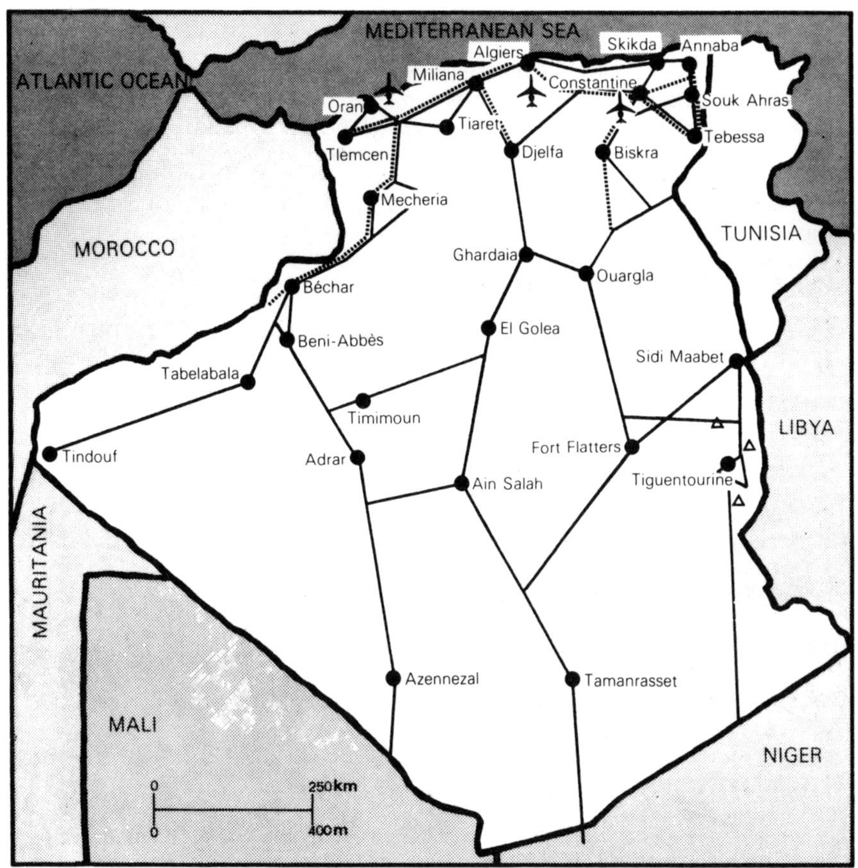

GEOGRAPHY

Algeria is bordered by Tunisia and Libya to the east, Morocco to the west and Niger, Mali and Mauritania to the south. The landscape is dominated by desert and mountains, but a wide, fertile belt (80km/50 miles wide) runs alongside the coast. The highest point in Algeria is Mount Tahat in the Sahara, which rises to a height of 3,000m/9,850ft.

Climate

Northern Algeria has a Mediterranean-type climate with average temperatures ranging from 13°C/55°F to 24°C/75°F. The temperature in winter rarely drops below 10°C/50°F. Summers are hot and humid with temperatures ranging from 27°C/80°F to 32°C/90°F. Greater variations of temperature occur south of the Saharan atlas where winter frosts are not uncommon at night. Most of the annual rainfall is during the winter months.

Agriculture

Algeria is a predominantly agricultural country with about 45% of the labour force employed in the agricultural sector. Most of the cultivable land is to be found in the northern coastlands. The former European-owned farms have now been taken over by the State and are managed by workers' committees – these account for about one-third of the total cultivable area and constitute some of the best growing land. A major land reform programme aims to increase productivity, reduce rural unemployment and increase the wages of agricultural workers.

Main Crops: wheat, barley, oats, grapes, citrus fruits, vegetables.

Mineral Resources: high-grade iron ore, phosphates, lead, zinc, antimony, oil and gas.

THE ECONOMY

Gross National Product (1976): US$15.3 billion.

Per Capita Income (1976): US$884.

Gross Domestic Product (1976): 68.7 billion Algerian dinars.

Foreign Trade (1976): Total Imports US$5.5 billion; Total Exports US$4.9 billion.

Main Trading Partners: Imports – France, West Germany, USA, Italy. Exports – USA, West Germany, France, Italy.

The Algerian economy is heavily centralised with the Government exercising control, through the Sociétés Nationales and Offices Nationales, of the key sectors of the economy such as banking, industry, mines, transport and tourism.

Since independence the economy has undergone a programme of rapid industrialisation consisting mainly of capital-intensive projects using local raw materials. Major projects include iron and steel works, oil refineries, gas liquefaction plants and the manufacture of engines, agricultural equipment and electrical goods. The industrial sector is the largest recipient of state investment and is seen as the key element in the Government's drive to achieve a minimum annual growth rate of 10% of the Gross Domestic Product.

Oil and gas are Algeria's main exports and increasing revenues from these products have enabled the Government to carry out its ambitious economic plans. However, the economy is not without its problems – large foreign debts swallow up a considerable proportion of export revenues, and there is a renewed necessity to find new and lucrative export markets for Algeria's natural gas in particular. The country's enormous reserves of natural gas could make Algeria the world's largest natural gas exporter in the 1980s.

Major Industries: oil and natural gas, food processing, textiles and clothing.

Main Commodities Traded: Imports – machinery, iron and steel, transport equipment, electrical equipment, and foodstuffs. Exports – crude oil and oil products, natural gas, iron and steel, wine, fruit, vegetables, metal ores and concentrates.

Oil Production (1977): 4,287 thousand metric tons per average calendar month.

Gas Production (1977 est.): 7,900 teracalories per average calendar month.

Algeria is a member of the Organisation of African Unity, OPEC and the Arab League.

HOW TO GET THERE

Air

Algeria's main international airport is Dar el Beida which is situated about 20km/12½ miles from the centre of Algiers. There are regular flights to Algiers from most European and Middle Eastern capitals. British Caledonian (Gatwick) and Air Algérie (Heathrow) operate several flights a week between London and Algiers.

Other major airlines flying to Algeria include Aeroflot, Air France, Alitalia, Egypt Air, Iberia, Lufthansa, Sabena, Saudia, Swissair and Tunis Air. There are regular flights from several French cities, Casablanca and Tunis to Annaba, Constantine and Oran.

Flying times to Algiers: from London 3 hours; from New York 11 hours; from Sydney 24 hours.

Rail

Daily services operate between Oran (Algeria) and Casablanca (Morocco), also between Annaba and Constantine and Tunis. In addition, an overnight rail service operates between Algiers and Tunis.

Road

The main points of entry into Algeria are: from Morocco at Maghnia; from Tunisia at El Kala, Souk Ahras and Tebessa; from Libya at Fort Thiriet; from Niger at In Guezzam; from Mali at Bardj Mokhtar.

ENTRY REGULATIONS

Visas

No visa is required by passport holders of Andorra, Denmark, Egypt, Finland, France, Guinea, Iceland, Iraq, Republic of Ireland, Italy, Jordan, Kuwait, Libya, Liechtenstein, Mali, Mauritania, Monaco, Morocco, Norway, San Marino, Spain, Sudan, Sweden, Switzerland, Syria, Tunisia, United Kingdom and Yugoslavia for a stay of up to 3 months.

All other nationals require visas obtainable from Algerian diplomatic missions abroad, or (for a maximum stay of 3 months) on arrival at the airport/frontier post.

No visa is required for transit passengers. A loading or transit permit, valid for 2–5 days, can be obtained on arrival in Algeria.

Visas are not normally granted to passport holders of Chile, South Korea, Malawi, Zimbabwe-Rhodesia, South Africa, Taiwan and Vietnam. Evidence in a passport of a previous or planned visit to Israel may adversely affect the granting of a visa.

Business travellers should support their visa application with a letter from their firm giving details of the business to be undertaken and confirming financial responsibility for the applicant.

Health Regulations

An International Certificate of Vaccination against smallpox is required for entry into Algeria. Valid yellow fever and/or cholera certificates are required by those persons arriving from infected areas.

Customs

Currency: Any amount of foreign currency may be imported into Algeria provided it is declared on the currency declaration form issued on arrival. The import and export of Algerian currency is limited to 50 dinars.

Duty-free articles: 200 cigarettes or 50 cigars or 400g of tobacco, one bottle of spirits and two bottles of wine. Samples of no commercial value provided they are not in a saleable condition. Samples of value can be temporarily imported against payment of a deposit which is refunded on re-export of the samples within a given period of time.

Prohibited articles: Arms and ammunition, narcotics, pornographic literature and contraceptives.

PRACTICAL INFORMATION FOR THE VISITOR

1. Currency

Monetary Unit – Algerian dinar, divided into 100 centimes.
Notes – 5, 10, 50, 100, 500 dinars.
Coins – 1, 10, 20, 50 centimes and 1, 5 dinars.

Visitors should avoid changing large amounts of foreign currency into dinars as they may experience difficulties in reconverting the dinars at the end of a stay in Algeria.

Travellers' cheques may be changed at specified branches of the Banque Nationale d'Algérie, the Banque Extérieure d'Algérie and the Crédit Populaire d'Algérie. In addition, there are exchange facilities at the international airports, the Algiers office of Air Algérie (1 Place Maurice Audin) and the air terminal in Algiers where travellers' cheques can be cashed and foreign bank notes exchanged.

Banking Hours:
0800–1500 Saturday to Wednesday

2. Electricity Supply

127 or 220V AC.

A wide variety of plugs are in use in Algeria.

3. Weights and Measures

The metric system is in use.

4. Media

The government-controlled Radiodiffusion Télévision Algérienne (RTA) operates three radio networks broadcasting in Arabic, French and Kabyle, and a national television network. Short daily broadcasts are made in English on the radio. No commercial advertising is accepted on the radio or television.

Newspapers:

Algeria's leading national dailies are *El Moudjahid* and *El Chaab*. Provincial dailies include *El Nasr* (Constantine) and *La République* (Oran). *Algérie-Actualités* is a weekly French language newspaper published in Algiers. An important weekly magazine is *Révolution Africaine*, the organ of the Front de Libération Nationale.

5. Medical Care

Sanitation in many Algerian towns is of a poor standard and the water supply is generally unsafe to drink, particularly during the hot summer months. Visitors should drink bottled mineral water which is readily available, or ensure that tap water has been properly boiled and filtered.

6. Telephone, Telex and Postal Services

International telephone calls are often subject to lengthy delays. Telegrams can be sent from any post office between 0800 and 1900 hours. The main post office in Algiers is at 5 Boulevard Mohammed Khémisti and a 24-hour service is maintained there. International telex facilities are available and there is a public call office in the post office at the above address.

All mail to and from Algeria should be despatched by air. All parcels, including those containing sales literature and commercial samples, are likely to be subject to Customs delays. Business travellers are advised to bring such sales material with them personally when visiting Algeria.

7. Public Holidays

Fixed Holidays:

1 January	*New Year's Day*
1 May	*Labour Day*
19 June	*Anniversary of June 19th*
5 July	*Independence Day*
1 November	*Anniversary of the Revolution*
25–26 December	*Christmas*

Muslim Holidays:

These follow the Muslim calendar and occur 10–12 days earlier every year. The dates of the Muslim holidays are approximate as they depend upon sightings of the moon, and may differ by one or two days from those given below. 1981 dates are:

18 January	*Prophet's Birthday*
31 May	*Ascension of the Prophet*
31 July –2 August	*End of Ramadan*
8–10 October	*Feast of the Sacrifice*
29 October	*Muslim New Year*
7–8 November	*Ashoura*

8. Time

GMT+1 (+2 March to September)

9. Internal Transport

Air

Air Algérie operate frequent internal services from Algiers to Annaba, Constantine, El Golea, Oran, Ouargala, Tamanrasset, Touggourt and several other smaller centres.

Airline Offices in Algiers:

Air Algérie	☎ 64 24 24/8.
Air France	☎ 63 16 10.

Aeroflot	☎ 60 50 22.
British Caledonian	☎ 61 45 87/64 12 20.
Lufthansa	☎ 64 27 36.
SAS	☎ 61 18 72.
Swissair	☎ 63 33 67/9.

Rail

Travel by rail in Algeria tends to be rather slow. Daily services operate from Algiers to Oran, Bougie, Skikda, Annaba and Constantine.

Road

Most main roads in Algeria, particularly in the north, are of a good standard and a large number of Saharan tracks have been surfaced recently.

Self-drive cars are available for hire in the main cities and towns. An International Driving Licence is required.

Car-Hire Firms in Algiers:

Africar	☎ 63 45 03.
Algérie Auto Tourisme	☎ 61 64 56.
Altour	☎ 77 93 45/77 12 82.
Avis	☎ 62 85 27.

Taxis are readily available in the main centres. Meters are in use in Algiers. There is a radio-operated taxi service in Algiers – ☎ 66 33 33.

10. Tipping

Taxis – 10% of the fare.

Porters – DA2 per bag.

Airport porters – DA5 per bag.

Hotels/restaurants – a service charge is usually included or added to the bill as a separate item.

11. Social Customs

Muslims in Algeria are forbidden by their religion to drink alcohol. However, Algerian law does not prohibit the sale or consumption of alcohol, and in fact many Algerians do drink it.

Most entertaining in Algeria for business purposes takes place in hotels or restaurants, although it is not uncommon for an Algerian to entertain foreign visitors at home. Algerian women do not often participate in business functions outside of the home.

For further information, refer to page 12 under 'Muslim Social Customs'.

USEFUL ADDRESSES (GENERAL)

Embassies and Consulates

Australian Embassy, 60 Boulevard Colonel Bougara, Algiers, ☎ 60 28 04/60 19 65.

British Embassy, Résidence Cassiopée, Bâtiment B, 7 Chemin de Glycines, B.P. 43, Algiers, ☎ 60 50 38/60 54 11/60 58 31.

Canadian Embassy, 27 bis rue d'Anjou, Hydra, B.P. 225, Algiers, ☎ 60 66 11.

Dutch Embassy, 23 Chemin Cheikh Bachir Brahimi, B.P. 72, Algiers, ☎ 78 28 28/9.

French Embassy, rue Larbi Alik, Hydra, Algiers.

French Consulate, rue Gouta-Sebti, Annaba and 28 Avenue Benlouizdad, Constantine and 3 Place Cayla, Oran.

West German Embassy, 165 Chemin Laperlier, B.P. 664, Algiers, ☎ 63 48 27/63 48 45/6.

Japanese Embassy, 3 rue du Docteur Lucien Raynaud, Algiers, ☎ 60 46 45/60 55 71.

Swiss Embassy, 27 Boulevard Zirout Youcef, B.P. 482, Algiers, ☎ 63 39 02/63 83 12.

US Embassy, 4 Chemin Cheikh Bachir Brahimi, Algiers, ☎ 60 14 25/ 60 11 86/60 17 16.

US Consulate, 14 Square de Bamako, Oran, ☎ 35 55 02/35 26 65.

Other addresses

Algerian National Tourist Office, 25–27 rue Khelifa Boukhalfa, Algiers, ☎ 64 68 64.

Wagons-Lits Tourisme Authorised Representative: Sonatour, 5 Boulevard Ben Boulaid, Algiers.

BUSINESS INFORMATION

Virtually all of Algeria's imports and exports are handled by state organisations which usually buy direct from the foreign manufacturer. Government control over foreign trade has resulted in the creation of state monopolies, and Algerian business life is dominated by government-owned and -controlled organisations, known locally as *Société Nationale* or *Office National.* Although state-owned, these organisations do not have the automatic guarantee of the Government, and are required to act as ordinary commercial concerns, responsible for their own purchases and debts.

Local commercial agents and distributors are now prevented from operating in Algeria. Foreign firms wishing to do extensive business in Algeria can establish a liaison office under a resident foreign manager to deal with the various state organisations.

Import and Exchange Control Regulations

All goods are subject to import controls of one kind or another, and require an import licence and/or the visa of the state organisation holding the import monopoly. The import of luxury consumer goods is usually prohibited. The holder of an import licence will normally be able to pay for the goods in foreign currency.

Business Hours

Government Offices and State Enterprises:

Winter –	0800–1200	Saturday to
	1430–1800	Wednesday
	0800–1200	Thursday
Summer –	0800–1600	Saturday to Wednesday
	0800–1200	Thursday

The Muslim week-end (Thursday afternoon and Friday) is observed in Algeria.

Business Events

The Algiers International Trade Fair is held each year in September/October. Enquiries about the fair should be addressed to: Algiers International Trade Fair, Palais des Expositions, Pins Maritimes, B.P. 571, Algiers.

BUSINESS SERVICES

Advertising

Agence Nationale d'Edition et de Publicité (ANEP), 1 Boulevard Pasteur, Algiers (posters, slides and filmlets).

Forwarding/clearing agents (state-owned)

SONATMAG, 1 rue de Cherbourg, Algiers, ☎ 66 92 92.
CNAN, rue de Chambery, Algiers, ☎ 64 52 69.

USEFUL ADDRESSES (BUSINESS)

Institut Algérien du Commerce Extérieur (COMEX), Palais Consulaire, 6 Boulevard Amilcar Cabral, Algiers, ☎ 62 70 44/7.

Chambre de Commerce et d'Industrie d'Annaba, Palais Consulaire, 4 rue du Cenra, Annaba.

Chambre de Commerce et d'Industrie de Constantine, 2 Avenue Zebane, Constantine.

Chambre de Commerce et d'Industrie d'Oran, 8 Boulevard de la Soummam, Oran.

Ministry of Commerce, 44–46 rue Mohammed Benlouizdad, Algiers, ☎ 66 33 66.

Ministry of Foreign Affairs, 6 rue Ibn Batram el Mouradia, Algiers, ☎ 60 05 85/9.

MAJOR CITIES AND TOWNS

Algiers

Algiers is the principal commercial and administrative centre of Algeria, as well as the seat of the Government. Much of the country's intellectual and artistic life also tends to be concentrated in Algiers.

In the heart of the city lies the Kasbah, an enchanting district of narrow, winding streets throbbing with local life and colour. The old fortress is to be found here as well as the Grand Mosque and the Sidi-Abderahmane Mosque. The area around the Admiralty is the centre of modern Algiers, while to the east of the city is the fishing port and fish market – the numerous restaurants specialising in seafood dishes are to be recommended.

Higher up out of the city is the district of Mustapha Supérieur which overlooks the city and the bay. There are two museums situated here which are well worth a visit – the Bardo Museum is an eighteenth-century villa and houses extensive collections of clothing, jewellery and musical instruments, and the Stephane Gsell Museum contains examples of Islamic art and archaeology as well as some Roman relics and antiquities.

The National Museum of Fine Arts has an important collection of paintings and sculptures reputed to be one of the finest in Africa.

Dar el Beida Airport is 20km/12½ miles from the centre of Algiers.

Hotels

The Ministry of Tourism hotel classification ranges from 4 star luxury, 4 star, etc., down to 1 star.

ALETTI (4 star), rue Asselah Hocine, ☎ 63 50 40/6.
Modern hotel on the promenade, near the city's commercial centre.
Rooms: 150.
Facilities: Restaurant, bar and coffee shop. Roof-top terrace. Garden.
Services: TC accepted in payment of bills.

AURASSI (4 star luxury), Avenue Frantz Fanon, ☎ 64 82 52.
Deluxe hotel overlooking the Bay of Algiers, 10 minutes from the city centre.
Rooms: 455 ❄, ⊛, ▭, ☎.
Facilities: 3 restaurants, cafeteria, coffee shop and bars. Nightclub. Tennis, swimming, sauna, gym and Turkish baths. Service shops.
Services: TC accepted in payment of bills. ⊟ Amex and Diners Club. Translation bureau.
Conference room – max. capacity 1,100.
Banquet rooms – max. capacity 230.

ST. GEORGE (4 star luxury), 24 Avenue Souidani Boudjema, ☎ 60 87 77.
Traditional Moorish-style hotel in garden setting, 10 minutes' drive from the city centre.
Rooms: 141.
Facilities: Restaurant and bar. Open-air restaurant in summer. Swimming and tennis.
Services: TC accepted in payment of bills. ⊟ Amex and Diners Club.
Banquet room – max. capacity 300.

Restaurants

In addition to the hotel restaurants, others in Algiers include: *Alhambra*, 29 rue Ben M'Hidi Larbi; *El Baçour*, 1 rue Patrice Lumumba, ☎ 63 50 92 – Algerian; *Le Carthage*, 1 chemin des Glycines, ☎ 60 28.63; *Taverna Romana*, rue Didouche Mourad, ☎ 60 26 76; *La Pagode*, 27 rue Victor Hugo, ☎ 66 46 80; *La Roue*, rue Claude Debussy, ☎ 66 66 52.

Entertainment

The National Theatre at Place Port Said stages colourful productions by Algerian artists and visiting groups from Eastern Europe, China, Cuba and other African countries.

French and English films can be seen in the city's numerous cinemas. The Aletti Hotel has its own nightclub and other popular nightspots are the *Blue Note*, 97 rue Didouche Mourad and the *Dar El Alia* with Oriental dancing.

Shopping

There are two state-run handicraft centres in Algiers – one at the airport and the other at 2 Boulevard Khemisti. Visitors should check the prices at either of these before purchasing goods in smaller shops. Hand-made goods on sale include pottery, leatherwork, wool and goat's hair carpets and rugs, inlaid silverwork, jewellery and basketwork.

Oran

Oran is Algeria's second largest city and is built on the coastal plateau spilling out over the hills beyond. The old town dates from the eighth century and was further extended by the Andalusian Arabs and the Spaniards who occupied the city from 1509 for almost 300 years.

Historic sights within the city include the sixteenth-century Santa Cruz Fortress on the Murdjadjo overlooking the city, and the Mosque of the Pasha of Sidi El Houari which dates from the eighteenth century.

Oran Airport is 20km/12½ miles from the city centre.

Hotels

GRAND (4 star), 5 Place du Maghreb, ☎ 33 01 81.
Traditional-style hotel in the city centre.
Rooms: 66 ▥, ▭ on request, ☎, ⚠.
Facilities: Restaurant and bar. Car hire.
Services: Credit cards not accepted. Dr. on call. $, ♿.
Conference room – max. capacity 20.

LES ANDALOUSES (3 star), Oran Les Andalouses, ☎ 0 4.

ROYAL, 3 Boulevard de la Soummam, ☎ 33 31 52.

WINDSOR, 1 rue Ben M'hidi, ☎ 33 31 75.

Restaurants

Apart from the hotel restaurants, others in Oran include: *Le Belvedere*, *Le Biarritz*, *La Comette* and *El Gallo*. *The Nahawand*, *El Djazair* and *Nuits du Liban* all specialise in Arab dishes.

BAHRAIN

State of Bahrain

Size: 660 sq.km/255 sq.miles.

Population: 350,000 (1978 estimate).

Distribution: 78% in urban areas.

Density: 460 persons per sq.km/1,191 per sq.mile.

Population Growth Rate: 3.2% p.a.

Ethnic Composition: 80% of the population are Bahraini nationals, 10% are from other Arab countries, and the remainder are mainly Asians, Europeans and North Americans.

Capital: Manama Pop. 95,000.

Major Towns: Muharraq Pop. 55,000; Issa Town – new town with projected population of 35,000.

Language: 90% of the population speak Arabic. Farsi and other Asian languages are spoken in non-Arab communities. English is widely used in business circles.

Religion: The Bahrainis are Muslims, with the population equally divided between the Sunni and Shia sects.

Government: A British Protectorate until 1971, Bahrain is now governed by the Amir and a Cabinet of appointed Ministers.

Bahrain has no formal political parties.

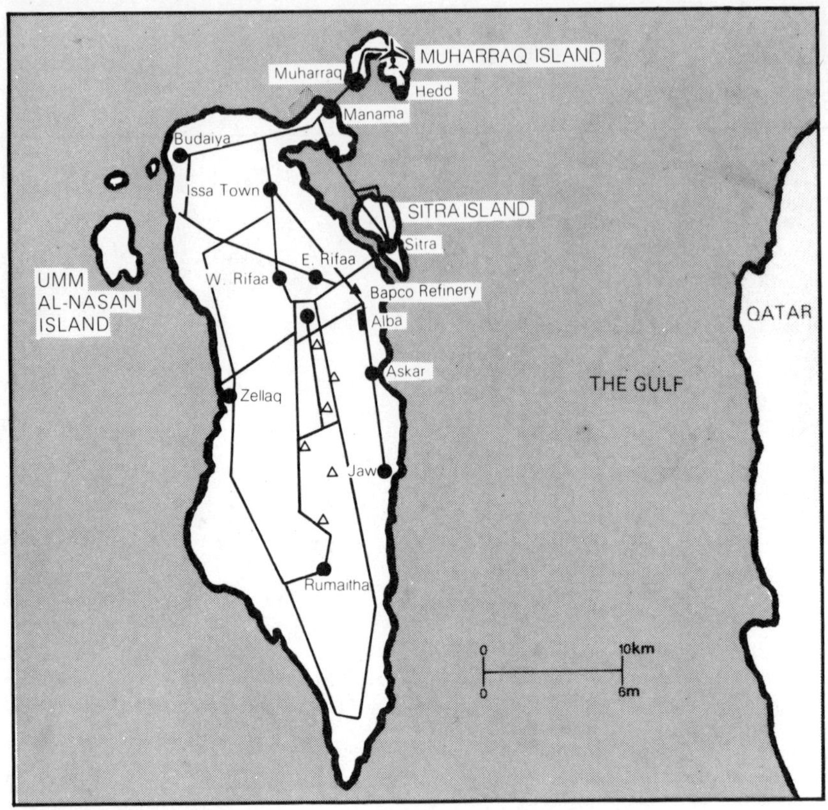

GEOGRAPHY

Bahrain consists of some thirty-five islands in the Gulf, 24km/15 miles east of Saudi Arabia. Bahrain Island is linked to Muharraq Island, the second largest in the group, by a causeway. The majority of the land area is low-lying, with a central range of hills reaching to a maximum height of 122m/400ft.

Climate

The climate is hot and humid in summer with temperatures reaching 44°C/110°F. December to March are the coolest months with temperatures ranging from 10°C/50°F to 20°C/68°F. Average annual rainfall is 7.6cm/3 inches.

Agriculture

A narrow fertile belt along the northern coast of Bahrain is virtually the only cultivable land. The fishing industry is important, and large quantities of shrimps are exported.

Main Crops: fodder crops (for cattle), vegetables and dates.

Mineral Resources: oil, gas, lime and gypsum.

THE ECONOMY

Gross National Product (1976 est.): US$1.2 billion.

Per Capita Income (1976): US$4,615.

Foreign Trade: Total Imports – US$1.16 billion (1975); Total Exports – US$1.28 billion (1976).

Main Trading Partners: Imports – UK, USA, Japan, China, Italy, West Germany. Exports – Saudi Arabia, Japan, Abu Dhabi, China, Iran.

The limited oil reserves of Bahrain, which are expected to run out at the turn of the century, have given an increased impetus to Bahrain to diversify its economy. Already a major entrepôt for Saudi Arabia and the Gulf States, a position liable to be strengthened by the completion of the causeway linking it to Saudi Arabia, Bahrain is developing a number of industries and services. The most notable advances have been made with its aluminium processing, natural gas, ship-repairing and offshore banking schemes. Alongside these schemes, the Government hopes to develop Bahrain as a tourist centre.

Oil production is controlled by the Bahrain Petroleum Company (BAPCO). The Bahraini Government has a 60% interest in the exploration and production rights, operations and related production of BAPCO.

Major Industries: oil and natural gas production, aluminium smelting, fishing.

Main Commodities Traded: Imports – machinery, foods, chemicals, industrial equipment, vehicles. Exports – crude oil, refined oil products, prawns, aluminium.

Bahrain is a member of the Arab League.

HOW TO GET THERE

Air

British Airways (Concorde) and Gulf Air operate daily services from London to Bahrain and there are regular flights from other European cities including Amsterdam, Paris, Rome, Geneva, Zurich and Vienna.

There are daily flights to Bahrain from Melbourne and Sydney and a weekly flight from Perth. Bahrain is also linked with a number of other places in the Far East and Asia including Bangkok, Singapore, Kuala Lumpur, Bombay, Hong Kong, Calcutta, Delhi and Manila.

Middle East Airlines operate a daily service from Beirut and there are regular flights from Cairo, Amman, Addis Ababa, Larnaca and several flights a day from Abu Dhabi, Dubai, Muscat, Doha, Dhahran and Kuwait.

Flying times to Bahrain: from London 8 hours (4½ hours by Concorde); from New York 12¼ hours; from Sydney 16 hours.

Muharraq International Airport is 6km/3½ miles from the centre of Manama.

ENTRY REGULATIONS

Visas

Visas are required by nationals of all countries except Kuwait, Qatar, Saudi Arabia and the United Arab Emirates. United Kingdom passport holders whose place of birth or country of residence is the UK and whose national status is 'British Subject' do not require visas.

All other nationals require visas obtainable from Bahraini diplomatic missions abroad.

Business travellers should support their visa application with documentary evidence that accommodation has been reserved, and a letter from their firm giving full details of the business to be undertaken and confirming financial responsibility for the applicant.

Visas are valid for 1 month for a stay which can vary in length up to 1 month. Visa applications for a stay of more than 1 month are usually referred.

Evidence in a passport of a previous or planned visit to Israel may adversely affect the granting of a visa.

Health Regulations

Smallpox and cholera vaccination certificates are required by all visitors. TAB (typhoid and paratyphoid) injections are recommended. Visitors arriving from infected areas are required to have yellow fever inoculations.

Customs

Currency: There are no restrictions on the amount of foreign or local currency which may be imported into or exported from Bahrain.

Duty-free articles: 400 cigarettes or 50 cigars or 8oz of tobacco, 8oz of perfume. Non-Muslims may import two bottles of wine or spirits free of duty. Personal goods and used articles. Trade samples carried by business travellers, provided they are not in a saleable condition.

Prohibited articles: Cultured, bleached or undrilled pearls produced outside the Gulf, arms and ammunition, black-listed goods on the Arab League boycott, pornographic literature.

PRACTICAL INFORMATION FOR THE VISITOR

1. Currency

Monetary Unit – Bahraini dinar (BD),
divided into 1,000 fils.

Notes – 100, 250 and 500 fils and 1, 5 and 10 dinars.
Coins – 5, 10, 25, 50 and 100 fils.

Banking Hours:
0730–1200 Saturday to Wednesday
0730–1100 Thursday

Offshore banking unit licences have been offered to more than thirty international banks by the Bahrain Monetary Agency in an attempt to establish Bahrain as a leading financial centre in the Gulf. There are approximately twenty commercial banks operating in Bahrain.

Major Commercial Banks in Manama:

Algemene Bank
P.O. Box 350, ☎ 255420.
Arab Bank
P.O. Box 395, ☎ 255988.
Bank of Bahrain and Kuwait
P.O. Box 597, ☎ 253388.
Banque de Paris et des Pays Bas
P.O. Box 5241, ☎ 253119.
Barclays Bank
P.O. Box 5120, ☎ 54046.
British Bank of the Middle East
P.O. Box 57, ☎ 255933.
Chartered Bank
P.O. Box 29, ☎ 255946.
Chase Manhattan Bank
P.O. Box 368, ☎ 251410.
Citibank
P.O. Box 548, ☎ 254755.
Crédit Suisse
P.O. Box 5100, ☎ 50677/50823.
Grindlays Bank
P.O. Box 793, ☎ 257687.
National Bank of Bahrain
P.O. Box 106, ☎ 258800.

Offshore Banks in Manama:

American Express International Banking Corporation
P.O. Box 93, ☎ 253660.
Bank of America
P.O. Box 5280, ☎ 250559.
Bank of Nova Scotia
P.O. Box 5260, ☎ 25522/256565.
Banque Nationale de Paris
P.O. Box 5253, ☎ 250321.
Canadian Imperial Bank of Commerce
P.O. Box 5484, ☎ 254385.
European Arab Bank
P.O. Box 5888, ☎ 250600.
Hongkong & Shanghai Banking Corporation
P.O. Box 5497, ☎ 252919.
Lloyds Bank International
P.O. Box 5500, ☎ 250069.
Manufacturers Hanover Trust (New York)
P.O. Box 5471, ☎ 254375.
Midland Bank Ltd
P.O. Box 5675, ☎ 257100.
National Westminster Bank
P.O. Box 820, ☎ 255546.
Swiss Bank Corporation
P.O. Box 5560, ☎ 257221.

Banking and exchange operations are controlled by the Bahrain Monetary Agency, P.O. Box 27, Manama, ☎ 712657.

2. Electricity Supply

230V AC 50Hz (Awali: 120V AC 50Hz).
Plugs: 3 flat pins.

3. Weights and Measures

The metric system is used.

4. Media

Radio Bahrain broadcasts mainly in Arabic with a few hours allotted each afternoon and evening to English-language programmes. The BBC World Service can be obtained easily along with the four radio channels transmitted by ARAMCO in Dhahran. Television programmes from the Gulf States, Saudi Arabia, Britain and the United States are all shown on Bahrain Television (colour). An English-language news summary is broadcast every day at 1900 hours.

Newspapers:

Akhbar al-Khalif is the leading Arabic daily and the *Gulf Daily News* and *Gulf Weekly Mirror* are the main English-language papers.

Other weekly newspapers and magazines include *Al-Bahrain Al-Youm*, *Al Adhwaa*, *Al-Jarida Al-Rasmiya* (Official Gazette).

The Bahrain Petroleum Company publishes a weekly Arabic paper called *Al-Najma al-Usbou*. *Al-Hiya Al Tijariya* is the monthly review published by the Bahrain Chamber of Commerce and Industry.

5. Medical Care

Western-trained doctors and dentists are readily available in Manama. The main hospital is the Sulmaniya Hospital, off Sulmaniya Road, ☎ 252761. The American Mission Hospital is on Shaikh Isa al-Kabir Road, ☎ 253449 (men)/253447 (women).

The Ruyan Pharmacy in Manama, ☎ 253751, is open 24 hours a day.

Tap water is usually safe to drink but care should be taken outside the capital. Bottled water and purified 'sweet' water are readily available, the latter being cheaper and also the one preferred by many visitors.

6. Telephone, Telex and Postal Services

Direct dialling is available from Bahrain to Europe and Qatar, UAE, Kuwait, Saudi Arabia and Iran, and the international telephone service is both quick and reliable.

Useful Telephone Numbers:

Emergency	☎ 999
Directory Enquiries	☎ 181
International Telephone Bookings	☎ 151
International Telephone Enquiries	☎ 191
Telegrams	☎ 131

Most large hotels have telex facilities and there is a public telex service at the Cable & Wireless Office on Al-Khalifa Road.

The Bahrain postal service is efficient and airmail letters to Europe take 3–4 days on average. The main post office is on Al-Khalifa Road, opposite Bab al-Bahrain, and there are branch post offices in Awali, Issa Town and Muharraq.

7. Public Holidays

Fixed Holidays:

1 January	*New Year's Day*
16 December	*Ruler's Accession Day*

Muslim Holidays:

These follow the Muslim calendar and occur 10–12 days earlier every year. The dates of the Muslim holidays are approximate as they depend upon sightings of the moon, and may differ by one or two days from those given below. 1981 dates are:

18 January	*Prophet's Birthday*
31 July –2 August	*Eid el Fitr* (end of *Ramadan*)
8–10 October	*Eid el Adha*
29 October	*Muslim New Year*
7–8 November	*Ashoura*

Business life is disrupted during the month of Ramadan, and visitors are expected to observe the religious code during this period – at least in public. This includes no smoking, eating or drinking during daylight hours.

The two-week period either side of the *Eid el Adha* pilgrimage is best avoided, as accommodation and flight seats within the vicinity of Saudi Arabia are very much in demand by Muslim pilgrims at this time.

8. Time

GMT+3

9. Internal Transport

Air
Bahrain has no internal air services.

Airline Offices in Manama:

Air France	☎ 254081.
Air India	☎ 254081.
British Airways	☎ 254621.
Gulf Air	☎ 322234.
JAL	☎ 253315.
KLM	☎ 253243.
Lufthansa	☎ 251477.
Middle East Airlines	☎ 255273/257015.
Qantas	☎ 254774/255375.
Saudia	☎ 251827/255357.
Singapore Airlines	☎ 253314.
TWA	☎ 253315.
UTA	☎ 252414.

Road
Traffic travels on the right-hand side of the road.

Taxi fare rates are fixed by the Government but drivers pay little attention to these. The official rate from the airport to Manama is BD1 but a charge of BD2–3 is usually made. All fares are subject to a 50% surcharge after midnight.

Self-drive cars are available for hire. An International Driving Licence is required.

Car-Hire Firms in Manama:

Avis, c/o Bahrain International Travel	☎ 253315/6.
Gulf Car Hiring Company	☎ 713288.
Hilton Garage	☎ 255026.
Husain Ali Slaibikh	☎ 252570.

10. Tipping

Taxis – no tip.

Porters – 100 fils per bag.

Hotels/restaurants – 10% of the bill if no service charge is included.

11. Social Customs

Bahrain is a less restrictive State for the foreign visitor than many of its neighbours. With the exception of Iraq, it is the only Arab country in the Gulf where alcohol can be purchased in retail shops without a permit.

Although many Muslim customs are observed, segregation of the sexes is not really adhered to, and women visitors are not prevented from driving or taking an active part in the business community.

For further information, refer to page 12 under 'Muslim Social Customs'.

USEFUL ADDRESSES (GENERAL)

Embassies in Manama

France: Mahooz 1785/7, P.O. Box 1034, ☎ 712596.

UK: Al Mathaf Square, P.O. Box 114, ☎ 254002/253446 and 257155 (commercial).

US: Shaikh Isa Road, P.O. Box 431, ☎ 714151.

Other addresses in Manama

Australian Consulate-General, Al-Fatah Building, Al Khalifa Road, ☎ 255011.

Australian Trade Commission, Al-Moayyed Building, Government Road.

New Zealand Consulate-General, Government Road, ☎ 259890.

Ministry of Information, P.O. Box 253, Jufair Road, ☎ 8711.

Thomas Cook Travco, Unitag House, Government Road, P.O. Box 799, ☎ 257444/258000.

Tourist Information Office, Muharraq Airport, ☎ 21648.

BUSINESS INFORMATION

Bahrain's excellent communications network and sophisticated financial structure have proved attractive to foreign firms who have been encouraged to invest by the numerous incentives offered by the Bahraini Government. Any foreign company seeking a licence to operate in Bahrain requires a Bahraini agent, who can apply for such a licence on the firm's behalf. Registration in the Commercial Register is also obligatory, and this also necessitates a local agent.

The appointment of an agent is difficult as Bahrain is a very small market for some commodities, and the provision of good after-sales services is rare.

Import Regulations

Import licences are not required except for the import of alcoholic drinks, arms, ammunition and certain other specified items.

Business Hours

Government Offices: 0700–1300 Saturday to Thursday

Business Houses: 0700–1200 / 1430–1700 Saturday to Wednesday; 0700–1200 Thursday

In Bahrain the week-end begins on Thursday afternoon and continues through Friday.

BUSINESS SERVICES

Consultants

Michael Rice Group – Middle East, P.O. Box 551, Manama, ☎ 51006. (Consultants to the Government of Bahrain and to numerous local and foreign businesses trading in Bahrain and other Gulf States.)

Arab Consult, P.O. Box 551, Manama, ☎ 51006. (P.R. Consultants to the Government of Bahrain.)

Insurance

Yousef Bin Ahmed Kanoo, Kanoo Building, Al Khalifa Road, P.O. Box 45, Manama, ☎ 254081.

Shipping

GISSCO, Hasan Mansouri Organisation, P.O. Box 5185, Manama, ☎ 252214.

Bahrain International Cargo Services, P.O. Box 45, Manama, ☎ 8726.

USEFUL ADDRESSES (BUSINESS)

Bahrain Chamber of Commerce and Industry, Al-Khalifa Road, P.O. Box 248, Manama, ☎ 253749/ 250678.

Ministry of Development and Industry, Government House, Government Road, P.O. Box 235, Manama, ☎ 253361.

Ministry of Foreign Affairs, P.O. Box 547, Manama, ☎ 252800.

Ministry of Information, Jufair Road, P.O. Box 253, Manama, ☎ 8711.

Ministry of Commerce and Agriculture and Economy, P.O. Box 53, Manama, ☎ 250813.

Cable & Wireless, Mercury House, Al Khalifa Road, P.O. Box 14, Manama, ☎ 256655.

MAJOR CITY

Manama

A mixture of the old and the new, Manama is constantly changing and keeping pace with the rapidly expanding business and commercial life of Bahrain. The oldest buildings in the city date back to the eighteenth century and include the tomb of Sheikh Ahmad al-Fatih and the Fort, now the headquarters of the State Police.

The focal point of modern Manama is Sheikh Sulman Square and nearby towers the minaret of the Juma Mosque, the tallest on the island. The main government and commercial buildings are along Government Road, and the Government House and the National Bank of Bahrain buildings stand out above the rest.

One of the town's most impressive and unusual buildings is the Palace near Ghudibiya Garden. This was built in the 1930s in a 'U' shape and has a large dining hall used for state banquets.

The Bahrain Museum is on Muharraq Island, linked to Manama by a causeway. The Museum houses the findings from the various archaeological sites in Bahrain, and also contains an extensive collection of diorite seals used some 4,000 years ago by Dilmun's merchants. Magnifiers are provided in the Museum to enable visitors to examine the intricate detail of the seals.

Muharraq Airport is 6km/3½ miles from the centre of Manama.

Hotels

There is no official hotel rating system in Bahrain.

BAHRAIN HILTON, King Faisal Road, P.O. Box 1090, ☎ 250000.
Modern deluxe hotel near the city centre, 10 minutes' drive from the airport.
Rooms: 298.
Suites available.
Facilities: Restaurants, bars and 24-hour coffee shop. Swimming. Shopping arcade. Health club and sauna.
Services: TC, FC. Amex, Carte Blanche, Diners Club, Eurocard and Master Charge. Dr. on call. S.
Business services.
Conference room – max. capacity 500.
Banquet rooms – max. capacity 350.

Delmon Hotel, Government Road, P.O. Box 26, ☎ 54761.
Luxury hotel in the centre of Manama, convenient for the main business and shopping districts.
Rooms: 120 ❄, ▥, ◉, ▭, ⌧, ⚠, ㉔. Suites available.
Facilities: Restaurants, bar and cocktail bar, 24-hour coffee shop. Swimming. Travel desk. 24-hour telex service.
Services: TC, FC. ⊟ Amex and Diners Club. **S**, ♂.
Conference room – max. capacity 400. Banquet rooms – max. capacity 200.

Gulf, P.O. Box 580, ☎ 712881.
Modern hotel overlooking Quadabiya Bay, 5 minutes' drive from the centre of Manama and 8km/5 miles from the airport.
Rooms: 250 ❄, ◉, ⌧, ⚠, ㉔.
Facilities: Restaurant, bars, 24-hour coffee shop. Swimming and tennis. Service shops including hairdresser. Car hire.
Services: TC, FC. ⊟ Amex and Diners Club. **S**, ♂.
Conference room – max. capacity 200.

Middle East, Shaikh Isa Road, P.O. Box 838, ☎ 54733.
Modern first-class hotel in the centre of Manama.
Rooms: 50 ❄, ◉, ▭ on request, ⚠, ㉔.
Facilities: Restaurant and bars. Car hire. Telex service.
Services: TC, FC. ⊟ Amex. Dr. on call. **S**, ♂.

Ramada Manama, P.O. Box 5750, ☎ 58100.
Modern hotel in the city centre opposite the Guest Palace.
Rooms: 125 ❄, ◉, ▭. Suites available.
Facilities: Restaurant (lobster and seafood tank) and cocktail bar. Nightclub. Swimming.
Services: ⊟ Amex and Diners Club.

Sahara, Municipality Road, P.O. Box 839, ☎ 50850.
Modern luxury hotel in the business centre of Manama.
Rooms: 40 ❄, ◉, ▭ on request, ⌧, ⚠, ㉔. Suites available.
Facilities: Restaurant and bar. TV lounge. Car hire.
Services: TC, FC. ⊟ Amex and Diners Club. Dr. on call. **S**, ♂.

Restaurants

There are a large number of restaurants in Bahrain. Since dining out is a major feature of social life in Bahrain, it is advisable to make a table reservation in advance, especially if dining in the hotel restaurants.

Excellent service and good food are offered by many of the hotel restaurants, including: *Bazaar Grill*, Hilton Hotel, ☎ 250000; *Falcon Room*, Gulf Hotel, ☎ 712881; *Alexander Room*, Tylos Hotel, ☎ 252660.

Further suggestions for eating out in Manama include: *Keith's Restaurant*, Quadibiya Road, ☎ 713163 – French; *The Pearl Restaurant/Nightclub*, Al-Khalifa Road, ☎ 252852; *The Chinese Restaurant*, New Palace Road, Quadibiya, ☎ 713603; *Gulf Star*, Muharraq Airport, ☎ 321418; *Dreamland*, Isa al-Kabir Road, ☎ 250128 – Continental, Chinese and Indian.

Nightclubs

Juliana's, Delmon Hotel, Government Road; *Zartaji*, near the Bristol Hotel, Shaikh Isa Road; *Saasha's*, New Palace Road, Quadibiya.

Entertainment

All the major hotels in Manama have swimming pools and the Delmon, Gulf and Hilton Hotels operate swimming clubs enabling non-residents to use their facilities for a small fee. There are plenty of stretches of unspoilt sandy beach where swimming is quite safe. Shaikh Isa's private beach at Zeltaq is open to some non-Bahrainis.

The main golf course (on sand) is the *Awali Golf Club* owned by the Bahrain Petroleum Company. Camel and horse racing takes place at the race course at Saafra on the Awali Road.

The *British Club*, off the Mutanabi Road, ☎ 8245, and the *American Club* on the Quadibiya Road, ☎ 712212, both have good sports and social facilities, and temporary membership is available for overseas visitors. The *Alliance Française*, Old Palace Road, ☎ 713111, is basically a cultural organisation which organises social activities such as dances, excursions and film shows.

Shopping

Best buys: pottery, cloth, jewellery, pearls, silver, brass and copperware.

The *souks* in Manama are near to Al-Khalifa and Government Roads. Just off the main *souk* are the cloth and jewellery markets. Much of the gold jewellery is above 18 carat and is sold according to weight. Bahraini pearls are of course renowned and are often made into original and beautiful pieces of jewellery.

A large stock of English books and magazines is available at the *Family Bookshop*, Shaikh Isa al-Kabir Road, ☎ 254288.

CYPRUS

Republic of Cyprus

Size: 9,251 sq.km/3,572 sq.miles. 254 sq.km/98 sq.miles of the total area are occupied by two British Sovereign Base Areas which are outside of the territory of the Republic of Cyprus. In 1975, 3,515 sq.km/1,357 sq.miles of northern Cyprus were established as the Turkish Federated State of Cyprus.

Population: 685,000 (1978 est.) (Greek Cypriots 500,000; Turkish Cypriots 125,000).

Distribution: 42.2% in urban areas.

Density: 67 persons per sq.km/174 per sq.mile.

Population Growth Rate: 0.8% p.a.

Ethnic Composition: About 75% of the population are Greek Cypriots, 18% are Turkish Cypriots, and the remainder is made up of Armenians, Maronites, Americans and British.

Capital: *Nicosia (now divided) Pop. 145,000.

Major Towns: Limassol Pop. 75,000; *Famagusta Pop. 15,000; Larnaca Pop. 32,000; Paphos Pop. 11,500; *Kyrenia Pop. 5,000.

*Partially or wholly controlled by the Turkish-Cypriot authorities.

Language: Greek and Turkish are the two main languages. English is widely spoken.

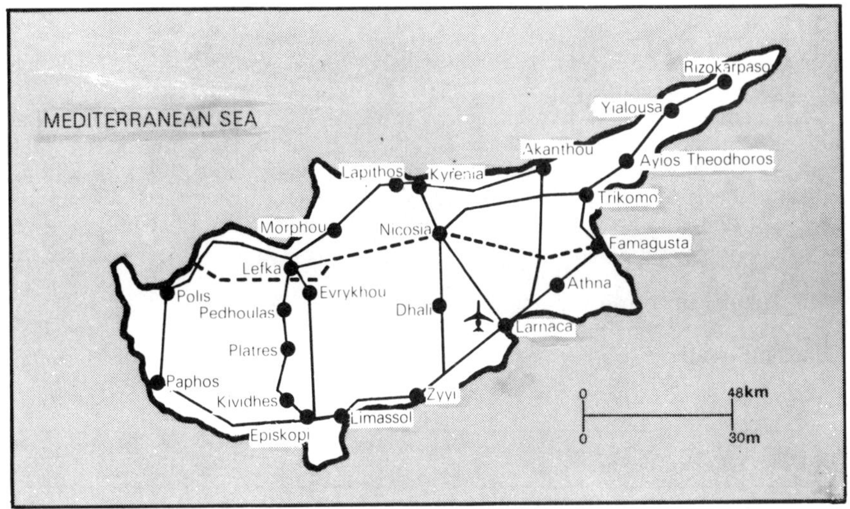

Religion: The Greek Orthodox Church is the principal religious body in Cyprus. There are Protestant and Roman Catholic minorities. The majority of the Turkish population are Muslims of the Sunni sect.

Government: Approximately 40% of Cyprus is under Turkish control, and the Government of Cyprus has *de facto* control only in the southern part of the island, despite the fact that it is recognised as the legitimate Government of the whole of Cyprus. The Turkish-controlled area has its own constitution providing for a legislative assembly within its boundaries, but this has been declared illegal by the Government of Cyprus. Cooperation between the two communities is restricted and centres mainly around matters such as public utilities, communications, etc.

The major political parties are: Greek Cypriot: Democratic Rally, Democratic Front, Communist Party, Socialist Party. Turkish Cypriot: National Unity Party (UBP), Turkish Republican Party (CPT), Communal Liberation Party (TKP) and Populist Party (HP).

GEOGRAPHY

Cyprus is predominantly flat except for two parallel mountain ranges – the Kyrenia range which stretches along the northern coast and the Troodos Mountains (highest point 1,952m/6,406ft) in the southwest. These two ranges are separated by a wide fertile plain called the Messaoria.

Climate

Summers are hot and dry with temperatures rising above 38°C/100°F. Winters are mild with average temperatures around 18°C/65°F during the day and 12°C/53°F at night. Most of the annual rainfall is in December–January. Snow falls in the Troodos Mountains in winter when temperatures are lower than in the coastal areas.

Agriculture

Cyprus is largely an agricultural country and agricultural produce accounts for a high percentage of the island's exports.

Approximately 70% of Cyprus's citrus groves, 100% of the tobacco farms and 60% of the cereal lands are now in the Turkish zone, but the Government of Cyprus has invested heavily in agriculture in order to replace these losses and bring agricultural production back to its former level. The Turkish-controlled area imports fresh and tinned foods from the Turkish mainland and has not yet been able to restore production to its pre-1974 level.

Main Crops: citrus fruits, potatoes, grapes, olives, vegetables.

Mineral Resources: iron pyrites, copper concentrates, chromite, asbestos, gypsum.

THE ECONOMY*

Gross National Product (1976): US$800 billion.

Per Capita Income (1976): US$1,242.

Gross Domestic Product (1977): C£425.3 million.

Foreign Trade (1976): Total Imports US$430 million; Total Exports US$257 million.

Main Trading Partners: Imports – UK, Greece, France, West Germany, Italy, Japan. Exports – UK, Syria, Libya, USSR, Greece.

*Figures for the area under the control of the Government of Cyprus.

Prior to the division of the island, the economy of Cyprus was based on three main pillars – agriculture, tourism and light industry. With the establishment of the Turkish-controlled area much of the country's productive resources fell into Turkish hands and the economy suffered a severe blow.

There have been extensive and largely successful efforts by the Government of Cyprus to revive the economy, particularly in the agricultural sector. Tourism has been badly affected with the loss of many hotels and apartments in Famagusta and Kyrenia, but a revival in the southern part of the island is planned. Unemployment has been another problem which was further aggravated with the influx of some 180,000 Greek Cypriots from the northern area.

By tradition, Britain is Cyprus's major trading partner but the Government is encouraging exports to new markets, in particular the Arab and COMECON countries, as part of its policy for economic revival.

Economic developments in the Turkish-controlled area have been hampered for a number of reasons: the lack of international recognition and therefore of export markets; shortage of trained labour; downturn in tourism and shortage of investment finance.

Cyprus has an association agreement with the EEC which allows concessions for citrus and other agricultural exports, and preferential rates of duty for imported goods of EEC origin.

Major Industries: light manufacturing including foodstuffs, clothing, footwear and consumer goods, petroleum refining, cement.

Main Commodities Traded: Imports – manufactured goods, food and livestock, mineral fuels, machinery and transport equipment, chemicals. Exports – food and livestock, manufactured goods, raw materials, cement, beverages and tobacco.

Detailed figures for the Turkish-controlled area are not available, but citrus fruits account for some 50% of total exports.

Cyprus is a member of the British Commonwealth.

HOW TO GET THERE

N.B. The airport and ports of Famagusta, Kyrenia, Karavostassi and Ercan in the Turkish-controlled area have been declared closed ports by the Government of Cyprus and travellers arriving at any of these are liable to a fine and deportation if they cross to the southern part of the island.

Travellers arriving at ports and airports controlled by the Government of Cyprus (Larnaca, Nicosia, Limassol) are not usually permitted by the Turkish authorities to enter the Turkish-controlled area but exceptions may be made for *bona fide* business travellers. Attitudes to border crossings are liable to change at short notice and travellers should check the latest regulations in advance.

Air

Larnaca is served by several international airlines and Cyprus Airways. Direct flights operate from London, Athens, Beirut and Israel, and several European and Middle Eastern centres, including Paris, Frankfurt, Cairo, Damascus, Dubai, Bahrain, Muscat, Berlin, Prague and Moscow. There are flights from Ankara to Tymbou Airport (Ercan) in the Turkish-controlled area. Nicosia Airport is closed to regular air traffic.

Flying times: from London 4 hours; from New York 12 hours.

Larnaca Airport is 5km/3 miles from the town centre, 64km/40 miles from the centre of Limassol, 48km/29 miles from the centre of Nicosia and 100km/62 miles from the centre of Paphos.

Sea

Larnaca and Limassol are the main ports in the southern part of Cyprus. A car-ferry service operates from Athens, Rhodes and Beirut, and there are regular sailings from Marseilles and Genoa.

ENTRY REGULATIONS

Visas

Cyprus Government-controlled area: Visas are required by nationals of all countries except all British Commonwealth countries, Austria, Belgium, Denmark,

Finland, France, West Germany, Greece, Iceland, Republic of Ireland, Italy, Japan, Liechtenstein, Luxembourg, Netherlands, Norway, San Marino, Spain, Sweden, Switzerland, USA and Yugoslavia.

Visas are valid for 3 months for a stay of up to 3 months maximum.

Transit visas are issued for a stay of up to 5 days.

Business travellers require a letter from their firm giving details of the business to be undertaken and the names and addresses of contacts in Cyprus.

Turkish-controlled area: Visitors to the northern part of Cyprus must comply with Turkish travel regulations. For further information, intending travellers should contact their nearest Turkish embassy or consulate.

Health Regulations

A certificate of vaccination against smallpox is not required for entry into Cyprus, but passengers arriving from areas in which smallpox, cholera or yellow fever are endemic must have the relevant certificates of vaccination. It is advisable to be vaccinated against typhoid.

Customs

Currency: There is no limit to the amount of foreign currency which may be taken into Cyprus, but all foreign currency, travellers' cheques, letters of credit, etc., must be declared on entry.

Sterling notes up to a value of £50 may be taken out of Cyprus together with any unspent foreign currency originally imported and declared on entry. Cyprus notes up to a value of C£10 may be exported.

Duty-free articles: Personal effects including typewriters, radios, cameras, etc. A deposit or security may be required to cover duty on valuable items of personal luggage but this will be refunded if the visitor, together with the articles concerned, leaves Cyprus within 12 months. 200 cigarettes or 250g of tobacco and one bottle of spirits. Samples which are not in a saleable condition are exempt from duty.

Articles liable to duty: Commercial samples which are likely to be sold. These may be temporarily imported provided the appropriate amount of customs duty is deposited or security is given for such an amount. Such samples must be re-exported within 6 months.

Prohibited articles: Firearms and ammunition. The export of antiques is strictly prohibited without the permission of the Cyprus Museum in Nicosia.

PRACTICAL INFORMATION FOR THE VISITOR

1. Currency

Monetary Unit – Cyprus pound (C£), divided into 1,000 mils. (In the Turkish-controlled area the Turkish lira is in circulation, although the Cyprus pound is generally accepted.)

Notes – 250, 500 mils, £1, £5.

Coins – 1, 3, 5, 25, 50, 100 mils.

All banks in Cyprus will cash travellers' cheques, but there may be some difficulty in obtaining foreign currency in Cyprus. Visitors are advised to make the necessary arrangements for currency before arriving.

Banking Hours:
0830–1200 Monday to Saturday
The Central Bank of Cyprus, P.O. Box 1087, Nicosia is the bank of issue.

The major banks have their head offices in Nicosia, with branches in the larger towns.

Domestic Banks (Greek Cypriot):

Bank of Cyprus Ltd
Phaneromeni Street, Nicosia.
Cyprus Popular Bank
Archbishop Makarios III Avenue, Nicosia.
Hellenic Bank.

Domestic Bank (Turkish Cypriot):

Turkish Bank Ltd
Kyrenia Street, Nicosia.

Major Foreign Commercial Banks in Nicosia:

Barclays Bank International Ltd
Eleftheria Square, P.O. Box 2081, ☎ 73052.
The Chartered Bank Ltd
corner of Evagoras and Archbishop Makarios III Avenues, P.O. Box 1047, ☎ 47242/48222.
Grindlays Bank
Paphos Gate Street (Head Office) and Stassinos Avenue.
National Bank of Greece
Archbishop Makarios III Avenue.
Turkiye Is Bankasi
Kyrenia Street.

2. Electricity Supply

240V AC 50Hz.
Plugs: 5 amp, 3 round pins or 13 amp, 3 flat pins.

3. Weights and Measures

The metric and imperial systems are understood, but Cyprus has its own internal system of weights and measures. The oke (2.8lb) is the standard measure of weight.
400 drams = 1 oke
44 okes = 1 Cyprus kantar
800 okes = 1 Imperial ton
180 okes = 1 Aleppo kantar (used in export circles)
1 liquid oke = 1⅛ quarts
1 Cyprus litre = 2⅘ quarts

4. Media

Cyprus has three radio networks: the Cyprus Broadcasting Corporation (CBC), which provides a commercial radio service in Greek, Turkish, Armenian and English; the British Forces Broadcasting Service (BFBS); and Radio Bayrak in the Turkish-controlled area.

Television programmes are transmitted by the Cyprus Broadcasting Corporation with news bulletins in Greek, Turkish and English. One of the CBC television channels – channel 8 – is now under Turkish control in the north of Cyprus.

Newspapers (daily):

Haravghi *Phileleftheros*	Greek
Bozkurt *Halkin Sesi*	Turkish

The *Cyprus Mail* is the only daily English-language newspaper. The Government of Cyprus publishes an official newspaper in English called the *Cyprus Bulletin*.

At least ten weekly papers are published in Cyprus, mostly on Mondays. Several journals and periodicals are also published and *Emporiki* (weekly) and *Echo* (monthly) are two of the principal Greek commercial magazines.

5. Medical Care

Tap water in Cyprus is safe to drink but, if preferred, bottled mountain water is available. It is advisable to wash all fruit.

Emergency medical services are obtainable through the General Hospitals in the main towns. Medical and dental treatment on the island are of a high standard and there are many English-speaking doctors in practice.

6. Telephone, Telex and Postal Services

Automatic dialling from Cyprus is available to Britain, the United States, Canada, Greece, West Germany, France and Israel, and further countries are being added to the list.

A 24-hour, 7 days a week, telegraph service is available from the Central Telegraph Office, Egypt Avenue, Nicosia, ☎ 77111.

Cyprus has international telex facilities but at present there are no public telex offices. In general, visitors may use the telex facilities at the larger hotels, or at the local branch of their bank.

All mail to and from Cyprus should be despatched by air.

Central Post Office, Metaxas Square, Nicosia, ☎ 703219.

7. Public Holidays

Fixed Holidays:

1 January	*New Year's Day*
6 January	*Epiphany*
19 January	*President's Name Day*
25 March	*Greek Independence Day*
1 May	*Labour Day*
15 August	*Assumption of the Virgin Mary*
28 October	*Ohi Day*
24–26 December	*Christmas*

In addition to the above, *Green Monday* (1st day of *Lent*), *Good Friday, Holy Saturday* and *Easter Sunday* are observed by the Christian community.

Muslim Holidays:

These follow the Muslim calendar and occur 10–12 days earlier every year. The dates of the Muslim holidays are approximate as they depend upon sightings of the moon, and may differ by one or two days from those listed below. 1981 dates are:

18 January	*Prophet's Birthday*
31 July –2 August	*End of Ramadan*
8–10 October	*Kurban Bairam*

These holidays are observed by the Turkish-Cypriot community.

Turkish offices are often closed for Turkish mainland holidays.

A number of wine and local arts festivals are held in Cyprus each year, particularly during the summer months. Intending visitors should contact their nearest Cyprus diplomatic mission for further details.

8. Time

GMT + 2

9. Internal Transport

Airline Offices in Nicosia:

Aeroflot	☎ 44985.
Air France	☎ 62101.
British Airways	☎ 42188/9.
British Caledonian	☎ 43132.
Cyprus Airways	☎ 41996/8 (also at Larnaca ☎ 54294 and at Limassol ☎ 73787).
Iberia	☎ 77151.
JAL	☎ 43394.
Lufthansa	☎ 43054.
Pan Am	☎ 43132.
PIA	☎ 3394.
Qantas	☎ 44666.
SAS	☎ 62101.
Swissair	☎ 45222.
TWA	☎ 42114.

Road

The principal towns are connected by bus and taxi services. There are several car-hire firms operating in Cyprus. Visitors wishing to hire a car require an International Driving Licence or a temporary Cyprus licence and two photographs. Traffic travels on the left-hand side of the road.

Car-Hire Firms:

Avis (Nicosia) ☎ 72062/62507.
Hertz (Nicosia) ☎ 77783/77974.

Taxis are efficient in general, and there is a standard charge for journeys within the towns. Shared service taxis run between the main towns at regular intervals and are the best form of inter-town travel.

10. Tipping

Taxis – tips are not usually expected but should be given for help with luggage.

Porters – not necessary as luggage handling is included in the airport service, but 50 mils may be given.

Hotels/restaurants – 10% service charge is added but a small, additional tip is appreciated.

11. Social Customs

The social customs of Cyprus differ slightly in the respective Turkish and Greek sectors, but the main features are very similar. Cypriots are by nature very hospitable and the custom of hand-shaking is extensively practised. Coffee is drunk in considerable quantity and it is impolite to refuse a cup. Most Turks are Muslims – alcohol is not prohibited, however, and there is not such a strict adherence to Islamic laws as in the more conservative Muslim states of the Arab world.

For further information, refer to page 12 under 'Muslim Social Customs'.

USEFUL ADDRESSES (GENERAL)

Embassies in Nicosia

Australia: 4 Annis Komninis Street, ☎ 73001.

France: 6 Ploutarchou Street, P.O. Box 1671, ☎ 65258.

West Germany: 10 Nikitaras Street, ☎ 44362/64.

UK: Alexander Pallis Street, P.O. Box 1978, ☎ 73131/7.

US: Therissos Street and Dositheos Street, ☎ 65151/5.

Other addresses

Dutch Consulate, 21 Archbishop Kyprianou Street, P.O. Box 203, Limassol, ☎ 66230/66235.

British Council, 17 Archbishop Makarios III Avenue, Nicosia, ☎ 42152.

Nicosia Rotary Club, c/o Ledra Palace Hotel, Nicosia, ☎ 63101.

Cyprus Tourism Organisation, 5 Princess Zena de Tyras Street, Nicosia, ☎ 44264.

Thomas Cook Authorised Representative: Hull, Blyth, Araouzos Ltd, 116 Archbishop Makarios III Avenue, P.O. Box 17, Limassol, ☎ 62223.

Other branches of Hull, Blyth, Araouzos Ltd, 67 Athens Street, P.O. Box 8, Larnaca, ☎ 52219; Palace Princess Zena de Tyra, 17 Evagoras Avenue, P.O. Box 244, Nicosia, ☎ 43132; Archbishop Makarios III Street, P.O. Box 12, Paphos.

BUSINESS INFORMATION

Cyprus will be regarded as having two essentially separate economies until such time as a settlement between the two communities is reached. The events of 1974 resulted in a considerable reduction in trade but a general recovery is now under way, particularly in the Cyprus Government-controlled area. It is difficult to estimate the trading situation in the Turkish-controlled area due to the lack of up-to-date figures.

Following the division of the island into two areas, there was a certain amount of trade between the two communities but since the introduction of a licensing system on imports by the Turkish authorities, it is now virtually impossible to supply goods to the northern area through a Greek-Cypriot agent. Since most agency agreements prior to 1974 were concluded with Greek Cypriots for the island of Cyprus as a whole, it might now be a breach of such an agreement to appoint another agent for the Turkish-controlled area. Some agreement may, however, contain a provision for direct indenting. Direct selling to Cyprus is largely confined to the supply of equipment for government use.

Import and Exchange Control Regulations

There are few import restrictions in the Cyprus Government-controlled area but specific import licences are required for certain foodstuffs, manufactured goods and machinery and for other goods which are in direct competition with locally manufactured goods.

Goods from EEC countries are subject to tariffs fixed under the Cyprus/EEC Association agreement. Commonwealth preference for imports into Cyprus has now been withdrawn.

Permission is needed from the Central Bank of Cyprus for the remittance of profits and the repatriation of capital.

Business Hours

Cyprus Government Offices:

Winter –	0800–1400	Tuesday, Wednesday, Friday
	0800–1400 1530–1730	Monday & Thursday
	0800–1300	Saturday
Summer –	0730–1330	Monday, Tuesday, Wednesday, Friday & Saturday
	0730–1330 1600–1800	Thursday

Business Houses:

Winter –	0830–1300 1430–1730	Monday to Friday
	0800–1300	Saturday

Summer – 0800–1300 } Monday to Friday
1600–1830 }
0800–1300 Saturday

Sunday is the weekly closing day and most shops and businesses are closed on Saturday afternoon.

August is the peak annual holiday period, and business travellers are advised to avoid a visit to Cyprus at this time.

Business Events

The Cyprus International (State) Fair is held annually in Nicosia in May/June. For further details contact: Cyprus International Fair, P.O. Box 3551, Nicosia.

BUSINESS SERVICES

Financial Houses

N. J. Dimitriou Ltd, P.O. Box 18, Larnaca (merchant bankers).

Cleanthis Christophides Ltd, P.O. Box 1312, Nicosia (merchant bankers).

Lombard Banking (Cyprus) Ltd, Evagoras Avenue, Nicosia.

Cyprus Development Bank Ltd, Nicosia.

Mortgage Bank of Cyprus Ltd, Nicosia.

USEFUL ADDRESSES (BUSINESS)

The Cyprus Chamber of Commerce & Industry, Hadjisavva Building (6th floor), Metaxas Square, P.O. Box 1455, Nicosia, ☎ 63339/62312. (Also address of **Nicosia Chamber of Commerce & Industry.**)

The Turkish Cypriot Chamber of Commerce, 99 Kyrenia Avenue, P.O. Box 718, Nicosia, ☎ 66477.

Limassol Chamber of Commerce & Industry, Spyros Araouzos Street, P.O. Box 347, Limassol, ☎ 62556.
(Also temporary address of **Famagusta Chamber of Commerce & Industry.**

Larnaca Chamber of Commerce & Industry, 30 Dimitriou Street, P.O. Box 287, Larnaca, ☎ 2027.

Paphos Chamber of Commerce & Industry, 18–20 Grivas Dhigenis Avenue, P.O. Box 68, Paphos, ☎ 2034.

Ministry of Commerce & Industry, 6 Drama Street, Nicosia, ☎ 705241.

MAJOR CITIES AND TOWNS

Nicosia

The demarcation line drawn up between the two communities of Cyprus runs directly through Nicosia, the capital of Cyprus since the seventh century.

The huge sixteenth-century Venetian walls of the old city lie surrounded by the modern, commercial buildings of the new part of the city, where restaurants, hotels, bars, nightclubs and other recreational facilities are to be found in abundance.

The Cyprus Museum must rank high on the list of sights to visit in Nicosia – it contains an extensive archaeological collection with many of the exhibits dating back as far as the sixth millennium B.C. Other buildings of historic interest include the cathedrals of St John and St Sophia, the Archiepiscopal Palace, the Folk Art Museum and another sight not to be missed is the Phaneromeni collection of icons.

Nicosia has an international conference centre and is the main administrative and commercial centre of the island.

Larnaca Airport is 48km/30 miles from the centre of Nicosia.

Hotels

The Cyprus Tourism Organisation grades hotels from 5 star to 1 star.

CYPRUS HILTON (5 star), Archbishop Makarios III Avenue, P.O. Box 2023, ☎ 64040.
Situated next to the US Embassy, 10 minutes' walk from the town centre.
Rooms: 143 ⚘, ▥, ⚽, ⌧, ⌂, ⊃. Suites available.
Facilities: Restaurant, grill room, 24-hr service restaurant. Golf, tennis, squash, swimming, 9-hole pitch and putt. Car hire.
Services: **TC**, **FC**. ⊟ Most major credit cards. **S**, ♂. Dr. on call.
Meeting facilities for up to 100 persons.
Banquet rooms – max. capacity 350.

CHURCHILL (4 star), 1 Achaens Street, P.O. Box 4145, ☎ 48858.
Modern hotel in the residential part of Nicosia.
Rooms: 52 ⚘, ▥, ⚽, ☐ in suites, ⌂, ⊃.
Facilities: Restaurants and bars. Facilities for exhibitions/shows and product demonstrations. Car hire.
Services: **TC**, **FC**. ⊟ Access, Amex, Barclay Visa, Carte Blanche, Eurocard and Master Charge. **S**, ♂. Dr. on call. Translation bureau and audio-visual equipment.
Conference room – max. capacity 150.
Banquet rooms – max. capacity 150.

PHILOXENIA (4 star), Elenja Avenue, P.O. Box 4812, ☎ 72181.
Modern hotel with panoramic view, built on a hill outside the town.
Rooms: 32 ⚘, ▥, ⚽, ⌧, ⌂, ⊃. Suites available.
Facilities: Grill room, coffee shop and bar. Car hire.
Services: **TC**, **FC**. ⊟ Credit cards not accepted. Dr. on call. **S**, ♂. Translation bureau and audio-visual equipment available.
Conference room – max. capacity 180.
Banquet rooms – max. capacity 300.

CLEOPATRA (3 star), 8 Florina Street, P.O. Box 1397, ☎ 45254.
Modern hotel in the town centre.
Rooms: 55 ⚘, ⚽.
Facilities: Restaurant, cafeteria, grill room and cocktail bar.
Services: ⊟ Amex, Bankamericard, Barclay Visa, Carte Blanche, Diners Club and Master Charge.

KENNEDY (3 star), 70 Regaena Street, P.O. Box 1212, ☎ 75131.
Modern hotel by the Venetian Walls within walking distance of the town centre.
Rooms: 95 ⚘, ⚽.
Facilities: Restaurant and bar. Roof garden and sun terrace. Meeting and banquet rooms.

Restaurants

Acropolis, 12 Leonidou Street, ☎ 64871; *Athineon*, 8 Makarios III Avenue, ☎ 44786; *Ekali*, 1 Spyridon Street, ☎ 33950; *Florida*, 122 Limassol Avenue, ☎ 22500; *Fournaki*, 129 Athalassa Avenue, ☎ 21960; *George's Kebab*, 7 Mnasiadou Street, ☎ 44736 – barbecues; *Mikis Tavern*, International Fair Road, ☎ 73925 – live music;

Pagoda, 11 Louki Akrita Street, ☎ 74245 – Chinese; *Psarotaverna*, 10 Crete Street, ☎ 48917 – seafood; *Rustic*, Grivas Dhigenis Avenue, ☎ 49434 – French; *Tina's*, 13 Ev. Pallikarides Street, ☎ 65276.

Nightclubs

Altamira, Makarios III Avenue, ☎ 43931; *Cosmopolitan*, 121 Prodromos Street, ☎ 43186 – with restaurant; *Cleopatra*, 8 Florina Street, ☎ 45254; *Elysée*, Pantheon Building, Evagoras Avenue, ☎ 73773; *Maxime*, 14 Zenas de Tyras Street, ☎ 45679; *Montparnasse*, Grivas Dhigenis Avenue, ☎ 51165; *Spider*, 48D Grivas Dhigenis Avenue, ☎ 43404 – disco.

Larnaca

Larnaca is a popular holiday resort with a long history dating back to the time of the early Greeks. It is built on the site of the Mycenaean city of Kition, home of the Stoic philosopher Zeno, and one can visit the excavations being carried out on the ancient city of Kition.

The Church of St Lazarus and the Phaneromeni megalithic monument are both worth a visit. On the shores of the Great Salt Lake where the pink flamingoes flock in their thousands, stands the shrine of the Tekke of Ummul Haram, the foster mother of the Prophet Mohammed.

Just outside the town, 384m/1,260ft up in the Troodos Mountains is the Stavrovouni monastery which contains a wooden cross reputed to be the original Cross.

Larnaca has a large oil refinery, and a deepwater port and tanker facilities have been built there.

Larnaca airport is 5km/3 miles from the town centre.

Hotels

SUN HALL (4 star), Athens Avenue, P.O. Box 300, ☎ 53341.
Modern hotel in the town centre.
Rooms: 112 on request. Suites available.
Facilities: Restaurant, grill room, bars and coffee shop. Tennis and swimming. Car hire.
Services: TC, FC. Amex. Dr. on call.
Conference room – max. capacity 450.
Banquet rooms – max. capacity 400.

FOUR LANTERNS (3 star), 19 Athens Avenue, P.O. Box 150, ☎ 52011.
Traditional-style hotel, built on the seafront near the town centre.
Rooms: 44.
Facilities: Restaurant and bar. Tennis nearby. Car hire.
Services: TC, FC, Access, Amex, Bankamericard, Barclay Visa, Carte Blanche, Eurocard and Master Charge. Dr. on call.
Conference room – max. capacity 300.
Banquet rooms – max. capacity 300.

Restaurants

Eraclis in the Municipal Gardens, ☎ 52150; *Garden of Allah*, 37 Lord Byron Street, ☎ 52571; *Kellari*, Sea Front, ☎ 53166; *Monte Carlo*, 20 Piale Pasha Street, ☎ 53815; *Nautical Club*, Piale Pasha Street; *Pafitis*, 5 American Church Street, ☎ 52608; *Pepis*, 43 Grivas Dhigenis Avenue, ☎ 52292; *Yenyktis*, 3 Galileos Street, ☎ 52639.

Nightclubs

Acapulco, Hermes Street, ☎ 54152 – cabaret; *Butterfly Discotheque*, 65 Makarios Avenue, ☎ 57333; *Golden Night*, 25 Galileos Street, ☎ 53492; *Nostalgia*, 57 Timayia Avenue, ☎ 56440; *Sand Beach Castle*, Piale Pasha Street, ☎ 55437 – with restaurant; *Spilia*, 28 Zenon Pierides Street – discotheque.

Limassol

Limassol is the second largest town on the island and is the main port of the Cyprus Government-controlled area. The Knights of St John of Jerusalem built the fortress of Kolossi here in 1210 and this was their headquarters until they were driven out by the Turks at the end of the sixteenth century.

The Episkopi Museum attracts many visitors, and at the site of the ancient city of Curium 24km/15 miles from Limassol, one can see some well-preserved Roman floors and mosaics. There are many citrus plantations and vineyards in the area and a 2-week wine festival is held every year in September.

Larnaca Airport is 64km/40 miles from the centre of Limassol.

Hotels

AMATHUS BEACH (5 star), P.O. Box 513, ☎ 66152.
Modern hotel 10km/6 miles east of Limassol.
Rooms: 208 ⚘, ▥, ◉, ☐ on request, ⚠, ☕. Suites available.
Facilities: Restaurant, fish tavern (summer only), coffee shop, nightclub and bars. Mini golf, tennis, sauna, swimming, water sports. Hotel bus service to Limassol.
Services: TC, FC. ⊟ Access, Amex, Barclay Visa, Carte Blanche, Eurocard and Master Charge. S, ♂. Dr. on call.
Conference room – max. capacity 200.
Banquet rooms – max. capacity 300.

APOLLONIA BEACH (5 star), P.O. Box 594, ☎ 65351.
Modern hotel on the beach, 4km/2½ miles from the town centre.
Rooms: 153 ⚘, ▥, ◉, ☐ on request, ⚠, ☕. Suites available.
Facilities: Restaurant, bar and coffee shop. Discotheque. Mini golf, tennis, swimming, water skiing and sailing. Hairdresser and boutique. Car hire.
Services: TC, FC. ⊟ Access, Amex, Barclay Visa, Carte Blanche, Diners Club, Eurocard and Master Charge. S, ♂. Dr. on call.
Conference room – max. capacity 300.
Banquet rooms – max. capacity 270.

CURIUM PALACE (4 star), Byron Street, P.O. Box 48. ☎63121.
Located in a residential area of the town next to the Municipal Gardens, just outside the town centre.
Rooms: 63 ⚘, ▥, ◉, ☐ on request, ⚠, ☕. Suites available.
Facilities: 2 restaurants and bars. Tennis, sauna and swimming. Car hire.
Services: ⊟ Access, Amex, Barclay Visa, Carte Blanche, Diners Club, Eurocard and Master Charge. S, ♂. Dr. on call.
Conference room – max. capacity 150.
Banquet rooms – max. capacity 280.

Restaurants

Butterfly, 153 Makarios Avenue, ☎ 73361 – rooftop restaurant with music; *Gino's*, 1 Larnaca Street, ☎ 71495 – Italian; *Koutouki*, 21 John Tsiros Street, ☎ 72071; *Ladas*, 1 Sadi Street, ☎ 65760 – seafood; *Palm Beach*, Limassol–Nicosia Road, ☎ 66431; *P'an Ku*, Limassol–Nicosia Road, ☎ 62302 – Chinese; *Ponteroza*, Yermasoyia Road; *Sobrero*, 122 Makarios Avenue, ☎ 56161; *Scotis*, corner 38 Makarios & Souli, ☎ 72573 – steak house; *Syrtaki*, 9 Larnaca Street, ☎ 55848 – tavern with music.

Nightclubs

ABC, 220 Leontis Street, ☎ 67675 – discotheque; *Balbonne*, Corner Makarios/Larnaca Road, ☎ 73800 – discotheque; *Can Can*, Corner Makarios/Nicosia Road, ☎ 53400; *Diana*, 163A Makarios Avenue, ☎ 71946; *Le Panache*, 86 Makarios Avenue, ☎ 67543; *Oroscope*, 200D Makarios Avenue, ☎ 72999; *Salamandra*, Polemidhia Road, ☎ 56200 – with restaurant; *Santogan*, 114 Makarios Avenue, ☎ 52508 – discotheque.

EGYPT

Arab Republic of Egypt

Size: 1,002,000 sq.km/386,872 sq. miles.

Population: 38.74 million (1977).

Distribution: approx. 45% in urban areas.

Density: Nile Valley/Delta region: 694 persons per sq.km/1,800 per sq. mile. Cairo: 96,500 persons per sq.km/250,000 per sq.mile.

Population Growth Rate: 2.3% p.a.

Ethnic Composition: The majority of the population belong to the Mediterranean sub-type exclusive to the Nile Valley. There are some negroid features in the Southern populace. The nomads in the Sinai area are related to Arabian tribal groups.

Capital: Cairo Pop. 8.5 million.

Major Cities: Alexandria Pop. 3.2 million; Giza Pop. 712,000; Suez Pop. 315,000; Port Said Pop. 313,000; Mansoura Pop. 212,000; Aswan Pop. 202,000.

Language: Arabic is the official language but English and French are widely used in business and commerce.

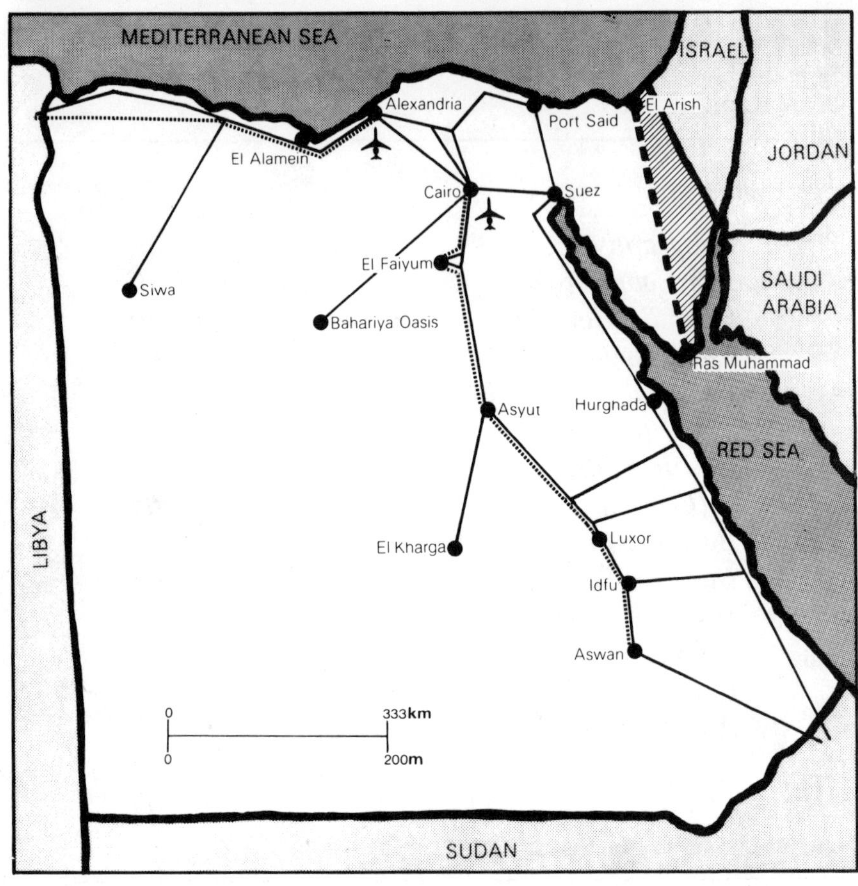

Religion: Islam is the state religion. 90% of the population are Sunni Muslims. The remainder are mostly Christians (especially Coptic) and Jewish. Freedom of worship is allowed.

Government: The Arab Republic of Egypt was founded in 1952. The People's Assembly, elected by universal suffrage, nominates the President who has extensive powers.

Following the abolition of political parties in 1953, the Arab Socialist Union (founded 1961) was the only recognized political organisation until 1976 when the ban was lifted.

GEOGRAPHY

Egypt is virtually a rainless country except for the Nile Valley and Delta regions (98% of the population live in these areas). The country is favourably located with access to Africa, Asia, the Red Sea and the Mediterranean. The Suez Canal (reopened 1975) provides the shortest route to countries in the Indian and Pacific Oceans from Europe. Apart from the fertile areas around the Nile, the remainder of Egypt consists largely of sparsely inhabited desert lands.

Climate

Hot and dry in summer, slightly cooler along the coast. Temperatures average 90°F/32°C in summer and 65°F/18°C in winter. Winter rains fall mainly on the Mediterranean coastal area.

A hot, dusty wind – the Khamsin – blows in from the desert during the summer months causing some discomfort.

Agriculture

Agriculture is the main activity in the Egyptian economy, contributing 30% of the Gross National Product and employing 47% of the total labour force. Various land reforms have resulted in a redistribution of land, and co-operatives are being established on a large scale in conjunction with the land reform.

Almost all agricultural production takes place in the Nile Valley and Delta. Irrigation is essential to agriculture in Egypt. The Aswan High Dam has increased the cultivated area by more than a million acres of land. Two to three different crops can be grown in one year in the Delta and central Egypt due to the high level of irrigation.

Main Crops: fodder crops, cotton, rice, fruit and vegetables.

Mineral Resources: phosphates, iron ore, manganese, salt and asbestos.

THE ECONOMY

Gross National Product (1976): US$13 billion.

Per Capita Income (1976): US$341.

Gross Domestic Product (1977): £E7,341 million.

Foreign Trade (1976): Total Imports – US$4.6 billion; Total Exports – US$1.8 billion.

Main Trading Partners: Imports – USA, France, Australia, USSR, West Germany. Exports – USSR, Japan, Czechoslovakia, Italy, West Germany, UK, East Germany.

There has been little growth in Egypt's industrial sector over the last decade, despite attempts by the Government to remedy the situation. The state control of the economy was loosened by the 'open door' policy inaugurated in 1974 on the initiative of President Sadat. This policy allowed for tax concessions to foreign investors and the setting up of free zones in Alexandria, Cairo, Port Said and Suez.

However, the 'open door' policy has not had the success which was anticipated, partly due to the continuing uncertainty surrounding the Egyptian economy, which has consequently deterred investors.

Over the last few years the Government has incurred vast debts, largely due to its huge military expenditure. With the signing of the peace treaty with Israel in March 1979, and the massive American loan aimed at reviving the economy, there is every hope that Egypt is about to experience a recovery in its economic position. However, as a result of the peace treaty, a number of Arab states have now withdrawn investment funds and this could have a damaging effect.

Egypt is also looking to expand its tourist trade and has undertaken an extensive hotel-building scheme.

Major Industries: agriculture, iron and steel, chemicals, fertilisers, petroleum, building materials, textiles.

Main Commodities Traded: Imports – Cereals, chemicals, machinery, electrical equipment, mineral products. Exports – Cotton (raw, yarn and fabrics), rice, crude oil, fruit and vegetables.

Crude Oil Production (1977): 1,753,000 metric tons per average calendar month.

Egypt is a member of GATT and enjoys a preferential trade agreement with the EEC.

HOW TO GET THERE

Air

Most international airlines have frequent, direct flights to Cairo – Egypt Air operates flights to Cairo from many world capitals.

Cairo International Airport is 22km/14 miles from the city centre – transport is readily available.

An airport tax of £E1 is payable on departure from Egypt.

Flying times to Cairo: from London 4½ hours; from New York 11½ hours; from Sydney 24 hours.

ENTRY REGULATIONS

Visas

No visa is required by passport holders of Algeria, Bahrain, Iran, Jordan, Kuwait, Lebanon, Morocco, Oman, Qatar, People's Democratic Republic of Yemen, Syria and Yemen Arab Republic.

All other passport holders require visas obtainable from Egyptian embassies and consulates abroad.

All persons entering Egypt must have the equivalent of £100 sterling in their possession, and passports must be valid for at least 6 months after the proposed date of departure from Egypt.

Evidence of a previous or planned visit to Israel in a passport may adversely affect the granting of a visa.

Business travellers require a supporting letter from their firm, giving details of the business to be undertaken and confirming their financial responsibility.

All visitors must register with the Police or the Ministry of Interior within one week of arrival. This can be arranged through hotels or travel agents.

Health Regulations

Smallpox vaccination certificates are required. Visitors from infected areas must have cholera and yellow fever inoculation certificates. TAB (typhoid and paratyphoid) injections are recommended.

Customs

Currency: Egyptian currency may not be taken into or out of the country. Any amount of foreign currency or travellers' cheques may be imported, but the amount taken out should not exceed the amount brought in. Currency declaration forms should be completed with care on arrival and surrendered on departure.

Duty-free articles: Personal effects including cameras, binoculars, jewellery – these must be declared however. Reasonable quantities of tobacco, wines, spirits and perfumes for personal use.

Samples (sent by mail or otherwise), provided their value does not exceed £E40 or if they are not in a saleable condition. Duty paid on samples with a value of £E40 or more is refundable if the samples are re-exported within one year.

Prohibited articles: Narcotics, drugs, cotton.

PRACTICAL INFORMATION FOR THE VISITOR

1. Currency

Monetary Unit – Egyptian pound (£E), divided into 100 piastres (PT) and 1,000 milliemes (mms).
Notes – 1, 5, 10 Egyptian pounds and 5, 10, 25 and 50 piastres.
Coins – ½, 1, 2, 5 and 10 piastres.

Travellers' cheques may be exchanged through authorised banks and their representatives, and transactions should be recorded on the currency declaration form.

Credit Cards: These are not in general use, but American Express and Diners Club are accepted in the larger hotels, restaurants and shops.

Banking Hours:
0830–1230 daily, except Friday and Sunday.
1000–1200 Sunday.

The Central Bank of Egypt, 31 Sharia Kasr el Nil, Cairo, ☎ 786681, is the government bank.

Domestic Commercial Banks in Cairo:

Arab African Bank
44 Abdel Khalek Sarwat Street, ☎ 916744.
Arab International Bank
35 Abdel Khalek Sarwat Street, ☎ 919252/916120.
Bank of Alexandria
49 Sharia Kasr el Nil, ☎ 913882/918245.
Banque du Caire
22 Sharia Adly Pasha.
Bank Misr
151 Sharia Mohammed Bey Farid, ☎ 71547/71753.
National Bank of Egypt
24 Sharia Sherif, ☎ 75434/41169/55563.

These banks have offices in Cairo, Alexandria and other main towns; also at Cairo Airport and in major hotels.

International Banks with Offices in Egypt:

Bank of America
15 Brazil Street, Zamalek, P.O. Box

2406, Cairo, ☎ 816722/813960.

Cairo Barclays International Bank
12 Midan el Sheikh Youssef, P.O. Box 2335, Garden City, Cairo, ☎ 22195/27950.

Bank of Credit & Commerce
1 Ahmed Orabi Street, Manshia Square, Cairo, and 9 Talaat Harb Street, Alexandria.

Chase National Bank (Egypt)
12 El Birgas Street, P.O. Box 2430, Garden City, Cairo, ☎ 25263.

American Express International Banking Corporation
23 Camal Eldin Aboul, Mahassen Street, Garden City, Cairo, ☎ 25360/26908.

Midland Bank Ltd
Group Representative Office, 3 Ahmed Nessim Street, Giza, Cairo, ☎ 987332.

2. Electricity Supply

220V AC 50Hz.
Plugs: 2-pin round.

3. Weights and Measures

The metric system, together with local systems, is in use.

4. Media

Egypt has a sophisticated TV and radio network, with an extensive foreign radio service broadcasting in some thirty-five languages (mainly European and African).

Over 400 newspapers and periodicals are published in Cairo and Alexandria, making Egypt the leading publisher in the Arab world.

Newspapers:

Leading dailies are *Al-Ahram* (circulation 780,000) and *Al-Akhbar* (circulation 500,000).

Weekly newspapers include *Akhbar al-Yom* (circulation 1,200,000) and *Asher Sa'a* (circulation 180,000).

The *Egyptian Gazette* is a weekly publication in English.

The *Egyptian Chamber of Commerce Bulletin* and the *Federation of Egyptian Industries Monthly Bulletin* are read in business and industrial circles and represent the trade press as such.

5. Medical Care

In the larger cities, hospitals and clinics offer good medical care. Hospitals in Cairo include:

Anglo-American ☎ 806163/5.
Italian ☎ 821641.

When swimming, keep to pools or the sea in order to avoid the risk of contracting bilharzia. It is advisable to take supplies of fly and insect repellent together with medication for gastro-intestinal disorders.

Drinking water in Cairo and Alexandria is safe, but elsewhere bottled water is recommended. Visitors should be cautious about unwashed fruit and vegetables outside of the better hotels and restaurants.

6. Telephone, Telex and Postal Services

International telephone, cable and telegraph services are available. Delays are frequent when telephoning within Egypt from one town to another. The Hilton and Sheraton Hotels in Cairo have public telex facilities open to residents only.

Telephone directories list Egyptians and Egyptian firms under the first letter of the first name. Only non-Egyptians are listed under the first letter of the last name.

Useful Telephone Numbers in Cairo:

Operator, ☎ 10.
International calls, ☎ 120.
Police, ☎ 912644.

Post Offices are open daily, except Friday. The Central Post Office, Alaba Square, Cairo, offers a 24-hour service.

7. Public Holidays

Fixed Holidays:

1 January	*New Year's Day*
8 March	*Syrian Revolution Day*
18 June	*Evacuation Day*
23 July	*Anniversary of the Revolution*
1 September	*Libyan Revolution Day*
6 October	*Armed Forces Day*
24 October	*Popular Resistance Day*
23 December	*Victory Day*

Muslim Holidays:

These follow the Muslim calendar and occur 10–12 days earlier every year. The dates of the Muslim holidays are approximate as they depend upon sightings of the moon, and may differ by one or two days from those given below. 1981 dates are:

18 January	*Prophet's Birthday*
31 July –2 August	*End of Ramadan*
8–10 October	*Kurban Biaram (Eid el Adha)*
29 October	*Muslim New Year*

Banks are closed on 1 January and on *Coptic Christmas, Coptic Palm Sunday* and *Coptic Easter*. Christian festivals are observed by Christian businesses in Egypt.

8. Time

GMT+2

9. Internal Transport

Air

Egypt Air operates flights between major cities: Cairo–Alexandria 45 minutes; Cairo–Luxor 80 minutes; Cairo–Aswan 1 hour, 45 minutes. For further information telephone Cairo 976477/900554.

Airline Offices in Cairo:

Aeroflot	☎ 42132.
Air France	☎ 971848.
Air India	☎ 31877.
British Airways	☎ 971447.
Egypt Air	☎ 985408.
JAL	☎ 817621.
KLM	☎ 971550.
Lufthansa	☎ 28322.
PIA	☎ 49630.
Pan Am	☎ 970444.
Qantas	☎ 971447.
Sabena	☎ 43525.
SAS	☎ 974588/7.
Swissair	☎ 976195.
TWA	☎ 979770.

Rail

Reliable train services operate from Cairo to Luxor, Aswan, Alexandria, Port Said, Suez and other towns. For further information, telephone Cairo 58458.

Road

There is no formal car-hire service in Egypt. Cars may be rented from larger hotels and through Avis. An International Driving Licence is required.
Avis Car Rental, Cairo:
☎ 28698.
☎ 811811 (Hilton Hotel).
☎ 963270 (Airport).
Taxis are available in all main towns at a moderate cost. Out-of-town and long-distance trips can be arranged and fares should be negotiated in advance. It may be necessary to enlist the help of hotel staff for this, since few taxi-drivers speak English.

10. Tipping

It is usual to tip for any kind of service in Egypt.

Taxis – 10%.

Porters – 5 piastres per bag.
Hotels/restaurants – 10%–12%.

11. Social Customs

Egypt is one of the more liberal Arab states with few restrictions placed on women. There is no strict segregation of the sexes. It is legal to drink alcohol.

For further information, refer to page 12 under 'Muslim Social Customs'.

USEFUL ADDRESSES (GENERAL)

Embassies in Cairo

Australia: 1097 Corniche el Nil, Garden City, ☎ 28190/28663.

Canada: 6 Mohammed Fahmi El-Sayed Street, Garden City, ☎ 23110.

France: 29 El-Giza Street, ☎ 848833.

West Germany: 20 Boulos Pacha Hanna Street, Dokki, ☎ 806015/17.

Japan: 14 Ibrahim Naguib Street, Garden City, P.O. Box 281, ☎ 33962.

Netherlands: 18 Hassan Sabri Street, Zamelek, ☎ 802024.

Switzerland: 10 Abdel Khalek Saroit, P.O. Box 633, ☎ 978171/2.

UK: Ahmed Raghal Street, Garden City, ☎ 20850/9.

US: 5 Latin America Street, Garden City, P.O. Box 10, ☎ 28219.

Other addresses in Cairo

American Express, P.O. Box 2160, 15 Kasr el Nil Street, ☎ 970138/970042.

Thomas Cook Overseas Ltd, 4 Champollion Street, P.O. Box 165, ☎ 46392/5 (also Bureau de Change at Cairo Airport).

Ministry of Information and Culture, ☎ 23529.

Ministry of Tourism, 5 Adly Street, ☎ 923000/979394.

Wagons-Lits Tourisme, Shepheards Hotel, Kasr el Ali Street, ☎ 31538.

Consulates in Alexandria

French Consulate, 2 Place Ahmed-Orabi, P.O. Box 474.

West German Consulate, 14 rue des Pharaons, ☎ 31587.

Swiss Consulate, 8 rue Moukhtar Abdel Halim Khalaf Saba Pacha, P.O. Box 1934, ☎ (03) 50726.

US Consulate-General, 110 Avenue Horreya, ☎ 25306/25607.

Other addresses in Alexandria

Egyptian Tourist Office, Saad Zaghloul Square, Ramleh Station, ☎ 25985.

Thomas Cook Overseas Ltd, 15 Midan Saad Zaghloul, P.O. Box 185, ☎ 27830.

BUSINESS INFORMATION

Egypt's 'open door' economic policy was introduced in 1974, partly as an attempt to break away from the Soviet sphere of influence. The new policy was designed to attract greater foreign investment which would improve both the country's employment situation and her foreign-exchange earning position.

However, foreign firms have been slow to invest in Egypt, largely due to problems surrounding foreign exchange. Investments were converted at the wholly unrealistic official exchange rate making them an unattractive proposition. The introduction of a parallel foreign exchange market together with a number of fiscal reforms has gradually led to an upward trend in investment, although it still remains insufficient for Egyptian needs.

The Egyptian market remains an attractive one, particularly for American exporters. However, a further liberalisation in the financial and economic structure may be necessary before foreign investors are fully convinced of the viability of wide-scale investment.

Individuals may act as agents for foreign firms provided their remuneration is in the form of a fee or salary, and not on a commission basis.

Import and Exchange Control Regulations

Exchange control is carried out through authorised banks under the direction of the Central Exchange Control.

Certain goods are liable to a number of taxes in addition to customs duty, and may attract excise duty, e.g., alcoholic drinks, fuel oil, sugar, coffee.

Major industries and commercial enterprises are state-controlled and generally speaking importing is in the hands of state trading companies. Import licences are not usually required for smaller shipments.

Free storage for a period of 8 days is granted at all ports.

Business Hours

Government Offices:
0800–1400 Saturday to Thursday

Business Houses:
0830–1330 and 1630–1900 Saturday to Thursday

Business Events

International Book Fair (annual), Cairo; Cairo International Trade Fair (annual); International Festival of Egyptian Fashion (annual), Cairo.

BUSINESS SERVICES

Translation Services

Middle East Observer, 8 Chawarby Street, Cairo.

Haddad Bureau de Traduction et Copie, 39 Sharia Talaat Harb, Cairo.

International Business Associates, 1079 Corniche el Nil, Garden City, Cairo (also offer secretarial services).

Bureau Technique de Traduction Juridique, Commercial et Littéraire, 28 Sharia Sesostris, Alexandria.

USEFUL ADDRESSES (BUSINESS)

Cairo

Cairo Chamber of Commerce, 4 Midan al-Falaki Street, Bab El-Louk.

The Federation of Egyptian Industries, 26 Sharia Sherif Pasha.

German-Arab Chamber of Commerce, 2 Sharia Sherif Pasha.

Camera di Commercio Italiana per l'Egitto, 33 Sharia Abdel-Khalek Sarwat, P.O. Box 19.

Alexandria

Egyptian Chamber of Commerce, Al-Ghorfa Eltegareia Street.

The Alexandria Chamber of Commerce, General Post Office.

MAJOR CITIES AND TOWNS

Cairo

Cairo stretches out along the banks of the Nile and offers an unusual combination of traditional and modern architecture, with ancient mosques and multi-storey office blocks crowding the city. The city has many fine museums displaying important collections of early Christian, Islamic and Oriental art. The Egyptian Museum in Tahrir Square contains an extensive collection of Egyptological findings.

The Ibn Tulun Mosque can be mounted by an outside staircase, and offers a good view of the city, as does the 180m-high tower of Cairo at Gezira.

Yet by far the most famous of all Egypt's offerings from the past are the Pyramids at Giza, together with the many tombs and the Sphinx. These are, in fact, only a small part of a whole series of ancient monuments stretching across the desert over a distance of about 70km/43 miles. From here one can view the whole Nile valley from west to east. Many of the better hotels are at Giza, 12km/7 miles from the centre of Cairo.

Cairo Airport is 22km/14 miles from the city centre.

Hotels

The Egyptian Tourist Board grades hotels from 5 star to 1 star.

CAIRO SHERATON (5 star), Galae Square, P.O. Box 11, Giza, ☎ 983000.
A modern, deluxe hotel near the Pyramids and Sphinx monument.
Rooms: 369 [symbols].
Facilities: Restaurant and nightclub, 3 bars. Gambling casino. Swimming. Shopping arcade.
Services: **TC**, **FC**. Amex, Bankamericard, Carte Blanche, Diners Club and Eurocard. **S**, [symbol].
6 conference rooms, each with maximum capacity of 400.

MENA HOUSE OBEROI (5 star), Pyramids Street, Giza, ☎ 855444.
Traditional hotel with extensive gardens and own golf course, 13km/8 miles from the centre of Cairo.
Rooms: 510 [symbols].
Facilities: Restaurant, 24-hr coffee shop, nightclub, bars. 18-hole golf course, swimming, tennis and riding.
Services: **TC**, **FC**. Amex, Diners Club and Eurocard. Dr. on call. **S**, [symbol].
Conference room – max. capacity 280.

MERIDIEN LE CAIRE (5 star), Corniche el Nil Street, P.O. Box 2288, Rodah, ☎ 845444.

Modern hotel in the city centre.
Rooms: 300.
Facilities: Oriental and French restaurants, bars, nightclub. Sauna and swimming.
Services: **TC**, **FC**. ⊟ Access, Amex, Diners Club, Eurocard and Master Charge. Dr. on call. ***S***.
Conference room – max. capacity 650.

NILE HILTON (5 star), Tahrir Square, ☎ 811811/815815.
Modern hotel overlooking the Nile, near the city centre.
Rooms: 400.
Facilities: 5 restaurants, bars, nightclub and casino. Shops, hairdressers and health club. Tennis, sauna and swimming.
Services: **TC**, **FC**. ⊟ Access, Amex, Carte Blanche, Diners Club, Eurocard and Master Charge. Dr. on call. ***S***.
Conference room – max. capacity 800.

SHEPHEARD'S (4/5 star), Corniche el Nil Street, Garden City, ☎ 33800.
Rooms: 290.
Facilities: Restaurant, banquet hall, 2 bars and casino. Golf, tennis and swimming at Gezira Sporting Club (5 minutes) by arrangement.
Services: **TC**, **FC**. ***S***.

Restaurants

Apart from the hotel restaurants, others in Cairo include:

Local Cuisine:
Versailles, 30 Mohammed Sakeb Street; *Sofar*, 21 Adly Street, ☎ 54360 (Lebanese); *Abu Shakra*, Kast el-Aini Street, ☎ 21521; *El-Shimy*, Talaat Harb Street, ☎ 49978; *El-Hatti*, 1 Midan Halim, ☎ 56055.

European Cuisine and other:
Estoril, 12 Talaat Harb Street, ☎ 72009; *Le Grillon*, 8 Kasr el Nil Street, ☎ 41114; *Löwenbrau/München*, 26–31 July Street, ☎ 59877; *Fu Ching*, 39 Talaat Harb Street.

Nightclubs

The Saddle Disco, Mena House Hotel, ☎ 855444; *Alhambra*, Cairo Sheraton, ☎ 983000; *Bateau Omar Khayyam*, ☎ 808553; *Sahara City*, beyond the Pyramids, ☎ 850673.

Entertainment

Many of the larger hotels have their own nightclubs with colourful floor shows and displays of Oriental dancing. The Sheraton Hotel has a gambling casino. A *son et lumière* display can be seen at the Pyramids (☎ 852880 for details) and at the Citadel (☎ 53260).

Sporting facilities include swimming, tennis, golf, horse riding, etc. Temporary membership is available from most clubs in the area.

Shopping

Khan el Khalili is the main shopping area in Cairo. Worthwhile purchases include jewellery, copper and ivory goods and inlaid mother-of-pearl work. Some genuine antiquities are for sale, but beware of modern reproductions.

Alexandria

Alexandria is Egypt's principal port and is well known for its beaches, making it a popular holiday resort for many Egyptians.

The city was once an important centre of worship for Christians, and the Graeco-Roman Museum and ruins of the Serapium Temple offer a glimpse into bygone ages. The chief Islamic monument – the mosque of Abu al-Abbas al-Mursi – can also be found here.

Alexandria Airport is 8km/5 miles from the city centre.

Hotels

CECIL (4 star), 16 Midan Saad Zaghloul, ☎ 807532.
Traditional, moderate first-class hotel on the seafront, within easy walking distance of the city centre.
Rooms: 85.
Facilities: Restaurant and American bar. Library and games room. Hairdresser. Ballroom.

PALESTINE (5 star), Montazah Palace, ☎ 66799.
Rooms: 234.
Facilities: Restaurant and bar. Garden nightclub and casino. Private beach, sailing and water skiing. Car-hire service.
Services: TC, FC. Credit cards not accepted.

SAN STEPHANO (4 star), El-Geish Avenue, ☎ 63580.
Rooms: 118.
Facilities: Restaurant and cafeteria. Nightclub, garden, barbecues, solarium.
Conference room.

Restaurants

Zafarian, Abu Kir (seafood); *Santa Lucia*, 40 Safeya Zaghloul Street (European); *Elite*, Safeya Zaghloul Street (European); *Pam Pam*, 23 Safeya Zaghloul Street.

Entertainment

Temporary membership is available at both the *Smouha* and *Sporting Clubs*, offering golf, horse racing, tennis and squash. Alexandria also has yachting, rowing and automobile clubs offering temporary membership to visitors.

Aswan

An attractive town, but temperatures in summer can rise to 40°C/104°F and the intense heat may cause great discomfort to the unacclimatised visitor.

Aswan Airport is 18km/11 miles from the town centre.

Hotels

CATARACT HOTELS, Abtal el Tahrir Street, ☎ 3222.
Adjacent hotels, one in traditional style and one modern, in quiet central location near the Nile.
Rooms: 288.
Facilities: Restaurant and bars. Dancing. Swimming, boating and tennis.
Services: TC, FC. Amex, Bankamericard and Diners Club.
Conference facilities.

ASWAN OBEROI, Elephantine Island, ☎ 3455.
The hotel is built in a picturesque location on an island overlooking the temples of Ramses II and Queen Nefertari.
Rooms: 150.
Facilities: Restaurant, bar and nightclub. Tennis, sauna and swimming.
Services: TC, FC. Amex and Diners Club. Dr. on call.
Conference room – max. capacity 150.

Luxor

Luxor is another popular resort town in a beautiful situation on the east bank of the Nile.

In ancient times Luxor was known as Thebes, and both within the town itself and in the surrounding area can be seen some of Egypt's most fabulous sights, rivalling even the Pyramids. A short ferry journey across the river and through an area of extremely fertile land will bring you to the Valley of the Kings and the Valley of the

Queens, containing some of the finest remains of ancient Egypt. The tombs of Tutankhamun, Ramses II, Ramses III and Queen Nefertari are to be found here together with those of a number of lesser pharaohs and nobles.

This area has been the scene of considerable archaeological excavation and other sites which have been discovered are the funeral temples of the kings, the temple of Medinet Habu and the remains of several other temples.

Luxor Airport is 12km/8 miles from the town centre.

Hotels

ETAP (5 star), El Bahr Street, ☎ 2160/2166.
Rooms: 120.
Facilities: Restaurant and bar. Garden. Swimming. Shops.

WINTER PALACE (5 star), El Nil Street, ☎ 2200.
Rooms: 260 [symbols].
Facilities: 2 restaurants and bars. Nightclub. Tennis and swimming.
Services: TC. [symbol] Amex. Dr. on call. Conference room – max. capacity 100.

IRAN

Every effort has been made to ensure that the information contained in this chapter is correct. However, due to the rapidly changing situation in Iran under the new Government, the publishers are unable to guarantee complete accuracy of information and cannot assume any direct responsibility in this connection.

Size: 1,648,000 sq.km/636,128 sq.miles.

Population: 35.21 million (1978 estimate).

Distribution: 44% in urban areas.

Density: 21 persons per sq.km/55 per sq.mile.

Population Growth Rate: 3% p.a.

Ethnic Composition: About 63% of the population are Persian, and 25% are of Turkish descent.

Capital: Tehran Pop. 4,400,000.

Major Cities: Isfahan Pop. 800,000; Mashed Pop. 600,000; Tabriz Pop. 555,000; Shiraz Pop. 380,000.

Language: Persian (Farsi) is the official and most widely spoken language, but many languages and dialects are spoken throughout Iran, the major ones being Azarbaijani Turkish, Lori, Kurdi, Gilaki and Mazandirani. Turkish is mainly understood in the northwest, and Arabic in the southwest of the country. English and French and some German are spoken in business and government circles.

Religion: 98% of the population are Muslims – 90% of these belong to the Shia sect and the remainder to the Sunni sect. Other religious communities include Christians (Armenians, Assyrians and others), and Jews.

Government: Iran was declared an Islamic Republic in March, 1979. Elections were held in August, 1979 in order

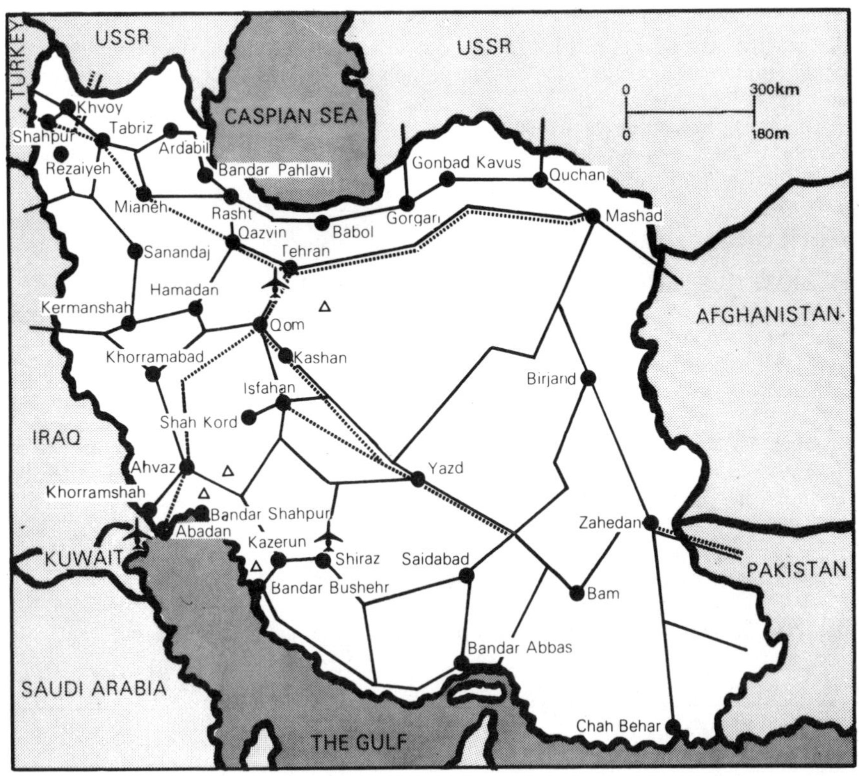

to establish a system of representative government, which will rule according to the precepts of the Islamic faith. The main political groups which fought the elections were the Ayatollah Khomeini's party, the National Democratic Front and the Iran National Party.

GEOGRAPHY

Iran is situated between the Persian Gulf to the south and the Caspian Sea to the north. It is bounded by Pakistan and Afghanistan to the east, the USSR to the north, and Turkey and Iraq to the west.

Most of the central region is composed of desert. This arid plateau area is surrounded by mountain ranges. In the north the Elburz mountain range rises above the tableland – the highest peak being Mount Damavand, 5,671m/18,606ft high. To the west lies the Zagros range with many peaks rising above 4,000m/13,100ft. The coastal regions of the Caspian Sea and Persian Gulf have narrow strips of lowland.

Climate

Tehran has an average temperature of 3°C/38°F in January and an average temperature of 29°C/84°F in July. The maximum temperature in the period July–

August is around 40°C/104°F. These temperatures in Tehran are the same for the plateau area as a whole. The Caspian and Gulf regions suffer from extreme heat and high humidity. Rainfall is very low and usually confined to the beginning of winter and spring.

The most pleasant times to visit Iran are the periods March–May and September–October. But the period 21–24 of March should be avoided, as this is the Iranian New Year holiday period.

Agriculture

About 35% of Iran's working population are engaged in the agricultural industry, which accounts for 25% of the Gross National Product. Widespread reforms have altered the structure of the agricultural sector. It has changed from being dominated by a few large landholders to being run in smaller units with more diverse ownership. Farm corporations and co-operatives have been created.

However, there have been teething problems in this area, with the result that productivity has been markedly low. A number of agro-businesses that were started have not responded well. A further hindrance to development has been the priority given by the Government to development of the industrial sector. Also the scarcity of water supplies has limited output.

Main Crops: wheat, rice, sugar beet, cotton, fruits.

Mineral Resources: oil, iron ore, copper, lead, zinc, gold, chromite ores, salt.

THE ECONOMY

Gross National Product (1976): US$69 billion.

Per Capita Income (1976): US$2,057.

Gross Domestic Product (1975): US$53,985 million.

Foreign Trade (1977): Total Imports US$10.4 billion; Total Exports US$23.5 billion.

Main Trading Partners: Imports – USA, West Germany, Japan, UK, France. Exports – Japan, West Germany, UK, Netherlands, France, Italy.

Recent upheavals in Iran—revolution and war with neighboring Iraq—have drastically reduced the country's oil output, but it still remains a major exporter. The country's ruling religious leaders have vowed to lessen Iran's dependence on oil, but there is no indication yet of their plans for redirecting the economy.

There have been a series of development plans undertaken since the Second World War to promote growth. The substantial price increase of oil in 1973, just after the implementation of the Fifth Development Plan, brought about a revision of policy that resulted in an even greater growth rate, twice the previous rate being aimed at. The growth rate in real terms was 33% in 1973/4 and reached 40% in 1974/5. Continuing unrest has, however, seriously cut back Iran's growth rate.

Aside from oil, priority sectors are steel and non-ferrous metals, mechanical and electrical industries and vehicle construction, chemicals and petrochemicals. More attention is being paid towards refining oil, although Iran's refineries have been damaged by war. Gas production is under way and Iran has vast known gas reserves.

Iran is utilising its hydro-electric power by the construction of a transmission line and grid network which will bring electric power to the industrial centres of Tehran, Isfahan, Ahvaz, Tabriz and Shiraz. Two nuclear power stations are under construction at Bushmore and the construction of several more is envisaged.

There has been an extension of mineral mining. Iran has quantities of zinc, lead, iron ore, chromite ores, coal and copper. The most important mining project is the Sar Cheshme copper mine near Kerman. It is hoped that Iran will be a major steel producer in the 1980s. The use of natural gas in direct reduction of iron ore is being explored, and one mill has already begun production using this method.

Expansion of the communications and transport system is taking place, and plans include the construction of more roads and railway track. In addition to the existing ports on the Persian Gulf which will be expanded, several new ports will be built.

Following the change of Government in Iran in 1979, many of the development projects and industrial contracts made by the Shah with countries such as the USSR and West Germany were abandoned. It is likely that some of these projects and agreements will come into force once again in the near future, but the general economic policy of Iran will undoubtedly change as the new Islamic Republic stabilises and the priority accorded to individual sectors of the economy changes.

Major Industries: food processing, chemicals, petrochemicals, textiles, cement, tanning, metallurgical products.

Main Commodities Traded: Imports – machinery, iron, steel, chemicals, drugs. Exports – oil, carpets, cotton, fruits, hides.

Crude oil production (1976): 293.9 million tonnes.

Iran is a member of the Organisation of Petroleum Exporting Countries (OPEC).

HOW TO GET THERE

Air

The main airports in Iran together with the distances from their respective city centres are: Mehrabad (Tehran) – 10km/6 miles; Isfahan – 5km/3 miles; Shiraz – 19km/12 miles; Abadan – 10km/6 miles.

From Europe: Iran is connected with the principal cities in Europe by the services of Air France, Alitalia, British Airways, Iran Air, KLM, Lufthansa, SAS and Swissair. The flying time from London to Tehran is 6 hours.

From North America: Iran Air and Pan Am fly direct to Iran. Flying time from New York to Tehran (non-stop) is 13¼ hours.

From the Far East and India: There are daily flights to Tehran from Bangkok, Delhi, Hong Kong and Tokyo. Also there are regular services linking Tehran with Bombay, Karachi, Singapore, Melbourne, Sydney and Peking.

From the Middle East: Iran is well connected with the major cities in the Middle East by the services of El Al, Gulf Air, Iran Air, Kuwait Airways and Syrian Airways.

There is an airport tax of 250 rials payable on departure from Iran.

ENTRY REGULATIONS

Visas

Visas are required by nationals of all countries except Belgium, Denmark, Finland, France, West Germany, Greece, Italy, Japan, Luxembourg, Morocco, Netherlands, Norway, Qatar, Saudi Arabia, Spain, Sweden, Tunisia, Turkey, United Kingdom (including Jersey and Guernsey) and Yugoslavia – for tourist purposes only, for a stay of up to 3 months which may be extended locally.

Nationals of all other countries and those travelling for reasons other than tourist ones require visas obtainable from Iranian embassies and consulates abroad. Visas will not be granted if the validity of the passport does not extend beyond the validity of the visa applied for.

Visa applications for business travellers should be accompanied by a letter from the applicant's firm stating the employee's name, full details of the business to be undertaken and with whom, the address of the person(s) with whom contact will be made, the length of stay and confirming financial responsibility for the applicant. Two photographs are also required.

Business visas are valid for 90 days. All visitors are required to register with the police on arrival, though registration at a hotel is sufficient. Any stay over 90 days necessitates a residence permit which is issued by the police on production of a work permit, obtained before arrival.

All business travellers (except UK passport holders) staying more than 15 days require exit visas. Any business traveller who spends 3 consecutive months or more in Iran must produce an Income Tax Clearance permit when applying for an exit visa. The Income Tax authorities usually complete the procedure within 72 hours.

Health Regulations

A valid International Certificate of Vaccination against smallpox is required for all persons entering Iran. A cholera vaccination is also required if the visitor has in the previous 5 days been in an infected area or has travelled from Afghanistan, Bahrain, Bangladesh, Burma, India, Iraq, Malawi, Malaysia, Pakistan, Philippines, Saudi Arabia, Singapore, Thailand and Vietnam. A vaccination certificate against yellow fever is also required if the visitor has, in the 6 days prior to arrival, visited an endemic zone.

Customs

Currency: There is no limit to the amount of foreign or local currency which may be taken into Iran. Visitors are allowed to leave the country with currency up to the value of 200,000 rials.

Duty-free articles: Clothing and articles of personal use. New articles and foodstuffs up to a value of 20,000 rials. 200 cigarettes or the equivalent in other tobacco products.

Articles liable to duty: Commercial samples of value may be imported on a duty-free basis subject to a bond to cover the payment of duties if the samples are not re-exported.

PRACTICAL INFORMATION FOR THE VISITOR

1. Currency

Monetary Unit – rial (Rs).
Notes – 20, 50, 100, 200, 500, 1,000, 5,000, 10,000 rials.
Coins – 1, 2, 5, 10, 20 rials.

Banking Hours:

Winter –	0800–1300	Saturday to
	1600–1800	Wednesday
	0800–1300	Thursday
Summer–	0730–1300	Saturday to
	1700–1900	Wednesday
	0730–1130	Thursday

Domestic Commercial Banks in Tehran:

Bank Melli Iran
Ferdowsi Avenue, ☎ 3231.
Bank of Iran and the Middle East
Ferdowsi Avenue, Koucheh Berlin, ☎ 314355.
Iranians' Bank
Takhte Jamshid Avenue, ☎ 892070.
Bank Barzargani
Maydan Sepah, ☎ 31504.
International Bank of Iran and Japan
750 Saudi Avenue, ☎ 304981.
Irano-British Bank
Saudi Avenue, ☎ 304361/8.

Foreign Commercial Banks in Tehran:

Bank of America
Bezrouke Building, Takhte Jamshid Avenue at Forsat, No. 40, P.O.Box 41-1828, ☎ 825588.
Bank of Boston
6 Azarshah, Sepahbod Zahedi Avenue, ☎ 890637.
Barclays Bank International
Bezrouke Building, Takhte Jamshid Avenue at Forsat, ☎ 825074.
Chase Manhattan Overseas
135 Khermande Shomali, ☎ 824896.
Citibank
Abbasabad Avenue, Darya-E-Noor Street, ☎ 627878.
Lloyds Bank International
199 Bisto Panj-E-Shahrivar Avenue, Abbasabad, ☎ 851487 (representative office).
Midland Bank Ltd
167 Takhte Tavoos, ☎ 851501 (representative office).

2. Electricity Supply

Tehran – 220V AC 50/60 Hz.
Plugs: 2 round pins.

3. Weights and Measures

The metric system is in use.

4. Media

Commercial advertising is used by Radio Iran and National Iranian Television which has three channels in Tehran and nineteen provincial stations.

Newspapers (daily):

Ayandegan (Persian); *Ettela'at* (Persian); *Kayhan International* (English); *Rastakhiz* (Persian); *Tehran Times* (Persian); *Bourse* (Trade).

Periodicals:

Ettela'at-e-Banovan (woman's weekly); *Ettela'at-e-Haftegi* (weekly); *Khandaniha* (twice weekly); *Jananan-l-Emruz*; *The Tehran Economist* (Persian and English editions); *Zan-e-Ruz*.

5. Medical Care

Tap water is only safe to drink in the main cities and towns. Elsewhere, it is advisable to drink only boiled water or use sterilising tablets.

The Caspian Sea area, especially from April to October, is still prone to incidents of malaria. Visitors should take precautions before going to this region; prophylactic tablets can be purchased locally. Visitors are advised to have typhoid and paratyphoid inoculations if intending to travel out of the main cities and towns. There is no free health service in Iran.

Hospitals in Tehran:

American Hospital, 59 Elizabeth II Boulevard, ☎ 655170.
Pars Hospital, Elizabeth Boulevard, ☎ 655051/5.
Sina Hospital, Sepah Avenue, ☎ 663984/649017.
Tehran Clinic, Shah Abbas Somali Avenue, Takhte Tavoos Avenue, ☎ 622931.

Hospitals in Isfahan:

Emergency Medical Centre, Saadatabad Avenue, ☎ 43028.
Isfahan Clinic, Sheikh Bahai Avenue, ☎ 30015/9.
Mehregan Hospital, Sheikh Bahai Avenue, ☎ 38848.
Soraya, Sepahbod Zahedi Avenue, ☎ 32114.

All-night Pharmacies in Tehran:

American Pharmacy, Pahlavi Square, ☎ 645290.
Takhte Jamshid Drug Store, Takhte Jamshid Avenue, ☎ 640386.
Takhte Tavoos Drug Store, Takhte Tavoos Avenue, ☎ 827240.

6. Telephone, Telex and Postal Services

There are public telephones on the streets of the major cities and in hotels, restaurants and cafés, etc.

International phone calls are costly and where booked through an operator can prove a lengthy business. PTT offices in Tehran at Sepah Square and Taj Avenue offer facilities for making international calls.

All telegrams must be sent from the Central Telegraph Office, Meydan Sepah, which operates 24 hours a day.

Telex facilities are located in most major hotels and there are also facilities at the Central Telegraph Office in Meydan Sepah.

All letters for abroad should be sent by air mail.

Central Post Office, Sepah Avenue, Tehran.
Central Post Office, Faiz Avenue, Isfahan.

Useful Telephone Numbers:

Police ☎ 02
Ambulance ☎ 68304 (Tehran); ☎ 7707 (Isfahan).

7. Public Holidays

Fixed Holidays:

21–24 March	*Iranian New Year (Now Ruz)*
2 April	*13th of Now Ruz*
5 August	*Constitution Day*
14 October	*Birthday of Imam Ali*

Muslim Holidays:

These follow the Muslim calendar and occur 10–12 days earlier every year. The dates of the Muslim holidays are very approximate; they depend upon sightings of the moon, and may differ by several days from those given below. 1981 dates are estimated as follows:

5 January	*Death of Imam Hussein*
18 January	*Prophet's Birthday*
18 June	*Birth of the 12th Imam*
25 July	*Death of Imam Ali*
31 July–2	*End of Ramadan*
26 August	*Death of Imam Jafar Sadeyh*

7 October	*Eid Qadir*
8 October	*Eid Qurban*
7-8 November	*Ashoura*

8. Time

GMT+4 (winter)
GMT+5 (summer)

9. Internal Transport

Air

Internal air services connect all the main cities and towns and are operated by Iran Air. The international airports at Tehran and Abadan handle domestic flights. Many of the major towns and cities are served by daily flights from Tehran. Abadan, Isfahan, Mashad and Shiraz have several flights to and from Tehran daily.

The international airport at Mehrabad is 10km/6 miles from Tehran. There are regular bus services connecting the airport with Tehran. Some hotels run their own bus service to and from the airport. Shared taxis are generally available at the airport together with limousine taxis.

Airline Offices in Tehran:

Aeroflot	☎ 829118/836164.
Air France	☎ 372622.
Air India	☎ 373108/371452.
British Airways	☎ 370105/9.
JAL	☎ 833067/9.
KLM	☎ 627562/627855.
Lufthansa	☎ 822070/8.
Pan Am	☎ 832051/61.
PIA	☎ 824095/9.
Qantas	☎ 370105.
SAS	☎ 892227/8.
Swissair	☎ 669457.
TWA	☎ 832071/2.

Rail

Tehran is linked by rail to Ahvaz, Abadan-Khorramshahr, Gorgan, Isfahan, Maragheh, Mashad, Tabriz, Yazd and Zarand. There is an express service between Mashad and Tehran. There are also weekly trains to Istanbul and Moscow. The railway station in Tehran is situated at the end of Pahlavi Avenue (☎ 530993/531051).

Road

There are good daily bus services to all the major towns and cities from Tehran; buses on the express routes are air-conditioned. Some of the main bus companies are Iran Peyma, Amir Kabir Street, ☎ 313171/3 and at Sevom Esfand, ☎ 301415/9; Mihan Tour, Ferdowsi Avenue, ☎ 302921/2; and TBT, Sepahbod Zahedi Avenue, ☎ 828180.

Self-drive and chauffeur-driven cars are available for hire in the main cities and towns. An International Driving Licence is required.

Traffic travels on the right-hand side of the road.

Car Hire:

Tehran

Avis	☎ 892231/3.
Hertz	☎ 827182/838720.
Kian Taxi	☎ 833387.
Tehran Taxi	☎ 891127/9.

Isfahan

Arya	☎ 41218.
Isfahan Taxi	☎ 55526/58769.
Sassan Tourist	☎ 28054/25054.
Sepahan	☎ 44364/5.

Taxis

There are three types of taxi service in Tehran: service, shared and telephone. The shared taxis are orange, and can cram in up to eight people at a time. Blue service taxis operate on the main avenues through the city. The telephone taxis can be booked in advance, but an hour's notice is usually necessary. Limousine taxis are probably the most convenient means of getting around Tehran and the other cities.

10. Tipping

Taxis – no tip.

Porters – 30–40 rials.

Hotels/restaurants – 15% of the bill if no service charge is included.

11. Social Customs

Iran is now governed according to strict Islamic law, so any visitors, especially women, who are increasingly becoming more limited in freedom of dress and movement, should be well acquainted with the various Muslim social customs. It should be remembered that Iranians are not Arabs, but stem from the Aryan race. Punctuality for social engagements is not strictly adhered to.

For further information, refer to page 12 under 'Muslim Social Customs'.

USEFUL ADDRESSES (GENERAL)

Embassies in Tehran

Australia: Shahryar Building, 248 Avenue Soraya, ☎ 833017.

Canada: 19 Davya-e-Noor Avenue, P.O. Box 1610, ☎ 623177.

France: 85 France Street, P.O. Box 2, ☎ 665321/640097/8.

West Germany: Ferdowsi Avenue, P.O. Box 48, ☎ 314111/15.

Japan: Pahlavi Avenue, 46 Nahid Street, P.O. Box 348, ☎ 225437/40.

Netherlands: Takhte Tavoos Avenue, Mooazami Street, P.O. Box 15, ☎ 896011/12.

Switzerland: 18 Pasteur Street, P.O. Box 45, ☎ 644063.

UK: Ferdowsi Avenue, ☎ 375011 (10 lines).

US: 260 Takhte Jamshid Avenue, P.O. Box 50, ☎ 820091/9.

Other addresses in Tehran

South African Consulate: Park Avenue No. 21, 22nd Street, P.O. Box 12, ☎ 621835/6/7.

American Express Authorised Representative: Near East Tours, 130 Takhte Jamshid Avenue, ☎ 294654.

Thomas Cook Authorised Representative: Near East Tours, Takhte Jamshid Avenue, ☎ 892161/5.

BUSINESS INFORMATION

At the time of going to press the economic situation in Iran is still clouded with uncertainty. Nobody can predict the intended economic policy of the Government. However it would seem reasonable to assume that the general pattern of development will not change drastically.

The continuing expansion of the country's steel, shipbuilding, and mining industries offers opportunities for foreign suppliers of machinery, materials and equipment. The development of the chemical, petrochemical, electrical and vehicle construction industries will require foreign goods and expertise. Major projects in the oil and gas industries will require technology and plant that could be provided by foreign companies. There has been a steady increase in the demand for consumer products and this has meant that opportunities exist for sales of items such as domestic equipment and appliances, china and furniture.

The best method of conducting any import trade is through the services of an agent. Agents in Iran tend to operate in specific areas of the market, rather than in a particular range of products. Major government contracts are often put up for tender. Any firms wishing to put in a tender must be able to produce bank guarantees of performance. Representation in Tehran should ensure adequate coverage of the whole country.

Khorranshahr is the main port but will soon be rivalled by Bandar-e-Abbas. Major industrial centres include Tabriz (tractors, diesel engines, textiles, machine tools), Isfahan (textiles, steel), Abadan (centre of the oil-refining industry) and Ahvaz (steel rolling, paper industries).

Import and Exchange Control Regulations

Iranian import regulations classify goods into two categories: 'authorised' and 'unauthorised'. 'Unauthorised' goods will only be allowed into the country if there is a shortage. 'Authorised' goods, if no Ministry approval is needed, may be freely imported. While no import licence is required, importers must register with the Central Bank – registration fee, 1 per cent. Some imports necessitate payment of a 15% deposit of the value of the order.

Business Hours

Government Offices:

0800–1600	Saturday to Wednesday, October to April.
0700–1300	Saturday to Thursday, May to September.

Business Houses:

0800–1300	Saturday to Wednesday,
1600–1900	October to April.
0800–1300	Saturday to Thursday,
1700–1900	May to September.

Business Events

The annual International Trade Fair is usually staged in Tehran in September and there are specialised trade fairs in Tehran each year.

BUSINESS SERVICES

Shipping

Arya National Shipping, 222 Karim Khan Zand Boulevard, Tehran, ☎ 894270.

Gray Mackenzie & Co, Amini Building, P.O. Box 870, Tehran, ☎ 314516/9.

Gulf Transportation Co, Karim Khan Zand Building, Nader Shah No. 4/2, Tehran, ☎ 897810.

Hansa Line, Aftab Shargh Building, Ferdowsi Avenue, Tehran, ☎ 311567.

Iran Express, Sea-Man Pak Co, 130 Soraya Street, Tehran, ☎ 825076/9.

Kavoon Co, 6 Nasser Street, Shadad Building, Tehran, ☎ 839234.

H. Nahai Bros, 688 Sepahbod Zahedi Avenue, Tehran, ☎ 893201.

USEFUL ADDRESSES (BUSINESS)

Tehran

Iran-American Chamber of Commerce, Iranian Bank Building, Takhte Jamshid Avenue, ☎ 895149/891168.

Iran-British Chamber of Commerce, Bezrouke House (side entrance, 3rd Floor), 140 North Forsat Avenue, Takhte Jamshid Avenue, ☎ 826705.

Iran Chamber of Commerce, Industries and Mines, 254 Takhte Jamshid Avenue.

Organisation for Investment and Economic Technical Assistance of Iran, Foreign Investment Department, Nasser Khosrow Avenue, ☎ 3251.

MAJOR CITIES AND TOWNS

Tehran

Tehran rests in the shadows of the Elburz mountain range which lies to the north of the city. It has only been the capital of Iran for 200 years and is very modern in comparison with the ancient Persian cities of Isfahan and Shiraz. Its fine boulevards are often completely congested by traffic and its modern facilities do not always match up to Western standards.

The city has a number of attractions to offer the sightseer. The finest places to visit are the Ethnological Museum, just off Nasser Khosrow Avenue – the museum illustrates many aspects of Iranian social life; the Tehran Contemporary Museum of Art in Farah Park; the National Arts Museum in Ruali Sina Avenue; the Archaeological Museum in Raphael Street – this museum contains a vast array of objects covering the many periods of Persian history; the Nagarastan Museum on Sepah and Kakh Streets – this museum houses a marvellous collection of ninteenth-century Persian art; the Bazaar in the southern part of the city (between Khayyam and Buzarjomehri Avenues) – a shopper's paradise, with stalls offering an incredible assortment of wares.

For tours of the city, it is best to visit the Tourist Information Office at 174 Elizabeth II Boulevard which arranges half-day and full-day excursions in Tehran. There is a bus service in the capital, but it has an inadequate number of vehicles to cater for the demand. Tickets are obtainable from the kiosks placed near the stops.

Mehrabad Airport is 10km/6 miles from the centre of Tehran.

Hotels

Hotels are officially rated deluxe, 4 star, 3 star, etc.

ARYA SHERATON (deluxe), 50 Bijan Street, ☎ 683021.
Modern, deluxe hotel 10km/6 miles from the city centre in the northern sector of the city.

Rooms: 204 [symbols]. Suites available.
Facilities: Restaurants, bars, coffee shop. Swimming. Parking and car hire.
Services: TC, FC. [symbol] Access, Amex, Bankamericard, Carte Blanche, Diners Club, Eurocard and Master Charge. [symbols]. Dr. on call.

Conference room – max. capacity 1,200.
Banquet room – max. capacity 1,000.

COMMODORE (4 star), 10 Takhte Jamshid Avenue, ☎ 666726.
Modern, first-class hotel in the city centre, 7km/4 miles from the airport.
Rooms: 200.
Suites available.
Facilities: Restaurants, bars. Swimming and sauna. Parking and car hire.
Services: TC, FC. Access, Amex, Carte Blanche, Diners Club, Eurocard, Master Charge. S. Dr. on call.
Conference room – max. capacity 1,000.
Banquet room – max. capacity 1,000.

INTER-CONTINENTAL (deluxe), Iran Novin Avenue, ☎ 655021/9.
Modern, deluxe hotel in the city centre, 10km/6 miles from the airport.
Rooms: 400.
Suites available.
Facilities: Restaurants, bars and coffee shop. Swimming and sauna. Tennis. Parking and car hire.
Services: TC, FC. Access, Amex, Carte Blanche, Diners Club, Eurocard, Master Charge. S. Dr. on call.
Conference room – max. capacity 600.
Banquet room – max. capacity 600.

ROYAL TEHRAN HILTON (deluxe), Shemiran Pahlavi Road, ☎ 290011/15.
Modern, deluxe hotel 10km/16 miles from the city centre encircled by a 22-acre exhibit and sports area.
Rooms: 554, on request. Suites available.
Facilities: Restaurants, bars. Shops and services. Tennis. Sauna, outdoor heated pool. Parking and car hire.
Services: TC, FC. Amex, Carte Blanche, Diners Club, Eurocard, Master Charge. S. Dr. on call.
Conference room – max. capacity 1,500.
Banquet room – max. capacity 1,000.

TEHRAN INTERNATIONAL (4 star), Kourosh-Kabir Road, ☎ 840081.
Deluxe resort hotel near to the city centre.
Rooms: 340.
Suites available.
Facilities: Restaurants, American bar and coffee shop. Indoor and outdoor pools. Sauna. Cinema.
Services: Amex, Diners Club.
Conference and convention facilities.

Restaurants

Iranian:
Khansalar, Jordan Avenue, Argentine Square, ☎ 685765; *Namakdoon*, Inter-Continental Hotel, Iran Novin Street, ☎ 655021/9; *Persian Garden*, Royal Tehran Hilton, Pahlavi Avenue, ☎ 290011; *Ravagh Teahouse*, Pahlavi Avenue, ☎ 295031; *Sarbad*, 25 Chahrivar Avenue, Abbasabad, ☎ 629792.

Chinese:
Chinese Pam Pam, Shahreza Avenue, ☎ 661272; *Chinese Paxy's*, Takhte Tavoos Avenue, ☎ 897253; *Chinese Restaurant*, 3 Abdoh, ☎ 890714.

French:
Chez Maurice, Royal Tehran Hilton, Pahlavi Avenue, ☎ 290031; *Lautrec*, Pahlavi Avenue, ☎ 222596; *Mirabelle*, 100 Villa Avenue, ☎ 824774; *Rotisserie Française*, Inter-Continental Hotel, Iran Novin Avenue, ☎ 655021/9; *Restaurant Suisse*, Forsat Street, ☎ 828516.

Other restaurants:
Piccola Roma, 212 Villa Avenue, ☎ 836592 (Italian); *Greek Tavern*, Vozara Avenue, 11th Street, ☎ 620656 (Greek); *Leon's Grill Room*, Hotel Leon, 306 Shahreza Avenue, ☎ 820605; *Maharaja*, Excelsior Hotel, Pahlavi Avenue, ☎ 665596; *Inner Room Piano Restaurant*, Takhte Tavoos Avenue (international).

Nightclubs

At the time of going to press, all nightclubs in Tehran were closed, due to the ruling of the Revolutionary Council.

Entertainment

Facilities for social and cultural events are provided by the following national associations: The *British Council*, 38 Ferdowsi Avenue, ☎ 303346; The *French Institute*, 58 Shahpour Ali Reza Avenue, ☎ 644202; The *German Goethe Institute*, Vozara Avenue, 7th Street, ☎ 627336; The *Iran-American Society*, Park Avenue, Abbasabad, ☎ 625545.

Tehran and its surrounds offer a wide range of sports and pastimes. There are indoor swimming pools at the *Ice Palace* and *Bowling Club*, City Recreation Centre. The Amjadieh Stadium, off Roosevelt Avenue, has public tennis courts. The *Imperial Country Club*, Pahlavi Avenue, *Taj Club* (to the north of Vanak Square), and *Nioc Club* all have tennis courts. *Tehran Riding School*, off Shemiran Road, and the *Imperial Country Club* offer horse-riding facilities. Many private clubs have squash courts.

Shopping

Best buys: carpets, ceramics, jewellery, pottery, textiles.
Opening hours for stores are 0900–1900 hours.
Some good shops to visit for various goods are: *Centre de l'Artisanat*, 381 Takhte Jamshid Avenue; *Markase Sanaye Dasti*, Shah Reza Avenue (handicrafts); *Atosa*, 2/132 Soraya Avenue (jewellery); *Turquoise Shop*, Lalezar Avenue (turquoise); *Iran Carpet Company*, 160 Ferdowsi Avenue, and *Azizi's Persian House*, 114 Ferdowsi Avenue (carpets).

Tourist Information

Tourist Information, 174 Elizabeth II Boulevard, ☎ 621291/8; also at airport and railway station. General information, ☎ 29029.

Iran Scene is a monthly publication for tourists.

Isfahan

Isfahan, the most picturesque city in Iran, with a fascinating history behind it, is situated to the south of Tehran. There is so much to see that it is impossible to fit everything in unless time is no problem, so here is a selection of places to visit: the Royal Square (Meydan) – this, together with the adjacent buildings, was built in the early seventeenth century; the Sheikh-e-Lutfullah Mosque, just by the Royal Square – completed in the first half of the seventeenth century, it was commissioned as a monument for the father-in-law of Shah Abbas I; Chahar Bagh Avenue, the main street, can be reached via Sepah Avenue which is located at the northwest corner of the Meydan; Ali Qapu (the Lofty Gate) which stands on the west side of the Meydan – the name includes as well as the gate the building behind it, in which there is a resplendent throne room and intricately decorated rooms; the Qaisariyeh Bazaar – built soon after the massive gate, it contains some interesting mosaics and paintings; the numerous mosques include the Masjed-e-Jomeh (Friday) mosque, the Masjed-e-Sorkhi (Red) mosque, the Masjed-e-Hakim (Hakim) mosque and the Masjed-e-Ali (Ali) mosque; the Manar-e-Ali (Ali Minaret) – probably the oldest minaret in Isfahan; the Manare-e-Sareban (Saberan Minaret) – the most elegant minaret in the city.

The city has a fairly good bus service. An alternative is to either use the taxis, orange (1st class) and black and white (low class), or to hire a car from one of the several car-hire firms which operate within the city. It is also possible to hire chauffeur-driven cars. For tours in and around the city use the main travel agents – Iran Travel, Isfahan Tourist and Near East Tours.

Hotels

KOUROSH INTERNATIONAL (deluxe), Farah Boulevard, ☎ 40230/39.
A modern first-class hotel, situated in the city centre, looking out over the Zayanderud river.
Rooms: 138 on request. Suites available.
Facilities: Restaurants, bars and coffee shop. Shopping arcade, beauty parlour, barber, airline office. Swimming. Car hire and parking.
Services: TC, FC. Access, Amex, Carte Blanche, Diners Club, Eurocard, Master Charge. Dr. on call.
Conference room – max. capacity 300.
Banquet room – max. capacity 150.
Custom-built conference room – max. capacity 1,000.

SHAH ABBAS (deluxe), Shah Abbas Avenue, ☎ 26010/7.
Famous luxury hotel situated in the city centre.
Rooms: 215.
Facilities: Restaurants and bars. Tennis and squash. Swimming and sauna. Car hire and parking.
Services: TC, FC. Amex, Carte Blanche, Diners Club.

Restaurants

Hatam, Fathieh Street, ☎ 26687 (Kebab restaurant); *La Fontaine*, Pole-Khadjoo, Moshtagh Avenue No. 7, ☎ 29951 (French); *Leon*, Korshid Street, ☎ 41276; *Moghadam*, Sheikh Bahai Street, ☎ 34901; *Noble*, Absharr Street, ☎ 43872 (Oriental dancing); *Shah Abbas*, Shah Abbas Hotel, Shah Abbas Avenue, ☎ 26010; *Shahrzad*, Abbasabad Avenue, ☎ 34474 (Iranian); *Soltani*, Chahar Bagh Avenue, ☎ 32239 (Iranian).

Shopping

Best buys: antiques, carpets, brass and silver articles, handicrafts, qalamqari (superlative hand-printed cotton fabrics).

The Qaisariyeh Bazaar is at the north end of the Meydan.

Tourist Information

Tourist Information Office, Shah Abbas Avenue, ☎ 27667 and at the airport, ☎ 28866. General Information ☎ 08.

IRAQ
Republic of Iraq

Size: 434,924 sq.km/167,924 sq.miles.

Population: 12,029,000 (1978 est.).

Distribution: 65% in urban areas.

Density: 26 persons per sq.km/67 per sq.mile.

Population Growth Rate: 3.3% p.a.

Ethnic Composition: 70% of the population are Arabs, 20% Kurds, and there are minority groupings of Armenians, Jews, Assyrians, Turkomans and Lurs.

Capital: Baghdad Pop. 2,987,000.

Major Cities: Mosul Pop. 892,000; Basra Pop. 1 million.

Language: Arabic is the official language and Kurdish is widely spoken in the northeast. English is widely understood in government and business circles, and some French is also spoken. The various languages of the ethnic minorities are also spoken.

Religion: 95% of the population are Muslim, both of the Sunni and Shia sects. There are Christian and Jewish minorities.

Government: The Revolutionary Command Council has supreme power in Iraq, although the 1970 Constitution envisaged a National Council with representatives from political, economic and social sectors – this has yet to be established.

The controlling party is the Regional Iraqi Command of the Arab Socialist Baath Party.

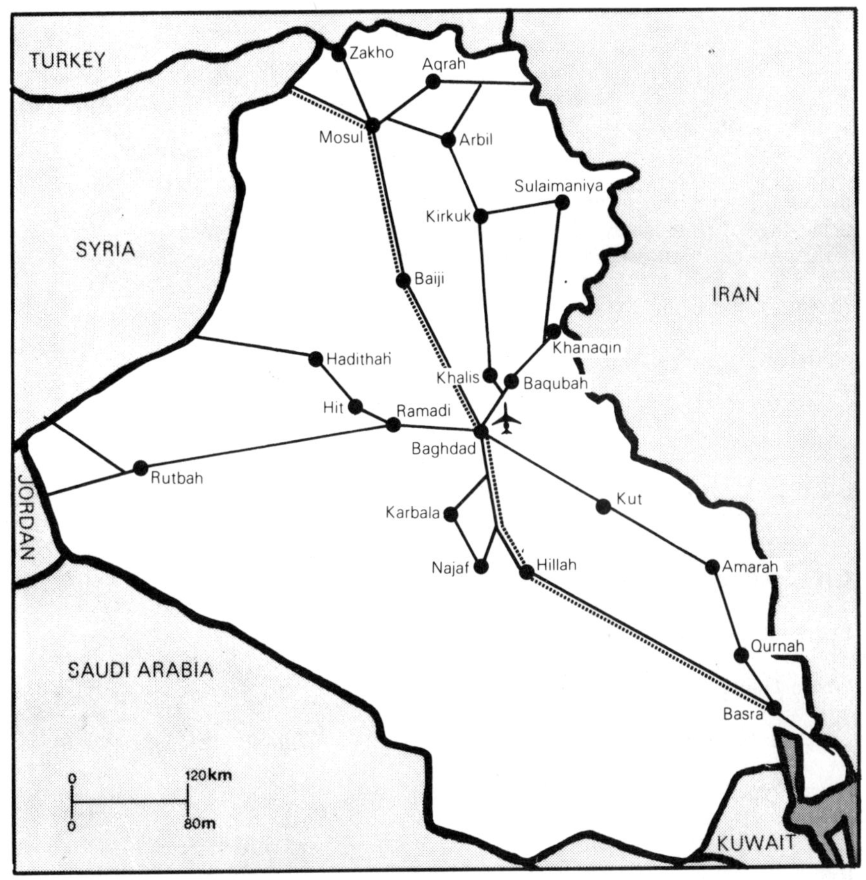

GEOGRAPHY

Iraq is bordered by Turkey to the north, Iran to the east, Kuwait, Saudi Arabia and the Gulf to the south, and Syria and Jordan to the east.

The landscape is one of contrasts with hills, mountains, deserts and marshes. The two rivers of ancient Mesopotamia – the Tigris and the Euphrates – flow almost the whole length of the country, from the Zagros mountains in the north, through the plains and marshes of the centre to the desert lands of the south and out into the Gulf.

Climate

Summers in Iraq are hot and dry with temperatures ranging from 25°C/77°F to 38°C/100°F and high humidity in southern areas. Winters are relatively cool with temperatures ranging from 11°C/52°F to 19°C/66°F.

Agriculture

With the expansion of the industrial sector less than one half of the population are engaged in working on the land, and today agriculture accounts for approximately 7% of the Gross National Product. However, Iraq is still the largest date exporter in the world.

With the increased oil revenues, Iraq has embarked on a number of schemes aimed at improving the productivity and growth rate of the agricultural sector and achieving self-sufficiency in food production. These schemes include nationalised farmlands, co-operatives, large-scale irrigation works and land reclamation.

Main Crops: cereals, dates, citrus fruits, rice, cotton.

Mineral Resources: oil, natural gas, salt, sulphur.

THE ECONOMY

Gross National Product (1976): US$15.5 billion.

Per Capita Income (1976): US$1,347.

Gross Domestic Product (1975): 3,802 million ID.

Foreign Trade (1976): Total Imports US$4 billion; Total Exports US$8.9 billion.

Main Trading Partners: Imports – Japan, West Germany, USA, France, UK. Exports – Italy, France, Brazil, Turkey, USSR, Spain.

Iraq is the third-largest exporter of oil in the Middle East. Oil revenues are being used to meet domestic needs and to develop new export possibilities, as well as to finance industrial diversification in order to reduce Iraq's imports. The country's major industries include oil, natural gas, chemicals, clothing, construction and food.

The rapid growth rate achieved by Iraq has brought with it a number of economic problems, such as a labour shortage and an over-extension of certain sections of the economy. The State has introduced a series of Development Plans calculated to reduce the growth rate and these measures have alleviated some of the problems to a certain extent.

Major Industries: oil, natural gas, chemicals, clothing, construction, food.

Main Commodities Traded: Imports – industrial machinery, iron and steel, automobiles, tea, sugar, clothing, pharmaceuticals. Exports – petroleum, agricultural products, livestock, cement.

Crude Oil Production (1977): 9,269,000 metric tons per average calendar month.

Iraq is a member of the Organisation of Petroleum Exporting Countries (OPEC) and the Arab League.

HOW TO GET THERE

Air

Iraqi Airways operate several flights a week to Baghdad from London and Paris and weekly flights from Amsterdam, Brussels, Copenhagen, Frankfurt, Geneva, Madrid, Munich, Rome and Vienna.

There are regular flights to Baghdad from Algiers, Amman, Beirut, Cairo, Casablanca, Damascus, Khartoum, Tripoli, Tunis, and from India, the Far East and most East European capitals.

Within the Gulf area there are good air links between Baghdad and Kuwait, Bahrain, Dubai, Abu Dhabi and Tehran.

There are no direct flights to Baghdad from North America.

Major airlines flying to Baghdad include Aeroflot, Air France, Air India, Alitalia, British Airways, Egypt Air, JAL, KLM, Lufthansa, MEA, PIA and Swissair.

Flying times to Baghdad: from London 5¼ hours; from New York 19 hours.

Baghdad International Airport is 16km/10 miles from the city centre.

ENTRY REGULATIONS

Visas

No visa is required by nationals of Algeria, Bahrain, Egypt, Jordan, Kuwait, Lebanon, Libya, Morocco, People's Democratic Republic of Yemen, Syria and the United Arab Emirates.

All other nationals require visas obtainable from Iraqi diplomatic missions abroad.

Visa applications should be made well in advance of the proposed visit as delays are likely to occur. Business travellers should support their application with a letter from the Church Authorities confirming the applicant's religion or their Baptismal Certificate, together with a letter from their firm giving details of the business to be undertaken in Iraq, the names and addresses of any contacts and confirming financial responsibility for the applicant. A letter from a travel agent or airline is also required, confirming that air tickets have been issued and giving details of the journey.

A letter of invitation from the company to be visited in Iraq or from the Iraq Government should also be submitted with the visa application.

Evidence in a passport of a previous or planned visit to Israel may adversely affect the granting of a visa.

Visas are valid for 3 three months for a stay of up to 30 days which can be extended in Iraq.

Transit visas are valid for up to 7 days. Applications for a transit visa should be supported by a ticket or booking letter from an airline or travel agent and proof of financial arrangements. Applicants should have their passport endorsed with the visa of the country they intend to visit after Iraq.

Business travellers staying in Iraq for more than 15 days must register with the local police authorities. Any visitor staying in Iraq for more than 30 days will require an exit visa which must be applied for at least 24 hours prior to departure from Iraq.

Health Regulations

Valid International Certificates of Vaccination against smallpox and cholera are required. TAB (typhoid and paratyphoid) injections are recommended.

Customs

Currency: There is no limit to the amount of foreign currency or travellers' cheques which may be brought in, but all foreign currency must be declared on arrival. There is a limit of ID25 to the amount of local currency which may be imported into Iraq, and the export of local currency is restricted to ID5.

Duty-free articles: 200 cigarettes, 50 cigars or 250g tobacco, 1 litre of wine or spirits and half a litre of perfume. Personal effects. Samples of no commercial value provided they are accompanied by a list endorsed by the Customs authorities of the country of origin.

Samples worth more than ID10 may be imported temporarily (for not more than 12 months) if the import duty is deposited and a licence obtained. The deposit is refundable on re-export of the samples within the time limit.

Prohibited articles: The import of most foreign newspapers and magazines is banned and these will be confiscated on arrival. Typewriters are also likely to be confiscated and only returned to the owner on departure from Iraq.

PRACTICAL INFORMATION FOR THE VISITOR

1. Currency

Monetary Unit – Iraqi dinar (ID), divided into 1,000 fils.
Notes – ¼, ½, 1, 5, 10 dinars.
Coins – 1, 5, 10, 25, 50, 100 fils.

Banking Hours:
Summer – 0800–1200 Saturday to Wednesday
0800–1100 Thursday
Winter – 0900–1300 Saturday to Wednesday
0900–1200 Thursday
Iraq's banking system is government-owned.

Major Banks with Head Offices in Baghdad:

Central Bank of Iraq (Bank of Issue)
Rashid Street, Shorja, ☎ 8889051.
Rafidain Bank
New Bank's Street.
Industrial Bank of Iraq
Khullani Square, ☎ 8889761.
Agricultural Bank of Iraq
Rashid Street, ☎ 8884191.
Estate Bank of Iraq
opposite Directorate General of Police, ☎ 8889091.

The Rafidain Bank is the only Iraqi bank dealing with normal business and commercial transactions and has numerous branches throughout the country.

2. Electricity Supply

220V AC 50Hz.
Plugs: 2 and 3 pin Continental.

3. Weights and Measures

The metric system is in use.

4. Media

Radio and television networks are controlled by the Iraqi Broadcasting and Television Establishment, part of the Ministry of Information.

Iraq Radio broadcasts 22 hours daily in several languages. An English news bulletin is broadcast on Iraqi television and radio every night, around 2200 hours.

Newspapers:

Al-Joumhouriya, *Al-Riyadhi*, *Al-Thaura* (Baath Party), *Tarik al-Shaab* (Communist Party), *Baghdad Observer* (English language).

Periodicals:

Among the numerous periodicals to be published in Baghdad are *Al-Fikr al-Jadid*, *Al-Iqtisad al-Iraqi*, and *Al-Amal al-Shaabi*.

Al-Naft wal Alaam is published monthly by the Iraq National Oil Company. *Commerce* is a quarterly publication of the Baghdad Chamber of Commerce which also issues weekly bulletins dealing with market conditions, commodity prices, etc. *Al Sinai* (Arabic and English) is the quarterly journal of the Iraqi Federation of Industries.

5. Medical Care

Well-qualified doctors and dentists are available in Baghdad. The Ibn Sina Hospital, Karradat Mariam, Haifa Street, Baghdad, ☎ 32134, is a private hospital with British medical staff. Medical City, North Gate, ☎ 8889001 is Baghdad's main general hospital.

Tap water is generally safe to drink in the cities and towns although its cloudy appearance and sediment are somewhat unpleasant.

6. Telephone, Telex and Postal Services

International telephone services from Iraq are extensive but frequent delays can be expected. Local calls in the main cities and towns can be made fairly quickly but inter-city connections are less reliable.

Useful Telephone Numbers (Baghdad):

Police	☎ 104
Ambulance	☎ 122

Some of the larger hotels have telexes, including the Baghdad Hotel, and there is a public telex service at the Central Post Office, Rashid Street in Baghdad.

There are branch post offices in Baghdad in Nidhal Street, opposite the Seventh Day Adventists' Church, in Saadoun Street and next to the Baghdad Hotel. The Poste Restante is located at the Nidhal Street post office.

All mail to and from Iraq should be sent by air.

7. Public Holidays

Fixed Holidays:

1 January	*New Year's Day*
6 January	*Army Day*
8 February	*Anniversary of 1963 Revolution*
21 March	*Nairuz Day*
1 May	*Labour Day*
14 July	*National Day*
17 July	*Baath Revolution Day*

Muslim Holidays:

These follow the Muslim calendar and occur 10–12 days earlier every year. The dates of the Muslim holidays are approximate as they depend upon sightings of the moon, and may differ by one or two days from those given below. 1981 dates are:

18 January	*Prophet's Birthday*
31 July –2 August	*Eid el Fitr* end of *Ramadan*)
8–10 October	*Eid el Adha*
29 October	*Al Hijra* (Muslim New Year)
7–8 November	*Ashoura*

The Muslim week-end (Thursday afternoon and Friday) is observed in Iraq.

8. Time

GMT+3

9. Internal Transport

Air

Iraqi Airways operate a daily service between Baghdad, Basra and Mosul.

Airline Offices in Baghdad:

Aeroflot	☎ 8881250.
Air France	☎ 96014.
Air India	☎ 99686.
British Airways	☎ 8886446.
Interflug	☎ 8889789.
Iraqi Airways	☎ 8880051/5519999.
JAL	☎ 96503.
KLM	☎ 92397.
Lufthansa	☎ 8889721.
Middle East Airlines	☎ 95128.
Pan Am	☎ 8888764.
PIA	☎ 8887181.
SAS	☎ 95592.
Swissair	☎ 92344.

Rail

The three major rail routes are: Baghdad–Basra; Baghdad–Kirkuk; Baghdad–Mosul.

Road

Self-drive and chauffeur-driven cars are available for hire. An International Driving Licence is required.

Car-Hire Firms in Baghdad

Sumer Cars, Saadoun Street, ☎ 92143.

Baghdad Cars, Masbah Square, ☎ 97721/90628.

Taxi drivers rarely keep to the official rates, preferring to switch off their meters and negotiate the fare at the beginning of each journey. The average fare within Baghdad is ID1. Fares are usually doubled after 2400 hours.

The fare between the airport and the city centre is often paid to an airport official who will refund the taxi driver. Be careful not to pay both the official and the driver as this is unnecessary.

10. Tipping

Taxis – no tip necessary.

Porters – 50–100 fils per bag.

Hotels/restaurants – 10% of the bill.

11. Social Customs

The majority of the population of Iraq are Muslims and strict attention should be paid to Muslim customs and mores. However, alcohol is available in the cities and large towns and is served in most restaurants.

The Iraqi authorities are very security conscious and visitors are advised to carry their passports with them at all times. Visitors should be careful when taking photos, especially near public buildings, port installations, etc.

For further information, refer to page 12 under 'Muslim Social Customs'.

USEFUL ADDRESSES (GENERAL)

Embassies in Baghdad

Australia: Masbah 141–377, ☎ 92356.

Canada: 47/1/7 Al Mansour, P.O. Box 323 Central Post Office, ☎ 5521459/5521932.

France: Karrada Dakhil, Kard el Pasha No. 9 J.3.1., ☎ 96061.

West Germany: Masbah Square, P.O. Box 2036, ☎ 92037/9.

Japan: 41/7/35 Masbah, P.O. Box 355, ☎ 95156/7.

Netherlands: 28/2 Nidhal Street, Saadoun Park, P.O. Box 2064, ☎ 8887175/6.

Switzerland: Masbah House, No. 41/2/35, Karradah Al-Sharkiah, P.O. Box 2107, ☎ 93091/3.

UK: Sharia Salah Ud Din, Karkh, ☎ 32121; Commercial Section, Shaheen Building, Saadoun Street, Kard al-Pasha, ☎ 99001/3.

US: 52/5/35 Masbah, Alwiyah, P.O. Box 2447, ☎ 96138/9.

Other addresses in Baghdad

State Organisation for Tourism, Alwiyah, Saadoun Street, ☎ 99306.

Thomas Cook Overseas Ltd, Saadoun Street, P.O. Box 2007, ☎ 89721/3.

BUSINESS INFORMATION

A series of Five-Year Plans, concentrating on the socialist sector of industry in particular, have given the Iraqi economy a definite boost in recent years. Nationalisations and various import restrictions have greatly reduced the private sector, which now represents no more than 5% in terms of imports.

Relations with the West (in particular the United States and Britain) have been strained in the past, and resentment towards US Middle East policy and British imperialism still runs strong in certain sectors. However, an economic rapprochement is under way and the Iraqi demand for US imports is now high.

The foreign business traveller is advised to become familiar with prevailing Iraqi attitudes and values which differ from those of other Arab countries. Since over 90% of imports are handled by government-controlled organisations, foreigners should be prepared to deal with a trained and efficient national bureaucracy.

Buying is usually done by public tender or occasionally by private invitation by state-trading organisations. Laws governing the appointment of agents are strict and any appointment must be approved by, and registered with, the Iraqi authorities. The effectiveness of an agent is severely limited by this policy.

Import and Exchange Control Regulations

Exchange transactions must be effected through the Rafidain and Central Banks. An import licence and exchange control permit are necessary for the import of all goods.

The importation of certain goods is prohibited, although this restriction may be waived in circumstances where national need prevails.

Business Hours

Government Offices:

Summer –	0800–1400	Saturday to Wednesday
	0800–1300	Thursday
Winter –	0830–1430	Saturday to Wednesday
	0830–1330	Thursday

Business Houses:

Summer –	0800–1400 1700–1900	Saturday to Wednesday
	0800–1300	Thursday

Winter –	0830–1430 1700–1900	Saturday to Wednesday
	0830–1330	Thursday

Business Events

Baghdad International Fair is held annually during the first 15 days of October. The general emphasis of the fair is on capital goods. For further information contact: Iraqi Fairs Administration, Baghdad International Fair, Damascus Street, Al-Mansour, Baghdad, ☎ 37130/1.

BUSINESS SERVICES

Interpreter and Translation Services

Albert Nisan, Gharibjan Building, Shorja, P.O. Box 11034, Baghdad, ☎ 86888.

Najib Franjia, Pachachi Building, Southgate, Baghdad.

Dar Al Alsun, Al Jamil Building, Khullani Square, Baghdad.

Dar al-Sharaq Al-Hadith, Pachachi Building, Southgate, Baghdad.

Khalid al-Ani, Faiha Building, Jamhouriya Street, P.O. Box 3119, Baghdad, ☎ 87835/66544.

Khayam Advertising Bureau, Mudbir Jassim Building, 7th Floor, Fatah Square, P.O. Box 5681, Baghdad, ☎ 99215.

USEFUL ADDRESSES (BUSINESS)

Federation of Iraqi Industries, Khullani Square, Baghdad, ☎ 80091/4.

Federation of Iraqi Chambers of Commerce, Baghdad Chamber of Commerce Building, Mustansir Street, Baghdad, ☎ 8888819.

Baghdad Chamber of Commerce, Mustansir Street, Baghdad, ☎ 8886111.

Mosul Chamber of Commerce, Khaled Ibn-al-Walid, P.O. Box 35, Mosul.

Ministry of Information, Jumhouriya Street, Tahrir Square, Baghdad, ☎ 69181.

Ministry of Trade, Karradat Miriam, Khullani Square, Baghdad, ☎ 8886141.

State Trade Organisation for Capital Goods, Jumhouriya Street, Al-Khullani Square, Baghdad, ☎ 8889703/5.

State Organisation for Exports, Yousif Rashid Al-Ani Building, Saadoun Street, Baghdad, ☎ 95424.

General Trade Establishment for Consumer Materials, Al-Masbah, Baghdad, ☎ 96076/98858.

MAJOR CITIES AND TOWNS

Baghdad

Baghdad was originally built on the west bank of the River Tigris in the first century A.D., and since that time the city has grown in size and spread its limits up until the present time when it spans both sides of the river. Amidst the tall office blocks and hotels stand the dwarfed minarets and churches and the old bazaars where much of the city's charm is to be found.

The city abounds with buildings of historic interest among which the Iraqi Museum is considered as one of the city's most prestigious attractions, and ranks as one of the finest archaeological museums in the Middle East. The unique collections within span several periods of ancient history from the Neolithic period through the Babylonian and Assyrian civilisations and on to the periods of Greek and Roman influence.

One cannot go far in Baghdad without coming across one of the city's numerous mosques. The most famous is the Shrine of Kadhimain on the outskirts but entry is forbidden to non-Muslims. The mosque of Abdul Qadir Gailani in Kifar Street is of outstanding beauty and the minaret of the Suq al-Ghazel Mosque in Jumhouriya Street is one of the few remaining intact from the Abbasid period.

Another fine site in Baghdad are the ruins of the Abbasid Palace in Mamuniyah Street, dating back to the twelfth century, and parts of this have recently been restored. The thirteenth-century Al Mustansiriyah School on the east bank of the Tigris is reputed to be the oldest university in the world.

Baghdad International Airport is 16km/10 miles from the city centre.

Hotels

There is no official hotel rating system in Iraq.

AMBASSADOR, Abu Nawas Street, ☎ 8886105.
Centrally located, overlooking the Tigris river.
Rooms: 66.
Facilities: Restaurant and bar. Car hire.
Services: **TC**, **FC**. Diners Club. **S**.
Conference room – max. capacity 200.

KHAYAM, Saadoun Street, ☎ 96176.
Modern, first-class hotel in the city centre.
Rooms: 78.
Facilities: Restaurant and bar. Bank and travel agency. Car hire.
Services: Amex and Carte Blanche. Dr. on call. Conference room.

BAGHDAD, Saadoun Street, ☎ 8889031.
Modern first-class hotel in the city centre.
Rooms: 200 and on request.
Facilities: Restaurants and bars. Travel agencies and banks. Post and Telegraph centre. Shopping arcade. Swimming. Car hire.
Services: **TC**, **FC**. Amex and Diners Club. **S**.

AL-ABBASI PALACE, Saadoun Street, ☎ 94384/6.
Rooms: 77.
Facilities: Restaurant and bar. Casino.

DIWAN, Saadoun Street, near Nasr Square, P.O. Box 3291, ☎ 888996.
Modern commercial hotel close to the city centre.
Rooms: 48.
Facilities: Restaurant and bar.
Services: Credit cards not accepted.

Restaurants

All restaurant prices are fixed by the Government. *Candles*, Tourism Administration Building, Saadoun Street; *Farouk*, Damascus Street, ☎ 32475; *Golden Plate*, Abu Nawas Street; *Fawanis*, Saadoun Street, ☎ 90522; *Strand*, Masbah Street, ☎ 92788; *Surab*, Nidhal Street, ☎ 90156; *Hammurabi*, Nidhal Street, ☎ 90559; *Pine Palace*, off Al-Fath Square.

Nightclubs

Moulin Rouge, Rashid Camp Road, ☎ 90809; *Embassy*, Al Masbah, ☎ 95971; *Baghdad*, Rashid Army Camp Street, ☎ 97945; *Select*, Saadoun Street, ☎ 99848; *Semiramis*, Saadoun Street, ☎ 99728; *Al Khayam*, Salhiyah, ☎ 34200.

Entertainment

Concerts are held at regular intervals in the Shab Hall and Al-Khuld Hall in Baghdad which attract Western performers as well as the Iraqi National Symphony Orchestra. Public performances are occasionally staged by the Russian-run School of Music and Ballet.

Soccer and horse racing are the city's most popular sporting attractions. Race meetings are held on Sundays, Wednesdays and Fridays (except during the hot summer months) at the Baghdad Race Course in Al-Mansur City.

The New British Club, Muasker Rashid Street, P.O. Box 2180, ☎ 93127, is a useful business meeting place. The club has good facilities (swimming pool, bar, dining room) and temporary membership can be obtained. Visitors requiring access to the club must be accompanied by a member.

The Aluriyah Club, Unknown Soldier Square, ☎ 95115, has a mixed Iraqi and expatriate membership. The club has good facilities including a restaurant, bar, swimming pool, squash and tennis courts and overseas visitors are admitted as guests of club members.

Shopping

The most interesting *souks* in Baghdad for the foreign visitor are the gold *souk*, the silk and textiles *souk* and the two antique *souks* near the Marjan Mosque. The Shorja *souk* sells a variety of goods while copper is the speciality of the Suq al-Safafir. The Suq al-Sagha is a silver bazaar near the Ahrar Bridge.

Iraqi handicrafts and souvenirs can be purchased at these shops: *Rural Crafts*, Saadoun Street, near Ali Baba Square; *Centre for Folkloric Handicrafts*, Ali Baba Square; *Handicrafts Shop*, Saadoun Street, around the corner from the Baghdad Hotel.

Basra

Basra lies on the edge of the desert and is the main date-producing area of Iraq. The city is divided by numerous canals and waterways and is Iraq's only direct link with the sea.

The city was founded in the seventh century A.D. by the Caliph Omar and was the capital of Iraq for a short time. During its long history the city has been under Turkish, Persian, Ottoman and British rule.

The inner area of Basra divides into three main areas: the Old City, the centre and the Maaqil (the port area). There are many reminders of the British period of rule within Basra and in fact much of the city's commercial life was dominated by the British up until the 1950s. Today the city has a cosmopolitan population, a sign of its transition into a modern, industrial city, with large numbers of expatriate workers from the Middle East and the Far East, including Japan.

The original site of the city was at Al-Zubair, 12km/7½ miles east of modern Basra, and several shrines dating back from the early days of Islam are to be found here.

It is said that the legendary Sindbad of *A Thousand and One Nights* fame began his journeys from Basra, and Sindbad Island in the Maaqil is reputed to have been his base.

The old airport in Basra has now been closed and Iraqi Airways use the air force base which is about 40 minutes' drive from the terminal at the Shatt al-Arab Hotel.

Hotels

SHATT AL-ARAB, Maaqil, ☎ 7701/7263.
Traditional hotel in the port area of Basra, overlooking the Shatt al-Arab.
Rooms: 88.
Facilities: Restaurant and bar. Bank and post office. Barber's shop. Air terminal.

UR HOTEL, Istiklal Street, Ashar, ☎ 217730/213252.
Modern hotel in central location, near the business district of Basra.
Rooms: 32.
Facilities: Restaurant and bar.

Restaurants

Venus, Khora Gardens – good quality Oriental food; *Sunside Restaurant*, Al-Thaura Street, ☎ 216220; *Ashtar Restaurant*, Al-Thaura Street; *Ali Baba*, Al-Thaura Street.

Entertainment

There are several bars in the Ashar district with live shows – the main one is the *Farrada* in Dinar Street.

Mosul

Mosul is the largest city in Northern Iraq and is an important trade and communications centre. The city has a long history dating back to 410 B.C. when it was mentioned by the Greek traveller Xenophon.

The city has many fine old buildings including the leaning minaret which is all that remains of the mosque built by Nur ed Din, the thirteenth-century Church of Shamoun al-Safa and the ruins of the old Turkish fortress of Bash Tabia. Another beautiful sight is the thirteenth-century palace of Qara Seraglio.

The Mosul Museum has some interesting archaeological exhibits from sites such as Nineveh, Nimrud and Assur, including some clay figures believed to date from the seventh millennium B.C.

Iraqi Airways use part of the Mosul air force base for flights to and from the city.

Hotels

AL-HIDARA AL-MAHALIYA, Cornish Street, ☎ 811271.
The hotel is run by the local governorate and overlooks the River Tigris.
Rooms: 71.
Facilities: Restaurant and bar.

RAFIDAIN HOTEL, Wadi Hajar, ☎ 71121.
Small hotel with a total of 10 rooms.

STATION HOTEL, Railway Station, ☎ 3083.
Small hotel with 31 rooms situated in Mosul's railway station.

Restaurants

Al-Ghabat Casino, off Dohuk Road; *Lake Casino*, near the Al-Ghabat Casino; *Nineveh Casino*, opposite the Nergal Gate of Nineveh – live music on Monday evenings.

Shopping

Best buys: textiles and carpets.

The Mosul *souk* is near the Old Bridge and sells a variety of goods often brought in by traders from outlying districts.

ISRAEL

State of Israel

Size: 20,700 sq.km/7,993 sq.miles (excluding territory occupied in 1967 war).

Population: 3,760,000 (1978).

Distribution: 86% in urban areas.

Density: 181 persons per sq.km/470 per sq.mile.

Population Growth Rate: 3% p.a.

Ethnic Composition: 85% of the population are Jewish, the rest are mainly Arab.

Capital: Jerusalem Pop. 366,300.

Major Cities: Tel Aviv Pop. 348,500; Haifa Pop. 227,200; Ramat Gan Pop. 121,000; Bat Yan Pop. 114,000.

Language: Hebrew is the principal language of Israel; Arabic is spoken by about 15% of the population. English and German are understood in business circles.

Religion: The majority of the population are Jewish; about 14% are Muslim and there are a small number of Christians.

Government: Israel has a Parliament consisting of one chamber (Knesset)

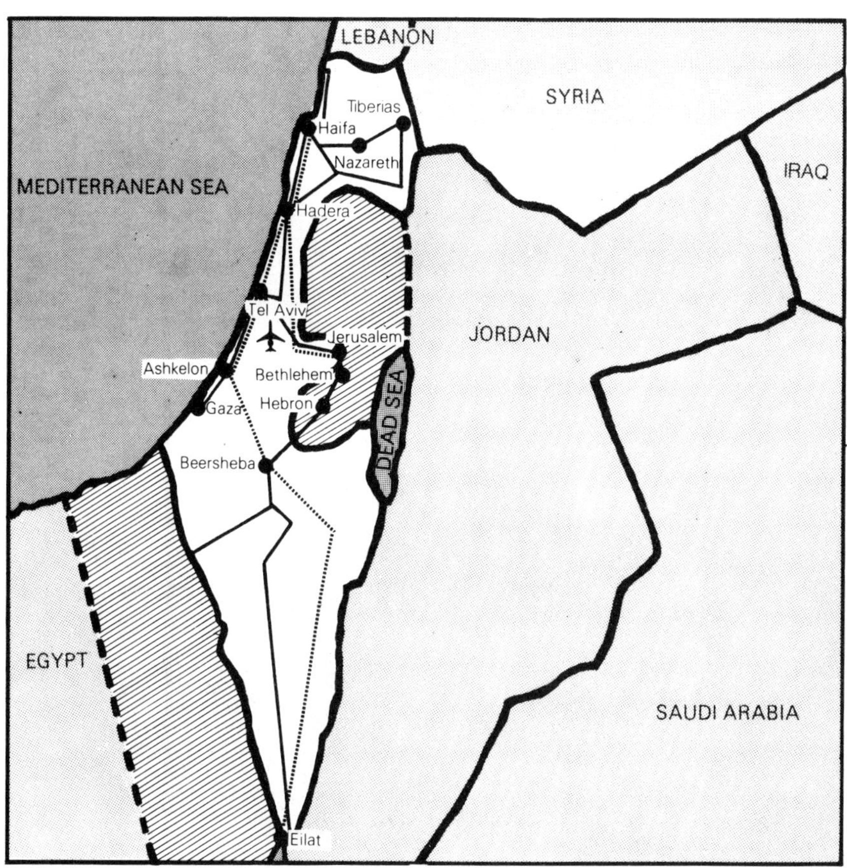

with 120 members elected by universal suffrage. A President is elected by the chamber. The major political parties are the ruling Likud Party, the Labour Party and the Democratic Movement for Change.

GEOGRAPHY

Israel is a relatively small country. The Mediterranean borders it on the east and it has borders with Lebanon to the north, Syria to the northeast, Jordan to the east and Egypt to the southwest.

On the west of the country is a 192km/120-mile-long and 24km/15-mile-wide coastal plain where the cities of Tel Aviv and Haifa are situated; two-thirds of the population live in this region. Down the centre of the country runs a mountain range that includes the hills of Galilee, Samaria and Judea. The Judean Hills run south to the Negev desert which occupies most of southern Israel (two-thirds of the total area of pre-1967 Israel). The Sea of Galilee, linked by the River Jordan to the Dead Sea, is on the eastern flank of Israel. Since the Israeli-Arab war of 1967, the West Bank region of the River Jordan and also the Golan Heights to the northeast have been occupied by Israel.

Climate

In summer there is virtually no rainfall and humidity can be around 75% in Tel Aviv and about 70% in Haifa. It is very hot with average summer temperatures between 23°C/74°F and 31°C/89°F.

The winter months (November to March) have an average temperature of around 18°C/64°F. Most of the rainfall occurs in these months. Winters are usually mild, especially in the coastal belt, but there is some snow in the hill regions. The Jordan valley has sub-tropical weather conditions.

Agriculture

Israel possesses a highly machine-intensive agricultural industry which is extremely efficient, contributing around 7% to the Gross National Product. Agricultural production is increasing at a rate of 7% annually.

Israel is almost self-supporting in foodstuffs, although cereals, beef, sugar and some animal foods are imported. The main exports are Jaffa oranges and grapefruit. Other exports that have increased are the out-of-season crops grown for the European market, such as flowers and fruit and vegetables.

Main Crops: citrus fruit, wheat, barley, durra, olives, melons, tomatoes, figs, cotton.

Mineral Resources: phosphates, potash, bromine, periclasse, oil.

THE ECONOMY

Gross National Product (1976): US$12.2 billion.

Per Capita Income (1976): US$3,516.

Gross Domestic Product (1975): US$12.1 billion.

Foreign Trade (1976): Total Imports US$4.1 billion; Total Exports US$2.4 billion.

Main Trading Partners: Imports – USA, UK, West Germany, Netherlands, Italy, Switzerland. Exports – USA, West Germany, UK, Netherlands, Hong Kong, France.

The Israeli economy has been beset by a number of problems over the last few years. Chief among these has been the increase in indebtedness, caused primarily by a huge military budget. The world trade recession, increases in commodity prices and inflation, which rose to 40% in 1976, have all contributed to the weakening of the economy.

Active measures have been taken to try and arrest the economic instability and boost the economy. These are aimed at reducing the balance of payments deficit and consumption and cutting public spending. The manufacturing industry and other export industries are to receive priority in government plans. Foreign investment has been encouraged by a number of fiscal measures that the Goverment has taken. However, Israel is still heavily dependent on the financial support of the United States.

Israel's manufacturing industries include metal-working, aircraft, clothing and textiles, electronics, chemicals, oil refining, petrochemicals and food. Areas of major growth over the next few years will be the metal-working and electronics industries. There are also large expansions planned in the chemical and petrochemical industries. The one other area where it is hoped to earn substantial revenues is the tourist industry. A steady increase in the number of tourists has taken place in the last few years. In 1977 there were 1,006,500 and the earnings from this source were the highest ever gained.

Major Industries: metal-working, aircraft, clothing and textiles, electronics, chemicals, petrochemicals.

Main Commodities Traded: Imports – rough diamonds, machinery, transport equipment, food and live animals, raw materials, chemicals. Exports – polished diamonds, citrus fruits, textiles, chemicals, fertilisers, metal products, minerals.

Israel is seeking to become a member of the European Economic Community (EEC).

HOW TO GET THERE

Air

The main airport in Israel is Ben-Gurion which is 19km/12 miles from the centre of Tel Aviv.

From Europe: Israel is connected with the principal cities in Europe by the services of Alitalia, Air France, Austrian Airlines, British Airways, Cyprus Airways, El Al Airlines, KLM, Lufthansa, Olympic Airways, SAS, Swissair and Taron.

The flying time from London to Tel Aviv is 4½ hours.

From North America: The only direct service linking New York and Tel Aviv is run by El Al. TWA and Canadian Pacific operate non-direct flights.

The flying time from New York to Tel Aviv is 13¼ hours.

There is an airport tax of IL30 for international flights.

ENTRY REGULATIONS

Visas

Visas and transit visas (valid for 5 days) are required by nationals of all countries except: Austria, Barbados, Belgium, Bolivia, Colombia, Costa Rica, Denmark, Dominican Republic, Dutch Antilles, Ecuador, El Salvador, Fiji, Finland, France,

Greece, Guatemala, Republic of Haiti, Holland, Hong Kong, Iceland, Jamaica, Japan, Lesotho, Liechtenstein, Luxembourg, Maldive Islands, Mauritius, Norway, Paraguay, Republic of the Philippines, Surinam, Swaziland, Sweden, Switzerland, Trinidad and Tobago, the United Kingdom – for tourist and business purposes, for a stay of up to 3 months, which can be extended locally.

Nationals of the following countries require a visitor's visa which will be issued free of charge at the port of entry: Argentina, Australia, Brazil, Canada, Central African Republic, Chile, Federal Republic of Germany (born after 1 January 1928), New Zealand, San Marino, South Africa, Uruguay and the USA for a stay of up to 3 months, which can be extended locally.

Visas are not required by persons holding diplomatic, service or special passports only, of Benin, Gabon, Gambia, Honduras Republic (diplomatic only), Ivory Coast, Madagascar, Liberia, Malawi, Nicaragua, Niger, Peru, Sierra Leone, Thailand, Togo, Upper Volta and Zaire.

All visitors are required to fill in an entry form AL 17 upon arrival.

It should be noted that travellers will probably be banned from entry into Arab countries after a visit to Israel and the same applies vice versa, if their passports show evidence of such a visit.

Visa applications should be accompanied by a letter of booking, from a travel agent or airline, giving full details and confirming that return or onward tickets are held.

Additionally, where the visit is for business reasons, a letter from the applicant's firm giving full details of the business to be undertaken and confirming financial responsibility for the applicant, also stating names and addresses of firms to be visited, is required. Accompanying the letter should be one photograph with the applicant's name on the reverse side in block letters.

A visa is valid for up to 3 months.

Health Regulations

A valid International Certificate of Vaccination against smallpox is required by all persons entering Israel from an infected area or a country in which smallpox was known to be endemic in 1975 – Bangladesh, Ethiopia, India and Pakistan.

Customs

Currency: There is no limit to the amount of foreign currency which may be taken into Israel. It is permissible to take out of the country foreign currency in any amount and Israeli currency of up to 1,000 Israeli pounds. Visitors should pay their bills in foreign currency as local taxes will not then be chargeable. A 15% service charge will still be payable.

Duty-free articles: Personal baggage. Binoculars, tape recorder, typewriter, etc. 0.75 litres of spirits, 0.75 litres of wine, 250g of tobacco or 250 cigarettes.

PRACTICAL INFORMATION FOR THE VISITOR

1. Currency

Monetary Unit – Israeli pound (IL), divided into 100 agorot.

Notes – 10, 50, 100 and 500 Israeli pounds.

Coins – 1, 5, 10, 25, 50 agorot and 1 Israeli pound.

On departure from Israel, visitors may exchange back Israeli pounds up to a maximum of $3,000. Any balance of Israeli currency over and above this sum can be reconverted upon presentation of receipts proving the conversion of foreign currency.

Banking Hours:
0830–1230 Monday to Friday
(Some banks also open in the afternoon.)
All banks are closed on Saturday.

Major Commercial Banks In Tel Aviv:

Bank Leumi Le-Israel BM
24–32 Yehuda Halevi Street.
Bank Hapoalim BM
50 Rothschild Boulevard
Barclays Discount Bank Ltd
103 Allenby Road.
First International Bank of Israel Ltd
39 Rothschild Boulevard.
Israel Discount Bank Ltd
27 Yehuda Halevi Street.
United Bank of Israel Ltd
6–8 Ahuzat Bait Street.
United Mizrami Bank Ltd
48 Lilienblum Street.

2. Electricity Supply

220V AC, single phase, 30 Hz (electric shavers and similar appliances may need adaptors).
Plugs: 2- and 3-pin with round or flat pins.

3. Weights and Measures

The metric system is in use although measurements of land are calculated by the dunam. 1 dunam = 1000 sq. metres; 1 acre = 4.047 dunams.

4. Media

Commercial advertising is accepted on the radio but not on television.

Newspapers (daily):

Ha'aretz
Davar
Jerusalem Post (English)

Newspapers (evening):

Yediot Aharonot
Maariv

Journals:

There are numerous daily and weekly business, economic and technical publications of which a selection are: *Journal of the Association of Engineers and Architects*; *Hassadeh*; *Hamashek Hahaklai*; *Hakablan ve Haboneth*; *Israel Economist*.

5. Medical Care

It is safe to drink the water in all of the major towns, but visitors are advised to use sterilising tablets or to drink mineral water outside of these towns.

All-night pharmacies are listed in the *Jerusalem Post*.

Visitors do not have to pay for any emergency treatment, but all other health and dental care must be paid for. Israel is well equipped in medical services with hospitals in every major town.

6. Telephone, Telex and Postal Services

There are public telephones on the streets, and at main post offices, hotels, bus stations, etc.

Public telephones accept tokens (aseemonim) which may be obtained from post offices and certain authorised kiosks.

Israel is linked with the United States and most European countries by direct dialling.

Telex services are available in most deluxe hotels in Tel Aviv and Jerusalem. Telex messages and telegrams can be sent from a public telex booth to most destinations. If arrangements are made, the charge for using this facility can be debited to the visitor's company in whichever country it is based.

A tax is added to the cost of all telegraphic and telephone communications at the rate of 12% per telex call, and 32% per telephone call.

Post office box numbers should be used wherever possible for all mail. Internal mail can take up to four days to reach its destination. All letters for abroad should be sent by air mail.

General Post Office, 23 Jaffa Street, Jerusalem.

General Post Office, 132 Allenby Street, Tel Aviv.

Useful Telephone Numbers:

Police ☎ 100
First Aid ☎ 101
Fire ☎ 102.

7. Public Holidays

Movable Jewish Holidays (1981):

19 April	*Passover (Pessach)*
20 April	**Passover (Pessach)*
21 April	**Passover (Pessach)*
22 April	**Passover (Pessach)*
23 April	**Passover (Pessach)*
24 April	**Passover (Pessach)*
25 April	*Passover (Pessach)*
7 May	*Independence Day*
8 June	*Pentecost (Shavuot)*
30 September	*New Year (Rosh Hashana)*
8 October	*Day of Atonement (Yom Kippur)*
13 October	*Tabernacles (Succot)*
14 October	**Tabernacles (Succot)*
15 October	**Tabernacles (Succot)*
16 October	**Tabernacles (Succot)*
17 October	**Tabernacles (Succot)*
18 October	**Tabernacles (Succot)*
19 October	*Rejoicing of the Law*
21 October	*(Simhat Torah)*

* These holidays are for half a day only.

The dates below are also recognised as holidays:

20 March	*Purim*
9 August	*Tisha B'av*

The Jewish Sabbath falls on a Saturday (day of rest); Friday is a half working day as are all days before full-day holidays.

8. Time

GMT+2 (+3 during Israeli summer time)

9. Internal Transport

Air

Internal air services in Israel are operated by Arkia Inland Airlines. There are scheduled flights between Jerusalem, Tel Aviv, Haifa, Rosh Pina, Masada, Eilat and Sharm el-Sheikh.

There are a number of charter services available to various parts of the country.

Airline Offices in Tel Aviv:

Air France	☎ 292333/5.
Arkia	☎ 262105.
British Airways	☎ 229251.
El Al	☎ 299333.
KLM	☎ 54141.
Lufthansa	☎ 53041/4.
Pan Am	☎ 247272.
Qantas	☎ 229251.
SAS	☎ 292233.
Swissair	☎ 243355.
TWA	☎ 51212.

Aircraft and Helicopter Charter in Tel Aviv:

Kanaf/Arkia, 75 Rehov Einstein, ☎ 423131.

Masok Helicopters & Air Services Ltd, 97 Sderot Rothschild.

Rail

There are rail services linking all the major towns and cities. Reservations can be made for a small fee. No trains run on the Sabbath and Jewish religious holidays.

Road

After air transport, this is probably the best way to travel. Israeli bus services operate on an urban and inter-urban basis. Egged, the National Bus Company, operates services throughout the country. Seats can be reserved in advance. Egged (Tel Aviv), ☎ (03) 31121.

Another means of road travel is by 'sherut'. A 'sherut' is a shared taxi, which can carry up to seven people. It follows a fixed route (often a bus route in major towns) between cities. It is possible to book seats in advance with some sherut companies. The companies listed below take reservations.

Tel Aviv – Aviv, ☎ 622888.
Arieh, ☎ 615011.
Jerusalem – Aviv, ☎ 227366.
Arieh, ☎ 224745.

All taxis are regulated by the Ministry of Transport and must either have a meter or a fare-sheet issued by the Ministry. However, since fares are constantly changing due to the economic climate, it is best to know the fare before you start. Taxis can be hailed in the street or booked by telephone.

Self-drive cars are available for hire in all the main cities and towns. An International Driving Licence is required or a national driving licence issued by a country which recognizes the Israeli licence and printed in French or English. If the licence is printed in another language, it must be accompanied by a certificate of confirmation in Hebrew.

Traffic travels on the right-hand side of the road.

Car-Hire Firms:

Tel Aviv – Avis, ☎ 36363.
Hertz, ☎ 264141.
Jerusalem – Avis, ☎ 525030.
Hertz, ☎ 231351.

10. Tipping

Taxis – no tip.

Porters – IL10–20.

Hotels/restaurants – 10% of the bill.

11. Social Customs

The Israelis are a very informal people and it is rare to see suits and ties being worn. It is always best to make an appointment to see somebody, but if the matter is urgent it would not be considered impolite to appear without an appointment. The correct term of greeting and saying goodbye is '*shalom*'. A small gift is not out of place, if being entertained in a private home.

Although social customs differ throughout Israel, it is usual to find that the Sabbath is observed and only Kosher eating habits are followed.

USEFUL ADDRESSES (GENERAL)

Embassies in Tel Aviv

Australia: 185 Hayarkon Street, ☎ 243152.

Canada: 220 Hayarkon Street, P.O. Box 6410, ☎ 228122/3.

France: 112 Promenade Herbert Samuel.

West Germany: 16 Soutine Street, P.O. Box 16038, ☎ 243111/15.

Japan: 4 Weizman Street, ☎ 257292/4.

South Africa: Yakhin House, 2 Kaplan Street, P.O. Box 7138, ☎ 256147.

Switzerland: 228 Hayarkon Street, Tel Aviv 63405, ☎ 244121/2.

UK: 192 Hayarkon Street, Tel Aviv 63405, ☎ 249171/8.

US: 71 Hayarkon Street, ☎ 54338.

Other addresses in Tel Aviv

Dutch Consulate, Shalom-Meyer Tower, 9 Achad Haam Street, P.O. Box 29109, ☎ 51177/51188.

American Express Authorised Representative: Meditrad Ltd, 16 Ben Yehuda Street, P.O. Box 4312, ☎ 294654.

BUSINESS INFORMATION

As Israel manages to cope with her economic difficulties, the opportunities for investment, foreign expertise and imports of materials and equipment increase. The Israeli Government is anxious to develop the manufacturing sector in its bid to increase exports, and it hopes that this stratagem, together with more productive investment, will bring about a reduction and eventually an end to dependence on foreign aid.

Israel's quest to join the EEC has meant that tariffs are being lowered gradually. In 1975 an agreement was reached with the Community that stipulates Israel will abolish all Customs duties on industrial imports from all member-countries of the EEC by 1989. By 1980 more than one half of such imports will not be subject to Customs duty. Some materials and goods designated for use in sectors regarded by the Government as high priority sectors are exempt from duty. The Kishon zone of Haifa and Eilat have been declared Free Port Zones.

The main channels through which the import trade is conducted are commission agents. Many of Israel's import orders are dealt with through the Government and the Jewish Agency. The Israeli Embassy or Consulate will be able to furnish details of all offices that represent Israeli importing organisations abroad.

The most important area of the Israeli market is the west coast of the country, where Tel Aviv and Haifa, the principal business centres, are situated. Representation in either of these two cities is recommended.

Approximately two-thirds (tonnage) of Israel's import trade passes through the port of Haifa. The main industries in this area include iron and steel, oil refineries, fertilisers, petrochemicals and glass.

Other industrial centres are: Petah Tikva (textiles, edible oils and soap, plastics and rubber); Beersheba (fertilisers, textiles, building materials); Ashdod (cosmetics, bus and lorry assembly, machinery, textiles) and Acre (textiles, prints and plastics).

Import and Exchange Control Regulations

Only some goods require import licences or need to comply to certain conditions such as Israeli standards.

There are no exchange controls.

Business Hours

Government Offices:

Summer 0730–1430
Winter 0730–1300 and 1345–1600

Business Houses:
June to October 0730–1430
November to May 0800–1300 and 1500–1800

All government offices and business houses close on Friday afternoon and all day on Saturday. They are open on Sunday.

BUSINESS SERVICES

Interpreting/translation

Most major hotels will be able to provide interpreters and translators when needed. Interpreting/translation services are offered by:

Israel Programme for Scientific Translations, Givat Shaul B', Jerusalem.
Brender Trans Copy, 63 Nahalat Binyamin, Tel Aviv.
STI Translations International Ltd, 31 Frishman Street, Tel Aviv.
Translators' Pool Ltd, 1 Rachel Street, Tel Aviv.

Shipping

Anglo-African Shipping Co of Israel Ltd, 68 Ibn Gvirol Street, P.O. Box 16177, Tel Aviv.
Cargo Ships – El Yam Ltd, 3 Habankim Street, Haifa.
Zim, 207–209 Hameginim Street, Haifa.

Insurance

Eliahu Insurance Co Ltd, 113 Allenby Street, Tel Aviv.
Manufacturers Life Insurance Co of Canada, 9 Ahad Ha'am Street, Tel Aviv.
Migdal-Binyan Insurance Co, 26 Se'adya Gaon Street, Tel Aviv.
Shiloach Insurance Co Ltd, 2 Pinsker Street, Tel Aviv.

USEFUL ADDRESSES (BUSINESS)

Beersheba

Beersheba Chamber of Commerce and Industry, P.O. Box 578, ☎ 73390.

Haifa

Haifa Chamber of Commerce, P.O. Box 176, 53 Derech Ha'atzmaut Road, ☎ 640921.

Jerusalem

The Government of Israel Investment Authority, 6 Pick Street, Kiryat-Moshe, P.O. Box 3426, ☎ 522261.

Jerusalem Chamber of Commerce, P.O. Box 183, 10 Hillel Street, ☎ 227241.

Tel Aviv

Anglo-Israel Chamber of Commerce, 99 Ahad Ha'am Street, ☎ 229165.

Federation of Israeli Chambers of Commerce, P.O. Box 501, 84 Hahashmonaim Street, ☎ 288224.

Israeli-German Chamber of Commerce, 3 Ahuzat Bayit Street, P.O. Box 29169, ☎ 53210/50343.

Manufacturers' Association of Israel, 13 Montefiore Street, ☎ 55261.

Tel Aviv–Jaffa Chamber of Commerce, P.O. Box 501, 84 Hahashmonaim Street, ☎ 288224.

MAJOR CITIES AND TOWNS

Jerusalem

Jerusalem, the capital and centre of government, is situated 52km/33 miles inland from the Mediterranean Sea in the Judean Hills. This historic city is revered by the followers of three of the great religions of the world: Christianity, Islam and Judaism. The city is crammed full with tourist attractions. Most of the ancient religious sites lie in the eastern half of the city but there is plenty to see in West Jerusalem as well. The Old City within East Jerusalem contains the most sacred religious sites to Jews, Christians and Muslims – the Wailing Wall, the Church of the Holy Sepulchre and the Dome of the Rock.

The Western (Wailing) Wall – the 'Kotel Ha'maaravi' – derives its name from the fact that people used to come and bewail the destruction of the Second Temple and the fate of the Jewish race. Also in this sector stands the Church of the Holy Sepulchre which contains the tomb of Joseph of Arimathea. It is situated on the Hill of Golgotha. Numerous sects share the church, and little chapels belonging to them are dotted about inside. In the southeast corner of the Old City is the Dome of the Rock. This is a beautifully ornate mosque standing on Temple Mount. Inside the mosque is the Rock from which the Prophet Mohammed is reputed to have ascended into heaven.

Other interesting places to visit are the Cathedral of St James in the Armenian Quarter; the Damascus Gate (1538) on the corner of Rehov Hatzanhanim and Nablus Road; the Garden of Gethsemane at the base of the Mount of Olives; the Hebrew University Medical Centre on the southwestern outskirts of the city near En Karem – it has a synagogue with stained-glass windows designed by Marc Chagall depicting scenes from the Bible; the Islamic Art Museum at 2 Rehov Hapalmach – the museum has a fine and varied collection of artwork; the Israel Museum at Temple Mount – this museum contains a large collection of Jewish and Middle-Eastern religious art, paintings by Picasso, Chagall, Braque, Leger, Soutine and others, sculptures by Moore, Daumier and Rodin, and also the famed Dead Sea scrolls; opposite the Israel Museum stands the Knesset (Parliament) – during the recess there are guided tours; the Mosque of El-Aksa at Temple Mount – a beautiful mosque (eighth century) with a silver dome; the Rockefeller Museum near the corner of Seleiman and Jericho Roads – this museum houses a vast collection of Middle-Eastern antiquities; the Tomb of the Virgin Mary at the Mount of Olives – the tomb itself is in the Greek Orthodox Church; the Via Dolorosa in the Christian and Muslim quarters – the road along which Christ walked to Calvary.

There are many tours of the city available by coach or chauffeured taxis. The majority of bus services that travel through the city leave from the Central Bus Station.

Ben-Gurion Airport is 60km/37 miles from the centre of Jerusalem.

Hotels

The Ministry of Tourism classifies hotels from 5 star to 1 star.

HILTON JERUSALEM (5 star), Givat Ram, ☎ 536151.
Modern, first-class hotel only 10 minutes from the city centre.

Rooms: 420
Facilities: Restaurants, bars and coffee shop. Tennis and swimming. Shops, travel agent and airline offices. Car hire. Parking (nearby).
Services: TC, FC. Access, Bankamericard, Carte Blanche, Diners Club, Eurocard, Hilton, Master Charge and

TWA. ***S***, . Dr. on call.
Conference room – max. capacity 900.
Banquet room – max. capacity 600.

INTER-CONTINENTAL (5 star), Mount of Olives, ☎ 282551/7.
Modern, first-class hotel 3km/2 miles outside the city centre on the Mount of Olives overlooking the city.
Rooms: 200 , , , , ☎, , . Suites available.
Facilities: Restaurant, bar and coffee shop. Tennis. Parking.
Services: **TC**, **FC**. Access, Amex, Bankamericard, Carte Blanche, Diners Club, Master Charge. ***S***, . Dr. on call.
Conference room – max. capacity 120.
Banquet room – max. capacity 120.

JERUSALEM PLAZA (5 star), 47 King George Street, ☎ 228133.
Modern, first-class hotel in the city centre.
Rooms: 310 , , , on request, ☎, , . Suites available.
Facilities: Restaurant, bars and coffee shop. Swimming and sauna. Parking.
Services: **TC**, **FC**. Amex, Carte Blanche, Diners Club, Eurocard, Master Charge, CP Hotels. ***S***, . Dr. on call.
Conference room – max. capacity 100.
Banquet room – max. capacity 250.

KING DAVID (5 star), King David Street, ☎ 221111.
Traditional, first-class hotel in the city centre.
Rooms: 262 , , , on request, ☎, , . Suites available.
Facilities: Restaurant, bar and coffee shop. Swimming and sauna. Parking.
Services: **TC**, **FC**. Access, Amex, Carte Blanche, Diners Club, Eurocard, Master Charge. ***S***, . Dr. on call.
No conference or banquet rooms.

SHALOM (4 star), Bayt Vagan, ☎ 422111.
Modern deluxe hotel 4km/2½ miles outside the city centre.
Rooms: 288 , , , , ☎, , . Suites available.
Facilities: Restaurant, bars and coffee shop. Swimming, sauna and solarium. Parking. Car hire.
Services: **TC**. Amex, Diners Club. ***S***, . Dr. on call.
Conference room – max. capacity 800.
Banquet room – max. capacity 500.

Restaurants

French:
Chez Maty, 24 King David Street, ☎ 223779; *Chez Simon*, 15 Shammai Street, ☎ 225602; *Hesse's*, 5 Ben Shetah Street, ☎ 226893; *Mishkenot Sha'ananim* (Kosher), Yemin Moshe Quarter, ☎ 225110.

Chinese:
The Mandarin, 2 Shlomzion Hamalka Street, ☎ 222890; *Mandi Tachi*, Horkenos Street.

Italian:
The Gondola, 14 King George Street, ☎ 225944; *Venezia*, Ben Shetah Street, ☎ 231793.

Jewish (Kosher):
Fefferberg (East European), 53 Yafo Street, ☎ 225788; *Dagim Beni* (Fish), 1 Yesharim Street, ☎ 222403; *Gerlitz* (East European), 18 Malchei Israel Street, ☎ 284342; *Savion* (Fish and seafood), 12 Aza Street, ☎ 32813.

Others:
Goulash Inn (Hungarian), En Karem, ☎ 419214; *Sea Dolphin* (Fish and seafood), Al Rashid Street, ☎ 282788; *Finks* (European), 13 King George Street, ☎ 234523; *The Khan Restaurant*, Kikar Remez, ☎ 719602; *Philadelphia* (Oriental), Haprahim Street, ☎ 289770; *Rama* (Oriental), 34 Agripas Road, ☎ 225665.

Nightclubs

The Khan in West Jerusalem and the *Taverna* on Nuzzeha Street are popular nightclubs with varied and entertaining floorshows. A nice piano bar to visit is the *Goliath Bar* by the King David Hotel. Two other good bars are the *Hesse* on Ben Shetah Street, and the *Key Bar* on Az-Zahra Street.

Entertainment

Jerusalem has several orchestras and ensembles which perform at regular intervals in the major concert centres in the city. The Cahana Ticket Agency, ☎ 222831, will be able to provide tickets for most of the musical concerts performed in Jerusalem. The Israeli Philharmonic Orchestra stages a season of winter concerts at Binyanei Haoma Hall on Yafo Street. The Jerusalem Theatre has a programme of fine films throughout the year. Jerusalem is also a venue for classical and modern ballet.

Shopping

Best buys: antiques, baskets, carpets, diamonds, handicrafts, jewellery, religious items.

Tourist Information

Government Tourist Information Offices, 24 King George Street, ☎ 241281, and Jaffa Gate, Old City, ☎ 282295/6.
Municipal Tourist Information Office, 34 Yafo Street, ☎ 228844.
Christian Information Centre, Jaffa Gate, Old City, ☎ 287647.
Jerusalem Information Service, ☎ 227305.

Tel Aviv

Tel Aviv, situated on the Mediterranean coast, is the commercial and industrial centre of Israel. This highly populated city is also the main entry point for visitors to Israel, via the international Ben-Gurion Airport which is 19km/12 miles from the city centre.

Tel Aviv now extends to the old Arab port of Jaffa, and the large municipal area is commonly known as Tel Aviv-Yafo. Within its boundaries are a myriad of exotic restaurants, nightclubs and bars dwarfed by the high-rise buildings that dominate the skyline. The main streets are Allenby, Ben Yehuda and Dizengoff, each offering an assortment of cafés and boutiques. Off Allenby Street is the Carmel open-air market, where you must be prepared to haggle over any goods you may wish to purchase. The same advice goes for visitors to the Flea Market off both sides of Aleystion Street in Jaffa.

Places of interest to visit include the following: Artists' House, 9 Alcharizi Street – contains exhibits of Israeli sculpture and painting; Jabotinsky Institute, 38 King George Street – an historical museum; Haaretz Museum, Ramat Aviv – this museum contains a large number of sections given over to displays of ancient glass, money, ceramics, exhibits from archaeological excavations of old cities, etc.; the Museum of Antiquities of Tel Aviv-Yafo, 10 Rehov Mifratz Shlomo (part of the Museum Haaretz) – this museum traces the history of the area; the Tel Aviv Museum, 39 Sderot Shaul Hamelekh – this museum displays works of art, and includes works by Chagall and Max Ernst amongst its collection.

Tours of the city are conducted by car or coach. The main tour operators are Egged Tours and United Tours.

Hotels

DAN (5 star), 99 Hayarkon Street, ☎ 241111.
Modern first-class hotel in the city centre.
Rooms: 320 [symbols], on request, [symbols]. Suites available.
Facilities: Restaurants, bar and coffee shop. Swimming. Shopping arcade. Car hire. Parking.
Services: TC, FC. [symbol] Access, Amex,

Eurocard and Master Charge. **S**. Dr. on call.
Conference room – max. capacity 250.

Diplomat (5 star), 145 Hayarkon Street 294422.
Modern, first-class hotel overlooking the Marina near the commercial centre.
Rooms: 300. Suites available.
Facilities: Restaurant, grill room, private beach, dining room, bar and coffee shop. Car hire. Parking. Swimming, sauna and health club. Shopping arcade.
Services: **TC**, **FC**. All major credit cards. **S**. Dr. on call.
Conference room – max. capacity 180.
Banquet room – max. capacity 350.

Hilton Tel Aviv (5 star), Independence Park, 244222.
Modern, first-class hotel in the city centre.
Rooms: 620. Suites available.
Facilities: Restaurants, bar and coffee shop. Car hire nearby. Parking. Swimming, sauna, tennis and health club.
Services: **TC**. Amex, Bankamericard, Carte Blanche, Diners Club. **S**. Dr. on call.
Conference room – max. capacity 1,200.
Banquet room – max. capacity 750.

The Plaza (5 star), 155 Hayarkon Street, 299555.
Modern, first-class hotel in the city centre.
Rooms: 350.
Facilities: Restaurants, bar and coffee shop. Car hire. Parking. Swimming. Private beach.
Services: **TC**, **FC**. Amex, Bankamericard, Carte Blanche, Diners Club. **S**.
Conference room.

Ramada Continental (5 star), 121 Hayarkon Street, 296444.
Modern, first-class hotel situated on the beachfront, a short walk from the commercial centre.
Rooms: 340. Suites available.
Facilities: Restaurants, bars and coffee shop. Car hire. Parking. Indoor swimming pool and sauna.
Services: **TC**, **FC**. All major credit cards. **S**. Dr. on call.
Conference room – max. capacity 500.
Banquet room – max. capacity 500.

Tel Aviv-Sheraton (5 star), 123 Hayarkon Street, 286222.
Modern, first-class hotel on the beachfront, a short walk from the commercial centre.
Rooms: 400, on request. Suites available.
Facilities: Restaurant, bars and coffee shop. Car hire. Parking. Swimming, sauna and massage.
Services: **TC**, **FC**. Access, Amex, Bankamericard, Barclay Visa, Carte Blanche, Eurocard and Master Charge. **S**. Dr. on call.
Conference room – max. capacity 250.

Restaurants

East European:
Acropolis, 46 Hamasyer Street, 32130; *Balkan Corner*, Rokach Boulevard, 417440; *Triana*, 12 Carlebach Street, 264949.

European:
Casbah, 32 Yirmiyahu Street, 442617; *Dolphin*, 16 Shalom Aleichem Street, 280970; *America House Restaurant*, 35 Shaul Hamelekh Boulevard, 268933; *Andromeda*, Old Jaffa, 821903.

French:
Alchambra, 30 Jerusalem Boulevard, Jaffa, 834453; *La Couronne*, 22 Pinsker Street, 299966; *Toutonne*, 1 Simtat Mazal Dayim, Old Jaffa, 820693; *La Versailles*, 37 Guelah Street, 55552.

Italian:
Casa Mia, Frishman Street, ☎ 239856; *Capriccio*, 288 Hayarkon Street, ☎ 451151/2; *Me & Me Pizzeria*, 293 Dizengoff Street, ☎ 443427; *Rimini*, 24 Ibn Gvirol Street, ☎ 266177.

Jewish:
Dan, 147 Ben Yehuda Street, ☎ 220988; *Keton*, 145 Dizengoff Street, ☎ 233679; *Martef Habira*, 46 Allenby Street, ☎ 55573; *Nitzan*, 113 Ben Yehuda Street, ☎ 226422.

Oriental:
Pninat Hakerem, 38 Hakovshim Street, ☎ 58779; *Shaul's Inn*, 11 Elyashiv Street, ☎ 53303; *Zion Exclusive*, 28 Peduyim Street, Kerem Hateimanim, ☎ 57323.

Seafood:
La Barchetta, 326 Dizengoff Street, ☎ 448405; *Dolphini*, 33 Yirmiyahu Street, ☎ 449722; *Shaldag Inn*, 256 Ben Yehuda Street, ☎ 445465; *Yordei Hasira*, 10 Yordei Hasira Street, ☎ 443654.

Entertainment

Tel Aviv has much to offer the visitor in the way of entertainment. The good hotels on the waterfront have piano bars and dancing on offer, as well as other types of entertainment. The Avia Hotel, located on the outskirts of the city, has an English-type pub and a nightclub – *The Jet Club*. Another nightclub, the *Omar Khayyam* in Jaffa, presents fine floorshows in a marvellous atmosphere, created by its 500-year-old surrounds of Arab stone. For more live entertainment try the *Cave*, the *Khalif*, the *Peacock* and the *Zorba*.

Theatres in the city include the Habima, Cameri and Soldier's House, which all perform plays in Hebrew. The Israeli Philharmonic Orchestra is based at the Mann Auditorium in which it performs regular concerts. On Allenby Street is the National Opera, the largest opera house in the country. The Israel Festival is held each year in July and August – this event embraces a wide range of performing arts.

Most of the top hotels have their own swimming pools, a few – such as the Hilton and Sheraton – possess their own beaches as well. Other recreational activities are tennis – again the big hotels offer facilities; horseback riding – *Gordon's Sports Farm* close by the Ramat Aviv Hotel; and boating – there are boats for hire at a number of places along the coast.

Shopping

Best buys: antiques, diamonds, handicraft, jewellery, leatherware.

LEATHER GOODS AND CLOTHING:
Leon Style, 33 Allenby Street; *Adam*, 40a Allenby Street: *Victor's Fashions*, 6 Ben Yehuda; *Danaya*, 7 Bograsov Street; *Snia*, 133 Dizengoff Street.

ARTS AND HANDICRAFTS:
Judean Gallery, 123 Ben Yehuda; *Domus*, 94 Ben Yehuda; *Wizo*, 87 Allenby Street; *Rachel*, 45 Ben Yehuda.

JEWELLERY:
Shalamon Diamonds Ltd, 24 Achad Ha'am Street; *Padani*, the Holiday Inn; *Topaz*, 121 Dizengoff Street; *H. Stern*, the Holiday Inn and Hilton Hotels.

Tourist Information

Israel Government Tourist Office, 7 Mendele Street, ☎ 223266/7.
Municipal Information Offices at Dizengoff Street, ☎ 223692, and at Kikar Namir, ☎ 278668.

JORDAN

The Hashemite Kingdom of Jordan

Size: 95,396 sq.km/36,832 sq.miles of which 5,607 sq.km/2,165 sq.miles has been under Israeli occupation since 1967.

Population: 2.78 million (1978).

Distribution: 50% in urban areas.

Density: 29.4 persons per sq.km/76 per sq.mile.

Population Growth Rate: 3.3% p.a.

Ethnic Composition: The population is almost 100% Arab.

Capital: Amman Pop. 750,000.

Major Cities (East Bank): Irbid Pop. 116,000; Kerak Pop. 113,000; Ma'an Pop. 55,000; Zarqa Pop. 220,000.

Language: Arabic is the official language. English is widely understood in business circles and some French is also spoken.

Religion: The majority of the population are Sunni Muslims, with a relatively large Christian minority located mainly in Amman and on the West Bank.

Government: Jordan is a constitutional monarchy with a bicameral national assembly. The responsibility

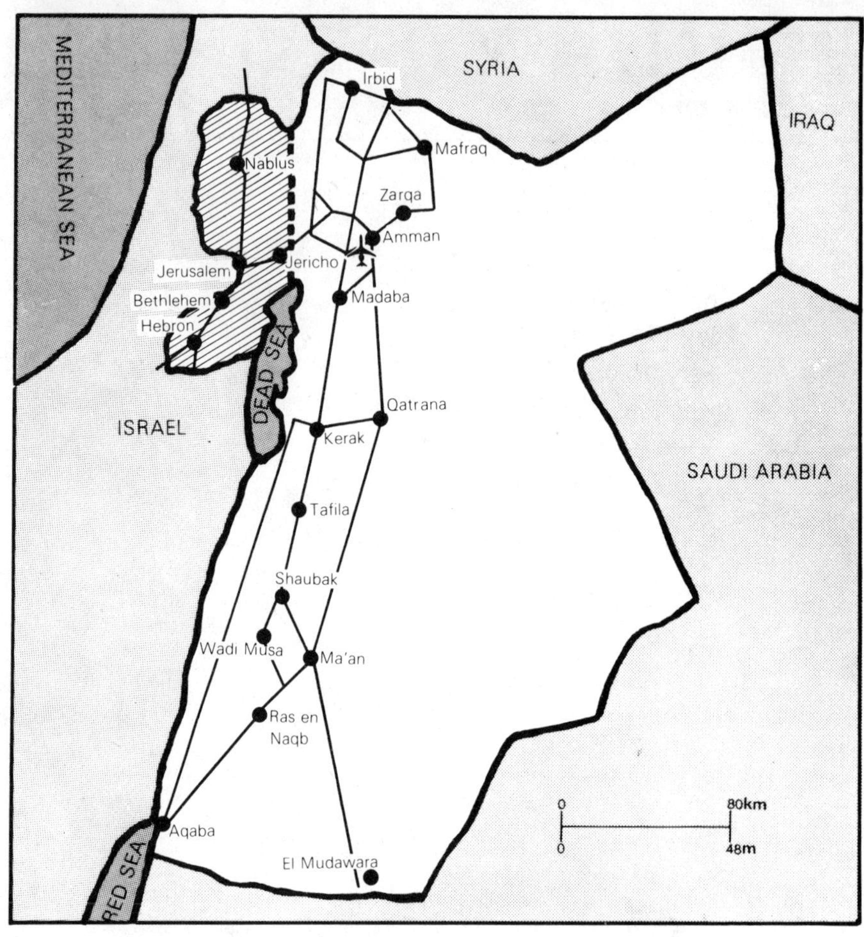

for the occupied West Bank has been assigned to the Palestine Liberation Organisation which was recognised as the sole representative of the Palestinian people by a summit conference of Arab leaders held in 1974.

All political parties were banned in 1957.

GEOGRAPHY

Jordan is bordered by Syria to the north, Israel to the west, Saudi Arabia to the south and east, and Iraq to the east. Most of Jordan is desert, with fertile areas confined to the valley of the River Jordan, which lies 392m/1,286ft below sea-level.

Climate

Hot and dry summers but cool evenings with the maximum temperature around 35.6°C/96°F. Winters are cold and damp with low temperatures around 2.2°C/28°F.

Rain falls mostly between November and March. Spring and autumn are the most popular times to visit Jordan.

Agriculture

Forty per cent of the total labour force is engaged in agriculture, which contributes between 18% and 25% of Jordan's Gross Domestic Product. Current economic plans aim at a 40% increase in agricultural income. Greater self-sufficiency in food, increased numbers of livestock, modernisation and mechanisation are all part of this goal. Farmers' associations and co-operatives are encouraged with government aid.

Main Crops: wheat, barley, olives, fruits and vegetables.

Mineral Resources: phosphates and limestone.

THE ECONOMY

Gross National Product (1976): US$1.4 billion.

Per Capita Income (1976): US$504.

Gross Domestic Product (East Bank only) (1977): 477.6 million Jordanian dinars.

Foreign Trade (1976): Total Imports US$1 billion; Total Exports US$150 million.

Main Trading Partners: Imports – West Germany, USA, Saudi Arabia, UK, Japan. Exports – Saudi Arabia, Syria, Iraq, Kuwait, Lebanon.

The historical background of Jordan, shaped by numerous political disorders in the Middle East, has not resulted in a smooth pattern of economic development. Imports have greatly exceeded exports (the ratio in 1975 was as high as 5:1). Sharp increases in oil prices have also hindered progress towards economic prosperity.

Jordan has few natural resources to exploit and exports are limited to phosphates (which account for almost one-half of all export earnings), fruits, vegetables and olive oil.

Jordan has sought to boost the economy by the introduction of a Five Year Development Plan, introduced in 1976, coupled with a reduction in overseas spending. Agriculture has been given priority under the plan in terms of investment, but other areas to receive attention include the fertiliser industry, based on the phosphate resources of Jordan, and the tourist industry, where the development of existing facilities and of new resorts will take place. Although the civil war in Lebanon reduced the size of the market for Jordanian exports, it did enable Amman to partially fill the vacuum left by the displacement of Beirut as one of the business centres of the Middle East.

Major Industries: phosphates, cement, petroleum products, clothing, cigarettes, furniture, plastics.

Main Commodities Traded: Imports – foodstuffs, machinery, vehicles, crude petroleum, textiles. Exports – fruits and vegetables, phosphates, cement, petroleum products, marble.

Jordan is a member of the Arab League.

HOW TO GET THERE

Air

ALIA, the Royal Jordanian Airline, operates flights to Amman from Houston, New York, London, Paris, Rome, Copenhagen, Frankfurt, Madrid and Bangkok.

There are also direct flights to Amman from Damascus, Baghdad, Cairo, Tehran, Kuwait and Bahrain. Twice-daily services operate between Amman and Beirut.

Other airlines which fly to Jordan are Alitalia, Aeroflot, British Airways, Egypt Air, KLM, Lufthansa and MEA.

Amman Airport is 5½km/3½ miles from the city centre.

Flying times to Amman: from Beirut 50 minutes; from London 5 hours; from New York 11 hours; from Houston 15 hours.

There is an airport tax of JD2 for passengers embarking from abroad.

Road

Taxis and buses run daily between Beirut, Damascus and Amman. The average time for the journey from Beirut to Amman is 6 hours.

ENTRY REGULATIONS

Visas

No visa is required by passport holders of Egypt, Iraq, Lebanon and Syria.

All other passport holders require visas obtainable from Jordanian embassies and consulates abroad.

Applications for a business visa (valid for 12 months) must be accompanied by a letter from the applicant's firm giving full details of the business to be undertaken and confirming financial responsibility for the applicant.

Visitors should ensure that their passport is valid for at least 3 months beyond the date of application for a visa.

Evidence in a passport of a previous or planned visit to Israel may adversely affect the granting of a visa.

Health Regulations

An International Certificate of Vaccination against smallpox is required, also cholera vaccination certificates if arriving from an infected area. TAB (typhoid and paratyphoid) injections are recommended.

Customs

Currency: There is no restriction on the import and export of foreign currency, but there is a limit of JD100 to the amount of local currency which may be imported or exported.

Duty-free articles: 200 cigarettes or 25 cigars or 200g of tobacco, 1 litre of wine or spirits and a reasonable amount of perfume. Personal effects such as cameras, portable typewriters, etc.

Commercial samples not exceeding JD5 in value, provided they are re-exported within 60 days. After a 60-day period they will be subject to the normal rates of duty. Medical samples, if clearly labelled as such, are exempt from duty.

PRACTICAL INFORMATION FOR THE VISITOR

1. Currency

Monetary Unit – Jordanian dinar (JD), divided into 1,000 fils.
Notes – 500 fils, 1, 5, 10 dinars.
Coins – 1, 5, 10, 20, 25, 50, 100, 250 fils.
Travellers' Cheques: Visitors are advised not to carry cheques and travellers' cheques issued by Barclays Bank, which are not currently accepted in Jordan.

Banking Hours:
0830–1330 Saturday to Thursday (cashiers close at 12.30)

The Central Bank of Jordan has the sole right to issue currency, supervise the banking institutions and engage in open-market operations.

Principal Banks in Amman:

Central Bank of Jordan
King Hussein Street, ☎ 30301.
Al-Ahli Bank
Redah Street, ☎ 25126.
Al Aqari Bank
Post Office Square, ☎ 36357.
Arab Bank
Faisal Street, ☎ 38161.
Arab Lands Company Bank.
Bank al-Mashrek SAL
King Hussein Street, ☎ 24161.
Bank of Credit and Commerce International
King Hussein Street, P.O. Box 7943, ☎ 38251.
British Bank of the Middle East
King Hussein Street, ☎ 36175.
Cairo Amman Bank
Shabsough Street, ☎ 39321.
Chase Manhattan Bank
P.O. Box 20191, Jebel Amman, ☎ 25131/2.
Citibank
Faisal Street, P.O. Box 5055, ☎ 38959/42276/7.
Grindlays Bank
King Hussein Street, ☎ 30104.
The Housing Bank
P.O. Box 7693, ☎ 42411.
Jordan Bank
Faisal Street, ☎ 24348.
Rafidain Bank
King Hussein Street, ☎ 24365.

2. Electricity Supply

220V AC 50Hz.
Plugs: 2-pin round.

3. Weights and Measures

The metric system is used.

4. Media

Jordan Television transmits programmes in both Arabic and English, and provides coverage of Jordan, Syria, Israeli-occupied territories, northern Saudi Arabia and southern Lebanon.

Newspapers:
Daily – *Al-Urdon*
Al-Dustour
Al-Rai
The Jordan Times (English)

Weekly –	*Al-Sabah*
	Akbar al Usbu
	Amman al-Masa
	Al-Aqsa
	Al-Hawadith
	Al-Sahafeh

5. Medical Care

Amman has many European-trained Arab doctors and many of the hospitals have good, modern facilities.

Jordan's Principal Hospitals:

Hussein Medical Centre, Amman, ☎ 44281.
Muasher Hospital, Amman, ☎ 23123.
Palestine Hospital, Amman, ☎ 25177.
University Hospital, Amman, ☎ 66121.
Al Rahma Hospital, Aqaba.
Ma'an Hospital, Ma'an.

The water supply in the main towns is safe, but elsewhere water should be boiled. Gastroenteritis is not uncommon, so visitors are advised to take suitable medication with them.

6. Telephone, Telex and Postal Services

Jordan has good internal telephone connections although some delay may occur during business hours. International telephone links are made via an earth satellite.

Useful Telephone Numbers:

Emergency (First Aid, Fire, Police), ☎ 19.
Trunk Calls (domestic), ☎ 10.
Trunk Calls (international), ☎ 17.

A telex system is in operation in Amman, and public telex facilities are available at the Jordan Inter-Continental Hotel. The main post office in Amman is on Prince Mohammed Street. There is also a post office at the Jordan Inter-Continental Hotel.

7. Public Holidays

Fixed Holidays:

22 March	*Arab League Day*
1 May	*Labour Day*
25 May	*Independence Day*
11 August	*Accession of King Hussein*
14 November	*King Hussein's Birthday*

Muslim Holidays:

These follow the Muslim calendar and occur 10–12 days earlier every year. The dates of the Muslim holidays are approximate as they depend upon sightings of the moon, and may differ by one or two days from those given below. 1981 dates are:

18 January	*Prophet's Birthday*
31 May	*Ascension of the Prophet*
31 July –2 August	*Eid el Fitr* (end of *Ramadan*)
8–10 October	*Eid el Adha*
29 October	*Hijira New Year*
7–8 November	*Ashoura*

8. Time

GMT+2

9. Internal Transport

Air

Daily flights operate between Amman and Aqaba (50 minutes).

Airline Offices in Amman:

Aeroflot	☎ 41510.
Air France	☎ 37184.
Air India	☎ 23135.
ALIA (The Royal Jordanian Airline)	☎ 22311/24131/4. (reservations).
British Airways	☎ 41430.
KLM	☎ 22175.
Lufthansa	☎ 41305.
MEA	☎ 36104.
Pan Am	☎ 22184.
PIA	☎ 22317.
SAS	☎ 22324.

Swissair	☎ 41906.
TWA	☎ 23430.

Road

Self-drive cars are available for hire in Amman. An International Driving Licence is required together with the driving licence from the visitor's country of residence. Traffic travels on the right-hand side of the road.

Car-Hire Firms in Amman:

Avis	☎ 41350.
	☎ 56347 (airport).
Bisharat Touring Car Company	☎ 41350/44355.
Jordan Tourist Co	☎ 44938.
National Rent-A-Car	☎ 39197.
Tyche Rent-A-Car	☎ 22195/25700.

Taxis are the cheapest method of travel and may be hired on a daily basis. Taxi sharing is quite common, and in Amman service taxis run on fixed routes with a standard charge per passenger.

10. Tipping

Taxis – no tip expected.

Hotels – 250–500 fils.

Restaurants – 250 fils.

11. Social Customs

Jordanian society is more obviously westernised than that of the Gulf States, and the position of women in public life and the abundance of entertainment facilities such as nightclubs, discotheques and bars bear witness to its 'liberal' nature.

The majority of the population are Muslims. Alcohol is not prohibited in Jordan – however, during the month of *Ramadan* visitors should refrain from drinking (including soft drinks and tea or coffee) and smoking during a business meeting with Jordanians.

For further information, refer to page 12 under 'Muslim Social Customs'.

USEFUL ADDRESSES (GENERAL)

Embassies in Amman

France: Mutanabi Street, P.O. Box 374, ☎ 41273/4.

West Germany: Al-Afghani Street 5, P.O. Box 183, ☎ 41351/2.

Japan: 4th Circle, Jebel Amman, P.O. Box 2835, ☎ 42486/8.

Switzerland: Abu Feras Street, P.O. Box 5341, ☎ 44416/7.

UK: Shahin Building, Ras Alain Road (off the Third Circle), ☎ 41064/43937/41261.

US: P.O. Box 354, ☎ 44371/6.

Other addresses in Amman

Dutch Consulate, Abu Jaber Building, Prince Mohammed Street, P.O. Box 312, ☎ 25162.

Tourist Authority Office, King Hussein Street, ☎ 42311/7.

American Express Authorised Representative: International Traders, King Hussein Street, P.O. Box 408, ☎ 25072/38213/42356.

BUSINESS INFORMATION

Jordan has a free-enterprise economy, although the Government has an important equity interest in many of the country's larger projects. Like many other Arab nations, Jordan is keen to encourage foreign investment and offers a number of incentives to foreign firms.

Agents representing foreign concerns must be Jordanian nationals residing in the country and registered with the Ministry of National Economy. Foreign firms will usually find it necessary to appoint a local agent, particularly when dealing with government and military tenders.

Import and Exchange Control Regulations

Import licences are required for all goods – the import of certain goods is prohibited. Goods for government and similar institutions are on open general licence, while others require specific licences – these are fairly easy to obtain and carry with them an allocation of foreign exchange.

Dealings in and the import of foreign currencies are restricted to licensed dealers and banks which operate in accordance with Central Bank orders.

Business Hours

Government Offices:

0800–1400 Saturday to Thursday
0930–1330 Saturday to Thursday during *Ramadan*

Business Houses:

0800–1300
1530–1930 Summer
0830–1330
1500–1830 Winter

Muslim business houses close on Fridays, and Christian business houses on Sunday.

BUSINESS SERVICES

Insurance

Arab Commercial Enterprises, P.O. Box 8663, Amman.

The United Insurance Co Ltd, Abu Jaber Building, King Faisal Street, Amman, ☎ 25828.

Forwarding/Clearing Agents in Amman

Arab Transit Goods Transport & Clearing Co, P.O. Box 324.

Cooperative Society for Clearance & Transport of Goods Ltd, P.O. Box 1920.

Issa El-Issa, P.O. Box 1063.

Jordan Clearing & Transport Goods Co Ltd, P.O. Box 1566.

Jordan Express Co, P.O. Box 2143.

Odeh Naber & Munir Bisharar Co, P.O. Box 1622.

Yassin Clearing & Transport Co, P.O. Box 579.

USEFUL ADDRESSES (BUSINESS)

Amman Chamber of Commerce, P.O. Box 287, Amman.

Amman Chamber of Industry, P.O. Box 1800, Amman.

Federation of Jordanian Chambers of Commerce, P.O. Box 287, Amman.

Irbid Chamber of Commerce, P.O. Box 13, Irbid.

Ministry of Trade and Industry, P.O. Box 2019, Amman.

Trade and Customs Department, Amman, ☎ 23186.

Aqaba Port Authority, Aqaba, ☎ 2432.

MAJOR CITIES AND TOWNS

Amman

Amman is built on seven hills, scattered with remains from the Greek, Byzantine, Roman and Islamic eras. Within the city itself is the Roman amphitheatre, dating from the second century.

Amman has developed at a lightning pace into a spacious and modern city. The *souk* (market) area lies in the heart of the city and is packed with small shops and stalls. The museum on the Citadel Hill houses a fascinating collection of relics dug up from various archaeological sites throughout Jordan, and these trace the country's history back thousands of years.

Amman Airport is 5½km/3½ miles from the city centre.

Hotels

The Ministry of Tourism hotel classification ranges from deluxe, 5 star, etc. down to 1 star.

JORDAN INTER-CONTINENTAL (deluxe), P.O. Box 35014, Jebel Amman, ☎ 41361.
A modern hotel, built on a hilltop and only 5 minutes from the city centre.
Rooms: 250 ⁂, ⁂, ⁂.
Facilities: Cocktail lounge and restaurant, coffee shop. Roof garden. Swimming. Shopping arcade, travel agency, airline office, post office, bank, optician. Taxi service. Car hire.
Services: TC, FC. ⊟ Amex, Bankamericard, Carte Blanche and Diners Club. ⁂, ⁂.
Conference room – max. capacity 350.

GRAND PALACE (4 star), P.O. Box 6916, Sport City Street, ☎ 61121.
Situated in the city centre.
Rooms: 160 ⁂, ⁂, ⁂.
Facilities: Restaurants, bar, coffee shop and cocktail lounge. Taxi service.
Services: TC, FC. ⊟ Amex.

AMBASSADOR (5 star), P.O. Box 19014, Shmeisani, ☎ 65161.
Modern hotel (built 1977), located near the city centre.
Rooms: 100, including 12 suites.
Facilities: Restaurant, bar, coffee shop. Shopping arcade. Banquet facilities. Taxi stand.

HOLIDAY INN (5 star), Al Hussein Ben Ali, P.O. Box 6399, ☎ 42350.
Built in 1978, the hotel is near the business centre.
Rooms: 216 ⁂, ⁂, ⁂, ⁂, ⁂, ⁂, ⁂.
Suites available.
Facilities: French, English and Oriental restaurants. Steakhouse. Rooftop sup-

per club and bar. Bars. Coffee shop. Discotheque. Shopping arcade. Swimming.
Services: **TC**, **FC**. ⊟ Amex. **S**, ♂. Dr. on call.
Conference room – max. capacity 500.
Banquet rooms – max. capacity 400.

PHILADELPHIA (4 star), Hashimi Street, P.O. Box 10, ☎ 25191.
Traditional first-class hotel in the city centre, facing the old Roman Theatre.
Rooms: 90 ♨, ♙, ☕.
Facilities: Restaurant, bar and cocktail lounge. Snack bar. Swimming.
Services: **TC**, **FC**. ⊟ Amex and Carte Blanche.
Conference room – max. capacity 160.

Restaurants
Most restaurants offer a selection of both European and Oriental food.
Babalu, Jebel Amman, ☎ 41116; *Elite*, Jebel Webdeh, ☎ 22103; *Istanbouli*, Jebel Amman, ☎ 38212; *Flying Carpet*, Shmeisani, ☎ 62181; *Jabri*, King Hussein Street, ☎ 24108; *Jordan*, Prince Mohammed Street, ☎ 38333; *Le Cesar*, Jebel Webdeh, ☎ 24421; *La Terrasse*, Shmeisani, ☎ 62831; *Omar Khayyam*, Prince Mohammed Street, ☎ 42910; *Seven Seas*, Prince Mohammed Street, ☎ 44085.

Nightclubs
Venus Club, Jebel Amman, ☎ 37236; *Le Cesar*, Jebel Webdeh, ☎ 24421; *Le Prive*, Jebel Abdoun, ☎ 44880; *Flying Carpet*, Shmeisani, ☎ 62181; *Wagon Club*, Jebel Abdoun.

Entertainment
The *Hussein Youth City*, the *Orthodox Club* and the *Royal Automobile Club* have their own swimming pools and tennis courts. A variety of sporting events are staged at the *Hussein Youth City* including motor and go-cart racing which are sponsored by the *Royal Automobile Club*.

Shopping
Best buys: glassware, mother-of-pearl articles, carved wooden objects, rugs.
SOUVENIR SHOPS IN AMMAN:
Arab Bazaar, Jebel Webdeh; *Jordan Souvenirs*, Prince Mohammed Street; *Khayyam Oriental Bazaar*, Jebel Webdeh; *Rabbath Amman Bazaar*, Jebel Al-Hussein; *Tamimi Fur Exhibition*, Ras El-Ein Street; *Tayke Souvenirs*, King Hussein Street.

Aqaba

Aqaba is Jordan's only seaport, and is also a popular and picturesque holiday resort. Aqaba offers every kind of watersport and all-the-year-round swimming. Skin diving is very popular here and some beautiful coral formations are to be found along the coast.

Hotels
CORAL BEACH (5 star), Palaces Street, P.O. Box 71, ☎ 3521.
Built on a private beach, 3km/2 miles from the town centre and 16km/10 miles from the airport.
Rooms: 94 ❄.
Facilities: Restaurant and bar. Swimming and watersports. Private beach. Diving club.
Services: **TC**, **FC**. ⊟ Amex. **S**, ♂.
Conference and banquet rooms – max. capacity 200.

HOLIDAY INN (5 star), Kings Boulevard, ☎ 2426.
A first-class hotel, 3km/2 miles from the town centre and 8 km/5 miles from the airport.
Rooms: 111 ♨, ▥, ❄, ☐, ♙, ☕. Suites available.
Facilities: Gourmet restaurant, cocktail

lounge and coffee shop. Live entertainment. Swimming. Car hire.
Services: **TC**, **FC**. ⊟ Amex. Dr. on call. **S**.
Conference room – max. capacity 200.
Banquet rooms – max. capacity 70.

Shopping

The two main souvenir shops in Aqaba are the *Abdeen Bazaar* and *Naief Store*, both in the New Market.

KUWAIT

State of Kuwait

Size: 19,940 sq.km/7,700 sq.miles.

Population: 1.13 million (1978).

Distribution: Two-thirds of the population live in the capital, Kuwait City, and its suburbs.

Density: 56 persons per sq.km/145 per sq.mile.

Population Growth Rate: 6% p.a.

Ethnic Composition: The majority of the population are Arabs with Indian, Pakistani and Iranian minorities. There are sizeable communities of Americans and Europeans living in Kuwait.

Capital: Kuwait City Pop. 700,000 including suburbs.

Major Towns: Ahmadi Pop. 18,719; Fahahil Pop. 32,506; Hawalli Pop. 130,302; Shuaiba Pop. 16,170.

Language: Arabic is the official language, but English is widely used in business circles.

Religion: 95% of the population are Muslims with Christian minorities of various denominations.

Government: The Amir is the constitutional ruler of Kuwait and is advised by a nominated Council of Ministers or Cabinet. In August 1976, the National Assembly was suspended for a 4-year period pending a review and revision of the Constitution.

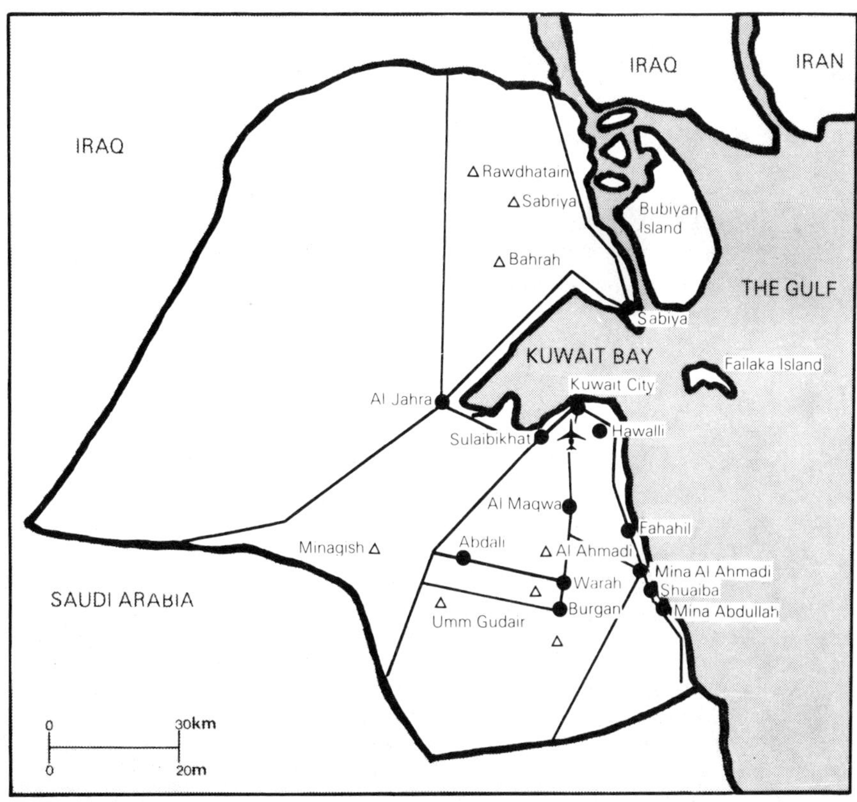

GEOGRAPHY

Kuwait is at the northwestern head of the Gulf, bordered by Iraq to the north and west, and by Saudi Arabia to the south. The country is virtually flat and consists mainly of sand and rock desert.

Climate

Summers are very hot with an average maximum shade temperature of 38°C/100°F. In July and August, this may rise to 50°C/122°F with humidity of 60–80%. Winters are cool with temperatures ranging from 7–20°C/45–68°F. Most of the rainfall comes between the months of January and March.

The north wind (*shimal*) occasionally causes severe sandstorms.

Agriculture

Agricultural development is hampered by the hot summer weather, water shortages and the infertile soil. Approximately 5% of the land is fertile, but only 1% is cultivated.

It is hoped that government agricultural experiments will result in an increase in Kuwait's food production, since at present Kuwait relies almost entirely on imports for its foodstuffs.

Mineral Resources: oil and natural gas.

THE ECONOMY

Gross National Product (1976 est.): US$12.6 billion.

Per Capita Income (1976): US$12,565.

Gross Domestic Product (1975): US$11,022 million.

Foreign Trade (1976): Total Imports US$2.39 billion; Total Exports US$9.4 billion.

Main Trading Partners: Imports – USA, Japan, West Germany, UK, Italy. Exports – Japan, UK, France, Singapore, Italy, Netherlands.

Oil is the key factor in the Kuwaiti economy and approximately 90% of exports consists of crude oil. In the early 1960s, revenues from oil sales and related royalties and taxes were used to finance large construction and development programmes, and large sums of money were injected into social provision and social services.

A policy of economic diversification, introduced in the mid-sixties, is now under way but progress is slow. This includes the stimulation of other industries as well as the processing of oil (refining, petrochemicals), but industrial development in general is limited by the absence of natural raw materials, except oil. However, a number of industries have been established, many of them wholly or partly owned by the Government. These include the manufacture of metal pipes, cement, bread, biscuits, asbestos products, fertilisers and car batteries. Shipping and aircraft maintenance are also key industries.

A large network of investment and financial agencies together with the newly created stock market exchange and insurance companies has established Kuwait as a leading financial centre. Kuwait is one of the largest Arab foreign investors and is in a position to make large overseas grants and loans on a world-wide scale, and in particular to other Arab countries through the Kuwait Fund for Arab Economic Development (KFAED).

Major Industries: oil and gas, fertilisers, construction and building equipment, cement, processed foods.

Main Commodities Traded: Imports – transport equipment, electrical machinery and appliances, machinery, textiles and clothing, foodstuffs. Exports – crude and refined oil, liquefied gas.

Crude oil production (1977): 650.8 million barrels.

Kuwait is a member of the Organisation of Petroleum Exporting Countries (OPEC) and the Arab League.

HOW TO GET THERE

Air

Major airlines flying to Kuwait include Kuwaiti Airways, Aeroflot, Air France, Alitalia, British Airways, Iberia, KLM, Lufthansa, MEA, SAS, Swissair, TWA.

British Airways, Kuwaiti Airways, Air India and PIA operate direct flights from London.

There are several flights a week from Athens, Frankfurt, Paris and Rome, and weekly flights to Kuwait from Amsterdam, Copenhagen, Geneva and Zurich. Air India operates two flights a week from New York. There are daily flights from Bombay, Beirut, Damascus and Cairo and also services from Amman, Aden, Tunis, Casablanca, Khartoum, Tripoli, Larnaca and Sana'a.

Within the Gulf Area, daily flights connect Kuwait with Bahrain, Dubai and Abadan.

Flying times to Kuwait: from London 6 hours; from New York 13 hours.

Kuwait International Airport is situated 16km/10 miles from the centre of Kuwait City. (Flight Information ☎ 710253.)

Road

A good road links Kuwait City with Basra (Iraq), and the journey can be made by taxi in approximately 3 hours.

ENTRY REGULATIONS

Visas

No visa is required by passport holders of Bahrain, Qatar, Saudi Arabia and the UAE. UK nationals with passports inscribed 'United Kingdom of Great Britain & Northern Ireland' or 'Jersey' or 'Guernsey & its Dependencies' with national status of 'British Subject' and place of birth or residence shown as the United Kingdom or Channel Islands do not require a visa, but should obtain a permit prior to departure.

Passport holders of all other countries require visas obtainable from Kuwaiti embassies and consulates abroad.

Applicants should state their religion on the visa/permit form. The entry of 'None' or 'Agnostic' may lead to a rejection of the application. Evidence in a passport of a previous or planned visit to Israel may adversely affect the granting of a visa.

Business travellers require a letter from their firm in support of the application, confirming financial responsibility for the applicant and giving details of the business to be undertaken.

Permits are valid for 3 months; the validity of a visa is variable.

Health Regulations

An International Certificate of Vaccination against smallpox is required. Persons coming from infected areas must have yellow fever and/or cholera vaccination certificates. TAB (typhoid and paratyphoid) injections are recommended.

Customs

Currency: Any amount of local and foreign currency may be exported and imported.

Duty-free articles: 100 cigarettes or 50 cigars or 8oz/227g of tobacco. (N.B. Most international brands of cigarettes are sold very cheaply on the local market.) Personal effects and commercial samples not intended for sale. Fully documented jewellery samples and other valuable samples should be accompanied by a bank guarantee amounting to 10% of their value.

Prohibited articles: Alcohol, pornographic literature.

PRACTICAL INFORMATION FOR THE VISITOR

1. Currency

Monetary Unit – Kuwaiti dinar (KD), divided into 1,000 fils.
Notes – 250, 500 fils and 1, 5, 10 dinars.
Coins – 1, 5, 10, 20, 50, 100 fils.

Banking Hours:
0800–1200 Saturday to Thursday
0830–1230 Saturday to Thursday during *Ramadan*

Currency is issued by the Central Bank of Kuwait, P.O. Box 526, Kuwait, ☎ 449200.

Major Domestic Banks:

Al Ahli Bank of Kuwait
P.O. Box 1387, ☎ 411101.
Bank of Bahrain and Kuwait
P.O. Box 24396, Safat, ☎ 417140/7.
Bank of Kuwait and the Middle East
Abdulla al Salem Street, P.O. Box 71, Safat, ☎ 421161/9.
Commercial Bank of Kuwait
Mubarak al Kabir Street, P.O. Box 2861, Safat, ☎ 411001.
Gulf Bank
Mubarak al Kabir Street, Commercial Area No. 5, P.O. Box 3200, ☎ 449501/20.
Industrial Bank of Kuwait
Al Ahli Bank Building, P.O. Box 3146, ☎ 442000.
Kuwait Real Estate Bank
P.O. Box 22822, ☎ 410110.
National Bank of Kuwait
Abdulla al Salem Street, P.O. Box 95, ☎ 422011.
Savings & Credit Bank
P.O. Box 1454, ☎ 420091.

2. Electricity Supply

240V AC 50Hz.
Plugs: 3 flat pins, 2- or 3-pin Continental.

3. Weights and Measures

The metric system is in use.

4. Media

Television programmes are mainly in Arabic, but Kuwait Radio broadcasts in Arabic, English and Urdu. English news bulletins are broadcast on Kuwait FM radio at 0830 and 2030 hours and on Kuwait television at 2000 hours. Advertising is accepted on television only.

Newspapers (daily):

Al Qabas, Al Suyasa, Al-Rai al-Amm, Kuwait Times, Arab Times.

There is virtually no trade or technical press in Kuwait. *Adhwa al Kuwait*, a weekly magazine, contains many advertisements. The *Kuwait Chamber of Commerce and Industry Magazine* is published monthly. The Kuwait Contractors' Federation publishes a monthly magazine called *Al Muqawil.*

5. Medical Care

Kuwait has a highly developed and efficient free health service with Arab and European specialists, doctors and dentists. There are also a number of private doctors and dentists in practice. Sabah Hospital ☎ 812919.

Amiri Hospital ☎ 422121.

Drinking water in the better hotels and in private houses is generally safe. Bottled mineral water and soft drinks are readily available.

During hot weather, many visitors suffer from headaches and lethargy due to a salt deficiency. Salt tablets should be taken regularly.

6. Telephone, Telex and Postal Services

Telegrams may be sent from the Chief Telegraph Office from 0700–2359 hours Saturday to Wednesday, and 0700–1200 hours on Thursday.

A 24-hour telex service is available at the main hotels and the main post office. Telexes can also be sent from the telecommunications centre in Abdullah al Salem Street near Safat Square (credit cards accepted) and from the offices of Teletex Services, near the Kuwait Hilton, ☎ 445779/445788. Telephone calls within Kuwait are free of charge. Most international calls have to be made through the operator.

Useful Telephone Numbers:

Police	☎ 109.
Fire	☎ 105.
Ambulance	☎ 422121.
Trunk Calls (Arab countries	☎ 104.
Trunk Calls (elsewhere)	☎ 102.
Telegraphic Enquiries	☎ 427033.

7. Public Holidays

Fixed Holidays:

1 January	*New Year's Day*
25 February	*Kuwait National Day*

Muslim Holidays:

These follow the Muslim Calendar and occur 10–12 days earlier every year. The dates of the Muslim holidays are approximate as they depend upon sightings of the moon, and may differ by one or two days from those given below. 1981 dates are:

18 January	*Prophet's Birthday*
31 May	*Ascension of the Prophet*
31 July –2 August	*Eid el Fitr* (end of *Ramadan*)
8–10 October	*Eid el Adha*
29 October	*Muslim New Year*
7–8 November	*Ashoura*

It is advisable to avoid a visit to Kuwait during the month of *Ramadan*: the consumption of food, drink and tobacco in public is prohibited during this period, restaurants are closed and government departments work shortened hours. *Ramadan* ends with a 3-day holiday when all businesses are closed.

The Muslim week-end (Thursday afternoon and Friday) is observed.

8. Time

GMT+3

9. Internal Transport

Air and Rail

Kuwait has no internal air or rail services.

Airline Offices in Kuwait:

Aeroflot	☎ 430227.
Air France	☎ 430224/6.
Air India	☎ 42033/438184.
British Airways	☎ 432106/9.
JAL	☎ 413454/433529.
KLM	☎ 423231.
Lufthansa	☎ 422493/420362.
Middle East Airlines	☎ 981046/423070.
Pan Am	☎ 420401.
SAS	☎ 439561/2.
Swissair	☎ 439561.
TWA	☎ 433529.

Road

Self-drive cars are available for hire. International Driving Licences are not valid, but a temporary driving licence, valid for 1 month, may be obtained on production of an International Driving Licence.

Car-Hire Firms in Kuwait:

Al Ghamim Company, ☎ 423327.
Automobile Club, ☎ 423008.
Avis, ☎ 417500.
Jazeera & Quoraini Transport Company, ☎ 980554.

Traffic travels on the right-hand side, and maximum speed limits are 45 kph (28 mph) in Central Kuwait and 70 kph (43 mph) in the suburbs.

The standard taxi fare within Kuwait City ranges from 500 fils to one dinar, but if the visitor intends making several calls, it is more economical to hire a taxi for a half or whole day. In this case, fares should be agreed upon in advance.

It is advisable to use a map in order to indicate your destination to taxi drivers.

The main telephone-operated taxi services are:
Ahmadi Taxi Hubara Club, ☎ 980044/5.
Carlton Hotel, ☎ 423171.
Gulf Taxi Company (24-hour service), ☎ 411450/7.

10. Tipping

Taxis – no tip necessary.

Airport porters – 100–250 fils per bag.

Hotel porters – small tip expected.

Hotels/restaurants – if no service charge is included, a 10% tip is usual.

11. Social Customs

Kuwait is one of the most conservative states in the Arab world. The sale and consumption of alcohol are banned by law, strict segregation of the sexes is enforced and the wearing of the veil is common practice.

In the past business visitors frequently managed to bring alcohol into the country for their own personal consumption. The general advice now is not to risk this – customs officials are very keen on checking the luggage of passengers arriving from Europe and the penalty for those found with alcohol in their possession could be a fairly lengthy jail sentence.

At social functions it is customary for guests to leave soon after drinking either tea or coffee. The practice of using the right hand when offering or receiving anything should be strictly adhered to.

For further information, refer to page 12 under 'Muslim Social Customs'.

USEFUL ADDRESSES (GENERAL)

Embassies in Kuwait

France: Qabazard Building, Istiqlal Street, P.O. Box 1037, ☎ 516144/516323.

West Germany: New House Building, Sour Street, P.O. Box Safat 805, ☎ 423031/32.

Japan: Al Rowdha, Plot No. 1, Street No. 13, Building No. 5, P.O. Box 2304, Safat, ☎ 518155/518259.

Netherlands: Al-Saleih Building, 14 Sha'ab District, P.O. Box 21822, ☎ 547573.

Switzerland: Kuwait Souk Building, Oman Street, P.O. Box 23954, ☎ 444725.

UK: Arabian Gulf Street, P.O. Box 2, ☎ 432047; British Embassy Commercial Department, Kuwait Investment Company Building (5th

Floor), Ahmad al-Jabir Street, P.O. Box 300, Safat, ☎ 439220/1/2.

US: Bnaid al-Gar, P.O. Box 77, Safat, ☎ 424156/8.

Other addresses

Thomas Cook Kuwait Travel and Tourism, Al Sabah Building, Fahad al Salem Street, P.O. Box 2156, Safat, Kuwait, ☎ 424803/424779/80.

BUSINESS INFORMATION

The business climate in Kuwait is encouraging to free enterprise and, following on in the tradition of the merchants who founded Kuwait, commercial endeavours are welcomed.

The wealth and opulence of Kuwait, derived from the enormous oil reserves, have created a kind of 'boom' society, and Kuwait has planned large investment and development projects. These include improved communications, the expansion of petroleum-related industries, more housing and medical facilities and increased hotel accommodation. Coupled together with these projects is an increase in the demand for heavy machinery, building and construction equipment, medical equipment, etc.

Only Kuwaiti nationals or firms whose ownership is at least 51% Kuwaiti may act as agents. Government purchases are made solely through Kuwaiti agents or companies who deal with all tender documents and bids.

Import and Exchange Control Regulations

No licence or exchange control formalities are required for physical imports into Kuwait, except for a number of items under the strict control of the authorities, e.g., arms and ammunition, alcoholic drink, explosives.

It is forbidden to import second-hand diesel-operated motor vehicles, fireworks, airguns, asbestos and welded iron pipes.

Foodstuffs, imports by government departments and oil companies, printed books, periodicals and newspapers and other items are exempt from customs duties.

Business Hours

Government Offices:

Summer –	0730–1300	Saturday to Wednesday
	0700–1100	Thursday
Winter –	0730–1330	Saturday to Wednesday
	0730–1130	Thursday
During *Ramadan* –	0830–1230 or 0900–1300	Saturday to Thursday

Business Houses:

Summer –	0730–1200 or 0800–1230	Saturday to Wednesday
	1500–1800 or 1530–1830	Saturday to Wednesday
	0730 or 0800–1230	Thursday

Winter –	0700–1200 or 0730–1230	Saturday to Wednesday
	1400–1700 or 1430–1800	Saturday to Wednesday
	0730 or 0800–1230	Thursday

BUSINESS SERVICES

Consultants

Kuwait Associated Consultants, P.O. Box 5443, Kuwait.
Middle East Management Consultants, P.O. Box 22462, ☎ 421843.

Accountants

Peat, Marwick, Mitchell & Company, P.O. Box 5996, ☎ 530000.
Abu-Ghazaleh & Co, (Price Waterhouse), Ford Agents Building, P.O. Box 4628, Safat, ☎ 433900.

Insurance

Al Ahliah Insurance Company, P.O. Box 1602, ☎ 435011.
Gulf Insurance Company, P.O. Box 1040, ☎ 423384.
Kuwait Insurance Company, P.O. Box 769, ☎ 420021.
Arab Commercial Enterprises, P.O. Box 2474, Safat, Kuwait, ☎ 430718/431498.

USEFUL ADDRESSES (BUSINESS)

Ministry of Commerce and Industry, Fahad al Salem Street, P.O. Box 2944, Kuwait, ☎ 422101.

Ministry of Information, Hilali Street/Mubarak al Kabir Street, P.O. Box 193, Kuwait, ☎ 427141.

Ministry of Planning, Hilali Street, P.O. Box 15, Kuwait, ☎ 423100.

Kuwait Chamber of Commerce and Industry, Chamber's Building, Ali al Salem Street, P.O. Box 775, Kuwait, ☎ 433864/6.

MAJOR CITY

Kuwait City

Kuwait City is a bustling, modern city with all the ingredients of a typical, American metropolis – fast cars, large office blocks, a vast range of consumer goods, restaurants, cinemas and shops in abundance. In contrast, most Kuwaitis wear traditional Arab dress and Arab customs and mores prevail.

The two Kuwait Towers built in the Gulf are a popular attraction – one is a water tower and the other a theatre, nightclub and revolving restaurant. Also worth a visit are the Kuwait National Museum and the artists' colony established in a restored merchant's house on the bay.

The Kuwait Natural History and Science Museum in Abdullah al Mubarak Street has an extensive collection of stuffed animals, including a whale, and there is a small planetarium and Space Hall attached to the Museum.

Probably one of the finest buildings in the city is the Seif Palace on Arabian Gulf Street which was built at the end of the nineteenth century and today houses the administrative headquarters of the Amir. The Palace interior consists of large areas of mosaic tilework of traditional Islamic design.

Kuwait International Airport is 16km/10 miles from the city centre.

Hotels

The Ministry of Tourism classifies hotels as deluxe, 4 star, 3 star, etc.

BRISTOL (4 star), Fahad al Salem Street, P.O. Box 3531, 439281/4.
First-class hotel in the city centre, overlooking beautiful gardens.
Rooms: 110 , , , on request, , .
Facilities: Restaurant with Oriental and European cuisine. Banquet facilities. Furnished flats available on a monthly basis. Car hire.
Services: **TC**, **FC**. Amex. **S**.

CARLTON (4 star), Fahad al Salem Street, P.O. Box 3492, 423171/5.
Modern hotel in the city centre, 15 minutes from the airport.
Rooms: 100 , , , , . Suites available.
Facilities: Restaurant with European and Oriental cuisine. Car hire. Swimming.
Services: **TC**, **FC**. Amex. **S**, .
Conference room – max. capacity 50.

KUWAIT HILTON (deluxe), Bnaid al Gar, P.O. Box 5996, 533000.
Ultra-modern, deluxe hotel, overlooking the Gulf, 3½km/2 miles from the city centre and 14½km/9 miles from the airport.
Rooms: 232 , , , , , , . Suites available.
Facilities: Restaurant with American, international and local cuisine. Supper club and coffee shop. Health club and sauna. Swimming, bowls and tennis. Free bus service to Kuwait City and airport. Car hire.
Services: **TC**, **FC**. Amex, Bankamericard, Carte Blanche, Diners Club, Eurocard and Master Charge. **S**, .
Conference rooms – max. capacity 900.

KUWAIT SHERATON (deluxe), Fahad al Salem Street, P.O. Box 5902, Safat, 422055.
Modern, deluxe hotel in the city centre.
Rooms: 263 , , , , , , . Suites available.
Facilities: Restaurant with European and Oriental cuisine. Rooftop restaurant with dancing. Coffee shop. Shopping arcade. Swimming, tennis and sauna. Car hire.
Services: **TC**, **FC**. Amex, Bankamericard, Carte Blanche, Diners Club, Eurocard and Master Charge. **S**. Dr. on call.
Conference room – max. capacity 500.

MESSILAH BEACH (4 star), Messilah Roundabout, P.O. Box 3522, Safat, 613466.
Townhouse-style hotel complex, located midway between the airport and Kuwait City.
Rooms: 320 , , , , , .
Facilities: Restaurant and coffee shop. Swimming, tennis and sauna. Nightclub. Shopping arcade, hairdresser and bank. Car hire. Free transport to and from city centre.
Services: **TC**, **FC**. Amex and Diners Club. **S**, .
Conference room – max. capacity 300.

UNIVERSAL (4 star), Mubarak al Kabir Street, 425361.
Modern, first-class hotel in residential

area, 16km/10 miles from the airport.
Rooms: 60 ⚘, ⊛.
Facilities and Services: Several restaurants including Chinese restaurant, coffee shop. Garden.
Conference room.

N.B. The sale or consumption of alcohol is prohibited throughout Kuwait – this applies to all hotels and restaurants.

Restaurants

The hotel restaurants are open to the public, except for lunch during *Ramadan*, and offer both European and Oriental dishes. Other restaurants in Kuwait include: *Caesar's*, behind Kuwait Sheraton Hotel – Chinese and Continental cuisine; *Adnan Jabri*, Fahad al-Salem Street, ☎ 434676 – Arab cuisine; *Golden Nest*, near Old Traffic Department; *Sharq* – Chinese; *Kuwaitia Towers*, KAC Building, ☎ 412400 – rooftop restaurant with nightclub; *Hubara Seafood*, Salmiyah, ☎ 616827 – seafood.

Nightclubs

Starlight Supper Club, Kuwait Hilton, Bnaid al Gar Street; *Al-Jawharah*, Messilah Beach Hotel; *Kuwaitia Towers*, KAC Building; *Al-Hambra*, Kuwait Sheraton, Fahad al Salem Street; *Marzouk Pearl*, Salmiyah Beach Road.

Entertainment

Kuwait offers many different sporting activities including sailing, scuba diving, power boating, riding, tennis and football. Horse racing takes place every Thursday (except during the height of summer) at the *Hunting and Equestrian Club* and at the *Ahmadi Governorate Horsemen's Association.*

During the summer, swimming races and sailing regattas are organised by the Government as part of a recreational programme which also includes dramatic and dance productions and firework displays.

Shopping

Most of Kuwait's *souks* are now housed in modern air-conditioned buildings and have lost much of their former charm and fascination to the Western visitor. Very few traditional items are on sale, the demand nowadays being for modern, imported consumer goods.

Some traditional articles can still be bought at the old *souk* off Palestine Street. The *Saled Ismail Sayed Abdul Rasool* shop specialises in antiques and has two branches – at Ali al Salem Street and off First Ring Road, near Silver Towers Grocery.

LEBANON

Republic of Lebanon

Many offices, banks and other facilities in Beirut which were closed down during the civil war have recently reopened, and it is likely that this trend will continue over the next few years. Whilst every effort has been made to ensure that the information given here is accurate and up-to-date, the publishers cannot assume any responsiblity in this connection.

Size: 10,100 sq.km/3,900 sq.miles.

Population: 3.06 million (1978).

Distribution: 60% in urban areas.

Density: 276 persons per sq.km/715 per sq.mile.

Population Growth Rate: 2.7% p.a.

Ethnic Composition: Over 90% of the population are Arabs, including large immigrant communities of Palestinians, Syrians and Jordanians. There is a sizeable minority of Armenians.

Capital: Beirut Pop. 1,200,000.

Major Cities/Towns: Tripoli Pop. 200,000; Saida (Sidon) Pop. 50,000; Zahlé Pop. 40,000.

Language: Arabic is the official language. French is widely used in business and government circles although English is now being increasingly spoken.

Religion: The population is basically made up of Christians and Muslims with the Christians forming a small majority. Most Christians belong to the Maronite sect and there are both Sunni and Shia Muslims.

Government: According to the Constitution, the President of the Lebanon must be a Christian (usually Maronite), the Prime Minister a Sunni Muslim and the President of the Chamber of Deputies a Shia Muslim. Similar to the offices of state in the Lebanon, the Chamber of Deputies is divided

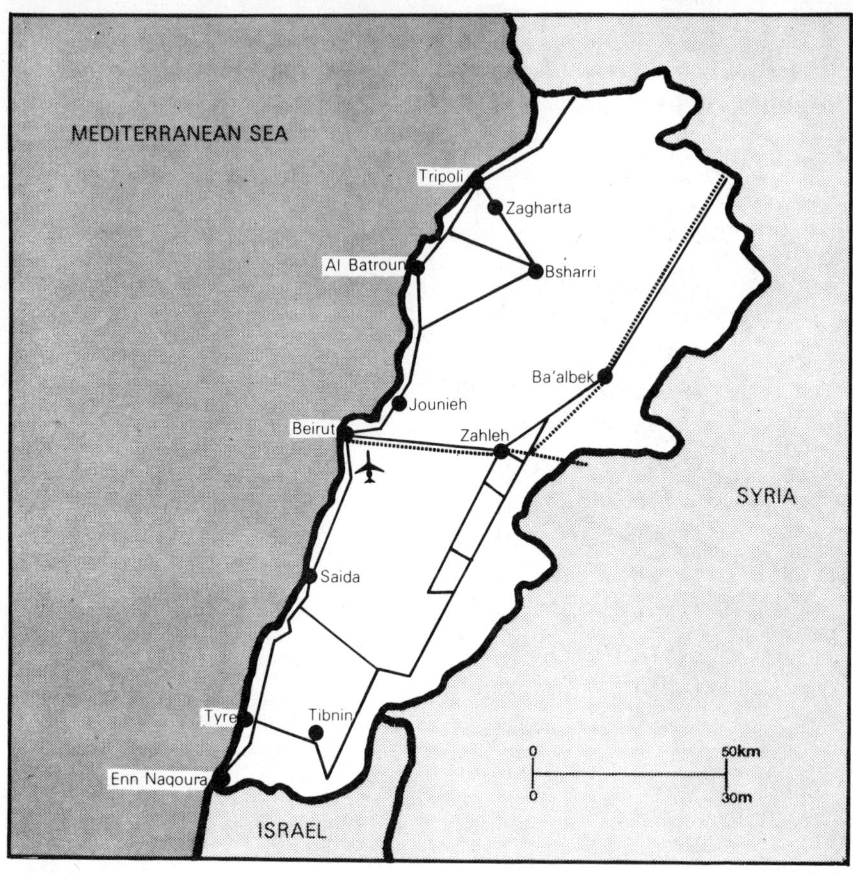

between the various religious sects with a basic ratio of six Christian deputies to every five Muslim deputies.

Representation in the Chamber of Deputies is governed by the proportional allocation of seats to religious groups, and this makes it difficult to give an accurate breakdown of the political parties in the Chamber of Deputies. Many deputies join in the parliamentary blocks such as the Democratic Front, Tri-Partite Coalition and the National Struggle Front.

The main political parties include Al Kataib (Phalangist Party), Al Wataniyin Al-Ahrar (National Liberal Party) and Al Takadumi Al-Ishteraki (Progressive Socialist Party).

GEOGRAPHY

The Lebanon lies at the eastern end of the Mediterranean and has borders with Syria to the north and east and with Israel to the south. The country is largely mountainous and approximately one-half of the land area lies at an altitude of over

9,846m/3,000ft. The narrow coastal plain is the principal fertile area and is the most densely populated part of the country.

The Bekaa Valley, which lies between the Lebanon mountains in the west and the Anti-Lebanon mountains in the east, is the other main fertile region of the Lebanon.

Climate

Summers in the Lebanon are hot and virtually rainless with temperatures averaging 29°C/84°F on the coast. Winters are mild and almost all the rain falls during the winter months, with snow in the mountains. Temperatures average 13°C/55°F on the coast and 0–10°C/32–50°F inland, depending on altitude.

Agriculture

Almost one-half of the Lebanon's exports are agricultural exports and the country supplies fruit and vegetables to Western Europe, the Gulf States and other Arab countries.

The coastal plain and the Bekaa Valley are the two main cultivated areas and terracing is used extensively in order to cultivate the higher land areas.

Main Crops: apples, citrus fruits, vegetables, grapes, olives, tobacco, cotton, sugar beet.

Mineral Resources: The Lebanon has scanty mineral resources which include small quantities of iron and lignite, and there are unconfirmed reports of sizeable oil resources both onshore and offshore.

THE ECONOMY

Gross National Product (1976 est.): US$2.5 billion.

Per Capita Income (1976 est.): US$1,000.

Gross Domestic Product (1979 est.): £L10.4 billion.

Foreign Trade (1976): Total Imports £L1,800 million; Total Exports £L500 million.

Main Trading Partners: Imports – USA, West Germany, France, Italy, UK. Exports – Saudi Arabia, France, UK, Libya, Kuwait.

The civil war in the Lebanon, together with the Israeli-Arab fighting (the southern Lebanon is increasingly used as a base by the Palestine Liberation Organisation for attacks on Israel), has had a drastic effect on the Lebanese economy – prices have risen dramatically due to a general lack of confidence and shortages, and today Beirut has one of the highest cost-of-living indexes in the world. The task of the Government is now one of reconstruction (in particular of the infrastructure) with the aim of restoring commercial activity to its pre-1975 level. Prior to unrest in this area of the Middle East, Beirut was a leading money market in the Arab world, and an important port for Middle East oil. The prosperity of the Lebanon rested largely on the goods and services she had to offer to her less-developed neighbours, in particular the entrepôt trade, and expertise in the construction and civil engineering fields.

Aided by grants from the USA, Western Europe and the Arab world, the Reconstruction and Development Council has the task of repairing the damage caused by the Civil War to both the private and public sectors and this, it is hoped, will lead to the restoration of confidence in the economy of the Lebanon in general.

The Lebanon is one of the most industrialised nations in the Middle East. A large proportion of the industrial concerns operate on a small, individual scale using a high percentage of imported raw materials and producing mainly consumer goods. There are two large oil refineries (Tripoli and near Saida (Sidon)) and two large cement plants in the region of Tripoli.

Major Industries: food processing, textiles, furniture, wood-working, clothing and footwear, oil refining.

Main Commodities Traded: Imports – precious metals and gems,* machinery and electrical equipment, textiles,* non-precious metals and products. Exports and Re-exports – precious metals, gems, etc., textiles, machinery and electrical equipment, vehicles, vegetable and fruit products.

* Transit trade.

The Lebanon is a member of the Arab League.

HOW TO GET THERE

Air

Major airlines operating services to Beirut include Aeroflot, Air France, ALIA, British Airways, Egypt Air, KLM, Lufthansa, Sabena, Swissair and TWA.

Middle East Airlines and Trans Mediterranean Airways (freight) are both based in Beirut.

Middle East Airlines operate a daily flight from London to Beirut and regular flights from Paris, Geneva, Milan, Zurich, Rome and Athens. Beirut has good air connections with the Gulf States and also with Cairo, Amman, Baghdad, Istanbul, Larnaka and Ankara.

Flying times to Beirut: from London 4¼ hours; from New York 11 hours; from Sydney 21 hours.

Beirut Airport is 16km/10 miles from the city centre.

Rail

A daily train service links Beirut with Aleppo in Syria. The journey takes between 10 and 13 hours.

Sea

There are regular, comfortable passenger services to the Lebanon from a number of ports in Italy, France and the Soviet Union.

Road

A first-class highway passing through the mountains connects the Lebanon with Damascus. Alternatively, it is possible to drive from Syria via Aleppo and Homs to Tripoli, and along the coastal road to Beirut.

ENTRY REGULATIONS

Visas

Nationals of all countries require visas which must be obtained in the applicant's country of origin from Lebanese embassies and consulates. Visas will not be granted on arrival in the Lebanon.

The validity of a passport must extend for at least 6 months beyond the proposed date of departure from the Lebanon.

Transit visas, valid for a stay of 15 days, are not granted for business purposes.

Business travellers should support their visa application with a letter from their firm giving full details of the business to be undertaken and confirming financial responsibility for the applicant.

Visas are usually valid for 6 months for a stay of variable length.

Evidence in a passport of a previous or planned visit to Israel may adversely affect the granting of a visa.

Health Regulations

An International Certificate of Vaccination against smallpox is required. Also cholera and/or yellow fever vaccination certificates if arriving from an infected area. TAB (typhoid and paratyphoid) injections are recommended.

Customs

Currency: There are no restrictions on the amount of local and foreign currency which may be taken into or out of the country.

Duty-free articles: 200 cigarettes or 50 cigars or 200g of tobacco and 1 litre of wines or spirits and 60g of perfume. Personal effects. Samples of no commercial value.

Articles liable to duty: Ordinary trade samples are subject to customs duty but may be temporarily imported by a travelling representative against a deposit equivalent to the amount of customs duty payable, and the deposit is refunded if the samples are re-exported.

Prohibited articles: Narcotics, pornographic literature, precious and semi-precious jewellery and jewelled watches.

PRACTICAL INFORMATION FOR THE VISITOR

1. Currency

Monetary Unit – Lebanese pound (£L), divided into 100 piastres.
Notes – 1, 5, 10, 25, 50, 100 pounds.
Coins – 1, 2½, 5, 10, 25 piastres.

Currency is issued by the Banque du Liban, Banque du Liban Street, P.O. Box 5544, Beirut, ☎ 341230.

Banking Hours:
0830–1230 Monday to Friday
0830–1200 Saturday

Prior to 1975, more than forty-five major international banks had offices in Beirut, together with some forty Lebanese commercial banks. During the civil war many foreign banks ceased operations in the Lebanon, but all banks officially reopened in January 1977.

Foreign Commercial Banks in the Lebanon:

Arab Bank Ltd
Riad Solh Street, P.O. Box 1015, Beirut, ☎ 250240.

British Bank of the Middle East
P.O. Box 11-1380, Beirut, ☎ 220745 (four branches in Beirut and one in Tripoli).

Chartered Bank
Riad Solh Street, P.O. Box 11-3996, Beirut, ☎ 221985/7.

Chase Manhattan Bank
Riad Solh Street, P.O. Box 11-3684, Beirut, ☎ 251581/5.

Citibank
Arab Bank Building, Riad Solh Street, P.O. Box 11-3648, Beirut, ☎ 240033/6.

2. Electricity Supply

110 or 220V AC 50 Hz.
Plugs: Continental 2-pin.

3. Weights and Measures

The metric system is in use.

4. Media

The Lebanese Broadcasting Station transmits domestic and foreign services in Arabic, French, English and Spanish.

There are two commercial television companies, Compagnie Libanaise de Télévision and Télé Orient, transmitting programmes in Arabic, French and English.

Newspapers (daily):
Al-Anwar, *Al-Jarida*, *Al-Nahar*, *L'Orient-Le Jour*, *Le Soir*, *Daily Star*.

Prior to the civil war, Lebanon had the most developed and competitive press in the Middle East and, as the major regional publishing centre, produced a large number of periodicals for the domestic, Middle Eastern and international markets.

Censorship laws were introduced in 1977, covering local and foreign news media.

5. Medical Care

The American University Hospital and the French Hôtel-Dieu Hospital are both situated in Beirut. A 24-hour service is operated by the pharmacies on a rota basis and most medicines can be obtained from them.

Visitors may suffer from minor stomach upsets and are advised to take suitable precautionary medicines.

Tap water is generally safe to drink, but bottled mineral water is readily available. Care should be taken with unpeeled and unwashed fruit and vegetables.

6. Telephone, Telex and Postal Services

Telephone services were badly damaged during the civil war but have now largely been repaired and the international service has been extended further.

A new telex system is in operation.

Postal services have now been re-established but are not very reliable. All mail to and from the Lebanon should be despatched by air.

7. Public Holidays

Fixed Holidays:

1 January	*New Year's Day*
9 February	*Feast of St Maron*
22 March	*Founding of the Arab League*

1 May	*Labour Day*
6 May	*Martyrs' Day*
15 August	*Feast of the Assumption*
1 November	*All Saints' Day*
22 November	*Independence Day*
25 December	*Christmas Day*
31 December	*Evacuation Day*

Muslim Holidays:

These follow the Muslim calendar and occur 10–12 days earlier every year. The dates of the Muslim holidays are approximate as they depend upon sightings of the moon, and may differ by one or two days from those given below. 1981 dates are:

18 January	*Prophet's Birthday*
31 May	*Ascension of the Prophet*
31 July –2 August	*End of Ramadan*
8–10 October	*Feast of the Sacrifice*
29 October	*Muslim New Year*
7–8 November	*Ashoura*

The movable Christian festivals of *Good Friday*, *Easter Monday* and *Ascension Day* are also official holidays.

All government offices and most business houses observe as holidays both the Christian and Muslim religious festivals, as well as the national and fixed holidays listed above.

8. Time

GMT+2

9. Internal Transport

Airline Offices in Beirut:

Air France	☎ 328700/350190.
British Airways	☎ 346347/9.
JAL	☎ 340620/4.
KLM	☎ 252525.
Lufthansa	☎ 347005.
MEA	☎ 274330/292220.
Pan Am	☎ 340153/4.
Swissair	☎ 353658/9.
TWA	☎ 221320.

Road

Road links are relatively good in the Lebanon and the journey from Beirut to Tripoli takes 2 hours. There are limited bus services within Beirut and from the city to the airport (16km/10 miles).

Self-drive and chauffeur-driven cars are available for hire. An International Driving Licence is required. Avis (Beirut), ☎ 240240/220316.

Both service and ordinary taxis operate in the Lebanon. Service taxis usually operate along fixed routes and are shared by a number of passengers. They operate within Beirut, also from Beirut to Damascus, Aleppo and Amman. Bookings can usually be made through a travel agent or the larger hotels. When using the ordinary taxis, visitors are advised to use those fitted with fare meters. If taxis without meters are used, the fare should be agreed upon before starting the journey.

10. Tipping

Taxis – no tip necessary.

Porters – £L1 per bag.

Hotels/restaurants – 10–12% of the bill if no service charge is included.

11. Social Customs

The population of the Lebanon is rigidly divided between the two main religious groups, the Christians and the Muslims, and much of the country is demarcated into separate regions for each religious community. Muslim social customs are relatively relaxed and the Christian sector is very westernised in its outlook.

Alcohol is not prohibited and can be offered to Muslims without offending them. Pork, ham or bacon should not be offered however.

Despite the recent troubles a fairly easy atmosphere prevails in Beirut although security is quite strict in some parts of the city, and especially at Beirut Airport.

For further information relative to the Muslim community in the Lebanon, refer to page 12 under 'Muslim Social Customs'.

USEFUL ADDRESSES (GENERAL)

Embassies in Beirut

Australia: Farra Building, 463 Bliss Street, ☎ 340776.

Canada: Centre Sabbagh, rue Hamira, ☎ 350660/5.

France: rue Clemenceau.

West Germany: rue Mansour Jourdak, B.P. 2820, ☎ 341255/7.

Japan: Olfat Salha Building, Corniche Chouran, P.O. Box 3360, ☎ 301301/301326.

Netherlands: Immeuble Sahmarani, 1st Floor, rue Kantari, B.P. 117, ☎ 220290/240126/7.

Switzerland: Immeuble Achou, rue John Kennedy, B.P. 172, ☎ 366390/1.

UK: Avenue de Paris, Ain el-Mreissé, ☎ 362500/362564.

US: Corniche at rue Ain el-Mreissé, ☎ 361800.

Other addresses in Beirut

National Council of Tourism in Lebanon, Bank of Lebanon Street, P.O. Box 5344, ☎ 340940.

Thomas Cook Overseas Ltd, Al-Moutawakel Building, Monseigneur Messara Street, Achrafié, P.O. Box 11-0085, ☎ (a.m.) 329569/332462 and (p.m.) 329221/346260.

American Express Authorised Representative: Amlevco Tours, Hotel Phoenicia Intercontinental, P.O. Box 11-1429, ☎ 367855/367760.

BUSINESS INFORMATION

The civil war, which disrupted the Lebanon's financial and commercial life so severely, resulted in a mass exodus of foreign interest which has yet to be fully reversed. However there are signs that those foreign businesses with sizeable assets are beginning to re-establish themselves in the Lebanon, and there is a renewed movement of Arab and international capital back into the Lebanese public sector. The rate at which this renewal of economic confidence occurs will largely depend on the success of internal reconstruction programmes and the final settlement of the political situation, concerning the Palestinian problem in particular.

Since 1977 branches of foreign banks must be approved and licensed by the Central Bank, but in general there are few restrictions applied to foreign business ownership. Fundamental changes in the laws governing foreign investment are expected with a view to encouraging the economic revival so badly needed in the country.

Import and Exchange Control Regulations

Import licences are required for all machinery, for the installation of manufacturing plants, for certain finished goods, communications equipment and foodstuffs such as wheat, barley, fruits, olives etc. Most other commodities do not require an import licence and exchange can be obtained without difficulty.

The import of goods from Israel and Zimbabwe-Rhodesia is prohibited. The import of arms, ammunition, narcotics and other similar products is either prohibited or reserved for the Government.

Business Hours

Government Offices:

Winter – 0800–1400 Monday to Thursday
0800–1100 Friday
0800–1330 Saturday
Summer – 0800–1330 Monday to Thursday
0800–1100 Friday
0800–1230 Saturday

Business Houses:

Winter – 0830–1330, 1500–1800 Monday to Friday
0830–1230 Saturday
Summer – 0800–1300 Monday to Saturday

The European week-end (Saturday afternoon and Sunday) is observed.

BUSINESS SERVICES

Insurance

Arab Commercial Enterprises, Hanna Building, Makdessi Street, P.O. Box 113-5112, Beirut, ☎ 340770/2.

Arab Commercial Enterprises, P.O. Box 487, Tripoli, ☎ 626099.

USEFUL ADDRESSES (BUSINESS)

Beirut Chamber of Commerce & Industry, Spears Street, Sanayeh, P.O. Box 11-1801, Beirut.

Association of Lebanese Industrialists, Justinian Street, P.O. Box 1520, Beirut.

Association of Banks in Lebanon, Riad el Solh Square, P.O. Box 976, Beirut.

Bourse Je Beizruth (Stock Exchange), P.O. Box 7641, Beirut, ☎ 235218.

MAJOR CITY

Beirut

Beirut was one of the liveliest and most prosperous cities of the Mediterranean and Middle East until the outbreak of the civil war. Much of the city, including hotels, banks, shops and offices, has been destroyed, together with the port of Beirut, and although the task of reconstruction is now under way, it will be several years before Beirut regains its former status and importance.

Beirut is a cosmopolitan city offering first-class hotels, cuisine of an excellent and varied nature and an abundance of sophisticated entertainment and leisure facilities. The cultural and intellectual life of the city are of the same high quality – several European countries and the United States have cultural institutes in the city where plays, concerts and exhibitions are staged at frequent intervals. Beirut also has a National School of Music and an Academy of Fine Arts.

Beirut International Airport is 16km/10 miles from the city centre.

Hotels

The Tourist Board classifies hotels by category and stars, i.e., 4 star A, 4 star B, 4 star C, 3 star A, 3 star B, etc.

BEIRUT CARLTON (4 star A), Général de Gaulle Avenue, P.O. Box 3420, 300240.
Modern hotel facing the Mediterranean, near the city centre and 6½km/4 miles from the airport.
Rooms: 140. Suites available.
Facilities: Restaurant, bars and lounge. Swimming and sundeck. Car hire.
Services: TC, FC. Amex and Diners Club. S.
Conference facilities.

BEIRUT INTERNATIONAL (4 star A), Général de Gaulle Avenue, P.O. Box 6110, 300016.
Modern first-class hotel in central location, overlooking the Mediterranean.
Rooms: 99, on request. Suites available.
Facilities: Restaurant and grill room, cocktail lounge, ballroom, rooftop restaurant, nightclub. Swimming, sauna, squash and bowling alley. Beauty salon and boutique. Car hire.
Services: TC, FC. Credit cards not usually accepted. Dr. on call. S.
Conference room – max. capacity 500.
Banquet rooms – max. capacity 200.

BRISTOL (4 star A), rue Madame Curie, P.O. Box 1493, 351400.
Traditional hotel, well situated near Beirut's business centre.
Rooms: 162, on request. Suites available.
Facilities: Restaurants, coffee shop and bars. Roof garden. Car hire.
Services: TC, FC. Credit cards not usually accepted. Dr.on call. S.
Conference room – max. capacity 600.
Banquet rooms – max. capacity 1,000.

LE VENDÔME INTER-CONTINENTAL (4 star A), rue Minet el-Hosn, 369280.
Modern deluxe hotel overlooking the sea, near the business centre of Beirut and 9½km/6 miles from the airport.
Rooms: 125. Suites available.
Facilities: French restaurant, bar, cocktail bar and tea room. Swimming. Car hire.
Services: TC. Amex, Diners Club and Carte Blanche. Dr. on call. S.
Conference room – max. capacity 100.
Banquet rooms – max. capacity 300.

BEIRUT COMMODORE (4 star B), Lyon Street, P.O. Box 3456, 350400.
Modern first-class hotel near the sea and the diplomatic area of Beirut.
Rooms: 48.
Facilities: Restaurant and grill room. Coffee shop, bar and nightclub. Swimming. Car hire.
Services: TC, FC. Credit cards not usually accepted. S.
Conference facilities.

RIVIERA (4 star B), Avenue de Paris, 362480.
Modern first-class hotel built on the sea front outside the city centre.
Rooms: 125, on request.

Facilities: European, Japanese and Indonesian restaurants. Bar and lounges. Private beach. Terrace. Car hire.
Services: **TC**, **FC**. Credit cards not usually accepted. **S**, **♂**. Dr. on call.
Conference room – max. capacity 200.
Banquet rooms – max. capacity 200.

Restaurants

In Beirut there are restaurants offering national specialities from many different countries including France, Italy, Germany, Scandinavia, China, Japan, India and Malaysia.

Two of the best restaurants for Arabic food are *Al Ajameh* in the *Souk* Tawileh and *Al Barmaki* on the rue Hamra.

One Lebanese national dish is *kibbe* made of lamb and cracked wheat or *burghol*, served raw, baked or fried in small pieces. *Arak* is the national drink and visitors will find Lebanese wines very good.

Entertainment

Beirut has many cinemas showing recent American, European, Indian and Arab films. The city is renowned for its night life and boasts a very unique club, the *Casino du Liban*, which is 25km/15½ miles from Beirut at Maamaltein. The *Casino* consists of gambling rooms, indoor and outdoor restaurants, a nightclub with floorshows and a theatre with a reputation for good-quality productions.

Swimming, sailing and waterskiing are some of the sporting activities offered in and around Beirut, and in the mountain areas skiing is becoming very popular, with new resorts being planned and developed. The city has its own race course and several riding clubs, as well as facilities for tennis and golf.

Shopping

Best buys: pottery, glassware, rugs, embroidery, hand-woven cloth.

LIBYA

Socialist People's Libyan Arab Republic

Size: 1,759,400 sq.km/679,128 sq.miles.

Population: 2.7 million (1977 estimate).

Distribution: 95% of the population live in the coastal region, mainly concentrated around Tripoli and Benghazi.

Density: 1.4 persons per sq.km/3.6 per sq.mile.

Population Growth Rate: 4.2% p.a.

Ethnic Composition: The majority of the population are Arabs with large numbers of Berbers, and in the south the population is predominantly black.

Capital: Tripoli (Western Province) Pop. 709,167.

Major Towns: Benghazi (Eastern Province) Pop. 331,180; Sebha (Southern Province) Pop. 112,318.

Language: Arabic is the official language and its exclusive use is encouraged by the Government in everything. Some English and Italian are spoken in business circles.

Religion: Most Libyans are Sunni Muslims with Christian and Jewish minorities, living mainly in Tripoli.

Government: The General People's Congress is the supreme legislative body in Libya, and has replaced the Revolutionary Command Council which emerged in 1969, following the abolition of the monarchy. Islamic socialism forms the basis of the Con-

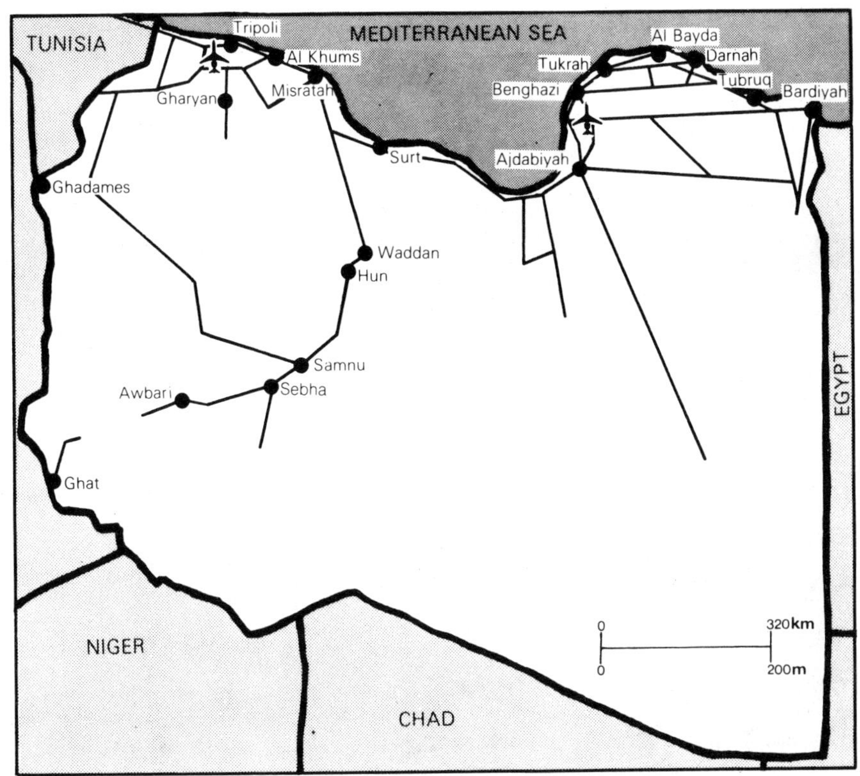

stitution, with an emphasis on popular power. Political power is exercised by People's Congresses and Committees, trade unions, etc., and the General People's Congress.

The Arab Socialist Union (founded 1971) is the only official political party, but has been virtually non-existent since the constitution was changed in 1977.

GEOGRAPHY

Libya lies on the Mediterranean coast of Africa and has borders with Tunisia, Algeria, Niger, Chad, Sudan and Egypt.

With the exception of a range of hills in the northwest known as the Jebel, Libya has few areas of high land; 90% of the country consists of sand and rock deserts and the only fertile land is the northern coastal fringe and a series of oases scattered across the country. Libya has no permanent rivers and sporadic rainfall causes frequent crop failure.

Climate

Most parts of Libya have a hot and arid desert climate, with no rainfall during the summer months. The climate along the coast is more temperate with temperatures of about 38°C/100°F in summer – humidity can exceed 90%. A hot, dry wind, the *ghibli*, blows in from the south causing a dramatic rise in temperature and some discomfort. Winters are cool with temperatures occasionally around freezing, particularly in the northern areas.

Agriculture

The discovery of oil in Libya resulted in a rural exodus and a decline in agricultural production which the Government is now anxious to reverse. A large percentage of development finance is being spent on various forms of agricultural development including land reclamation, irrigation and experimental farms. Subsidies are given to the farming community, and Libya aims to achieve self-sufficiency in meat and cereals by the 1980s.

Main Crops: barley, olives, citrus fruits, dates, almonds, tobacco.

Mineral Resources: oil, natural gas, iron ore, gypsum, potassium.

THE ECONOMY

Gross National Product (1976): US$14 billion.

Per Capita Income (1976 est.): US$5,583.

Gross Domestic Product (1977): 5,732 million Libyan dinars.

Foreign Trade (1976): Total Imports US$4,625 million; Total Exports US$8,603 million.

Main Trading Partners: Imports – Italy, West Germany, France, Japan, UK. Exports – USA, Italy, West Germany, Spain, UK.

Libya is the world's tenth-largest oil exporter and the majority of the country's income comes from oil revenues. Substantial oil reserves together with increased production and higher oil prices are enabling Libya to pursue a policy of economic diversification which, it is hoped, will give the economy a more balanced structure.

Progress is slow, and at times uncertain, and this is partly due to a shortage of skilled labour as well as to a certain unwillingness on the part of both foreign and domestic private investors to invest on a large scale.

Libya has a separate development budget with the main emphasis on industrialisation, housing and the infrastructure. Heavy industries such as iron and steel are still in their infancy. Manufacturing is largely confined to the processing of agricultural produce; other important light industries are tobacco, furniture, textiles and clothing. Growth in this sector should eventually reduce Libya's dependence on imported goods, especially on consumer items.

Major Industries: oil, natural gas, food processing, tobacco, building materials.

Main Commodities Traded: Imports – machinery, iron and steel pipes, manufactured goods, food products. Exports – crude oil, barley, olives, citrus fruits, hides and skins, tobacco.

Crude Oil Production (1976): 92 million tonnes.

Libya is a member of the Organisation of Petroleum Exporting Countries (OPEC), the Arab League and the OAU (Organisation of African Unity).

HOW TO GET THERE

Air

Major airlines flying to Tripoli and Benghazi (Benina Airport) are: Aeroflot, Alitalia, British Caledonian, KLM, Lufthansa, Swissair, TWA and UTA.

There are regular flights to Libya from Rome, London, Frankfurt, Athens, Cairo, Paris, Tunis, Algiers and Zurich. British Caledonian operate six direct flights a week to Tripoli from London and a weekly flight to Benghazi.

Flying times to Tripoli: from London 3 hours; from New York 15 hours.

An airport tax of 500 dirhams is payable on departure from Libya. This does not apply to Libyan nationals or transit passengers. Foreign business travellers may be charged income tax at Benina Airport, Benghazi, based on the number of days spent in Libya over the previous 12 months. This does not apply at Tripoli Airport so travellers are advised to use this route into Libya.

A bus service operates between Tripoli Airport and the main hotels in the city – the fare is 500 dirhams each way.

Tripoli International Airport is 35km/21 miles from Tripoli, and Benina Airport is 29km/18 miles from Benghazi.

Road

The road which runs along the North African coast for some 1,830km/1,140 miles provides a through route from Cairo via Libya to Tunis and on to Algiers and Casablanca. Persons wishing to cross the border into or out of Libya to Tunisia or Egypt should enquire if the border is open.

ENTRY REGULATIONS

Visas

Nationals from the following countries do not require visas: Algeria, Bahrain, Jordan, Kuwait, Mauritania, Morocco, Oman, Qatar, Saudi Arabia, Somalia, Sudan, UAE, Yemen Arab Republic and the People's Democratic Republic of Yemen.

All other nationals require visas, obtainable from Libyan Embassies and Consulates abroad.

Libyan government regulations require that a passport holder's particulars must be in Arabic before a visa can be issued. An 'open stamp' which must then be completed in Arabic is necessary and the visa form also must be completed in Arabic. Arrangements for the stamp are usually made by the passport-issuing authority.

British passport holders can obtain the appropriate stamp at all United Kingdom passport offices and at selected British Embassies and High Commissions abroad. Arrangements for translations into Arabic can be made through the Thomas Cook Passports, Visas and Reservations Department, 45 Berkeley Street, London.

Visas are normally valid for entry within 90 days of issue and for a stay of up to one month. Business travellers are advised to plan their visit so that they leave Libya within the period of validity of their visa. The validity of passports should extend for at least 3 months from the date of issue of visas.

Business travellers require a letter from their firm giving details of the business to be undertaken in Libya and the names of business contacts there.

Evidence in a passport of a previous or planned visit to Israel may adversely affect the granting of a visa.

All visitors must register with the immigration authorities within 7 days of arrival in Libya.

Health Regulations

An International Certificate of Vaccination against smallpox is required. Also yellow fever and/or cholera certificates if entering from an African country. TAB (typhoid and paratyphoid) injections are recommended.

Customs

Currency: No more than 20 Libyan dinars in bank notes may be taken into or out of the country. There are no restrictions on the amount of other currencies or travellers' cheques. All monies must be declared on entry and departure on a currency declaration form issued on most flights to Libya.

Duty-free articles: 200 cigarettes, 500g tobacco and 250ml perfume. Personal effects.

Accompanied samples, providing the business traveller can prove the existence of a Libyan agent. A deposit equivalent to the amount of duty payable may be charged and this is refunded on departure.

Prohibited articles: Alcohol.

PRACTICAL INFORMATION FOR THE VISITOR

1. Currency

Monetary Unit – Libyan dinar (LD), divided into 1,000 dirhams.

Notes – 250, 500 dirhams and 1, 5, 10 Libyan dinars.

Coins – 1, 5, 10, 20, 50, 100 dirhams.

Travellers' cheques should be cashed only at banks or hotels and visitors should ensure that their currency declaration form is stamped by the cashing authority. Credit cards are not normally accepted in Libya.

Banking Hours:

Winter – 0900–1300 Saturday to Thursday

Summer – 0800–1230 Saturday to Thursday
1600–1700 Saturday and Wednesday

The Central Bank of Libya is the bank of issue and operates the exchange control. Its Commercial Banking Division has branches throughout the country.

The Central Bank of Libya
Sharia Gamal Abdul Nasser, P.O. Box 1103, Tripoli, ☎ 33591.
Sharia Omar Mukhtar
P.O. Box 249, Benghazi.

Commercial Banks in Libya:

Masraf al Jumhouriya
Sharia Magarief, P.O. Box 396, Tripoli, ☎ 33553.
Sharia Gamal Abdul Nasser, P.O. Box 1291, Benghazi.

Masraf al Wahda
Sharia Magarief, P.O. Box 374, Tripoli, ☎ 34016.
Sharia Gamal Abdul Nasser, P.O. Box 1320, Benghazi, ☎ 94527.

National Commercial Bank
Maidan Al-Shuhada, P.O. Box 2553, Tripoli, ☎ 37191.
Municipality Square Branch, P.O. Box 1279, Benghazi.

Umma Bank
1 Sharia Omar Mukhtar, P.O. Box 685, Tripoli, ☎ 34031.
P.O. Box 221, Benghazi, ☎ 93377.

Sahara Bank
Sharia 1 September, P.O. Box 270, Tripoli, ☎ 32771.
Sharia Omar Mukhtar, P.O. Box 2151, Benghazi, ☎ 92766.

2. Electricity Supply

125V AC 50Hz in the Western Province and 220V AC 50Hz in the Eastern Province.
Plugs: 2-pin round Continental.

3. Weights and Measures

The metric system is in use.

4. Media

Radio broadcasts are transmitted in Arabic and English from Tripoli and Benghazi. Libya has a colour television network. There are no commercial radio or television programmes.

Newspapers:

Al Fajr Al Jadid (daily) and *Al Johad* (three times a week). The circulation of both these newspapers ranges from 16,000 to 25,000. The *Libyan Press Review* is a daily news-sheet in English published in Tripoli. *Arab Oil* is a monthly publication in Arabic and English.

5. Medical Care

There has been a sharp decline in the number of European doctors and dentists working in Libya since the Revolution.

The main towns have a high standard of cleanliness and there are no great health hazards. Tap water is safe to drink in the larger towns.

Government Hospital,
Tripoli ☎ 30585.
Emergencies ☎ 34682.
Government Hospital,
Benghazi ☎ 92131.
Emergencies ☎ 89666.

6. Telephone, Telex and Postal Services

Direct dialling is available from Libya to most European countries. Delays can be expected with trunk calls, especially during the mornings.

Useful Telephone Numbers:

Tripoli – Emergency, Police, Fire, First Aid, ☎ 41471.
Benghazi – Fire ☎ 95555, Police ☎ 99.

Libya has limited telex facilities.

Daily international and internal air mail services operate from Tripoli and Benghazi. Post offices are open 7 days a week with restricted services on Fridays.

7. Public Holidays

Fixed Holidays:

8 March	*Syrian Revolution Day*
28 March	*Evacuation Day* (UK)
25 May	*Sudan National Day*
11 June	*Evacuation Day* (US)
23 July	*Egyptian National Day*
1 September	*Libyan Revolution Day*
7 October	*Evacuation Day* (Italian)

Muslim Holidays:

These follow the Muslim calendar and occur 10–12 days earlier every year. The dates of the Muslim holidays are approximate as they depend upon sightings of the moon, and may differ by one or two days from those given below. 1981 dates are:

18 January	*Prophet's Birthday*
31 July	
–2 August	*Eid el Fitr*
8–10 October	*Eid el Adha* (3–4 days)
29 October	*Muslim New Year*

Friday is the official weekday holiday. Banks, government offices, business houses, etc. are closed on Fridays and work on Sundays. Most oil companies are closed on Saturdays.

8. Time

GMT+2

9. Internal Transport

Air

Libyan Arab Airlines operate hourly services between Tripoli and Benghazi. Also regular services to Ghadames, Sebha, Marsa Brega, Beida, Tobruk and Kufrah.

Airline Offices in Tripoli:

Aeroflot	☎ 41257.
Air France	☎ 34362.
British Airways	☎ 33518.
British Caledonian	☎ 33516/7.
KLM	☎ 34348.
Libyan Arab Airlines	☎ 44206.
Lufthansa	☎ 32990/44488.
PIA	☎ 46229.
SAS	☎ 38048/37407.
Swissair	☎ 36046/7.
TWA	☎ 35840/1.

Road

International Driving Licences are not required. Self-drive cars are available for hire in Tripoli and Benghazi, also chauffeur-driven cars but these are very expensive. Driving is on the right-hand side of the road. All traffic signs and signposts are in Arabic script.

Car-Hire Firms in Tripoli:

Alta Rentacar, 124 Sharia Imgarief.
El Rahila, Sharia Omar Mukhtar.
Otal, 10–16 Sharia Ikball.

Taxis in Libya are expensive with a minimum charge of LD1 for a single journey within Tripoli or Benghazi. Visitors are advised to negotiate all fares on a time basis before engaging a taxi.

10. Tipping

Taxis – no tip necessary.

Porters – 50 dirhams per bag.

Hotels and restaurants – 10% service charge is usually included in the bill.

11. Social Customs

Strict observance of traditional Islamic customs is kept by most of the Muslim population of this predominantly Muslim nation. The sale and consumption of alcohol is prohibited. There is also strict segregation of the sexes.

For further information, refer to page 12 under 'Muslim Social Customs'.

USEFUL ADDRESSES (GENERAL)

Embassies in Tripoli

France: Omar Lofti Saad Street, Quartier Garden City, P.O. Box 312.

West Germany: Sharia Hassan el Mashai, P.O. Box 302, ☎ 33827.

Japan: 37 Sharia Abi Ben Kaab Street, Garden City, P.O. Box 3265, ☎ 46090/46381.

Netherlands: Sharia Gelal Bayar 20, P.O. Box 3801, ☎ 41549/41550.

Switzerland: Jeraba, P.O. Box 439, ☎ 32416.

UK: 30 Sharia Gamal Abdul Nasser, ☎ 31191/5.

US: Sharia Mohammad Thabit, P.O. Box 289, ☎ 34021/6.

Other addresses

Tourist Department, Sharia Adrian Pelt, Tripoli.

American Express Authorised Representatives: The Libyan Travel Bureau, Reufeh El Ansari Street, Tourist Building, P.O. Box 306, Benghazi, ☎ 3083/2565.
North African Maritime and Travel Enterprises, 73/75 Baladia Street, P.O. Box 253, Tripoli, ☎ 40565/40562.

Secretariat for Information and Culture, Sharia Baladia Street, Tripoli, ☎ 34081.

BUSINESS INFORMATION

In accordance with Libya's Development Plans, about 17% of total investment has been allocated to agricultural development and some 15% to the industrial sector. Agricultural expansion should mean an increased demand for fertilisers and agricultural machinery. Industrial diversification, while aiming to reduce Libya's dependence on imported consumer goods, will necessitate an increase in the amount of imported capital goods as well as the need for technical advice and consultancy services.

Opportunities for direct foreign investment in Libya are limited and until now have been mainly confined to the petroleum industry and related industries. The Libyan Government tends to engage foreign contractors on a particular project which, on completion, is then handed back to Libyan operators. Foreign firms offering technical advice or working in a consultative capacity may be allowed to operate in Libya through wholly foreign-owned branches.

Agents must be Libyan nationals or, in the case of a company, wholly owned by Libyans. Because of the distance separating Benghazi and Tripoli, it is usually necessary to appoint separate agents for each market.

It is important to remember that all correspondence with government officials and all trade literature should be written in Arabic.

Import and Exchange Control Regulations

A permit is necessary for the transfer of foreign exchange from Libya, and prior approval from the Central Bank of Libya is required for the issue of exchange permits.

Certain goods, particularly those for use in the petroleum industry, are exempt from import duties.

A licence is required to import all goods – this may be an open general licence or, in the case of a wide range of items including some foodstuffs, precious metals, gems and furniture, a specific licence is required. The import of alcohol is strictly forbidden, and there is a ban on imports from South Africa, Zimbabwe–Rhodesia, Portugal and Israel.

Business Hours

Government Offices:

Winter – 0800–1400 Saturday to Thursday
Summer – 0700–1300 Saturday to Thursday
(In addition, government employees may work voluntarily from 1530–1730, except on Thursdays.)

Oil Companies:

0730–1230
1400–1630 Sunday to Thursday

Business Houses:

0900–1300
1600–1930 Saturday to Thursday

Business Events

Tripoli International Trade Fair (held annually in March). For further information contact: Fairs General Board, P.O. Box 891, Tripoli.

BUSINESS SERVICES

Translation services

Tripoli:

Ibrahim Hafez Translation Bureau, 31 Giaddat Omar Mukhtar, ☎ 33885.

Bakkush Services Agency, 39 Beirut Street, P.O. Box 2463, ☎ 44659/ 44038.

United Agents, Khweldi Building, Entrance B, 1st Floor, Khaled Ben Waled Street, P.O. Box 3791, ☎ 39633/ 40320.

Benghazi:

Abdul Majid Ben Sa'oud, Sharia Gzeir, P.O. Box 126, ☎ 92597.

USEFUL ADDRESSES (BUSINESS)

Chamber of Commerce, Industry and Agriculture for the Western Province, Sharia Al Jumhouriya, P.O. Box 2321, Tripoli, ☎ 34539/36855.

Chamber of Commerce, Industry and Agriculture for the Eastern Province, Sharia Gamal Abdul Nasser, P.O. Box 208, Benghazi, ☎ 92490/ 94526.

Secretariat for Agriculture and Agrarian Reform, Sidi Masri, Tripoli, ☎ 37338.

Secretariat for Industry and Minerals, Alfath Road, Tripoli, ☎ 40150.

Secretariat for Petroleum, Sadoon Swehli Street, Tripoli, ☎ 33195.

MAJOR CITIES AND TOWNS

Tripoli

The history of Tripoli dates back to Phoenician and Roman times, although there are few remaining traces of these origins today – with the exception of the arch of Marcus Aurelius in the old city.

Modern Tripoli is more a product of the period of Italian occupation, with wide streets and spacious open areas. The old city is of most interest to visitors with the sixteenth-century castle overlooking the harbour and port and the maze of narrow winding alleys and traditional *souks* or markets. The Castle houses a museum containing sections on the archaeology, ethnography, epigraphy and natural history of Libya.

Visitors are advised not to photograph the port.

Tripoli International Airport is 35km/21 miles from the centre of Tripoli.

Hotels

The Department of Tourism classifies hotels as deluxe, 1st class, 2nd class, etc.

LIBYA PALACE (1st class), Sharia Sidi Issa, P.O. Box 727, ☎ 31181.
First-class hotel in the city centre.
Rooms: 400 , , , , on request, .
Facilities: American bar. International restaurant and bar. Roof garden. Swimming pool. Hairdresser. Car hire.
Services: **TC**, **FC**. Amex and Diners Club. Dr. on call. .
Conference room – max. capacity 500.
Banquet room – max. capacity 500.

UADDAN (deluxe), Sharia Sidi Issa, P.O. Box 337, ☎ 30041.
Modern hotel near the city centre, overlooking the sea.
Rooms: 96 , , , on request.
Facilities: Restaurant and bars. Nightclub and casino. Cinema and theatre. Swimming pool. Hairdresser and beauty parlour.
Services: **TC**, **FC**.
Conference room – max. capacity 400.

MEDITERRANEAN (1st class), off Sharia Omar Mukhtar, P.O. Box 6607, ☎ 43016.
Modern hotel beside the sea, half a mile from the city centre.
Rooms: 290 , , . Suites available.
Facilities: Restaurant and bar. Hairdresser. Bank. Swimming.

Restaurants

Apart from the hotel restaurants, others in Tripoli are: *Excelsior*, *Caravan*, *Le Paris*, and several *Wadi al-Rabee* restaurants.

N.B. Alcohol is forbidden by law and is not served in Libyan hotels and restaurants.

Entertainment

Tripoli has several cinemas, but no regular theatre or concert hall. There are a number of municipal beaches around the town, but swimming is generally better further outside Tripoli.

Sporting activities available include football, golf, horse-racing, ten-pin bowling and tennis.

Shopping

Weavers, coppersmiths, goldsmiths and leatherworkers can be seen at work in the *souks* and their goods are on display for sale.

Benghazi

Benghazi is the main town in Libya's Eastern Province with a population of more than 300,000. Part of the modern town is built on top of the ancient city of Berenice, formerly inhabited by both the Greeks and the Romans.

Benghazi was severely damaged during the Second World War and many of the buildings dating from the periods of Turkish and Italian rule were destroyed.

Benina Airport is 29km/18 miles from the centre of Benghazi.

Hotels

GEZIRA PALACE (deluxe), Ali Wouraieth Street, P.O. Box 285, ☎ 96001.
Deluxe hotel overlooking the sea.
Rooms: 150 on request.
Facilities: Restaurant and bar. Swimming pool.

OMAR KHAYAM (deluxe), Sharia Gamal Abdul Nasser, P.O. Box 2148, ☎ 95100.
Deluxe hotel near the city centre, overlooking the sea.
Rooms: 186.
Facilities: Restaurant and bar. Swimming pool. Car hire.
Services: Amex. Dr. on call.
Conference room – max. capacity 200.
Banquet room – max. capacity 500.

Restaurants

Apart from the hotel restaurants, the two main restaurants in Benghazi are the *Palace* and the *Vienna.*

Entertainment

Two cinemas, the *Berenice* and the *Rex*, show foreign films. There is no theatre or concert hall in Benghazi.

MOROCCO

Kingdom of Morocco

Size: 458,730 sq.km/177,069 sq.miles.

Population: 18,000,000 (1977 estimate).

Distribution: 35% in urban areas.

Population Growth Rate: 2.6% p.a.

Ethnic Composition: The majority of Moroccans are Arab; although 35% are of Berber origin.

Capital: Rabat Pop. 900,000.

Major Cities: Casablanca Pop. 1,900,000; Fez Pop. 399,000; Marrakech Pop. 407,000; Meknes Pop. 376,000; Tangier Pop. 189,000.

Language: Arabic is the official language, although certain Berber tribes have their own dialects. Most Moroccan government officials and business people speak French, with some Spanish spoken in the north. English is rarely used.

Religion: The majority of the population are Muslims. There is a sizeable Jewish community and the majority of Europeans (French and Spanish) are Roman Catholics.

Government: Morocco is an independent, hereditary monarchy. The King presides over the Cabinet and appoints its members, including the Prime Minister. The House of Representatives is

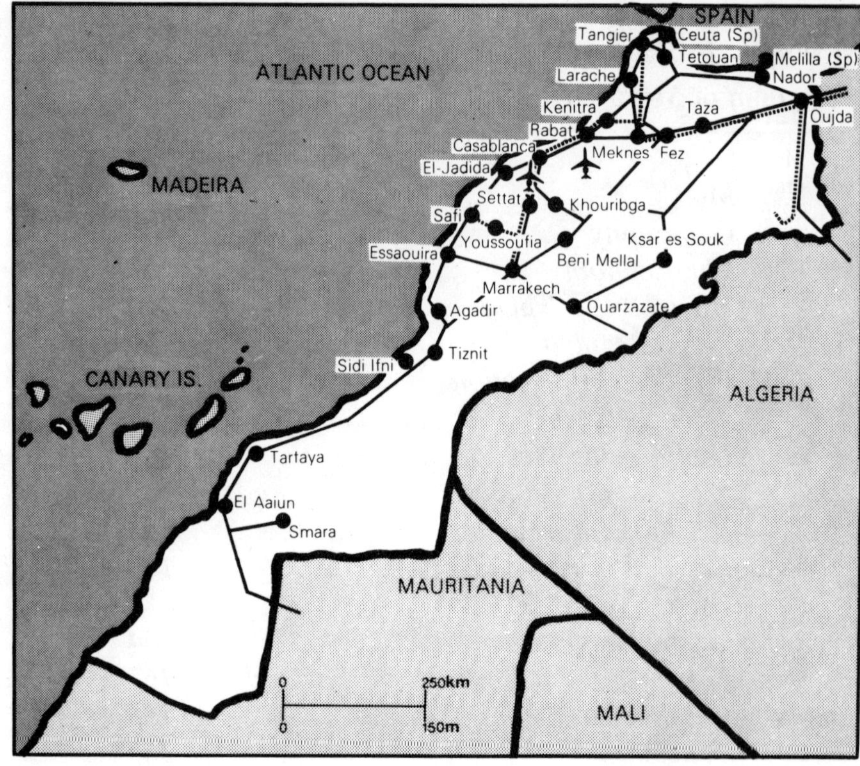

the legislative body and two-thirds of its members are elected by direct, universal suffrage. All legislation must have the approval of the King.

The main political parties in Morocco are the Istiqlal, the Union Nationale des Forces Populaires (UNFP), the Union Socialiste des Forces Populaires (USFP) and the Mouvement Populaire. Increasing control by the monarchy over the Government has weakened the political parties and until recently the Istiqlal and the UNFP refused to participate in the Government for this reason. The former is now one of four opposition parties whose leaders are Cabinet members.

GEOGRAPHY

Morocco is bordered by Algeria to the south and the southeast and by Mauritania – the partition of the Spanish Sahara was agreed between Mauritania and Morocco in 1976 when the new frontier was established. The Moroccan annexation of the Western Sahara is not recognised by Algeria, which is actively backing the Polisario Front who claim independence for the entire area, and are engaged in guerrilla activities against the occupying Moroccan troops.

The landscape is one of great contrast with the dominant feature being the Atlas Mountain range – the High Atlas to the south reaches a height of more than 4,000m/13,130ft. Between these mountains and the Atlantic stretch the fertile plains where the majority of the population is concentrated, while to the south and east lie the dry steppes, eventually merging into the Sahara desert.

Climate

The Moroccan climate is essentially of the Mediterranean type, although inland temperatures are more extreme. Summer temperatures around the coast average 22°C/72°F while inland they may rise to 38°C/100°F and over. Winters are mild with average temperatures of 10°C/50°F in the coastal regions, but below 5°C/41°F in the mountain areas.

Agriculture

Approximately 70% of the working population are engaged in agriculture, which accounts for about 25% of Morocco's Gross Domestic Product. Agriculture is sharply divided into the modern and traditional sectors – the majority of Moroccan farms are small with crops grown for local consumption, while the larger farms, established by European settlers, concentrate on production for market and export purposes.

This situation is gradually changing and land formerly owned by foreigners is now being redistributed and co-operatives have been established.

Main Crops: cereals, citrus fruits and vegetables. The cultivation of sugar beet, cotton and sunflowers is expanding rapidly.

Mineral Resources: phosphates, iron ore, lead, zinc, copper.

THE ECONOMY

Gross National Product (1977): US$7,890 million.

Per Capita Income (1976): US$477.

Foreign Trade (1976): Total Imports US$3.2 billion; Total Exports US$2.7 billion.

Main Trading Partners: Imports – France, USA, West Germany, Spain, Italy, Iraq, UK. Exports – France, West Germany, Italy, UK, Spain, Poland.

Morocco is the world's largest exporter of phosphates and, due to a number of substantial price increases, phosphates now dominate the country's export structure and account for some 55% of total exports by value.

The 1973–1977 Five-Year Plan concentrated on the development of phosphate mining and food-processing industries as well as general industrial expansion and the development of tourism. Manufacturing industries have grown rapidly, particularly in the fields of textiles, construction materials, chemicals and food processing (mainly for export).

Morocco's traditional visible trade deficit is largely offset by receipts from tourism and remittances from Moroccan workers overseas, together with the revenue from phosphates which represent Morocco's chief source of foreign-exchange earnings.

Future development plans are expected to concentrate on the expansion of light manufacturing industries and agricultural and social development, with less emphasis on large industrial projects.

The EEC is Morocco's major trading partner and a trade agreement between the EEC and Morocco was concluded in 1976. Morocco also has growing economic links with the major Arab oil producers, especially Saudi Arabia and Kuwait.

Major Industries: phosphates, sugar refining, textiles, chemicals, food and tobacco processing.

Main Commodities Traded: Exports – phosphates, fruits and vegetables, canned fish. Imports – sugar, wheat, crude oil, machinery, chemicals.

Morocco is a member of the Arab League and the Organisation of African Unity (OAU).

HOW TO GET THERE

Air

There are international airports at Agadir, Casablanca, Fez, Marrakech, Rabat and Tangier, and all are linked by direct flights to many European cities.

Royal Air Maroc flies from Algiers, Brussels, Cairo, Dakar, Frankfurt, Geneva, Las Palmas, Lisbon, London, Madrid, Marseille, Milan, Montreal, New York, Paris and Tunis.

Major airlines flying to Morocco are Aeroflot, Air France, Alitalia, British Airways, British Caledonian, Iberia, Pan Am and Sabena.

Flying times to Casablanca: from London 3¼ hours; from New York 8 hours.

Distances of airport from city centres:

Agadir	8km/5 miles	Meknes/Mezergues	2km/1 mile
Casablanca	30km/18 miles	Rabat/Sale	2km/1 mile
Fez/Sais	10km/6 miles	Tangier/Boukhaf	12km/7 miles
Marrakech/Menara	3½km/2 miles		

Sea

Frequent passenger and car ferries operate from Gibraltar, Algeciras and Malaga to Tangier.

Road

The ferry services mentioned above carry cars – alternatively there is access to Morocco from Algeria at Oujda.

The following documents are needed to take a car into Morocco: International Certificate of Motor Insurance (green card) or Moroccan Insurance Certificate, International Driving Licence, car registration book.

Rail

There is a direct connection from Paris via Bordeaux, Madrid, Algeciras and ferry to Tangier, and on to Casablanca. Regular services to Morocco run from Oran in Algeria.

ENTRY REGULATIONS

Visas

Nationals from the following countries do not require visas: Andorra, Argentina, Australia, Austria, Bahrain, Belgium, Brazil, Canada, Chile, Congo, Denmark, Egypt, Finland, France, Greece, Guinea, Iceland, Indonesia, Iran, Iraq, Ireland, Italy, Ivory Coast, Japan, Kuwait, Lebanon, Liberia, Liechtenstein, Luxembourg, Mali, Mexico, Monaco, Netherlands, New Zealand, Niger, Norway, Oman, Pakistan, Peru, Philippines, Puerto Rico, Qatar, Romania, San Marino, Saudi Arabia, Senegal, Spain, Sudan, Sweden, Switzerland, Tunisia, Turkey, United Kingdom (including the Channel Islands), USA, Venezuela and Yugoslavia.

Visitors from all these countries may stay for a period of up to 3 months, after which they must register with the police if an extension of their stay is required.

Nationals from all other countries require visas, obtainable from Moroccan embassies abroad. Applications from holders of Indian, Jordanian, Libyan, Palestinian and Syrian passports are always referred at additional cost to the applicant. Visitors arriving in Morocco without the necessary visa can obtain a permit for a 72-hour stay, provided they hold an outward ticket.

Nationals of Israel, Zimbabwe-Rhodesia and South Africa are not usually permitted to enter Morocco.

Evidence in a passport of a previous or planned visit to Israel may adversely affect the granting of a visa.

Health Regulations

International Certificates of Vaccination against smallpox, cholera and yellow fever are only required if arriving from infected areas. However, all visitors are advised to have smallpox and TAB (typhoid and paratyphoid) inoculations.

Customs

Currency: No Moroccan currency may be imported or exported by travellers. There are no restrictions on the amount of foreign currency which may be brought into Morocco. It is sometimes difficult to re-exchange Moroccan currency on departure, so it is advisable to change only small amounts of foreign currency at a time while staying in Morocco.

Duty-free articles: 400g tobacco, 200 cigarettes or 50 cigars, one bottle of wine or spirits. Personal effects such as cameras, tape recorders, typewriters, etc., limited to one of each item per person.

Commercial samples temporarily imported on payment of a deposit which is refundable if the samples are re-exported within 12 months.

PRACTICAL INFORMATION FOR THE VISITOR

1. Currency

Monetary Unit – dirham (DH), divided into 100 centimes.

Notes – 5, 10, 50, 100 dirhams.
Coins – 1, 2, 5, 10, 20, 50 centimes and 1 dirham.

Banking Hours:

Winter – 0815–1130 Monday to
1415–1630 Friday
Summer – 0830–1130 Monday to
1500–1700 Friday

The Banque du Maroc, 22 Avenue Mohammed V, B.P. 445, Rabat, ☎ 20531/30026 is the national central bank of issue. All banks formerly under foreign control are now at least 50% Moroccan-owned.

Major Commercial Banks:

Banque Marocaine du Commerce Exterieur
174 Boulevard Mohammed V, Casablanca.

Arab Bank Ltd
174 Boulevard Mohammed V, Casablanca.

Banque Marocaine pour l'Afrique et l'Orient (formerly British Bank of the Middle East)
80 Avenue Lalla Yacout, Casablanca, ☎ 72401/67441/26887.

All the major banks have branches in the cities and main towns.

2. Electricity Supply

Casablanca, Rabat, Tangier: 110/220V AC 50Hz.
Marrakech: 115V AC 50Hz.
Fez: 110V AC 50Hz.
Plugs: 2-pin round.

3. Weights and Measures

The metric system is in use.

4. Media

Radiodiffusion Télévision Marocaine broadcasts in Arabic, French, Berber, Spanish and English. Television programmes are in both French and Arabic. A foreign radio service from Morocco is broadcast in Arabic, French and English.

Newspapers:

Casablanca: *Le Matin*; *Maroc Soir*; *Al-Bayane*. Rabat: *L'Opinion*; *Al Alam*; *Al Anba*.

A wide range of weekly and monthly periodicals is also published. There is no regular trade press.

5. Medical Care

The better health facilities are located in Casablanca and Rabat.

It is not advisable to drink tap water, and care should be taken with fresh fruit and vegetables. Typhoid and paratyphoid are endemic and TAB inoculations are recommended.

6. Telephone, Telex and Postal Services

International telex facilities are available. The following hotels have telex facilities available to non-residents:
Rabat – Hilton Hotel, Tour Hassan Hotel.
Casablanca – El Mansour Hotel, Marhaba Hotel.

7. Public Holidays

Fixed Holidays:

1 January	*New Year's Day*
3 March	*Fête du Trône*
1 May	*Labour Day*
9 July	*King Hassan's Birthday*
18 November	*Independence Day*

Muslim Holidays:

These follow the Muslim calendar and occur 10–12 days earlier every year. The dates of the Muslim holidays are approximate as they depend upon sightings of the moon, and may differ by one or two days from those given below. 1981 dates are:

18 January	*Prophet's Birthday*
31 July–2 August	*Eid el Fitr*
8–10 October	*Eid el Adha*
29 October	*Hijra New Year*

Local festivals or *moussems* are held in different parts of Morocco throughout the year. Times vary according to the Muslim calendar.

Sunday is the weekly holiday in Morocco.

8. Time

GMT

9. Internal Transport

Air

Internal air services connect Casablanca, Rabat, Tangier, Marrakech, Agadir, Fez, Tetouan, Oujda and Al Hoceima.

Airline Offices in Casablanca:

Air France	☎ 274242.
Air India	☎ 271122.
British Caledonian	☎ 278079/260958.
Iberia	☎ 279600.
KLM	☎ 272729.
Lufthansa	☎ 223027/223210.
Pan Am	☎ 271122.
PIA	☎ 221018/269273.
Royal Maroc	☎ 271122.
SAS	☎ 224184.
Swissair	☎ 271234.

Rail

A daily service operates from Casablanca to Tangier (6 hours). Also, services operate from Casablanca to Marrakech, Rabat, Fez, Meknes and onwards to Oujda and the Algerian border.

Road

Good bus services to all parts of the country are run by the Compagnie des Transports Marocains.

There are two kinds of taxis: the *petit* taxis, normally painted red, offer the cheapest service but do not carry baggage, as do the larger taxis.

Car-Hire Firms:

Avis

Agadir	☎ 2755.
Casablanca	☎ 272424.
Marrakech	☎ 30745.
Rabat	☎ 20888.
Tangier	☎ 33031.

Hertz

Agadir	☎ 3939.
Casablanca	☎ 223220.
Fez	☎ 22812.
Marrakech	☎ 31680.
Rabat	☎ 34475.
Tangier	☎ 33322.

Locoto

Casablanca	☎ 270500.

An International Driving Licence is required.

10. Tipping

Taxis – large: 10%
small: 50 centimes to DH1.

Hotels/restaurants – a service charge of 10–15% is usually added to the bill. A small tip of DH2–3 is usual for hotel porters.

Porters – DH1 to DH1.50 per bag, depending on weight.

11. Social Customs

The customs and mores of the people living in Morocco's cities and large towns basically centre around the Arab culture, while in rural areas Berber traditions still prevail. However, both cultures are unified in their observance of the Islamic faith.

Alcohol is not prohibited in Morocco although its availability is likely to be restricted during the month of *Ramadan.*

Within the business community the Muslim code of practice is less strictly adhered to and, under the influence of the French and Spanish communities, social customs tend to be more along European lines.

For further information, refer to page 12 under 'Muslim Social Customs'.

USEFUL ADDRESSES (GENERAL)

Embassies in Rabat

Canada: 13 Bis rue Jaafar es Sadiq, Rabat-Agdal, B.P. 709, ☎ 71375/76.

France: 6 Avenue Mohammed V, ☎ 20421/26.

West Germany: 7 rue Mohammed El Fatih, B.P. 235, ☎ 32532.

Japan: 19 Avenue Tarik Ibn Ziad, ☎ 22159/30146.

Netherlands: 40 rue de Tunis, B.P. 329, ☎ 33512/3.

Switzerland: Square de Berkane, B.P. 169, ☎ 24695/31024.

UK: 17 Boulevard de la Tour Hassan, B.P. 45, ☎ 20905/6.

US: 2 Avenue de Marrakech, B.P. 99, ☎ 30361/30362.

Other addresses in Rabat

National Office of Tourism, 22 Avenue d'Alger, ☎ 21252.

Syndicat d'Initiative, rue Patrice Lumumba, ☎ 23272.

Wagons-Lits Tourisme, 1 Avenue Al Amir Moulay Abdallah, ☎ 22645/6.

Consulates in Casablanca

British Consulate-General, 60 Boulevard d'Anfa, B.P. 762, ☎ 261440.

Dutch Consulate-General, Algemene Bank Marokko S.A., Place du 16 Novembre, Immeuble des Habous, Passage du Grand Socco, B.P. 478, ☎ 221712/221820.

French Consulate, Avenue du Prince Moulay Abdallah, B.P. 36.

West German Consulate, 42 Avenue de l'Armée Royale, B.P. 165, ☎ 264872/3.

Swiss Consulate, 79 Mahaj Al-Hassan At Tani, (Avenue Hassan II), B.P.5, ☎ 260211/12.

US Consulate-General, 8 Boulevard Moulay Youssef, B.P. 80, ☎ 260521/23.

Other addresses in Casablanca

Wagons-Lits Tourisme, 60 rue de Foucauld, ☎ 261211/4.

American Express Authorised Representative: Voyages Schwartz, 112 Avenue du Prince Moulay Abdallah, ☎ 222946/273133.

Consulates in Tangier

British Consulate-General, 52 rue d'Angleterre, B.P. 2033, ☎ 35895/7.

French Consulate, 2 Place de France, B.P. 401.

Dutch Consulate, Immeuble 'Miramonte', 47 Avenue Hassan II, ☎ 31245.

West German Consulate, 47 Avenue Hassan II, ☎ 21600.

US Consulate-General, Chemin des Amoureux, ☎ 35904.

Other addresses in Tangier

Syndicat d'Initiative, rue Velazquez, ☎ 35486.

National Office of Tourism, 29 Boulevard Pasteur, ☎ 32996.

Wagons-Lits Tourisme, 86 rue de la Liberté, ☎ 31640.

American Express Authorised Representative: Voyages Schwartz, 76 Avenue Mohammed V, ☎ 33459/33471.

Other American Express Authorised Representatives:

Voyages Schwartz, rue de Hotel Deville, Immeuble 'Frères', Agadir.
Voyages Schwartz, rue Mauritania, Immeuble 'Mouataouakil' 1, Marrakech, ☎ 33321.

Other Wagons-Lits Tourisme Offices:

26 Avenue des Forces Armées Royales, Agadir, ☎ 3528.
Immeuble du Grand Hotel, Boulevard Mohammed V, Fez, ☎ 22958.
122 Avenue Mohammed V, Marrakech, ☎ 31687.
Immeuble Sifiche, 1 Zenkat Ghana, Meknes, ☎ 21995/6.
Place Mohammed V, Oujda, ☎ 2520.

BUSINESS INFORMATION

Development plans in Morocco are relatively ambitious and are likely to suffer without a recovery in phosphate earnings – there are optimistic signs that the export demand for phosphates will increase while there is a general recovery in world trade and an increased demand for fertilisers. Imports will be reduced wherever possible to improve the country's trade deficit.

State participation in industry is high and is increasingly being carried out in conjunction with local private enterprise and foreign companies. At the same time strict measures have been introduced to control speculation and reduce inflation – food prices rose by 19% in 1976.

The majority of agents importing foreign goods are based in Casablanca. Agency agreements are governed by the general rules on liabilities and contracts under Moroccan law.

Import and Exchange Control Regulations

Although Morocco is in the franc zone, exchange control measures apply to transactions within that area as well as with the rest of the world.

Certain restrictions regarding import licences have been relaxed and for some imported goods an *engagement d'importation* is sufficient to clear goods through Customs. A *certificat d'importation* issued by the Ministry of Commerce may be necessary for certain specified goods.

Business Hours

Government Offices:

Winter –	0830–1200 1430–1800	Monday to Friday
	0800–1300	Saturday
Summer –	0830–1200 1600–1900	Monday to Friday
	0800–1300	Saturday

During Ramadan – 0900–1400 Monday to Friday

Business Houses:

0900–1200
1500–1800/1900 } Monday to Friday

Most business houses are open on Saturday morning.

Many business people and government officials are on holiday from mid-July to mid-August when some businesses virtually close down. Visitors are advised to avoid a trip to Morocco during this period, and also during the period of Ramadan.

Business Events

An International Trade Fair is held every other year (1981, 1983, etc.) in Casablanca, usually during the spring. For further information contact: International Fair, 11 rue Jules Mauran, Casablanca.

BUSINESS SERVICES

Translation

Ecole Berlitz, 10 Avenue de l'Armée Royale, Casablanca, ☎ 268932.

Assimil, 71 rue Allal ben Abdullah, Casablanca, ☎ 267567.

Publicity Agencies

Casablanca:

Agence Marocaine de Publicité, 88 Boulevard Mohammed V.

Havas Maroc, 61 Avenue de l'Armée Royale.

Publivente, 71 rue Allal ben Abdullah.

Tangier:

Luri, 18 rue Sanlucar.

USEFUL ADDRESSES (BUSINESS)

Chambre de Commerce et d'Industrie de Casablanca, 98 Boulevard Mohammed V, B.P. 423, Casablanca.

La Fédération des Chambres de Commerce et d'Industrie du Maroc, 11 Avenue Allal Ben Abdullah, B.P. 218, Rabat.

British Chamber of Commerce for Morocco, 291 Boulevard Mohammed V, Casablanca.

Chambre Française de Commerce et d'Industrie du Maroc, 15 Avenue Mers Sultan, B.P. 73, Casablanca.

Office de Commercialisation et d'Exportation, 45 Avenue des Forces Armées Royales, Casablanca.

Confédération Générale Economique Marocaine (C.G.E.M.), 23 Boulevard Mohammed Abdouh, Casablanca.

Ministry of Information, Rabat, ☎ 31705/32016.

Ministry of Finance, Rabat, ☎ 27171/30552.

Ministry of Trade, Industry, Mines & Merchant Shipping, Rabat, ☎ 51073/27511.

MAJOR CITIES AND TOWNS

Rabat

Rabat was founded in the twelfth century but only regained its former importance when the French established the city as the administrative capital of Morocco at the beginning of this century. The modern aspect of Rabat with its broad avenues and luxurious homes and office blocks dates from this period, yet blends in well with the old city. The ancient city of Chellah to the east is one of Rabat's most interesting sights, although only the ruined mosque and ancient tombs remain to be seen today.

The Kasbah of the Oudaias has many fascinating attractions including a small carpet factory open to visitors, and various craftsmen working out in the open street. The Museum of Moroccan Arts is here too. The Royal Palace and Mosque and other government offices occupy the centre of the city in an enclosed area called the *Mechouar*.

Sale Airport is 2km/1 mile from the centre of Rabat.

Hotels

The Ministry of Tourism hotel classification ranges from 5 star to 1 star.

RABAT-HILTON (5 star), Aviation-Souissi, B.P. 450, ☎ 72151.
A deluxe hotel, built in extensive grounds, 5 minutes' drive from the city centre.
Rooms: 259 [symbols]. Suites available.
Facilities: International and Moroccan cuisine. Coffee shop, cocktail lounge and bar. Shops. Swimming, tennis and golf. Nightclub. Hairdresser and boutique. Car hire.
Services: TC, FC. [symbol] Amex, Carte Blanche, Diners Club and Eurocard. Dr. on call. [symbols].
Conference rooms – max. capacity 1,000.
Banquet rooms – max. capacity 900.

DE LA TOUR HASSAN (5 star), 26 Avenue Abderrahman Annega, B.P. 14, ☎ 21401.
Modern, deluxe hotel in the heart of the city – luxuriously decorated throughout in the Moorish style.
Rooms: 150.
Facilities: Restaurant, dining room and rooftop supper club with international and Moroccan cuisine. Swimming and sauna. Hairdresser and boutique. Golf. Conference and banquet rooms.

RABAT CHELLAH (4 star), 2 rue d'Ifni, ☎ 24052.
Modern, first-class hotel in city centre.
Rooms: 100 [symbols].
Facilities: Restaurant, grill and bar. Boutique.
Services: TC, FC. [symbol] Amex and Diners Club. Dr. on call. [symbols].
No conference facilities.

Restaurants

The larger hotels offer both international and Moroccan cuisine. Restaurants in Rabat include:
L'Oasis, 7 rue al Osgofia (French/Moroccan), ☎ 22185; *Kabbaj Palace*, rue Mokhtar el Souissi (Moroccan), ☎ 34241; *Koutoubia*, 10 rue Pierre Parent (Moroccan), ☎ 26125; *Chez Pierre*, Avenue Mohammed V (French), ☎ 23090; *Le Capri*, Place des Alaouites (Italian), ☎ 33281; *Hong Kong*, 261 Avenue Mohammed V (Chinese), ☎ 23594; *Le Mandarin*, Avenue Soumaya, ☎ 24699.

Nightclubs

Aquarium, Boulevard Mohammed V; *El Farah*, Hotel de la Tour Hassan, ☎ 21401; *Hilton Hotel Night Club*, ☎ 72243; *La Cage*, Place Bremond, ☎ 20334; *L'Entonnoir*, Place Bremond, ☎ 34132.

Entertainment

Tennis – *Olympique Marocain*, ☎ 22351.
Riding – *Club Equestre*, route du Zaers, ☎ 50294.
Golf – *Dar Es Salaam Royal Club* (18 holes), ☎ 20205.
Souissi Royal Golf Club (9 holes), ☎ 40359.
Sailing – *Royal Yacht Club*, ☎ 20264.

Shopping

The main shopping area is concentrated around Avenue Mohammed V and Avenue Allal ben Abdallah. Traditional Moroccan wares are sold in the *Medina* and visitors will find a fine selection of carpets, leatherwork, pottery, jewellery and embroidered goods.

Casablanca

Casablanca is Morocco's main port and, as the principal commercial and industrial centre of the country, has developed into a modern, bustling, European-style city. In contrast, the city is skirted by a mass of *bidonvilles* or shanty towns with severe problems of overcrowding and poverty.

Unlike Fez or Marrakech, Casablanca does not abound with buildings and places of great historic interest. The *souks* in the *Medina* are notably tourist-orientated. The new *Medina* in the eastern part of the city houses the Royal Palace, Great Mosque and Mahakma (law courts) – the latter are open to non-Muslims and constitute a fine example of modern Moorish architecture.

Casablanca Airport is 30km/18 miles from the city centre.

Hotels

EL MANSOUR (5 star), 27 Avenue de l'Armée Royale, ☎ 265011.
A deluxe hotel in the heart of Casablanca's business centre.
Rooms: 250. Suites available.
Facilities: International and Moroccan restaurants. Coffee shop and bar. Sauna and massage. Boutique and hairdresser.
Services: **TC**, **FC**. Amex and Diners Club. Dr. on call. Airline, car-hire and travel agency services. **S**.
Conference rooms – max. capacity 1,200.
Banquet rooms – max. capacity 800.

MARHABA (5 star), 63 Avenue de l'Armée Royale, ☎ 224199.
Modern, first-class hotel situated in the heart of the business district.
Rooms: 135. Suites available.
Facilities: Restaurants and cocktail lounge. Roof terrace. Sauna and massage. Boutique and hairdresser. Travel agency. Car hire.
Services: **TC**, **FC**. Amex and Diners Club. Dr. on call. **S**.
Conference and banquet rooms – max. capacity 300.

ANFA PLAGE (4 star), Boulevard de la Corniche, ☎ 58242.
Modern hotel in residential centre, near the sea.
Rooms: 130. Suites available.
Facilities: 2 restaurants and 3 bars. Swimming and tennis. Nightclub. Hairdresser.
Services: **TC**, **FC**. Amex and Diners Club. Dr. on call. **S**.
Conference room – max. capacity 30.
Banquet rooms – max. capacity 200.

TRANSATLANTIQUE (4 star), 79 rue Colbert, ☎ 60761/2.
First-class hotel in the heart of the business centre.
Rooms: 60.
Facilities: Restaurant and cocktail lounge.

Restaurants

Seafood:
La Mer, El Hank, ☎ 21084; *Le Petit Rocher*, El Hank, ☎ 21195; *Le Cabestan*, El Hank, ☎ 21060; *A Ma Bretagne*, Ain Diab, ☎ 52111; *Le Clapotis*, Ain Diab, ☎ 58144.

Moroccan:
Al Mounia, 111 rue du Prince Moulay Abdallah, ☎ 22686; *Sijilmassa*, Ain Diab, ☎ 58233; *L'Etoile Marocaine*, 107 rue Allal Ben Abdallah, ☎ 64781.

Spanish:
La Corrida, rue Gay-Lussac, ☎ 78155; *Tio Pepe*, Boulevard de la Corniche, ☎ 58189.

Others:
Don Camillo, 13 rue de Verdun (Italian), ☎ 61644; *Viking*, 22 rue Ferhat Hachad (Scandinavian), ☎ 78266; *La Pagode*, 95 rue Ferhat Hachad (Chinese), ☎ 77185.

Nightclubs

Don Quichotte, 44 Place Mohammed V, ☎ 22051; *Embassy*, 2 Boulevard Mohammed V, ☎ 65707; *Le Bahia*, Boulevard de la Corniche, ☎ 58242; *La Notte*, Boulevard de la Corniche, ☎ 58361; *La Rose Orientale*, 4 rue Nolly, ☎ 75589; *Puerta del Sol*, 7 Avenue Hassan II, ☎ 22772.

Entertainment

Tennis – *Tennis Romandie*, ☎ 51640.
Golf – *Golf Club d'Anfa* (9 holes), ☎ 51026.

Shopping

Along the Boulevard Mohammed V are many fine shops, mainly filled with French-imported goods which tend to be very expensive. The government-controlled *Maison de l'Artisanat*, opposite the Hotel Marhaba, sells goods at fixed prices and will arrange shipment abroad.

Tangier

Tangier's proximity to Europe has established it as a city with an international flavour, and yet it has retained much of the traditional Moroccan charm. The old city overlooking the port is of the most interest and adjoins the Gran Socco, believed to be the original site of the Forum in the Roman city of Tinghis. This is the heart of Old Tangier where the Kasbah is to be found, containing many fine buildings, the Museums of Moroccan Art and Antiquities and the 300-year-old Royal Palace. The Great Mosque which dates from the late seventeenth century stands in the old town.

Boukhaf Airport is 12km/7 miles from the centre of Tangier.

Hotels

LES ALMOHADES (5 star), Avenue des Forces Armées Royales, B.P. 311, ☎ 36025.
Deluxe hotel facing the sea, about 1 mile from the city centre.
Rooms: 150 [symbols]. Suites available.
Facilities: International and Moroccan restaurants. Bars and discotheque. Sauna, swimming and tennis. Shops and hairdresser. Car hire.
Services: TC, FC. ⊟ Amex and Diners Club. Dr. on call. [symbols].
Conference room – max. capacity 300.
Banquet room – max. capacity 220.

EL MINZAH (5 star), 85 rue de la Liberté, ☎ 35885.
Deluxe hotel in traditional Moorish style, 12km/7½ miles from the airport.
Rooms: 100 [symbol]. Suites available.
Facilities: Restaurant with French and Moroccan cuisine. Bar, coffee shop, evening entertainment. Swimming, tennis and golf.
Services: ⊟ Amex and Diners Club.
Conference and banquet rooms.

INTER-CONTINENTAL (5 star), Boulevard de Paris, ☎ 36053.
Modern, deluxe hotel near the city centre.

Rooms: 130 (in some rooms), , , . Suites available.
Facilities: 2 restaurants (European and Moroccan), Oriental nightclub. Discotheque. Roof terrace. Sauna and swimming. Boutique. Car hire.
Services: TC, FC. Amex, Bankamericard, Carte Blanche, Diners Club, Eurocard and Master Charge. Dr. on call. , .
Conference room – max. capacity 100.
Banquet rooms – max. capacity 200.

CHELLAH (4 star), 47–49 rue Allal Ben Abdallah, 36388.
First-class hotel near the city centre, 500 yards from the beach.
Rooms: 180 , , , , , , .
Facilities: Restaurant, lounge bar and nightclub. Heated swimming pool. Boutique. Car hire.
Services: TC, FC. Amex. Dr. on call. , .
Conference and banquet rooms – max. capacity 350.

GRAND HOTEL VILLA DE FRANCE (4 star), 143 rue de Hollande. 31475.
Built in traditional style, the hotel overlooks the Kasbah and the Straits of Gibraltar.
Rooms: 60.
Facilities: Restaurant (Moroccan and French cuisine), bars and patio. Swimming. Boutique.

Restaurants

Moroccan:
Damascus, 2 Avenue du Prince Moulay Abdallah, 34730; *Hammadi*, rue d'Italie, 34514; *Marhaba*, Kasbah, 37643.

French:
La Grenouille, rue Rembrandt, 39042; *Guittas*, rue San Francisco, 37333; *Alhambra*, rue Docteur Fumey, 21021; *La Clairière*, route du Cap Spartel, 33885.

Spanish:
Manila, Boulevard Pasteur, 34632; *Montero*, rue Belgique, 39114; *Pilo*, rue de Fez, 34569; *Romero*, Avenue du Prince Moulay Abdallah, 32277.

Others:
Les Ambassadeurs, Avenue du Prince Moulay Abdallah (Italian), 35704; *La Pagode*, rue Balmes (Vietnamese and Chinese), 38086.

Nightclubs

African Rhythms, Avenue Prince Heritier, 33439; *Churchill Club*, 11 rue Sanlucar, 26662; *Koutoubia Palace*, 7 rue Sanlucar, 39525; *Morocco Palace*, Avenue du Prince Moulay Abdallah, 39814.

Entertainment

Tennis – *Tennis Emsallah*, 38026; *Tennis Municipal Club*, 37324.
Golf – *Country Club*, Boubanah (9 holes), 38925.
Sailing and sea fishing – *Yacht Club*, 39939.

Shopping

Every variety of bazaar and shop can be found in the *Medina* where gold, silver, brass, copper, silk and wool goods are on sale. Bargaining is an integral part of any sale.

OMAN

Sultanate of Oman

Size: 310,800 sq.km/120,000 sq.miles.

Population: 820,000 (1978).

Distribution: 19% in urban areas.

Density: 4 persons per sq.km/10 per sq.mile.

Population Growth Rate: 3.1% p.a.

Ethnic Composition: The majority of the population are Arabs – many being expatriates from India, Pakistan and East Africa.

Capital: The capital area stretches from Muscat through Muttrah to Seeb and has a population of approximately 50,000.

Major Towns: Nizwa Pop. 10,000; Salalah Pop. 10,000; Sohar Pop. 6,000.

Language: Arabic is the official language, but English is widely used in government and business circles.

Religion: Islam is the main religion and the official creed of Ibadhi is used. There are also Sunni Muslims and a minority of Shia Muslims.

Government: Oman is a sultanate and the Sultan is also the acting Prime Minister. He presides over the Council of Ministers which is responsible for internal administration. The southern region of Dhofar has its own administration, headed by the Sultan and Governor of Muscat.

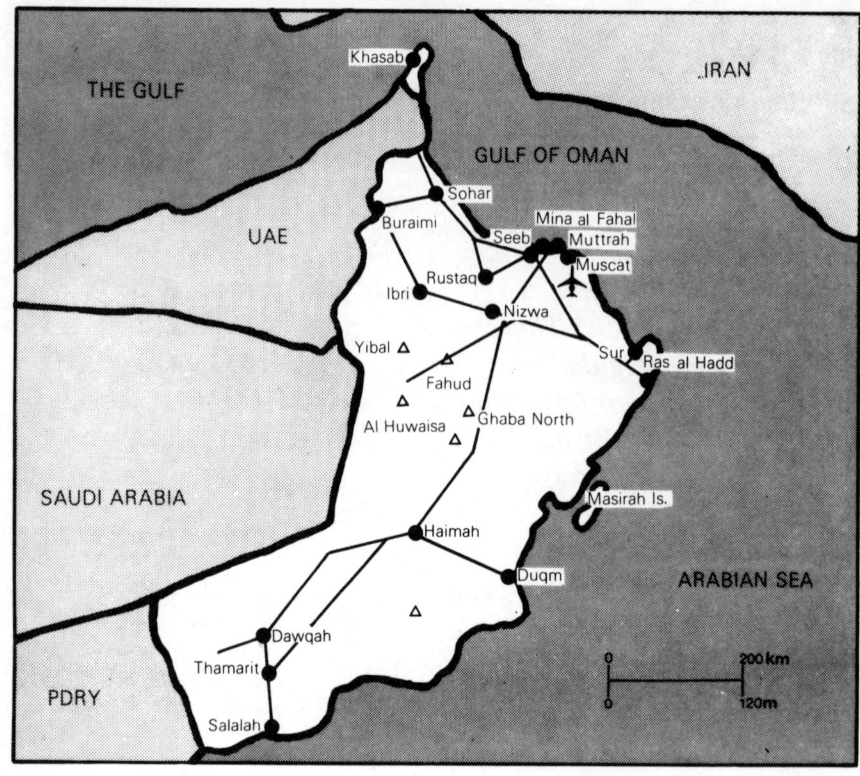

GEOGRAPHY

Oman is situated at the eastern corner of the Arabian peninsula and has borders with the UAE, Saudi Arabia and the People's Democratic Republic of Yemen. The landscape is varied with stretches of desert, areas of rich vegetation, particularly along the coastal plains, and mountain ranges rising to 3,000m/9,800ft.

Climate

Oman has an arid, sub-tropical climate. Hot, humid summers with temperatures reaching 47°C/117°F along the coast, where humidity can exceed 85%. Winter temperatures range from 16°C/61°F to 32°C/90°F. Visitors will find that the best time to visit Oman is from November to March.

Agriculture

The cultivated area is estimated at 40,000 hectares/90,000 acres, of which 38% lies along the Batinah coast and 50% in a series of interior oasis areas.

Approximately 75% of the population is dependent on agriculture and pastoralism. The use of land for agricultural purposes is dependent on water supplies and the Government is undertaking a 10-year water-development plan.

Fishing is also important, providing employment for around 10% of the population and an essential food supply.

Main Crops: dates, alfalfa, limes, wheat, fruits, vegetables.

Mineral Resources: oil, copper, asbestos, manganese, coal.

THE ECONOMY

Gross Domestic Product (1976): US$1.8 billion.

Per Capita Income (1976): US$2,250.

Gross Domestic Product (1977): 872.9 million rial Omani.

Foreign Trade (1976): Total Imports US$673 million; Total Exports US$1.3 billion.

Main Trading Partners: Imports – UK, United Arab Emirates, Japan, West Germany, USA, India. Exports – Japan, Spain, UK, West Germany, Brazil.

Oman began exporting oil just over a decade ago, and since that time government income has increased multifold, particularly since the sudden rise in oil prices in 1973/4. Many large-scale development projects were started in the mid-seventies following this boom, and large sums of capital were invested. The subsequent drop in oil production created a liquidity problem, and until recently Oman has been involved in paying off past debts.

The Government plans to develop new sources of income to supplement oil revenues, and to increase capital investment in income-generating projects. These include the development of new industrial areas producing cement, iron and steel, liquefied gas and a copper mining and smelting project.

Government budgets continue to show a deficit due as much to high defence and internal security expenses as to a decrease in oil income, and the resulting cuts in government expenditure have tended to produce an overall slow-down in terms of foreign trade.

Major Industries: oil, cement, flour, construction materials, furniture, food processing.

Main Commodities Traded: Imports – foods, machinery, manufactured goods, materials, clothing. Exports – oil, dates, fish, limes.

Oil Production (1976): 133.8 million barrels.

Oman is a member of the Arab League.

HOW TO GET THERE

Air

Regular flights operate between Muscat and London, Paris, Amsterdam, Karachi, Bombay and Beirut, Amman, Cairo and the Gulf capitals.

Gulf Air and British Airways operate direct flights from London.

Other major airlines flying to Oman include Air India, Royal Jordanian Airlines, Middle East Airlines, PIA and Saudi Arabian Airlines.

Flying times to Oman: from London 7 hours; from New York 13 hours.

Seeb International Airport is 40 km/26 miles from Muscat. (Flight information ☎ 610456/610036.)

An airport tax of RO2 is payable by all passengers on departure from Oman.

ENTRY REGULATIONS

Visas

Passport holders of all countries require visas obtainable from Omani Embassies abroad. No tourist or transit visas are issued. Visa applications by business travellers should be supported by a letter from the applicant's firm stating full details of the business to be undertaken and confirming financial responsibility for the applicant.

In addition, applicants who already have connections in Oman must obtain a letter from the firm or government department they wish to visit in Oman, stating the name(s) of person(s) visiting Oman, their dates of arrival and duration of their stay in the country.

Applicants who do not already have connections in Oman should seek advice from their nearest Omani Embassy.

For visits to relatives or friends in Oman, a 'No Objection Certificate' is required, obtainable through such relatives and friends.

Evidence in a passport of a previous or planned visit to Israel may adversely affect the granting of a visa. No visitor is allowed to enter Oman without a visa or 'No Objection Certificate'.

Health Regulations

International Certificates of Vaccination against smallpox and cholera are required by all persons entering Oman. TAB (typhoid and paratyphoid) injections are recommended.

Customs

Currency: There are no restrictions on the amount of local or foreign currency which may be taken into or out of Oman.

Duty-free articles: Personal effects, cigarettes and tobacco for personal consumption.

Articles liable to duty: Samples are technically liable to duty, although duty is in fact charged at the discretion of the Customs officials.

Prohibited articles: Alcohol and pornographic literature.

PRACTICAL INFORMATION FOR THE VISITOR

1. Currency

Monetary Unit – rial Omani (RO), divided into 1,000 baizas.
Notes – RO 1, 5, 10, 20 and 100, 250, 500 baizas.
Coins – 2, 5, 10, 25, 50, 100 baizas.

Banking Hours:
0800–1200 Saturday to Wednesday
0800–1130 Thursday
(Opening times are one hour later during *Ramadan*)

Currency is issued by the Central Bank of Oman, P.O. Box 534, Muscat, ☎ 745021.

Major Commercial Banks in Oman:

Arab Bank Ltd
P.O. Box 991, Muscat, ☎ 722831.
Bank of Credit & Commerce International
P.O. Box 840, Muscat, ☎ 701007.
Banque de Paris et des Pays-Bas
P.O. Box 425, Muscat, ☎ 722740.
The Chartered Bank
P.O. Box 210, Muscat, ☎ 722011/3.
Bank of Oman, Bahrain & Kuwait
P.O. Box 920, Muscat, ☎ 722966.
British Bank of the Middle East
P.O. Box 234, Muscat, ☎ 772041.
Citibank
P.O. Box 918, Muscat, ☎ 722662.
Grindlays Bank Ltd
P.O. Box 91, Muscat, ☎702023.
National Bank of Oman
P.O. Box 1272, Muttrah, ☎ 773131.

The Oman Development Bank (40% government-owned) has been established to assist development, in particular in the private sector.

2. Electricity Supply

220V AC 50Hz.
Plugs: 2- or 3-pin round or 3-pin flat.

3. Weights and Measures

The metric system is in use.

4. Media

Radio programmes are broadcast in Arabic. There is a daily English-language radio programme from 1300–1500 hours, with news bulletins at 1300 and 1430 hours. Oman has a colour television network. Advertising is not accepted on either radio or television.

Newspapers:

Al Watan; Oman; Gulf Weekly Mirror; Times of Oman; Akhbar Oman. The following magazines and journals are also published: *Al Aqida* (weekly); *Al Usra* (weekly); *Tijarat* (quarterly trade magazine); *Al Nahda* (fortnightly).

5. Medical Care

Oman has a good network of hospitals and clinics throughout the country. There are some doctors and dentists in private practice.

Muscat Hospital	☎ 722508.
Al Rahmah Hospital, Muttrah	☎ 722453.
Al Nadha Hospital, Ruwi	☎ 701255.
Al Khoula Hospital, near Mina al Fahal	☎ 600455.

Treatment from a British doctor and dentist is available at the Medident Centre, Flats 2 and 3, Apartment Block No. 17, Road 'O', Medinat Qaboos East, ☎ 600668.

Dysentery, TB, malaria and eye diseases are endemic and it is advisable to take along suitable medications as a precaution against these. Food and drink should be taken with caution outside of the good hotels and restaurants.

6. Telephone, Telex and Postal Services

There is a radio-telephone link between Muscat and the Gulf ports, London and other European capitals.

Due to the short supply of telephones in the capital area, many business firms are awaiting installation of this facility.

Useful Telephone Numbers:

Police Headquarters	☎ 600099.
Ruwi Police	☎ 701770.
Muscat Police	☎ 722611.
Muttrah Police	☎ 772226.
Muscat Fire Station	☎ 722666.
Overseas Operator	☎ 195.

Oman has a 24-hour telegram service. Telex messages can be sent from the public counter at the OMANTEL office in Muscat.

All mail, to and from Oman, should be despatched by air.

7. Public Holidays

Fixed Holidays:

18 November *National Day**
19 November *Sultan's Birthday*

*The dates of the *National Day* holidays are variable, and are not fixed until a few days before the holiday.

Muslim Holidays:

These follow the Muslim calendar and occur 10–12 days earlier every year. The dates of the Muslim holidays are approximate as they depend upon sightings of the moon, and may differ by one or two days from those given below.

1981 dates are:

18 January	*Prophet's Birthday*
31 May	*Ascension of the Prophet*
31 July–2 August	*End of Ramadan*
8–10 October	*Eid el Adha*
29 October	*Hijra (Muslim) New Year*

The Muslim week-end (Thursday afternoon and Friday) is observed.

8. Time

GMT + 4

9. Internal Transport

Air

Gulf Air operates daily flights to Salalah in Dhofar, but passengers must obtain permission in writing from the Office of the Governor of the Capital of Muscat. Tickets are sold only at the airport approximately 1 hour prior to departure. Permission to travel on the return flight must be sought in a similar way from the Wali of Dhofar.

Airline Offices in Oman:

Air France (Muscat)	☎ 734626.
British Airways (Muscat)	☎ 702410/3.
British Airways (Salalah)	☎ 461132.
British Caledonian (Muscat)	☎ 734600.
Lufthansa (Muscat)	☎ 734292.
MEA (Muscat)	☎ 701482.
Pan Am (Muscat)	☎ 702251.
TWA (Muscat)	☎ 734811/3.

Road

Self-drive and chauffeur-driven car-hire facilities are available through the major hotels.

Car-Hire Firms in Oman:

Avis (Ruwi), ☎ 722498.
Avis (Qurum), ☎ 600500 (c/o Muscat Inter-Continental Hotel).

International Driving Licences are valid for 3 months. Traffic travels on the right-hand side of the road.

Taxis operate between the capital area (Muscat/Ruwi/Muttrah) and the airport. Fares are usually subject to negotiation.

10. Tipping

This is not necessary whenever the 10% service charge is levied. Negotiated taxi fares usually include a tip.

11. Social Customs

Oman is rather conservative in outlook and clings to the more traditional

Muslim way of life. However, alcohol is available in Oman but sale of it to the public is heavily restricted. It is sold in hotel bars and restaurants. Visitors should remember that the penalties for drunkenness in public are very severe.

For further information refer to page 12 under 'Muslim Social Customs'.

USEFUL ADDRESSES (GENERAL)

British Embassy, P.O. Box 300, Muscat, ☎ 722411/5.

Dutch Consulate, Mina al-Fahal, P.O. Box 81, Muscat, ☎ 607225.

French Embassy, P.O. Box 591, Muscat, ☎ 722916.

West German Embassy, P.O. Box 3128, Muscat, ☎ 702164.

US Embassy, P.O. Box 996, Muscat, ☎ 722021.

BUSINESS INFORMATION

The reduction in Oman's oil income, together with accumulated debts and the large amount of recurrent expenditure necessary to maintain the country's infrastructure, has led to the adoption of new economic objectives. These are largely based around the development of non-oil industries which will supplement and eventually replace oil revenues – and for this reason the Omani Government is eager to encourage foreign participation.

Exemption from certain business regulations are granted to projects designated as Economic Development Projects.

Foreign participation in a local firm cannot exceed 65% and companies engaging in agency-type business must have at least 51% Omani ownership.

Foreign firms importing into Oman will find the appointment of an agent necessary, but this can prove difficult due to a shortage of technical staff capable of meeting the requirements of the foreign company. The market for imported goods is relatively small, and for many commodities is virtually non-existent.

Import and Exchange Control Regulations

Import licences are required for alcoholic drinks, firearms, narcotics, explosives and a few other restricted or prohibited items. Most other goods carry a 2% *ad valorem* duty, but goods imported by the Government are free of duty, as are many foodstuffs and agricultural equipment, fertilisers, etc.

Business Hours

Government Offices:

0730–1400 Saturday to Wednesday
0800–1300 Thursday

(Starting times are a half-hour later and finishing times are one hour earlier during Ramadan.)

Business Houses:

0830–1330
1600–1800 Saturday to Thursday

(These times are variable.)

BUSINESS SERVICES

Accountants

Saba & Company, P.O. Box 790, Muscat, ☎ 2145.

Consultants

Brian Colquhoun & Partners, P.O. Box 402, Muscat.
Gibb, Perlmutter & Partners, P.O. Box 592, Muttrah, ☎ 3393.
Whitehead Consulting Group, P.O. Box 699, Muscat, ☎ 2806.
Sir William Halcrow & Partners, P.O. Box 220, Muttrah, ☎ 3290.

Insurance

Arab Commercial Enterprises, P.O. Box 1063, Muttrah, ☎ 734473.

Shipping

Oman United Agencies, P.O. Box 70, Muscat, ☎ 702410.
Gulf Agencies, P.O. Box 3740, Ruwi, ☎ 773374.

USEFUL ADDRESSES (BUSINESS)

Omani Chamber of Commerce, P.O. Box 4400, Ruwi–Muscat, ☎ 702259.

Ministry of Commerce & Industry, P.O. Box 550, Muscat, ☎ 722036.

MAJOR CITY

The Capital Area

The capital city area is a lively metropolis which has undergone a huge modernisation programme, but still retains some of its old charm (and inconveniences!). The majority of the recreational pleasures and entertainment centre around outdoor activities (see under Entertainment below).

The history of Muscat dates back to its time as a Portuguese stronghold in the sixteenth century, and the Jalali and Mirani forts were built either side of the cove to defend the city from the invading Turkish armada.

The architecture within the city shows a variety of influences: Arab, Persian, Indian, African and Portuguese. One of Muscat's oldest houses is Beit Ghaliya, near the Bab al Kabir gate, constructed in the early nineteenth century. The inner city is a walled city with four main entrance gates, and the Sultan's Palace which lies within the walled city is worth a visit.

Muttrah lies about 3km/1½ miles to the west of Muscat and is the site of the new port of Mina Qabous. Within the walled town is a second walled area known as the Sur al-Lawatiyah or quarter of the Khojas. The Khojas who live here are merchants, originally of Sindhi origin, and have been in Oman for several generations now and are Omani citizens.

The Oman Museum at Qurum houses a series of exhibitions designed to portray the culture and history of Oman over the ages, and deals with its archaeology, the people and their land and Islamic art and architecture.

Seeb International Airport is 40km/26 miles from the centre of Muscat.

Hotels

Al Falaj, P.O. Box 456, Ruwi, ☎ 702311/702430.
Modern hotel approximately 5km/3 miles from the centre of Muscat.
Rooms: 150.
Facilities: Restaurant, grill, bar and coffee shop. Tennis, squash and swimming. Twice-weekly cinema. Car hire. Shops.
Services: TC, FC. Amex. S. Dr. on call.
Conference room – max. capacity 200.
Banquet room – max. capacity 500.

Gulf, P.O. Box 4455, Ruwi, ☎ 600100.
Modern hotel located between the airport and Muscat, facing the Qurum beach.
Rooms: 120 (in suites).
Facilities: Restaurant and lounge, American bar, coffee shop. Swimming, squash and tennis. Car hire.
Services: TC, FC. Amex. S. Dr. on call.
Conference room – max. capacity 30.
Banquet room – max. capacity 180.

Muscat Inter-Continental, P.O. Box 1398, Muttrah, ☎ 600500.
Luxury hotel, built on the beachfront at Qurum.
Rooms: 308.
Facilities: Main restaurant, coffee shop, poolside snack bar, nightclub. Swimming. Shops.
Services: Amex, Carte Blanche and Diners Club. Dr. on call.
Conference rooms – max. capacity 1,080.
Banquet rooms – max. capacity 630.

Ruwi, P.O. Box 5195, Ruwi, ☎ 702244.
Modern hotel in the centre of Ruwi, 10km/6 miles from the centre of Muscat.
Rooms: 100 available.
Facilities: Restaurant and bar. Swimming pool.
Conference facilities.

Restaurants

Most visitors eat in the hotel restaurants which are open to non-residents. A few restaurants have opened up in the capital area:
The Palm Tree, Ruwi (Arab specialities); *The Taj Restaurant*, Muttrah, ☎ 702532/734880 (Indian); *The Muscateer*, near Darsait roundabout; *The Qurum Private Club*, Qurum, ☎ 600543 (visitors are granted honorary membership).

Entertainment

Most hotels have their own clubs for the use of their swimming pools, tennis and squash courts, etc. Oman has vast stretches of sandy beaches with safe swimming, and sailing and fishing are also available, as well as water-skiing and scuba diving.

There are several sports clubs in Oman including the *Royal Ghalla Wentworth Golf Club* at Mina al-Fahal and the *Oman Yacht Centre*, Al-Rowdha beach, near Muscat.

A special attraction for foreign visitors is the camel racing which is held on National Day and other official and religious holidays at the old airstrip at Seeb along the Batinah Coast.

Ruwi has three air-conditioned cinemas featuring English-language and Oriental films.

Shopping

The two main *souks* (Muttrah and Muscat) offer a colourful display of goods including gold and silver jewellery (usually sold by weight), Omani coffee pots, incense burners, traditional Omani pottery, onyx articles and woven cloth. Local Omani handicrafts can be purchased in the gift shop owned by the Ministry of National Heritage and situated in the Gulf Hotel at Qurum.

QATAR
State of Qatar

Size: 10,360 sq.km/4,000 sq.miles.

Population: 180,000 (1978 estimate).

Distribution: 70% of the population lives in the capital, Doha.

Density: 8 persons per sq.km/20 per sq.mile.

Population Growth Rate: 3.1% p.a.

Ethnic Composition: The expatriate and non-Qatari population is estimated at 60% of the total population. Apart from Qatari Arabs, there are large numbers of Indians, Pakistanis and Northern and Gulf Arabs. The European and American community numbers around 4,000.

Capital: Doha Pop. 150,000.

Major Town: Umm Said Pop. 6,000.

Language: Arabic is the official language and English is widely used in business circles.

Religion: Most Qataris are Sunni Muslims of the Wahabi sect – there is a minority of Shia Muslims, mainly of Iranian origin.

Government: The Amir, as Prime Minister, heads a 14-member Council of Ministers.

Following the constitution of 1970, the rulership of Qatar is hereditary in the Al-Thani family.

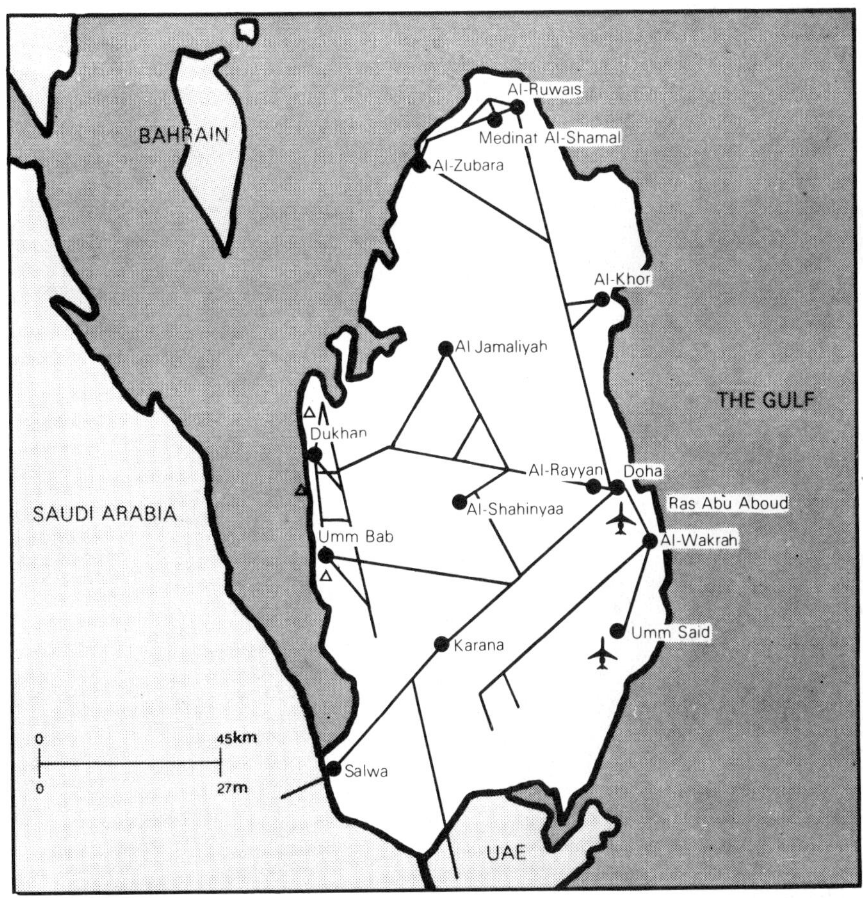

GEOGRAPHY

Qatar is a peninsula extending northwards into the Gulf. Qatar has borders with Saudi Arabia and the Emirate of Abu Dhabi.

The landscape is almost totally flat with rocky areas in the north and centre, and sandy plains and desert to the south. There is little natural vegetation.

Climate

The climate is hot and humid in summer with midday temperatures reaching 44°C/111°F and humidity of 85% and more. During the period from December to March the climate is more pleasant with temperatures ranging between 10°C/50°F and 20°C/68°F. The average annual rainfall is 3 inches.

Agriculture

This is severely limited by climatic problems and limited water resources. Government research into agriculture is extensive and aid is given to farmers in the form of machinery, technical advice, fertilisers, etc.

Qatar is self-sufficient in vegetables with small surpluses remaining for export, and aims to reach total self-sufficiency in foodstuffs.

Government poultry farms and livestock projects together with irrigation schemes are currently being developed. Qatar also has a shrimp export industry.

Main Crops: tomatoes, vegetables, alfalfa.

Mineral Resources: oil, gas.

THE ECONOMY

Gross National Product (1976 est.): US$4.2 billion.

Per Capita Income (1976 est.): US$42,000.

Foreign Trade (1976): Total Imports US$835 million; Total Exports US$2.2 billion.

Main Trading Partners: Imports – Japan, UK, USA, West Germany, France, Dubai, Italy, Kuwait. Exports – Bangladesh, India, Vietnam, USA, Saudi Arabia, China.

Qatar's economy is almost exclusively based on oil and since 1948 there has been a steady development of the country's resources. Additional sources of natural gas, as yet not fully exploited, will supplement oil revenues substantially.

In common with other Gulf States, Qatar is aiming at industrial diversification and the reduction of its dependence on imported materials for industrial projects. The economy is relatively stable and much of the unspent oil revenues has been invested. Qatar's infrastructure is severely underdeveloped and steady progress is now being made in this area. Labour shortages are another problem experienced by Qatar. Hospitals, schools, roads and port facilities are all being built in an attempt to provide Qatar with the mechanisms necessary for a modern, industrial state.

In the industrial sector, the emphasis on heavy industry is reflected by the establishment of a gas liquids plant, iron ore reduction plant and cement and petrochemical industries. A number of light industries producing badly needed consumer goods have also been developed.

Major Industries: oil, gas, cement, petrochemicals, iron and steel, fertilisers.

Main Commodities Traded: Imports – electrical equipment, machinery, transport equipment, foodstuffs and consumer goods. Exports – oil (96% of total).

Qatar is a member of the Organisation of Petroleum Exporting Countries (OPEC) and the Arab League.

HOW TO GET THERE

Air

Major airlines flying to Qatar include: Air France, Air India, Alia, British Airways, Egypt Air, Gulf Air, MEA and PIA.

British Airways and Gulf Air operate seven direct flights per week from London to Doha. Gulf Air also operates flights from the other Gulf States and Iran to Doha.

Flying times to Doha: from London 7½ hours; from New York 14 hours.

Doha International Airport is 6½km/4 miles from the city centre.

ENTRY REGULATIONS

Visas

Nationals of Bahrain, Kuwait, Oman, Saudi Arabia and the United Arab Emirates do not require visas. Also British nationals by origin whose place of birth or residence is in the UK or the Channel Islands do not require visas.

All other nationals require visas, obtainable from Qatari Embassies abroad. Business travellers may obtain a 72-hour visa at Doha Airport provided their visit is sponsored by a reputable Qatari.

Applications for visas must be accompanied by a 'No Objection Certificate' obtainable from the Qatari Immigration Department, Ministry of the Interior, P.O. Box 2433, Doha, Qatar. A letter from the applicant's firm giving full details of the business to be undertaken and confirming financial responsibility for the applicant is required.

Evidence in a passport of a previous or planned visit to Israel may adversely affect the granting of a visa.

Health Regulations

An International Certificate of Vaccination against smallpox is required, also certificates of vaccination against yellow fever and cholera if travelling from an infected area. TAB (typhoid and paratyphoid) injections are recommended.

Customs

Currency: There are no restrictions on the amount of currency which may be taken into or out of Qatar.

Duty-free articles: Cigarettes, personal effects and commercial samples.

Prohibited articles: Alcoholic drink.

PRACTICAL INFORMATION FOR THE VISITOR

1. Currency

Monetary Unit – Qatar riyal (QR), divided into 100 dirhams.
Notes – 1, 5, 10, 50, 100, 500 riyals.
Coins – 1, 5, 10, 25, 50 dirhams.

All monetary issues are under the control of the Qatar Monetary Agency, P.O. Box 1234, Doha, ☎ 5987.

Banking Hours:
0730–1130 Saturday to Thursday.

Major Commercial Banks in Doha:

Arab Bank Ltd
P.O. Box 172, ☎ 324745/321570.
Bank Almashrek
P.O. Box 338, ☎ 23981.
Bank of Oman
P.O. Box 173, ☎ 26281.
Bank Saderat Iran
P.O. Box 2256, ☎ 24440.
Banque de Paris et des Pays-Bas
P.O. Box 2636, ☎ 26291.
British Bank of the Middle East
P.O. Box 57, ☎ 22646/23124.
Chartered Bank Ltd
P.O. Box 29, ☎ 23321/325700.
Citibank
P.O. Box 2309, ☎ 24416.
Commercial Bank of Qatar,
P.O. Box 3232, ☎ 321010.
Grindlays Bank
P.O. Box 2001, ☎ 26141.
Qatar National Bank
P.O. Box 1000, ☎ 23092.
United Bank of Pakistan
P.O. Box 242, ☎ 321420.

2. Electricity Supply

240–415V AC 50Hz.
Plugs: 3 flat pins.

3. Weights and Measures

Metric is the official system but some imperial measures are still in use.

4. Media

Radio Qatar broadcasts in Arabic and English. Qatar has a colour television network. News bulletins are transmitted by Radio Qatar at 1800 hours and on the television at 2200 hours.

Newspapers:
Al-Arab (daily) and the *Gulf Weekly Mirror* are the main newspapers in circulation. The following periodicals are published in Qatar: *Al Ouroba; Al Doha* (Ministry of Information); *Al Ahad; Al Khalig al Jadeed; Diaruna wal Alam* (Ministry of Finance and Petroleum).

Middle East Trade, published by Middle East Trade Publications Ltd, London, is also available in Qatar.

5. Medical Care

Visitors may suffer from stomach upsets caused by the heat and are advised to take along suitable precautionary medicines. Doha has good efficient medical facilities – the following is a selection of some of the main hospitals and clinics:
Rumailah Hospital, ☎ 22651 – major and minor complaints. Accidents and Casualty.
Women's Hospital, ☎ 321601 – maternity and gynaecological patients.
Polyclinic, ☎ 22339 (near the Guest Palace) – Saturday to Thursday mornings for general practitioner and specialist surgery. In the afternoon general practitioner only.
Bin Omran Clinic, ☎ 87379 (near American Embassy).
East Clinic, ☎ 325278 (near the Museum) – Saturday to Thursday: 0700–1030; 1500–1630.
Dental Care:
Main Clinic, ☎ 22425 (near the Museum) – Saturday to Thursday: 0700–1300.

6. Telephone, Telex and Postal Services

Direct dialling is available from Doha to Bahrain, the United Arab Emirates, Kuwait and the United Kingdom.

Useful Telephone Numbers (Doha):

Emergency ☎ 999.
International Operator ☎ 15.
Directory Enquiries ☎ 18.

All external telegraph and telephone services are operated by Cable and Wireless on behalf of the Government. Telegrams can be sent from the Cable and Wireless Office between 0600 and 2300 hours. International telex facilities are available in Qatar at the Cable and Wireless Building in Musarib Street.

The main post office in Doha is opposite Government House. All mail should be sent by air mail.

7. Public Holidays

Fixed Holidays:

22 February *Accession of the Amir*
3 September *Independence Day*

Muslim Holidays:

These follow the Muslim calendar and occur 10–12 days earlier every year. The dates of the Muslim holidays are approximate as they depend upon sightings of the moon, and may differ by one or two days from those given below.

1981 dates are:

18 January *Prophet's Birthday*
31 May *Ascension of the Prophet*
31 July–2 August *End of Ramadan*
8–10 October *Eid el Adha*
29 October *Muslim New Year*

Friday is the weekly holiday in Qatar.

8. Time

GMT+3

9. Internal Transport

Air

Qatar has no internal air services.

Airline Offices in Doha:

Air France ☎ 321427/26788.
Air India ☎ 27747.
British Airways ☎ 22555/25498.
British Caledonian ☎ 328051.
Gulf Air Co ☎ 22555/7.
JAL ☎ 321880.
KLM ☎ 22555.
Lufthansa ☎ 22555/7.
Middle East Airlines ☎ 22288.
PIA ☎ 4949.
SAS ☎ 22555/6.
Swissair ☎ 22555/6.
TWA ☎ 23453/23465.

Road

The major towns are linked by a good road network. Self-drive cars are available for hire. Visitors require a temporary driving licence issued by the Police Traffic Department on presentation of their own licence with four passport-size photographs.

Car-Hire Firms in Doha:

Al-Sada Co-op Co ☎ 5037/29494.
Khalaf Services ☎ 24205.
National Motors Hire Service ☎ 23868.
Pananghai Services ☎ 25778.
Rent-a-Car ☎ 28100/26649.

Taxis may be hired on an hourly or daily basis. Meters are not fitted so fares should be negotiated in advance. There is a fixed rate for the journey from the airport to the hotels and from the hotels to the centre of Doha.

10. Tipping

Taxis – no tip necessary.

Porters – QR1 per bag.

Hotels – a service charge is added to the bill.

Restaurants – 10% of the bill unless a service charge is included.

11. Social Customs

Qatar is still a relatively conservative state and the majority of the population are strict Wahabi Muslims adhering rigidly to Muslim customs and mores. However, women are now less restricted in Qatar, e.g., they are allowed to drive, and the indigenous female population is gradually being integrated into the business community.

Severe restrictions are placed on the sale and consumption of alcohol. Alcohol can be obtained in the bar of the Gulf Hotel but this is only open to hotel residents.

For further information, refer to page 12 under 'Muslim Social Customs'.

USEFUL ADDRESSES (GENERAL)

Embassies in Doha

France: Shaikh Suheim Street, P.O. Box 2669, ☎ 25216.

Japan: Shaikh Suheim Street, Off Salwa Circle, P.O. Box 208, ☎ 26152/3.

UK: P.O. Box 3, ☎ 321911/4.

US: Farig Bin Omran, P.O. Box 2399, ☎ 87701/2/3.

BUSINESS INFORMATION

In order to achieve its development objectives Qatar is dependent on imports and constitutes a good market for construction equipment, vehicles, foodstuffs and technical services.

Foreign firms considered to be contributing to the country's development and industrial projects are given various direct and indirect forms of aid.

Foreign businesses must have at least 51% Qatari ownership but this condition may be waived under special circumstances.

Commercial agencies are restricted to Qatari nationals registered with the Ministry of Commerce and Economy.

Import Regulations

Import licences are required for alcoholic drink, arms and ammunition and dangerous drugs. The import of cultured pearls is prohibited, except when made up into jewellery. All firms wishing to import must be registered with the Ministry of Commerce and Economy.

Many business people leave Qatar during the hot summer months and trade tends to slacken over this period. Visitors are advised to avoid a visit to Qatar at this time.

Business Hours

Government Offices:
0600–1300 Saturday to Thursday

Business Houses:
0730–1200
1430–1800 Saturday to Thursday

BUSINESS SERVICES

Consultants

Arab Engineering Bureau, P.O. Box 1148, Doha, ☎ 22964.
Doha Consultants, P.O. Box 2380, ☎ 26662.

Cargo services

P & O operate cargo services to Qatar every 10 days from the United Kingdom and every 20 days from Antwerp in Belgium.

An overland truck service runs between Qatar and Jeddah in Saudi Arabia where Ro-Ro Ships bring cargo from Western Europe.

A number of international air charter firms operate air freight services into Doha: *TMA*, *Tradewinds*, *Cargolux*, *Transmeridian*, *Caledonian* and *IAS Cargo*.

USEFUL ADDRESSES (BUSINESS)

Ministry of Industry and Agriculture, P.O. Box 1966, Doha, ☎ 25211.

Ministry of Economy and Commerce, P.O. Box 1968, Doha, ☎ 5394.

Ministry of Finance and Petroleum, P.O. Box 83, Doha, ☎ 4054.

Qatar Chamber of Commerce, P.O. Box 402, Doha, ☎ 25131.

Industrial Development Centre, Doha, ☎ 29211.

MAJOR CITY

Doha

In the space of relatively few years the small fishing village of Doha has been transformed into a modern city whose architects are to be congratulated on their good planning and preservation of the old atmosphere of the village. The city's public buildings have been well designed in the tradition of Arab and Islamic architecture.

The Clock Tower is the focal point of the modern city with the massive new Emeiri Palace alongside. The National Museum on Corniche Road East contains some fascinating exhibits depicting the history of Qatar during the early days of traditional Bedouin life. Near to the Museum is an aquarium.

The Grand Mosque with its towering minaret is an impressive landmark in Doha. The rapid economic development of modern Qatar is traced in the National Development Exhibition near the Clock Tower.

Doha Airport is 6½km/4 miles from the city centre.

Hotels

There is no official hotel rating system in Qatar.

GULF HOTEL, P.O. Box 1911, ☎ 25251. Deluxe hotel, 5 minutes' drive from the city centre.
Rooms: 320 [symbols]. Suites available.
Facilities: Restaurant and coffee shop.

Rooftop restaurant. Tennis, squash, swimming, bowling centre, sauna. Marina and private beach. Shops. Car hire.
Services: TC, FC. ⊟ Amex and Diners Club. S. Dr. on call. Translation bureau and audio-visual equipment.
Conference facilities for groups up to 1,000.

New Doha Palace, Moushareb Road, P.O. Box 710, ☎ 26131.
Centrally located, close to the business area and 5km/3 miles from the airport.
Rooms: 89, on request.
Facilities: Restaurant (European and Oriental cuisine).
Services: TC, FC. ⊟ No credit cards accepted. S. Dr. on call.
Conference room.

Oasis Hotel, Ras Abboud Road, P.O. Box 717, ☎ 328221.
Luxurious hotel on seafront, 3km/2 miles from the airport.
Rooms: 100. 8 suites.
Facilities: Restaurant. Swimming and sailing. Cinema. Beach Club. Hairdresser and boutique. Travel office.
Services: TC, FC. ⊟ Credit cards accepted if represented in Qatar. S.
Conference room – max. capacity 25.

Restaurants

All three hotels listed above have public restaurants. Other restaurants are: *Strand* (Lebanese); *Montazah Park; Rendezvous; Doha Airport Restaurant; Abu Nuwas*, Kharaba Street.

Doha has several snack bars.

Alcohol is not usually served in hotels and restaurants.

Entertainment

Doha has limited sports facilities and the best of these are to be found at the exclusive *Doha Club* where guests may be admitted with a member. Several oil companies have their own social clubs and in some cases their own tennis or squash courts.

Doha has its own race-course and camel races are held there from time to time. The miles of unspoilt sandy beaches along the coast are ideal for bathing and fishing.

Shopping

Best buys: copper and brassware, antiques.

The *souks* are situated in the area of the Clock Tower but visitors will be disappointed to find that the principal *souk* mainly sells imported, modern consumer goods. There is an area where copper and brass pots, bowls and other utensils are sold and the occasional genuine antique.

SAUDI ARABIA

Kingdom of Saudi Arabia

Size: 2,240,000 sq.km/864,640 sq.miles.

Population: 9.52 million (1978).

Distribution: Almost 50% of the population live in urban areas.

Density: 4.2 persons per sq.km/11 per sq.mile.

Population Growth Rate: 2.9% p.a.

Ethnic Composition: Saudi Arabia has a predominantly Arab population.

Capital: Riyadh Pop. 750,000.

Major Cities/Towns: Jeddah Pop. 700,000; Mecca Pop. 400,000; Medina Pop. 200,000; Dammam–Dhahran–Al-Khobar Pop. 150,000.

Language: Arabic is the official language. English is widely used in the oil industry and in business circles.

Religion: Islam is the only religion which may be practised – the majority of the population are Sunni Muslims. The holy city of Mecca is the centre of the Islamic faith and is forbidden to all non-Muslims.

Government: Saudi Arabia is a monarchy and the King appoints the Council of Ministers, which is largely composed of members of the royal family. Significant political power is also wielded by the many sheikhs (hereditary tribal chiefs by tradition) and religious leaders.

Saudi Arabia has no political parties.

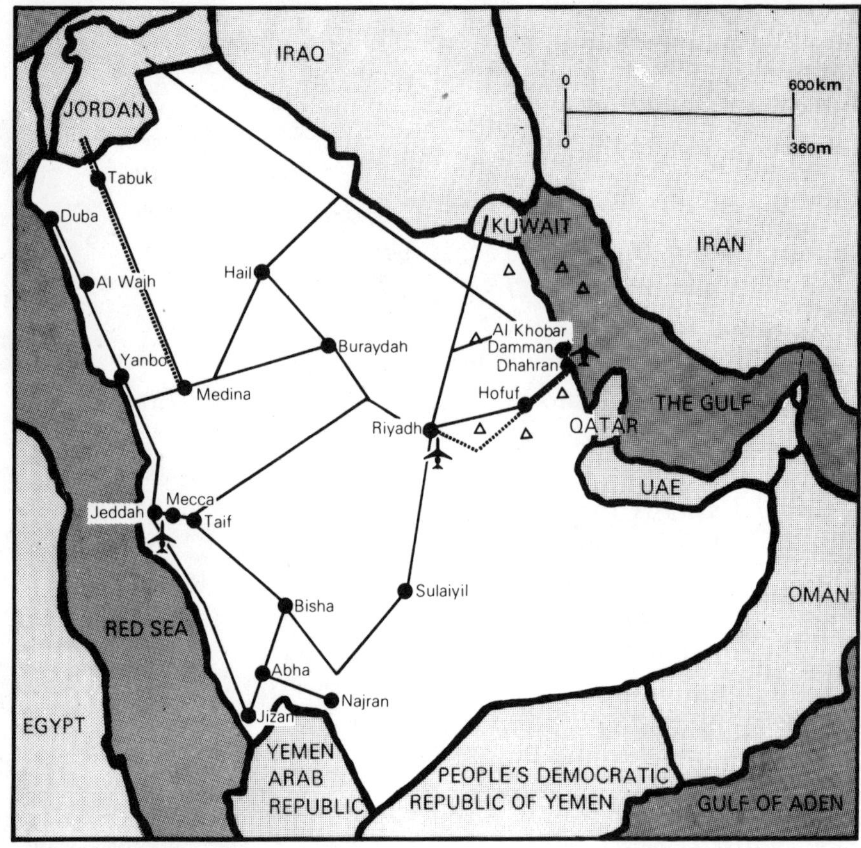

GEOGRAPHY

Saudi Arabia is the largest country in the Middle East and has borders with Jordan, Iraq and Kuwait to the north, with the two Yemen Republics to the southwest and with the United Arab Emirates and Oman to the southeast. Two great deserts – the Rub al-Khali (Empty Quarter) and the Nefud – dominate the country, which is divided into four provinces: Al Hasa, Najd, Hijaz and Asir. The highest land (over 2,000m/6,560ft) is in the west by the Red Sea and slopes gradually to the coastal lowlands along the Gulf in the east.

Climate

Saudi Arabia has a desert climate although within the country itself there are sizeable temperature and rainfall extremes. Summer temperatures are high with humidity reaching 90% or more in the coastal regions (particularly around Jeddah). Inland, temperatures can rise to 54°C/130°F in summer with a drastic drop during the winter months when heavy rains or frosts are not uncommon. Coastal temperatures and weather conditions are generally more equable and during the short winters (December to mid-February) temperatures are cool.

Agriculture

The scarcity of water supplies, and poor communications between production areas and markets, have hindered the development of the agricultural sector of the economy. At present, although half the labour force is engaged in agriculture, this sector contributes only 3% of the Gross National Product. Less than 1% of the total land arca is under cultivation.

The steady increase in the population, together with a corresponding rise in food imports, has added more pressure on the Government to improve the agricultural sector. A 40% increase in irrigated land is being aimed for by 1980, the water being tapped from underground sources. Wheat, poultry, and cattle production have been encouraged by the implementation of loans, subsidies, and the removal of restrictions on the import of agricultural machinery.

Main Crops: melons, dates, alfalfa, vegetables, barley, millet, sorghum.

Mineral Resources: oil, natural gas, gypsum, copper, salt, silver, gold, iron, zinc, lead.

THE ECONOMY

Gross National Product (1976): US$49 billion.

Per Capita Income (1976): US$8,430.

Gross Domestic Product (1976): SR193,100 million.

Foreign Trade (1976): Total Imports US$12.5 billion; Total Exports US$45 billion.

Main Trading Partners: Imports – USA, Japan, West Germany, UK, Italy. Exports – Japan, France, Italy, UK.

Saudi Arabia is the largest oil-producing nation within OPEC and supplies about 13% of the world's annual needs, while oil revenues account for 90% of the total national budget revenue.

Despite a substantial trade surplus, the economy has suffered over recent years from a high inflation rate with prices rising by 32% in 1976. One explanation for this given by the Saudis is the exploitation by foreign suppliers and contractors. In addition, the import of skilled labour and of materials required for development plans has undoubtedly contributed to a high rate of inflation. Nevertheless, a high growth rate has been maintained and there is continued development and expansion of the country's infrastructure. (The planned growth rate for the period 1976–1980 was 10.2%.)

Plans to reduce Saudi Arabia's dependence on oil reserves include the development and improvement of agriculture (irrigation, better links between farming areas and markets, etc.) and the expansion of the manufacturing sector with an emphasis on export-orientated industries using local raw materials.

Oil production in Saudi Arabia continues to rise and there is evidence of considerable reserves still to be exploited. Meanwhile the overriding problem facing the Government seems to be to control inflation while maintaining the growth rate which is needed for development.

Major Industries: oil, gas, building materials, petrochemicals, steel.

Main Commodities Traded: Imports – foodstuffs, textiles and clothing, machinery and electrical equipment. Exports – crude oil, petroleum products.

Oil Production (1976): 428.7 million tonnes.

Saudi Arabia is a member of the Organisation of Petroleum Exporting Countries (OPEC) and the Arab League.

HOW TO GET THERE

Air

Saudi Arabia has three international airports, at Jeddah, Riyadh and Dhahran. There are several direct flights a week from London to Jeddah and Dhahran (British Airways), and from London to Jeddah and Riyadh (Saudia). Direct flights also operate to Jeddah from Amsterdam, Beirut, Frankfurt, Geneva, Paris and Rome.

Jeddah also has good connections with other Middle East centres and the Indian sub-continent. There are frequent flights between Jeddah and Bahrain, Dubai, Kuwait, Cairo, Damascus, Tripoli, Bombay, Hong Kong, Jakarta and Singapore.

Dhahran and Riyadh airports deal with a smaller volume of traffic than Jeddah. Both cities have good connections with the rest of the Gulf States and with many European and Middle Eastern cities including London, Paris, Rome, Amman, Cairo, Damascus and Sanaa. There is a daily service to Dhahran from Karachi and weekly flights from Bombay, Colombo and Delhi.

Major airlines serving Saudi Arabia include Air France, Air India, Alitalia, British Airways, Lufthansa, KLM, MEA, Sabena, Saudia and Swissair.

Flying times to Jeddah: from London 6 hours; from New York 14 hours; from Sydney 19 hours.

Distances of airports from nearest city/town: Jeddah 2½km/1½ miles; Riyadh 2km/1 mile; Dhahran 8km/5 miles from Al-Khobar.

ENTRY REGULATIONS

Visas

All visitors to Saudi Arabia must be in possession of a passport which is valid for at least 6 months beyond the proposed stay in Saudi Arabia. Nationals of all countries require visas obtainable from Saudi embassies abroad.

Any woman travelling to Saudi Arabia for business purposes must have prior special authorisation. The business firm or contact in Saudi Arabia should request the Foreign Ministry to cable such an authorisation to the Saudi Embassy or Consulate abroad where the visa application is being made. The cable, when received, will give an application number which is then advised to the applicant. A normal application should then be made, quoting the number given by the Foreign Ministry.

Business travellers should support their visa application with a letter from their firm giving full details of the business to be undertaken and confirming financial responsibility for the applicant. It is essential that the name and address of the contact(s) in Saudi Arabia be mentioned in the letter

Transit visas are valid for a stay of up to 3 days. The validity of entry visas is variable.

An exit visa, obtainable locally, is usually required although business travellers may be exempt from this regulation. Business travellers must, however, obtain Income Tax clearance supported by a guarantor of Saudi Arabian nationality. Visitors leaving Saudi Arabia may be required to deposit their passport with the airline on the day before departure. Check this on arrival in the country.

Evidence in a passport of a previous or planned visit to Israel may adversely affect the granting of a visa.

All passengers are advised to take at least two additional photos with them – these may be required on arrival.

Health Regulations

An International Certificate of Vaccination against smallpox is required, also certificates for yellow fever and/or cholera vaccinations if arriving from an infected area.

Cholera, polio and TAB (typhoid and paratyphoid) immunisations are all recommended.

Customs

Currency: There is no restriction on the amount of currency that may be taken into or out of the country.

Duty-free articles: Articles for personal use, 600 cigarettes, 100 cigars or 500g of tobacco and a reasonable amount of perfume. A deposit may be charged on such items as typewriters, but this is refunded if the articles are re-exported within 90 days.

Articles liable for duty: Samples of no commercial value and others of minimal value are admitted free of duty. Other commercial samples are subject to the payment of customs duty – this is refunded if the samples are re-exported within 12 months.

Prohibited articles: Alcoholic beverages, narcotics, contraceptives, pornographic literature, pig meat, pig-meat products and pig-skin articles. The import of arms and ammunition is restricted and other restrictions, mainly on religious grounds, are in force.

PRACTICAL INFORMATION FOR THE VISITOR

1. Currency

Monetary Unit – Saudi riyal (SR), divided into 100 halalah.

Notes – 1, 5, 10, 50, 100 Saudi riyals.
Coins – 5, 10, 25, 50 halalah.

Credit cards are not widely used, but American Express and Diners Club cards are accepted in the major hotels, restaurants and shops.

Banking Hours:

0830–1200 1700–1900	Saturday to Wednesday
0830–1130	Thursday

The central bank is the Saudi Arabian Monetary Agency, P.O. Box 394, Airport Street, Jeddah, ☎ 31306/31130.

Domestic and Foreign Banks in Jeddah:

Arab Bank Ltd
P.O. Box 344, ☎ 22896.
British Bank of the Middle East
P.O. Box 109, ☎ 23251.
Citibank
P.O. Box 490, ☎ 47661/47557.
General Bank of the Netherlands
P.O. Box 67, ☎ 21078.
National Commercial Bank
P.O. Box 3555, ☎ 23974.
Riyadh Bank
P.O. Box 1047, ☎ 32417.

Another important domestic bank is:
The Saudi Credit Bank
Riyadh, ☎ 29625.

2. Electricity Supply

100/120V AC 60Hz or 220V AC 50Hz, depending on the area.
Plugs: 2-pin Continental round.

Electrical standards vary throughout Saudi Arabia and the supply is sometimes erratic. Visitors should not always rely on using their own electrical appliances in hotels.

3. Weights and Measures

The metric system is in use.

4. Media

Saudi Arabian Radio broadcasts in both Arabic and English and there are now five commercial television stations.

Newspapers:
The two main daily newspapers (Arabic) are the *Al-Medina* (Jeddah) and the *Al-Riyadh* (Riyadh). Publications in English include two daily newspapers: the *Saudi Gazette* and *Arab News* (both in Jeddah) and two daily news-sheets: the *Saudi Review* and the *Riyadh Daily*.

The *Saudi Economic Survey* (weekly) provides useful information about business and also gives details of development projects, trade and industrial regulations and government tenders.

The Chambers of Commerce of Jeddah, Mecca, Riyadh and Dammam all publish monthly magazines which carry advertising.

5. Medical Care

Western-trained doctors and dentists are available in the major towns, and many of the foreign embassies hold a list of local practitioners.
Jeddah hospitals with a 24-hour emergency service are:
Dr. Daghestani Hospital, Mecca Road.
Jeddah Clinic, Shara al-Matar,
☎ 27715.
Lebanese Hospital, Medina Road,
☎ 52944.
Riyadh Hospitals:
National Hospital, Siteen Street
☎ 61211.
Obeid Hospital, Faradaq Street,
☎ 62695.

The famous King Faisal Hospital accepts only referred cases and has no emergency service.

Water supplies are generally safe in the better hotels, but visitors are advised to drink bottled water where possible. Caution should be exercised with fresh fruit and vegetables. Suitable medicines for stomach upsets are advisable.

Visitors are likely to suffer from heat exhaustion during the hot summer months, and it is advisable to take extra salt, in tablet or solution form.

6. Telephone, Telex and Postal Services

Internal telephone communications have improved considerably and a further expansion of services is planned. It is now possible to dial Riyadh and the Eastern Province from Jeddah.

International communications are good from Jeddah, Riyadh and the Dhahran/Al-Khobar area. There are direct-dial connections with Bahrain and Kuwait and links are to be established with Western Europe, the United States and other countries in the Middle East.

Useful Telephone Numbers:

Fire ☎ 98.
Ambulance ☎ 97.
Police ☎ 99.
Trunk calls ☎ 90.
International calls ☎ 91.

Public telex facilities are available in Jeddah, Riyadh and Dhahran. Several of the larger hotels also have telex facilities.

All mail to and from Saudi Arabia should be sent by air. The main post office in Jeddah is off the lower end of King Abdul Aziz Street and the Riyadh post office is at the north end of Wazir Street.

Most hotels sell stamps and have a collection service.

DHL International Courier Service has an office in Riyadh, off Hassa Street, ☎ 63756.

7. Public Holidays

Fixed Holiday:

5 September *National Day*

Muslim Holidays:

These follow the Muslim calendar and occur 10–12 days earlier every year. The dates of the Muslim holidays are approximate as they depend upon sightings of the moon and may differ by one or two days from those given below. 1981 dates are:

31 July–2 August	*Eid el Fitr (end of Ramadan)*
8–10 October	*Eid el Adha*

Friday is the weekly holiday, although some shops may remain open on that day.

8. Time

GMT+3

9. Internal Transport

Air

Saudia operate internal services between Jeddah–Riyadh 75 minutes; Riyadh–Dhahran 45 minutes; Jeddah–Dhahran 90 minutes.

An economy-class service called *Arabian Express* is now in operation between Jeddah and Riyadh, and Riyadh and Dhahran. Seats on these flights cannot be reserved (except where a booking is made from abroad). Tickets count as boarding passes, and seats are allocated on a first-come, first-served basis just before the flights leave.

Airline Offices in Jeddah:

Air France	☎ 32468.
Air India	☎ 31026.
British Airways	☎ 56424/22937.
JAL	☎ 21172/25437.
KLM	☎ 24684.
Lufthansa	☎ 23324/28714.
MEA	☎ 21141/34661.
Pan Am	☎ 23731.
Qantas	☎ 42591/43033.
SAS	☎ 58975/58988.
Saudia	☎ 21222 reservations.
	☎ 21111 information.
	☎ 21666 confirmation.
Swissair	☎ 56233/5.
TWA	☎ 22228.

Rail

A daily passenger service in each direction links Riyadh and Dammam. The journey takes 8 hours.

Road

Good roads link the three main towns. Self-drive and chauffeur-driven cars are available for hire. In general visitors are advised to hire a chauffeur-driven car as there are a number of formalities and restrictions concerned with private motoring and some of these may prove awkward.

Car Hire:

Jeddah

Arabian Car Rental, ☎ 33965.
Avis, ☎ 52930.
Sahary Rent-A-Car, ☎ 21032.
Saudi Hotel Car Rental, ☎ 20451, (agents for Godfrey Davis).

Dammam

Hanco, ☎ 29000 ext. 281.

Riyadh

Sahary Rent-A-Car, ☎ 34500 ext. 5.

Visitors need an International Driving Licence (preferable) or a Driving Licence from their country of residence.

Taxis are available in the main towns and can be hired on a daily basis. Taxi fares are officially controlled but these rates are not always observed so it may be necessary to bargain with the driver.

10. Tipping

Taxis – no tip.

Porters – SR1 per bag.

Hotels/restaurants – a 15% service charge is usually included. Any additional tip is optional.

11. Social Customs

Saudi Arabia is a strict Muslim country where religion is taken very seriously. Most Saudis will stop work at various times during the day in order to pray, and this practice should be respected by foreigners.

Religious occasions take precedence over all others and during the month of *Ramadan* and the annual *Hajj* (pilgrimage) including the fortnight either side of it business life tends to be disrupted.

Airline seats are usually fully booked during the time of the *Hajj* and hotel accommodation is scarce.

Alcohol is prohibited in Saudi Arabia and the penalties for offenders are extremely severe.

Restrictions on women in Saudi Arabia are harsh and non-Muslim women will find many of these difficult to accept. Women are not permitted to drive and are expected to dress with extreme modesty and sobriety. Full-length skirts and long sleeves are the safest form of dress.

Since the Islamic faith forbids the representation of the human body, it is advisable to refrain from taking photographs of people without first obtaining permission.

For further information, refer to page 12 under 'Muslim Social Customs'.

USEFUL ADDRESSES (GENERAL)

Embassies in Jeddah

Australia: off Al-Hamra Road, Ruwais Quarter, P.O. Box 4876, ☎ 51303.

Canada: 6th Floor, Commercial and Residential Centre, King Abdul Aziz Street, P.O. Box 5050, ☎ 34597/8.

France: Sheikh Mohammad Bin Abdul Wahab Street, P.O. Box 145, ☎ 21233/21447.

West Germany: Abubakur Al-Siddieck Street, P.O. Box 126, ☎ 53545/53344.

Japan: Palestine Road, P.O. Box 1260, ☎ 52402/52405.

Netherlands: Medina Road, P.O. Box 1776, ☎ 53611/2.

Switzerland: Medina Road, P.O. Box 1016, ☎ 51387/58359.

UK: Jeddah Towers, P.O. Box 393, ☎ 52544/52628 and 27122/27306 (commercial section).

US: Palestine Road, Ruwais, ☎ 53410/54110/52188; Commercial Centre, ☎ 24226/32949.

Other addresses

American Express Authorised Representatives: ACE Arab Commercial Enterprises, King Abdul Aziz Street, P.O. Box 6152, Jeddah, ☎ 23731/31151, and Aziziah Building, King Faisal Street, P.O. Box 667, Riyadh, ☎ 20021/2.

BUSINESS INFORMATION

The development of Saudi Arabia's infrastructure together with the rapid expansion of the industrial sector has created a boom in civil engineering, and many foreign contractors are currently working for the Saudi Government. A strong market for capital equipment exists alongside construction opportunities, although building materials are increasingly being produced locally. Domestic electrical goods are also very much in demand.

Foreign investment is encouraged by the Saudi Government as part of a general policy of growth in the private sector. A minimum of 25% local participation is usually required when foreign firms are setting up in Saudi Arabia, except in the trading sector where participation must be wholly Saudi.

The appointment of an agent is essential as goods may only be imported by Saudi nationals. In addition, bidding for government contracts may only be undertaken by residents of Saudi Arabia.

Import and Exchange Control Regulations

There are several restrictions on imports into Saudi Arabia: goods from Israel, South Africa and Zimbabwe-Rhodesia are banned; no alcohol may be imported; licences are required from the Ministry of the Interior for the import of arms and ammunition; prior permission from the Ministry of Health is required for the import of pharmaceutical products. In addition, there are a number of special regulations governing the import of foodstuffs.

There are no exchange control restrictions in operation in Saudi Arabia.

Business Hours

Government Offices:

0730–1430 Saturday to Wednesday
Thursday and Friday are official holidays.

Business Houses: There are no standard hours, but approximate ones are as follows:

Jeddah:	0900–1330 1630–2000	Saturday to Thursday
Riyadh:	0830–1200 1630–1930	Saturday to Thursday
Eastern Province:	0730–1200 1430–1700	Saturday to Thursday
ARAMCO, Dhahran:	0700–1130 1300–1630	Saturday to Wednesday

Visitors are advised to avoid Saudi Arabia at least a fortnight either side of the *Eid el Adha* pilgrimage when normal business activity is disrupted. Business hours are also considerably shorter during the month of *Ramadan*, and most Saudis are available during the day only for a short period around noon.

In addition, many Saudis are away on holiday or on business trips abroad during the summer months.

Business Events

An International Trade Fair is held each year in the spring. For further details contact: The Saudi International Trade and Industry Fair Organisation, King Abdul Aziz Street, P.O. Box 4571, Jeddah.

BUSINESS SERVICES

Advertising

Mecca Advertising, P.O. Box 3029, Jeddah, ☎ 24043/32821.

Tihama (Advertising and Public Relations), P.O. Box 5455, Jeddah, ☎ 22132.

Insurance

Abdullah Ali Riza, P.O. Box 8, Jeddah, ☎ 22233.

Arab Commercial Enterprises, P.O. Box 1084, Jeddah, ☎ 23454/28666, and P.O. Box 667, Riyadh, ☎ 22585/7.

Consultants

Consulting Centre, P.O.Box 1888, Riyadh, ☎ 62347.

Saudi Marketing Research Bureau, P.O. Box 1796, Jeddah, ☎ 32433, and P.O. Box 1848, Riyadh, ☎ 26208.

Saudi Research & Investment Office, Prince Mansour Building, King Abdul Aziz Street, Jeddah.

USEFUL ADDRESSES (BUSINESS)

Jeddah Chamber of Commerce & Industry, P.O. Box 1264, Jeddah, ☎ 31059/23535.

Riyadh Chamber of Commerce & Industry, P.O. Box 596, Riyadh, ☎ 22700/22600.

Eastern Province Chamber of Commerce & Industry, P.O. Box 719, Dammam, ☎ 21134.

Saudi-British Economic Co-operation Office, P.O. Box 487, Riyadh, ☎ 60607.

Industrial Studies & Development Centre, P.O. Box 1267, Riyadh, and P.O. Box 1001, Jeddah.

Mecca Chamber of Commerce & Industry, P.O. Box 1086, Mecca, ☎ 21134.

Medina Chamber of Commerce & Industry, P.O. Box 443, Medina, ☎ 25190/25775.

The Saudi Industrial Development Fund, Washim Street, P.O. Box 4143, Riyadh, ☎ 33703/33710/33745.

Ministry of Commerce, Airport Street, Riyadh, ☎ 23400.

Ministry of Oil & Mineral Wealth, Airport Street, Riyadh.

MAJOR CITIES AND TOWNS

Riyadh

The capital of the Kingdom of Saudi Arabia since its creation in 1925, Riyadh has expanded at an alarming pace over the last 50 years. Today it is a truly modern city with good communications, services and facilities which have developed since the discovery of oil, as is the case in many other Arab states.

The Royal Palace is in Riyadh and another landmark of interest is the elegant water tower which rises over the city. The Masmak Fort off Thimairi Street is preserved as an item of cultural heritage. Another attraction in Riyadh is the Museum of Archaeology and Ethnology on Imam Abdul Aziz Bin Mohammed Street. Modern audio-visual and display techniques are extensively used in this, Saudi Arabia's first museum, and there are some good exhibits depicting the life of the early Arabian settlers. Many of the exhibits in the section devoted to the land of Dilmun are sumptuous with exquisite and priceless pieces of jewellery and gold coins.

Riyadh Airport is 2km/1 mile from the city centre.

Hotels

There is no official hotel rating system in Saudi Arabia.

INTER-CONTINENTAL, Mazaar Street, P.O. Box 3636, ☎ 34500.
New, luxury hotel 5 minutes from the airport and 10 minutes from the city centre.
Rooms: 197. Cabanas available. 450 new rooms scheduled to open 1980/81.
Facilities: Restaurant (international and Oriental cuisine), coffee shop. Tennis and swimming. Car hire.
Services: TC, FC. Amex, Bankamericard, Carte Blanche, Diners Club. Dr. on call.
Conference and banquet facilities.

AL-YAMAMAH, Airport Road, P.O. Box 1210, ☎ 28200.
First-class hotel near the business centre and the government ministries.
Rooms: 145. Suites available.
Facilities: Restaurant, breakfast room. Swimming. Garden.
Services: TC, FC. Diners Club.
Conference room – max. capacity 250.
Banquet rooms – max. capacity 250.

ATALLAH HOUSE, Mazaar Street, P.O. Box 1975, ☎ 35965/35767.
Modern, first-class hotel centrally located midway between the airport and the city centre.
Rooms: 82, 6 suites, 10 bungalows.

Facilities: 2 restaurants, coffee shop. Swimming. Hairdresser. Car hire.
Services: **TC**, **FC**. ⊟ Amex and Diners Club. **$**, ♂. Telex service. Dr. on call.
Conference room – max. capacity 180.

AL KHEREIJI, Batha Street, P.O. Box 1075, ☎ 39913/19, Reservations ☎ 35600.
Modern hotel near the business centre and the government ministries.
Rooms: 336 🚿, 🚗, ▭, ☎, △, 📺. Suites available.
Facilities: Restaurant and snack bar. Pool room, table tennis. Cinema. Car hire.
Services: **TC**, **FC**. ⊟ Amex and Diners Club. **$**, ♂. Dr. on call.
Conference room – max. capacity 60.
Banquet rooms – max. capacity 200.

SAUDIA, Nasriah Street, P.O. Box 244, ☎ 24051.
Modern hotel in the city centre.
Rooms: 100 🚿, ▭, ☎, △. Suites available.
Facilities: Restaurants, coffee shop. Swimming. Garden and terrace. Hairdresser. Cinema. Car hire.
Services: No credit cards.
Conference room – max. capacity 60.

Restaurants

The Inter-Continental and Saudia Hotels both have good restaurants. During the summer months, the Al-Yamamah Hotel has a garden restaurant open in the evenings only.

Other restaurants in Riyadh include the *Shangri-La*, off Airport Road, ☎ 62431 – Chinese; *Sindbad Restaurant*, Shara Al-Jamaa, ☎ 26557 – steak specialities; *Semiramis*, Shara Al-Wazir, ☎ 23841 – Lebanese; *Roma*, off Jareer Street, ☎ 67838 – Italian; *60 Restaurant*, near Petromin Roundabout, ☎ 60706.

Entertainment

Riyadh has very limited social amenities and those likely to appeal to the Western visitor are mostly concentrated in the compounds of the large foreign companies. The establishment of cinemas, nightclubs, discotheques etc. is prohibited under the laws of Wahabism.

Horse racing takes place at the *Equestrian Club* on Monday afternoons and the programme includes a camel race. Many of the hotels have swimming pools but mixed bathing is not allowed in any public pools, including hotel pools.

Shopping

Most of the *souks* in Riyadh are in the vicinity of the Palace of Justice and Batha Street. There are separate *souks* exclusively for gold, silver, pottery, fabrics, rugs, etc.

Jeddah

The port of Jeddah dates back some 1,200 years and is today the largest port on the Red Sea. As the commercial and diplomatic centre of Saudi Arabia, Jeddah has grown rapidly like Riyadh, although some of the old character of the city has been retained. The contrast between the old and the new is best seen in the *souk* (market), where women in traditional Arab dress with loaded baskets on their heads file past the modern, luxury department stores.

In accordance with the strict laws of Islamic faith, at prayer time the market stallholders will hasten to the mosque while prayers and music are transmitted aloud over the city.

The huge water tower in the Khozam Palace gardens is the most distinctive landmark in Jeddah, and offers a panoramic view of the city from the top. There are a few old houses left in Jeddah and one of the finest is that of the Nasif family in Alawi Street – the house is now being restored as an ethnic museum. A wander through the old town is always worthwhile and much of it has remained untouched with its distinctive Arab character well preserved.

Jeddah Airport is 2½km/1½ miles from the city centre.

Hotels

N.B. Hotel accommodation in Jeddah is very difficult to obtain during *Ramadan* and the high season, and prices invariably double.

JEDDAH PALACE, Bab-al-Jadidd, P.O. Box 473, ☎ 32387/32255.
Modern, first-class hotel in the city centre.
Rooms: 120. Suites available.
Facilities: Restaurant, cafeteria. Swimming, tennis, sauna and health centre. Car hire.
Services: TC, FC. Amex.
Conference room – max. capacity 1,000.

KANDARA PALACE, Airport Road, P.O. Box 473, ☎ 23155.
Modern, first-class hotel near the airport, 5 minutes' drive from the city centre.
Rooms: 400.
Private villas available.
Facilities: Restaurant (international and Oriental cuisine), coffee shop and 24-hour snack service. Garden, swimming, sauna and tennis. Hairdresser. Airline office and travel agency. Car hire.
Services: TC, FC. Amex and Diners Club. Dr. on call.
Conference and banquet rooms – max. capacity 600.

AL-ATTAS, P.O. Box 1299, ☎ 20609.
AL-ATTAS OASIS, P.O. Box 1789, ☎ 20211.
Adjacent, modern, first-class hotels off Shar'a al-Matar. Under the same management.
Rooms: 250.
Facilities: Restaurant and coffee shop. Swimming and tennis. Barber's shop. Banquet room.

JEDDAH KAKI, Airport Road, P.O. Box 2559, ☎ 48071.
Modern hotel near the airport and the business centre of Jeddah.
Rooms: 220. Suites available.
Facilities: Restaurant (international and Oriental cuisine), cabana club. Swimming. Hairdresser. Airlines counter.
Services: Amex and Diners Club. Telex service.

JEDDAH AIRPORT, Airport Road, ☎ 33155.
Modern, first-class hotel situated midway between the airport and the city centre.
Rooms: 69. 18 suites.
Facilities: Restaurant and cafeteria. Shops. Swimming and tennis.
Services: TC, FC. No credit cards.
Conference room.

Restaurants

Apart from the restaurants in the main hotels, others include: *Kaymak*, Tariq al-Medina – Lebanese; *Koreana*, Shara Al-Sharafiyah; *Topkapi*, Khalid bin Walid Street; *Al Riyadh*, Sharafiyah; *Il Castello*, off Khalid bin Walid Street – Italian; *Shangri-La*, behind Jeddah Shopping Centre – Chinese; *Shalimar*, behind Jeddah Shopping Centre – Indian; *American Steak House*, near Zebmarket; *Rebeia International*, Madaris Road – Indonesian.

Jeddah also has a number of snack bars.

Entertainment

A favourite week-end activity (Thursday afternoon and Friday) is to go to the beach. The Creek is the most popular area, but many foreigners prefer to drive farther out of Jeddah to the various beaches dotted along the Red Sea. Bikinis are acceptable on these beaches although the Arab population still immerse themselves fully clothed in the water.

Shopping

In the *souk* visitors will find fine copper and silverware and other traditional Oriental goods. Also an excellent selection of fresh fruits.

Dhahran–Dammam–Al-Khobar

Dhahran is the main centre of a group of towns situated close together in Saudi Arabia's Eastern Province. Dhahran is the headquarters of the Arabian American Oil Company (ARAMCO) and, as the main port in the east of the Kingdom, is an important commercial centre.

The Oil Exhibit Centre which is visited by thousands of people each year is situated by the east gate of the Aramco compound, and depicts the development of Saudi Arabia's oil industry.

Dammam has grown rapidly like its neighbours, and is today the administrative capital of the Eastern Province. The town has succeeded in retaining much of its Arabian character and the population seems relatively untouched by Western influence. Exotic Oriental goods such as Shisha pipes, incense, spices, etc., are sold in the market place and it is not unusual to see Bedouin women from the desert selling their hand-made wares.

A large proportion of the foreign residents attached to the various companies in the Dhahran–Dammam–Al-Khobar area live in Al-Khobar. The town was once a small *dhow* port and a few *dhows* still make the journey each day between Al-Khobar and Bahrain, leaving in the morning and arriving 3 to 4 hours later in Manama.

Dhahran Airport is 8km/5 miles from Al-Khobar.

Hotels

AL-GOSAIBI, P.O. Box 51, Dhahran Airport, Al-Khobar, ☎ 42466.
Modern, luxury hotel near Dhahran Airport and the centre of Al-Khobar.
Rooms: 300, 39 suites, 25 villas.
Facilities: Roof restaurant (international and Oriental cuisine), 24-hour coffee shop, poolside snack bar. Cinema and recreation centre. Swimming.
Services: Amex.
Conference rooms – max. capacity 500.

AL KHAJAH, P.O. Box 45, Al-Khobar, ☎ 43122.
Well situated on the fringe of the business centre of Al-Khobar, 15 minutes from Dhahran Airport.
Rooms: 142.
Facilities: Chinese restaurant, 24-hour coffee shop.

Other hotels in the area include:
DAMMAM HOTEL, P.O. Box 1928, Dammam, ☎ 21926.

GULF FLOWER HOTEL, Street No. 9, Al-Khobar Road, Dammam, ☎ 22170.

Restaurants

Maxims, King Abdul Aziz Avenue, Al-Khobar; *Kaymat Glace Shangri-La*, Al-Khobar (Chinese); *Arirang*, Dhahran Road, Al-Khobar (Korean and Japanese); *Dragon Inn*, 10th Street, Al-Khobar (Chinese); *Strand*, King Abdul Aziz Boulevard, Al-Khobar (European).

Entertainment

Many of the foreign companies in the area have good recreational facilities which visitors known to company employees can occasionally use. In the Azizia district, 15km/9½ miles south of Al-Khobar, there are a number of good public beaches, and sailing and water-skiing are both popular.

Shopping

There is a large gold *souk* in Dammam where jewellery is sold by weight. Most of the shops in the three towns sell consumer goods of little interest to the souvenir hunter. The *Batik Shop* in Al-Khobar is worth a visit, and has a large selection of light, colourful cottons.

SUDAN

Democratic Republic of Sudan

Size: 2,502,673 sq.km/966,283 sq. miles.

Population: 16.95 million (1978).

Distribution: Over 60% of the population live in the central area of Sudan, around Khartoum and the Nile River.

Density: 6.2 persons per sq.km/16 per sq.mile (40 per sq.km/104 per sq.mile in Khartoum Province).

Population Growth Rate: 2.5% p.a.

Ethnic Composition: Sudan has many different ethnic groups. A large percentage of the population are Muslim Arabs living in the northern and central areas, together with the Nubians.

Black peoples occupy much of the western part of the country where there has been mixing with migrants from West Africa. The south is inhabited by many different tribes with the Nilotic tribe predominating.

Capital: Khartoum Pop. 333,920.

Major Cities/Towns: Omdurman Pop. 299,400; Khartoum North Pop. 150,990; Port Sudan Pop. 127,120; Wad Medani Pop. 106,776; El Obeid Pop. 90,060; Atbara Pop. 66,116; Juba Pop. 56,737.

Language: Arabic is the official language, spoken by about half of the population. More than 100 languages are spoken throughout the Sudan and the Nilotic and Nilo-Hamitic languages are spoken by approximately 23% of the population. English is the most widely spoken foreign language.

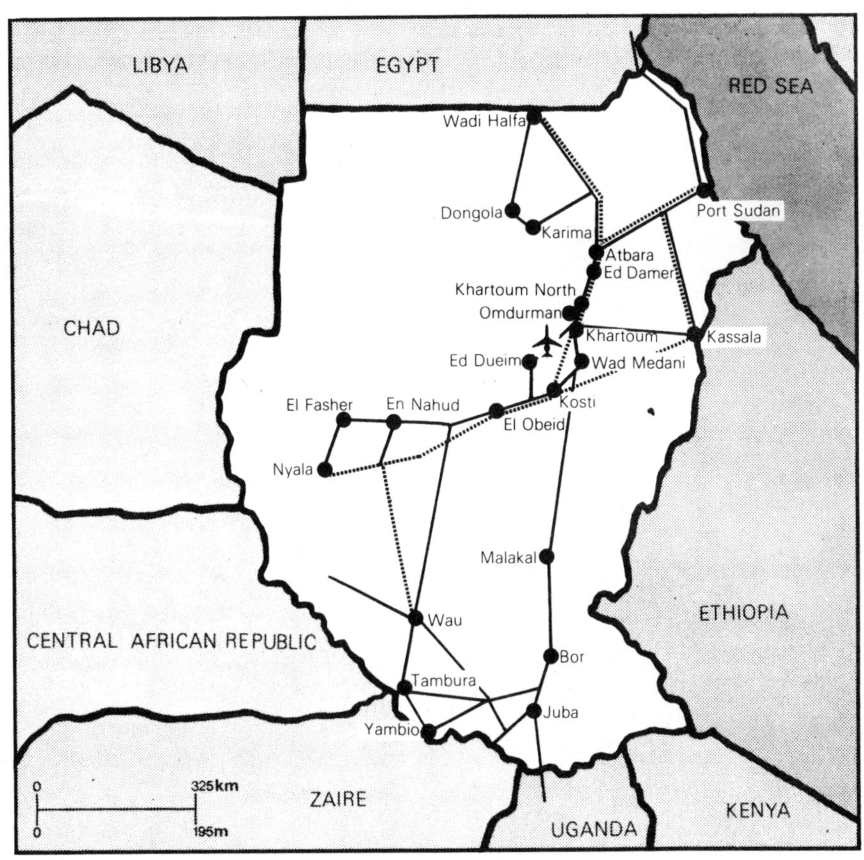

Religion: The population is predominantly Muslim with 80% belonging to the Sunni Sect. There are small Christian communities and pagan worship is widespread amongst the southern tribes.

Government: The Head of State of the Sudan is the President who is responsible for maintaining the Constitution and appointing the Prime Minister and other government ministers. A 250-member People's Assembly is formally vested with legislative power.

In 1972 the Southern Region of Sudan gained regional autonomy within a federal structure of government and is governed by a High Executive Council.

The Sudanese Socialist Union is the only legal political party.

GEOGRAPHY

Sudan is the largest country in Africa and is almost equal to Western Europe in size. It has borders with Egypt to the north, Ethiopia to the east, Kenya, Uganda and Zaire to the south and the Central African Republic, Chad and Libya to the west.

From the geographical angle, the country is very varied with desert, savannah and tropical rain forest. The White and Blue Niles flow through southern Sudan, joining at Khartoum to form the main Nile River.

The greater part of the country consists of an immense plateau which is separated from the Red Sea coast to the east by a range of hills. Much of southern Sudan consists of savannah and tropical rain forest with large areas of swampland, while the north is a desert region through which the Nile flows, providing the chief means of communication.

Climate

Sudan has a tropical climate although conditions differ considerably in the various regions. Rainfall is highest in the south and over much of Sudan it is unreliable and severe crop failures are not uncommon.

From mid-April to June the weather is extremely hot and dry with increasing humidity from July to September. Temperatures in Khartoum range from 32°C/90°F in December to 42°C/108°F in June. The southern provinces are cooler but with greater humidity in summer. The period from October to mid-April is the most pleasant time to visit the Sudan.

Agriculture

Sudan is predominantly an agricultural country and depends heavily on agriculture for export earnings and employment. Irrigation is widespread and several large dams have been built – the Sennar Dam on the Blue Nile irrigates about 1.8 million acres known as the Managil Extension, and the Roseires Dam will eventually provide all-year-round irrigation for 3 million acres of land.

Commercial farming is largely confined to the north, while in the south traditional methods of agriculture and livestock rearing prevail. Cotton is the chief cash crop, accounting for approximately 55% of Sudan's total exports by value. The Gezira cotton-growing scheme in the triangle formed by the White and Blue Niles is one of the largest single agricultural enterprises in Africa.

Attempts are being made to increase the cultivation of other cash crops such as sugar, groundnuts and castor seed in order to reduce the country's dependence on cotton. With the development of large-scale irrigation, Sudan's agricultural potential is enormous and many of the new schemes are being financed with the help of Arab oil-producing nations.

Main Crops: cotton, sugar, groundnuts, gum arabic, oil seeds, sorghum (dura), millet, dates.

Mineral Resources: Various mineral deposits have been located, but exploitation to date is very limited. Known mineral deposits include copper, iron ore, chromite, manganese, gold, salt.

THE ECONOMY

Gross National Product (1976): US$4.3 billion.

Per Capita Income (1976): US$236.

Gross Domestic Product (1974): £S1,511 million.

Foreign Trade (1976): Total Imports US$853 million; Total Exports US$483 million.

Main Trading Partners: Imports – Iran, India, UK, China, USA, West Germany. Exports – Italy, France, China, West Germany, USA, Saudi Arabia.

The Sudanese economy is primarily based on agriculture and trade is mainly concerned with the export of primary or processed agricultural products and the import of both capital and consumer goods needed by a developing country.

Sudan is almost self-sufficient for its major food items and current agricultural development plans are aimed at reaching total self-sufficiency in foodstuffs. Cotton still remains Sudan's chief means of earning foreign exchange which leaves the country in a vulnerable position where the balance of payments is concerned.

Agriculture and irrigation are the chief beneficaries of government development funds, together with the associated food-processing industries. New sugar factories are being built and a major development of the cotton-spinning and weaving industry is envisaged. On a smaller scale, there has been a recent expansion in the field of the light manufacturing industries – mainly producing basic consumer goods such as soap, shoes, soft drinks and beer. The exploitation of Sudan's various mineral deposits is also to be stepped up.

The Six-Year Development Plan (1977/8 to 1982/3) should go a long way towards solving many of the Sudan's problems related to under-development. Transport and communications, health, education and welfare are all scheduled to benefit from increased investment.

Major Industries: light manufacturing, e.g., foodstuffs, soap, textiles, footwear, etc., paper products, sugar, cement.

Main Commodities Traded: Imports – machinery and equipment, vehicles, manufactured goods and foodstuffs, chemical and petroleum products. Exports – cotton, groundnuts, sesame, gum arabic.

Sudan is a member of the OAU (Organisation of African Unity) and the Arab League.

HOW TO GET THERE

Air

Khartoum Civil Airport is the main international airport, located 5km/3 miles from the city centre.

Major airlines flying to the Sudan are Aeroflot, Alitalia, British Airways, Egypt Air, Lufthansa, MEA, SAS, Saudi Arabian Airlines and TWA. Sudan Airways operate between Khartoum and Bahrain, Egypt, Ethiopia, West Germany, Greece, Kenya, Italy, Iraq, Lebanon, Libya, Saudi Arabia and the United Kingdom.

Flying times to Khartoum: from London 8 hours; from New York 15½ hours.

An airport charge of £S1 is payable by all passengers embarking on international flights from Khartoum Airport.

Taxis are available at the airport and, on request, airlines will arrange for transport from hotels to the airport.

ENTRY REGULATIONS

Visas

Nationals of all countries require visas which should be obtained in advance from Sudanese embassies and consulates abroad.

Business travellers require a letter from their firm giving the fullest details of the business to be undertaken in Sudan, the full names and addresses of contacts and the actual amount of funds available to the applicant.

N.B. When filling out the visa application form, applicants should ensure that the information regarding the details of their trip is as precise and complete as possible.

Visas are valid for 3 months from the date of issue for a stay of up to one month. Travellers should ensure that the validity of their passport extends for 3 months beyond the date of issue of the visa.

Visitors staying for more than 3 days in the Sudan must register on arrival with the Aliens Department of the Ministry of the Interior. Visitors intending to travel outside of the Three Towns district of Khartoum, Khartoum North and Omdurman should first notify the Ministry of the Interior of their destination.

Evidence in a passport of a previous or planned visit to Israel may adversely affect the granting of a visa.

Health Regulations

All visitors must have valid certificates of vaccination against smallpox and cholera. Visitors wishing to travel to the south of Sudan should also have a valid certificate of vaccination against yellow fever.

Travellers entering Egypt or the UK from Sudan are required to have a yellow fever certificate or a *location certificate* certifying that they have not been in a yellow fever area. These can be obtained from the offices of the Khartoum Municipality 24 hours or less before departure.

Customs

Currency: There is no limit to the amount of foreign currency which may be taken into the Sudan. All currency, including travellers' cheques and letters of credit, must be declared on entry and exit. The import and export of Sudanese currency is prohibited.

Visitors should exchange their travellers' cheques and foreign currency at authorised exchange points only, and the currency declaration form must be endorsed. This has to be shown to the Customs authorities on departure.

Duty-free articles: Personal effects, 250g tobacco or 200 cigarettes or 50 cigars and 2 pints of spirits.

Articles liable to duty: All commercial samples are subject to the usual import regulations. When dutiable samples accompany a traveller and are re-exported within 12 months, the payment of Customs duty is refunded.

PRACTICAL INFORMATION FOR THE VISITOR

1. Currency

Monetary Unit – Sudanese pound (£S), divided into 100 piastres (PT) and 1,000 milliemes (mms).
Notes – 25, 50 piastres and 1, 5, 10 Sudanese pounds.
Coins – ½, 1, 2, 5, 10 piastres.

Several major hotels and airline offices in Khartoum now accept internationally recognised credit cards but their use is not widespread throughout the Sudan.

Banking Hours:
0830–1200 Saturday to Thursday
All commercial banks in the Sudan were nationalised in 1970. The banking system now consists of the Bank of Sudan which is the central bank, five commercial banks and three specialised banks. A number of foreign banks have recently been allowed to open branches in Khartoum.

Bank of Sudan
Sharia Gamaa, P.O. Box 313, Khartoum, ☎ 70761/5.

Commercial Banks in Khartoum:
Bank of Khartoum
8 Sharia Gamhouria, P.O. Box 1008, ☎ 81071/2 /70666.
El Nilein Bank
Sharia Khalifa, P.O. Box 466, ☎ 73939.
People's Co-operative Bank
Sharia Qasr, P.O. Box 992, ☎ 73555.
Sudan Commercial Bank
P.O. Box 1116, ☎ 71468.
Unity Bank
Sharia Barlaman, P.O. Box 408, ☎ 74200/6.

Specialised Banks in Khartoum:
Agricultural Bank of Sudan
Sharia Gamhouria, P.O. Box 1363, ☎ 77424/5/77466.
Industrial Bank of Sudan
UN Square, P.O. Box 1722, ☎ 71223.
Sudanese Estates Bank
Sharia Baladia, P.O. Box 309, ☎ 81061/2/78062.

Foreign Commercial Banks in Khartoum:
Bank of Credit and Commerce International
P.O. Box 5, ☎ 73970.
Chase Manhattan Bank
P.O. Box 2679, ☎ 78740/78703.
Citibank
P.O. Box 2743, ☎ 76623/76654.
Faisal Islamic Bank
P.O. Box 2415, ☎ 75367.
National Bank of Abu Dhabi
P.O. Box 2463, ☎ 74892.

2. Electricity Supply

240V AC single phase.
Plugs: 2-pin round.

3. Weights and Measures

The metric system is used in commercial circles and imperial measures are also used. Important local measures to be noted are:
Kantar (100 Rotls) used for cotton = 315lb seed cotton or 100lb lint cotton.
Feddan = 1.038 acres.

4. Media

The Sudanese Broadcasting Service transmits radio programmes in Arabic, English, Somali and eight Sudanese languages. Both television and radio carry advertising. Enquiries should be addressed to: El Gorashi Advertising and Printing Corporation, P.O. Box 536, Khartoum.

Newspapers (daily):
Al Ayam; Al Sahafa.

The press was nationalised in 1970. The Ministry of Information and Culture sponsors a number of publications including the *Nile Mirror* and *Sudanow* (both in English).

Two Arabic journals printed in England – *Anglo-Arab Trade* and *Middle East Trade* – both circulate in Sudan, together with a number of other foreign trade publications. The *Journal of the Engineering Society* is published bi-annually and the Sudan Chamber of Commerce publishes its own journal.

5. Medical Care

Malaria is endemic in many parts of Sudan and visitors should take anti-malarial measures as recommended by their doctor. Gastroenteritis, hepatitis and bilharzia are additional health risks, often resulting from poor sanitation.

Although the water supply in Khartoum and other large towns is safe to drink, visitors are advised to drink boiled or filtered water. Visitors should take extra salt, in tablet or solution form, during the hot summer months.

6. Telephone, Telex and Postal Services

Telegrams may be sent from the main Khartoum Post Office 24 hours a day. International telephone and telex communications have improved considerably since the Satellite Tracking Station came into use.

All mail to and from Sudan should be despatched by air.

7. Public Holidays

Fixed Holidays:

1 January	*Anniversary of Sudan Independence*
3 March	*Unity Day*
25 May	*Revolution Day*
12 October	*Republic Day*
25 December	*Christmas*

Muslim Holidays:
These follow the Muslim calendar and occur 10–12 days earlier every year. The dates of the Muslim holidays are approximate as they depend upon sightings of the moon, and may differ by one or two days from those given below. 1981 dates are:

18 January	*Prophet's Birthday*
31 May	*Ascension of the Prophet*
31 July –2 August	*(end of Ramadan)*
8–10 October	*Kurban Bairam*
29 October	*Muslim New Year*
7–8 November	*Ashoura*

Easter is a public holiday for all Christians in the Sudan.

8. Time

GMT+2

9. Internal Transport

Official permits are required for most journeys within the Sudan. Visitors spending the night in a town outside of the Three Towns district must register with the local police.

Air

Sudan Airways operate regular, internal services to Atbara, Juba, El Obeid, Port Sudan, Wad Medani and other towns. The provincial airport charge is PT50.

Airline Offices in Khartoum:

Aeroflot	☎ 71150.
Air France	☎ 74479.
Air India	☎ 74583.
British Airways	☎ 74577/9.
Lufthansa	☎ 71322.
MEA	☎ 80968.
Pan Am	☎ 80971.
SAS	☎ 81011/81015.
Sudan Airways	☎ 76411/76414.
Swissair	☎ 80196/80229.
TWA	☎ 76413.

Rail

Trains in the Sudan are generally clean and comfortable but tend to be very slow. There are trains from Khartoum to Port Sudan, Wadi Halfa, El Obeid, Nyala, Wau, Kosti and Kassala. Sleeping cars and catering facilities are available on the main routes.

Road

Motorists should enquire about road conditions and administrative restrictions before commencing a journey through the country. Sudan has few tarred roads and conditions during the rainy season (July–September) are bad.

Self-drive cars are available for hire. Traffic drives on the right-hand side of the road.

Taxis are not metered and fares should be arranged before starting a journey. Collective taxis can be found in Khartoum market place.

10. Tipping

Taxis – no tip expected.

Porters – 5 piastres per bag.

Hotels/restaurants – 10% of the bill.

11. Social Customs

More than three-quarters of the population are Muslims and most Muslim customs are observed in Sudan. Alcohol is not prohibited however.

Segregation of the sexes is generally practised and women rarely attend social and business functions.

For further information, refer to page 12 under 'Muslim Social Customs'.

USEFUL ADDRESSES (GENERAL)

Embassies in Khartoum

France: 6H East Plot 2, 19th Street, P.O. Box 377.

West Germany: 53 Baladia Street, Block No. 8 D.E., Plot No. 2, ☎ 77990/77995.

Japan: House No. 24, Block 10 A.E., 3rd Street, New Extension, P.O. Box 1649, ☎ 44549/44554.

Netherlands: Sharia El Mahdi, corner Gama' Avenue, P.O. Box 391, ☎ 777889.

Switzerland: New Aboulela Building, P.O. Box 1707, ☎ 71161/72365.

UK: New Aboulela Building, Sharia Barlaman, P.O. Box 801, ☎ 70760/70766/9.

US: Gamhouria Avenue, P.O. Box 699, ☎ 74611/74700.

Other addresses

Ministry of Culture and Information, Khartoum, ☎ 74949/74955.

Sudan Tourist Corporation, P.O. Box 2424, Khartoum, ☎ 70230.

Thomas Cook Authorised Representatives: Sudan Travel and Tourist Agency, P.O. Box 769, Khartoum, ☎ 72119/70919, and Tigani World Wide Travel Organisation, 76 Sharia Gamhouria, P.O. Box 936, Khartoum, ☎ 76996.

BUSINESS INFORMATION

In 1970 most of the foreign interests operating in the Sudan were nationalised and replaced by government-owned trading companies. However, a large proportion of the nationalised companies have now been handed back to their original owners, and this has given rise to renewed activity in the private sector. The Development and Promotion of Industrial Investment Act (1972) and the Act to Organise and Encourage Investment in Economic Services (1973) were both designed to attract foreign investment.

About 75% of the country's industrial activity is located in the Khartoum area, although a number of important government organisations are outside of this region. Of particular importance are Sudan Railways at Atbara, the Sudan Gezira Board near Wad Medani and the Ministry of Irrigation and Hydro-Electric Power also at Wad Medani.

Firms wishing to trade in the Sudanese market generally require a local agent who must be registered with the Ministry of Commerce and Supply, and have a current licence to operate.

Personal contact is highly valued in the Sudan and periodic visits by representatives of foreign companies are very important and also facilitate the choice of a good local agent.

Import and Exchange Control Regulations

Import regulations are strict and most goods require a Specific Import Licence, although some goods can be imported under an Open General Licence. The importation of goods from Israel, South Africa, Zimbabwe-Rhodesia and Portugal is prohibited.

Sudan operates its own exchange control under the supervision of the Bank of Sudan. All payments must be made through banks authorised to deal in foreign exchange. All advance payments require the prior approval of the Exchange Control Authorities.

Business Hours

Government Offices:

Khartoum –	0800–1400	Saturday to Thursday
Other centres –	0630–1400	Saturday to Thursday (with an interval for breakfast)

Business Houses:

0830–1330 1700–2000	Saturday to Thursday

Friday is the weekly holiday in the Sudan.

Business Events

In 1978 Khartoum staged its first International Trade Fair and this has become an annual event, taking place in January/February of each year on a permanent site by the Blue Nile. Further details can be obtained from the Director General, Sudan Exhibitions and Fairs Corporation, P.O. Box 2366, Khartoum.

BUSINESS SERVICES

Agents who will arrange collection/despatch of samples include:

Commercial & Shipping Company, P.O. Box 308, Khartoum. (Forwarding Department, P.O. Box 74, Port Sudan.)

Ezzel din Ali Osman, P.O. Box 544, Port Sudan.

May Trading & Services Ltd, P.O. Box 215, Khartoum. (Forwarding Department, P.O. Box 17, Port Sudan.)

Palestine Trading Company, P.O. Box 251, Khartoum, and P.O. Box 6, Port Sudan.

Sudan Shipping Line Ltd, P.O. Box 1731, Khartoum. (Forwarding Department, P.O. Box 426, Port Sudan.)

USEFUL ADDRESSES (BUSINESS)

Sudan Chamber of Commerce, P.O. Box 81, Khartoum, ☎ 72346/76518.

Ministry of Finance, Planning & National Economy, Sharia Gama'a, P.O. Box 194, Khartoum, ☎ 70288.

Ministry of Commerce & Supply, P.O. Box 194, Khartoum.

Sudan Development Corporation, P.O. Box 710, Khartoum.

Sudanese Industries Association, P.O. Box 2563, Khartoum.

MAJOR CITY

Khartoum

Khartoum is the capital of the Three Towns (Khartoum, Khartoum North, Omdurman) which lie at the junction of the Blue and White Niles. Omdurman is considered to be the national capital, Khartoum the commercial and administrative capital and Khartoum North the industrial capital of Sudan. All three towns are joined together by a series of bridges which span the two rivers.

The modern city of Khartoum is built with wide avenues, spacious open areas and large, white colonial-style buildings, but one can still find the old narrow streets and colourful market-places tucked away behind the main area of the city.

The People's Palace has a fine collection of antique field guns, swords and other military equipment dating from the time of General Gordon.

Omdurman was built in the nineteenth century by the Mahdi when he laid siege to Khartoum and General Gordon's forces. It subsequently became the capital of the Mahdi's empire until it was captured in 1898 by the British and Egyptian armies under Lord Kitchener. The Mahdi's tomb can be visited, and adjacent to it stands the Khalifa's Museum, named after the Mahdi's successor Khalifa Abd Ullahi.

The flat-roofed, baked mud houses in Omdurman are good examples of Sudanese architecture. In the shaded, narrow streets visitors will find many small shops and stalls and the bazaar where traditional Sudanese handicrafts are sold – ivory and ebony carved goods, silverware, beadwork and slippers, bags, wallets and belts made from leopard and lizard skins.

Khartoum Airport is 5km/3 miles from the city centre.

Hotels

There is no official hotel rating system in Sudan.

Khartoum Hilton, P.O. Box 1910, 74100/78930.
Luxury, modern hotel built at the junction of the Blue and White Niles, 2½km/1½ miles from the centre of Khartoum.
Rooms: 274.
Facilities: Restaurant, grill room, nightclub, coffee shop and lobby bar. Airline office, shops, barber's shop. Tennis, sauna, swimming, bowling alley, billiards. Health club.
Services: TC, FC. Amex. Dr. on call.
Conference room – max. capacity 434.
Banquet rooms – max. capacity 324.

Khartoum Meridien, P.O. Box 1716, 75970.
Modern, first-class hotel in the city centre, 10 minutes' drive from the airport.
Rooms: 150, on request.
Facilities: Restaurant and bar. Sauna and swimming. Garden.
Services: TC, FC. Amex. Dr. on call.
Banquet room – max. capacity 150.

Sudan, Sharia el Nil, P.O. Box 1845, 80811.
Modern hotel in the city centre.
Rooms: 80. Suites available.
Facilities: Restaurant and bar. Gift shop, hairdresser. Squash.
Services: TC, FC. Amex. Dr. on call.

Restaurants

Good international cuisine can be found in the restaurants of the Hilton, Grand, Sudan and Sahara Hotels. Other restaurants in Khartoum include: *St James*, Sharia Gamhouria; *Blue Nile Casino*, Khartoum North; *The Gordon Cabaret* (dinner and dancing), 72045; *Shish Kebab Restaurant.*

Nightclubs

Hilton Hotel (open-air nightclub) 74100; *Hamad Floating Casino*, Sharia el Nil, Khartoum; *Blue Nile Cafeteria*, Sharia el Nil, Khartoum; *Jimmy's Night Club*, Khartoum.

Entertainment

Khartoum has several cabarets and cinemas and the National Theatre, Sharia el Nil, Omdurman, 51549 stages productions from October to June.

A number of sporting clubs offer swimming, tennis, golf, polo, cricket, and hockey. Race meetings are held regularly in Khartoum on Fridays during the winter. Khartoum also has a zoo where most of the country's native animals can be seen.

A number of interesting cruises operate along the Nile, and launches for up to fifteen persons can be hired at 24 hours' notice.

The *Sudan Club*, P.O. Box 322, Khartoum, is an exclusively British club offering limited accommodation for men and women. The *Club* has a restaurant and bar and library facilities, and also offers swimming, badminton, volleyball, snooker, billiards, squash and tennis for residents. Visiting business travellers can obtain temporary membership on application to the Secretary.

Shopping

Best buys: hides and skins, jewellery, ivory and ebony carved goods.

A selection of Khartoum shops specialising in particular goods is as follows: *Sudan Folklore House*, 67 Sharia El Qasr, 71729 – ivory and skins; *Sudan Crafts*, Sharia El Qasr, 77367 – souvenirs; *Khartoum Tannery*, P.O. Box 134, Khartoum South – hides, skins, chamois.

SYRIA

Syrian Arab Republic

Size: 184,000 sq.km/71,000 sq.miles.

Population: 7,840,000 (1978).

Distribution: 50% in urban areas.

Density: 40 persons per sq.km/103 per sq.mile.

Population Growth Rate: 3.3% p.a.

Ethnic Composition: 90% of the population are Arabs. The various minority groupings include Circassians, Armenians, Turks and Kurds.

Capital: Damascus Pop. 1,054,000.

Major Cities/Towns: Aleppo Pop. 778,500; Hama Pop. 162,000; Homs Pop. 314,750.

Language: Arabic is the official language. Both French and English are used in government and business circles.

Religion: Approximately 86% of the population are Muslims – mainly of the Sunni sect. The Christian minority is of various denominations and is centred around Aleppo.

Government: The Constitution of 1973 defines Syria as a popular, democratic, socialist republic and provides for a 7-year President, a 4-year People's Assembly and a Council of Ministers. The Baath Arab Socialist Party is the ruling political party in alliance with the Communist and Socialist parties. Islamic law forms the basis of all state legislation.

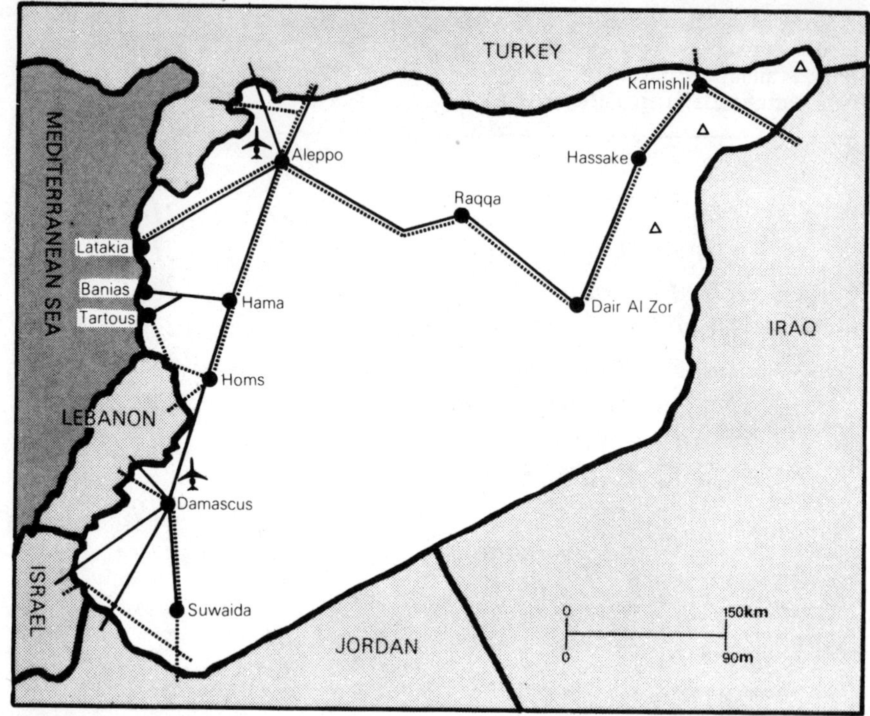

GEOGRAPHY

Situated on the east coast of the Mediterranean, Syria has borders with Turkey to the north, Iraq to the east, Jordan and Israel to the south and with Lebanon to the southwest.

The country divides naturally into four major regions: the narrow coastal plain, the highland region in the north and northwest which includes the Anti-Lebanon mountains, the central and eastern fertile plains and the semi-arid steppes and Syrian Desert in the south and southeast. The Euphrates river flows mainly through the interior plains region.

Climate

The Syrian climate is pleasant with hot, dry summers and relatively cold winters. Rainfall in winter ranges from 40″ in the west to 1″ in the desert region. Summer humidity is low except in the north/west coastal regions. In Damascus average temperatures range from 23°C/73°F in summer to 10°C/50°F in winter.

Agriculture

Approximately 75% of the arable land in Syria is irrigated and yet harvests are often drastically affected by seasonal variations in rainfall. The main cultivated areas are the coastal strip, the northeast and the mountain areas.

Many irrigation and agricultural development projects are under way, particularly in the Euphrates basin involving several East European nations. Simultaneously, Syria is aiming to develop her agricultural infrastructure in order to provide better transportation, storage and processing facilities.

Main Crops: cotton, grains, sugar beet, fruit and vegetables, tobacco.

Mineral Resources: oil, phosphates, asphalt, gypsum, rock salt.

THE ECONOMY

Gross National Product (1976): US$2.6 billion.

Per Capita Income (1976): US$342.

Gross Domestic Product (1977): £Syr25,993 million.

Foreign Trade (1976): Total Imports US$2.3 billion; Total Exports US$1 billion.

Main Trading Partners: Imports – West Germany, Italy, France, USA, Japan, Switzerland. Exports – Italy, West Germany, Belgium/Luxembourg, UK, USSR, Yugoslavia.

The Syrian economy is essentially state-controlled and the State Trading Organisations are responsible for over 65% of total imports and 75% of total exports. There has been an upsurge in the private sector, however, following a general liberalisation of economic policy in 1973.

The 1973 Arab/Israeli war and Syria's recent involvement in the Lebanon have been a heavy strain on the economy and many development projects are currently suspended. The closure in 1976 of a major pipeline which carried Iraqi oil across Syria to the Mediterranean terminals has resulted in a substantial loss of revenue for Syria and has further damaged the balance of payments situation. Despite financial aid from Arab oil-producing nations, prospects for the economy remain very much in the balance, and growth is difficult to predict pending a settlement of the Lebanese problem.

Plans to increase industrial and mining production are still in force and Syria aims to achieve self-sufficiency in agriculture by 1981. The Euphrates is to be developed both agriculturally and industrially and the dam at Tabqa will double electricity production and create larger areas of irrigated land suitable for cultivation.

Major Industries: oil, textiles, cement, glass, clothing, food processing.

Main Commodities Traded: Imports – machinery and transport equipment, manufactured goods, food and livestock, raw materials. Exports – oil and oil products, textiles, clothing, fertilisers.

Crude Oil Production (1977): 890,000 metric tons per average calendar month.

Syria is a member of the Arab League and has applied for membership of the Organisation of Petroleum Exporting Countries (OPEC).

HOW TO GET THERE

Air

Syrian Arab Airlines fly to Syria from Beirut, Berlin, Cairo, Delhi, London, Moscow and Paris. Major airlines operating through Damascus include Aeroflot, Air France, Alitalia, British Airways, KLM, Lufthansa, SAS and Pan Am.

Flying times to Damascus: from London 4¾ hours; from New York 13 hours.

There is an airport tax of £Syr10 payable on departure from Syria.

Damascus Airport is 29km/18 miles from the city centre.

Road

Syria has good road links with Beirut and Amman and there are regular bus and shared taxi services to both these destinations.

ENTRY REGULATIONS

Visas

Visas are required by nationals of all countries except: Algeria, Bahrain, Egypt, Iraq, Jordan, Kuwait, Lebanon, Libya, Mauritania, Morocco, Oman, Qatar, Saudi Arabia, Sudan, Tunisia, UAE, Yemen Arab Republic and People's Democratic Republic of Yemen.

Visas are obtainable from Syrian embassies and consulates abroad.

Entry visas are usually valid for only one entry and for a stay of up to 2 weeks without any residence formalities. If a longer stay is intended, the visitor must report, with two photographs, to the Department of Security and Police. Visitors staying in Syria for any length of time should register with their own embassy or consulate.

Transit visas are valid for a stay of up to 3 days. Emergency visas can be obtained at Damascus Airport and the land frontiers.

Visit visas are valid for re-entry into Syria if the visitor leaves for a neighbouring country and returns to Syria within one month of the date of first entry.

Evidence in a passport of a previous or planned visit to Israel may adversely affect the granting of a visa.

Business visitors should support their visa application with a letter from their firm giving full details of the business to be undertaken, the full itinerary for the proposed visit and confirming financial responsibility for the applicant.

Health Regulations

An International Certificate of Vaccination against smallpox is required. Cholera and typhoid vaccinations are recommended.

Customs

Currency: There is no restriction on the amount of foreign currency which may be taken into or out of Syria. There is a limit of £Syr100 to the amount of Syrian currency which may be exported or imported. A currency declaration may have to be made on arrival and departure.

Duty-free articles: Articles for personal use are admitted free of duty. Limited amounts of personal jewellery may be taken into or out of Syria without completing a customs declaration form. The admission of and export of gold coins and bars, jewellery and pearls for commercial purposes are subject to strict customs regulations. Samples of no value.

Articles liable to duty: Samples of commercial value may be temporarily imported for a period of 3 months (which may be extended) subject to the normal import duty being deposited. The deposit is returned if the samples are re-exported within the time limit.

PRACTICAL INFORMATION FOR THE VISITOR

1. Currency

Monetary Unit – Syrian pound (lira), divided into 100 piastres (or qirsh).
Notes – 1, 5, 10, 25, 50, 100, 500 £Syr.
Coins – 5, 10, 25, 50, 100 (£Syr1) piastres.

Travellers are advised to obtain some Syrian currency before arriving in Syria; travellers' cheques are not always accepted at exchange offices at Damascus Airport or at land frontiers.

Banking Hours:
0800–1400 Saturday to Thursday.

The Syrian banking system is government-owned.

Domestic Commercial Banks in Damascus:

Central Bank of Syria (bank of issue)
Shabander Square, P.O. Box 2254, ☎ 16800/24800.
Commercial Bank of Syria
Mouawiah Street, P.O. Box 933, Harika (specialised bank for internal and foreign trade – branches across the country).
Other banks include the Agricultural Bank, the Industrial Development Bank, the Popular Credit Bank and the Real Estate Bank.

2. Electricity Supply

Damascus: 115/200V AC or 220/380V AC 3 phase 50Hz.
Aleppo: Domestic electricity is supplied on the same system as in Damascus, but at 115V AC.

3. Weights and Measures

The metric system is used, but cloth is occasionally measured in yards.

4. Media

Television broadcasting is government-controlled and the commercial service accepts advertising. Further information is available from the Directorate of Television, Advertising Section, Omayad Square, Damascus, ☎ 11200.
English-language news programmes can be heard daily on the radio:
0900/1030 Medium Wave 344m and 280m
2230/2400 Medium Wave 344m, 280m and 228m

Newspapers (daily):

In Damascus: *Al-Baath; Al-Thaura; Tishrin.* In Aleppo: *Al-Jamahir al-Arabia.*

There are a number of weekly newspapers and periodicals, all with limited circulation. No foreign language newspapers are published in Syria; the *Financial Times* and the *Economist* are often available.

5. Medical Care

A number of English-speaking European and American trained doctors can be found in Damascus, Aleppo and other large towns.

Tap water is safe in Damascus, but elsewhere it is best to boil the water or drink bottled mineral water. Raw fruit should be peeled and salads should only be eaten in the better hotels and restaurants (unless one is sure they have been thoroughly washed).

6. Telephone, Telex and Postal Services

There is an adequate inter-urban telephone service and communication with Amman is also available. International services are not very developed, but telegraphic communications are generally quick and reliable.

There is no public telex service, but facilities are available at many of the larger hotels.

The main post office in Damascus is open from 0800–2000 hours every day. Postal orders for foreign currency are not obtainable in Syria.

7. Public Holidays

Fixed Holidays:

1 January	*New Year's Day*
8 March	*Syrian Revolution Day*
17 April	*Independence Day*
1 September	*Union of Syria–Egypt–Libya*
25 December	*Christmas Day*

Muslim Holidays:

These follow the Muslim calendar and occur 10–12 days earlier every year. The dates of the Muslim holidays are approximate as they depend upon sightings of the moon, and may differ by one or two days from those given below. 1981 dates are:

18 January	*Prophet's Birthday*
31 July –2 August	*Eid el Fitr (3–4 days)*
8–10 October	*Eid el Adha*
29 October	*Muslim New Year*

The Christian festival of *Easter* (Latin and Greek Orthodox) is also a public holiday.

8. Time

GMT+2 (+3 May to September)

9. Internal Transport

Air

Syrian Arab Airlines operate services between Damascus, Aleppo, Deir-ez-Zor, Qamishly, Palmyra and Latakia.

Airline Offices in Damascus:

Aeroflot	☎ 111363.
Air France	☎ 116865/119567.
British Airways	☎ 228221/3.
JAL	☎ 223988/220854.
KLM	☎ 113395/6.
Lufthansa	☎ 111165/119593.
Pan Am	☎ 112500/1.
PIA	☎ 111755/6.
SAS	☎ 116604/118801.
Swissair	☎ 223424/112500.
TWA	☎ 223988.

Road

Regular bus and shared taxi services are available to all parts of the country.

All vehicles entering Syria must take out Third Party Insurance at the border (valid for 10 days). A *Carnet de Passages en Douanes* and International Driving Licence are required.

Driving is on the right-hand side of the road and there is a speed limit of 40kph (25mph) in towns, although this may be lower in the town centre itself.

Visitors are advised to use taxis for local and inter-town trips. Fares should be negotiated with the driver before starting a journey.

10. Tipping

Taxis – usually no tip.

Porters – 50–100 piastres per bag.

Hotels/restaurants – 10% of the bill if a service charge is not already included.

11. Social Customs

Syria is a Muslim country but less strict than some in attitude towards observance of religious customs. Alcohol is available in the main centres.

For further information, refer to page 12 under 'Muslim Social Customs'.

12. Photography

No attempt should be made to photograph anything remotely concerned with the armed forces, or anything near defence installations, including such things as radio transmission aerials. Visitors should also be careful about photographing Syrian peasants who tend to regard the camera with suspicion. A responsible official or police officer should be consulted if there is any doubt.

USEFUL ADDRESSES (GENERAL)

Embassies in Damascus

France: rue Ata Ayoubi, B.P. 769.

West Germany: 53 rue Ibrahim Hanano, B.P. 2237, ☎ 336070/71.

Japan: No. 15 Avenue Al-Jala'a, B.P. 3366, ☎ 339421/338273.

Netherlands: Abou Roemaneh, Place Abou-Alaa-Al-Maari No. 116, B.P. 702, ☎ 336871/337661.

Switzerland: Malki, 31 rue M. Kurd Ali, Immeuble Hazzam, B.P. 234, ☎ 335474.

UK: 11 Kotob Building (3rd Floor), Mohammad Kurd Ali Street, B.P. 37, ☎ 332561/3.

US: Abu Rumaneh, No. 2 Al Monsur Street, B.P. 29, ☎ 332315/332814.

Other addresses

Tourist Information, Boulevard du 29 mai, B.P. 201, Damascus.

American Express Authorised Representative: Amlevco Tours, Mouradi Building, rue Fardous, B.P. 507, Damascus, ☎ 111652/119553.

Thomas Cook Authorised Representative: Khoury Bros., Sharia Al-Nasar, B.P. 157, Damascus, ☎ 112500.

Ministry of Information, Damascus, ☎ 111702.

Ministry of Culture and National Guidance, Damascus, ☎ 331557.

Ministry of Tourism, Damascus, ☎ 114918.

BUSINESS INFORMATION

The State Trading Organisations, based in Damascus, have a virtual monopoly of the public sector in Syria, although a recent reassertion of the private sector has established Aleppo as an important trading centre. Nevertheless, Damascus remains the main centre for business activity.

The import of many basic foodstuffs, raw materials, pharmaceuticals, fertilisers, vehicles, tractors, tyres etc. is reserved to the State Trading Organisations which often insist on dealing direct with foreign suppliers and not through local agents. Where other products are concerned, business is best done through a local agent – this is essential when dealing with government departments and official bodies.

Only firms owned by Syrian nationals may hold agencies of foreign suppliers. The majority of agents are based in Damascus and Aleppo. It may prove difficult to find a Syrian agent as the activities of private importers have been reduced by the high incidence of nationalisation and state trading.

Import and Exchange Control Regulations

Imports into Syria are classified as either prohibited or permissible – prohibited imports are generally those goods manufactured locally which the authorities wish to protect. An import licence must be obtained for all permissible imports.

Importation and exportation to and from designated Free Zones are exempt from restrictions and exchange regulations. The General Authority for Free Zones supervises the administration and exploitation of the Free Zones and markets in Syria. Free Zones currently administered by the General Authority are: Damascus, Adra, Damascus International Airport, Aleppo, Latakia and Tartous.

Exchange control regulations are stringent and there has been a unified rate of exchange since 1973.

Business Hours

Government Offices:

	0800–1400	Saturday to Thursday

Business Houses:

Winter:	0900–1400 1600–1900	Saturday to Thursday
Summer:	0830–1330 1700–2000	Saturday to Thursday

Government offices, banks and Muslim firms close on Friday and remain open on Sunday. Christian firms generally close on Sunday and remain open on Friday, although some follow the Muslim custom.

During the month of Ramadan, government offices open daily from 0900–1400. Work in most business houses usually slows down at this time.

Business Events

The Damascus International Fair is held annually in July–August. For further details contact: The General Directorate of the Damascus International Fair, 67 Boulevard de Baghdad, Damascus.

USEFUL ADDRESSES (BUSINESS)

Chamber of Commerce, Mouawia Street, Harika Quarter, P.O. Box 1040, Damascus, ☎ 111339/118339.

Chamber of Industry, Mouawia Street, Harika Quarter, P.O. Box 1305, Damascus.

Chamber of Commerce, Moutanabbi Street, Aleppo, ☎ 14236.

Chamber of Industry, Moutanabbi Street, Aleppo.

Ministry of Economy and Foreign Trade, Damascus, ☎ 113513.

Aftomachine (Foreign Trade Organisation for Machinery and Equipment), Fardous Street, B.P. 3130, Damascus, ☎ 118480.

Aftometal (Foreign Trade Organisation for Metals and Building Materials), Joumhouriya Street, B.P. 3136, Damascus, ☎ 223731.

Gota (General Organisation for Trade and Artisan Products), B.P. 15, Damascus.

Tafco (Foreign Trade Organisation for Chemicals and Foodstuffs), B.P. 893, Joumhuriya Street, Damascus.

MAJOR CITIES AND TOWNS

Damascus

The ancient city of Damascus dates back over 4,000 years. The Anti-Lebanon mountains form a picturesque background to the city, although the outskirts are gradually expanding and creeping up onto the surrounding hillside.

The city contains many ruins and relics from its Christian past, including the site of John the Baptist's tomb – the Ummayad Mosque, and the House of Hanania which once served as St Paul's refuge. Other buildings of historic interest in Damascus are the Sulaimaniya Mosque, the Al-Azm Palace and the National Museum which houses an extensive collection of Islamic art, including many ancient, illustrated copies of the Koran.

Damascus Airport is 29km/18 miles from the city centre.

Hotels

The Ministry of Tourism classifies hotels as deluxe, 1st class, 2nd class, etc.

DAMASCUS SHERATON (deluxe), Omayad Square, P.O. Box 4795, ☎ 224200.
New hotel in striking Oriental style, Standing in its own gardens near the diplomatic area of the city and 5 minutes from the centre.
Rooms: 350. Suites available.
Facilities: Grill room, cocktail lounge, coffee shop and nightclub. Tennis, sauna and swimming. Shopping arcade. Hairdresser. Travel agency.
Services: TC, FC. Amex, Bankamericard, Carte Blanche, Diners Club and Eurocard. Dr. on call.
Conference room – max. capacity 550.
Banquet rooms – max. capacity 500.

DAMASCUS INTERNATIONAL (1st class), Bahsa Street, P.O. Box 5068, ☎ 112400.
First-class hotel in the city centre.
Rooms: 150, on request. Suites available.
Facilities: Restaurant (international and Oriental cuisine), bars and nightclub. Car hire.
Services: TC, FC. Amex. Dr. on call.
Conference room – max. capacity 150.
Banquet rooms – max. capacity 300.

INTERNATIONAL AIRPORT HOTEL, P.O. Box 4101, ☎ 225401.
First-class hotel near the airport, 26km/16 miles from the city centre.

Rooms: 48, soundproof, ☎.
Facilities: Restaurant (Oriental and European cuisine), 24-hour coffee shop, bars, nightclub and casino. Swimming, tennis and riding. Shopping arcade. Car hire.
Services: TC, FC. Carte Blanche. S. Airport transfer available.
Conference room – max. capacity 50.

MERIDIEN DAMAS (deluxe), Avenue Choukry Kouwalty, P.O. Box 5531, ☎ 229200.
Modern hotel facing the Damascus International Fair, 5 minutes' walk from the business centre of the city.
Rooms: 372, ☎. Suites available.
Facilities: Restaurants and bars, discotheque. Tennis, sauna and swimming. Shopping arcade.
Services: TC, FC. Amex and Diners Club. S. Dr. on call.
Conference room – max. capacity 800.
Banquet rooms – max. capacity 600.

NEW OMAYAD (1st class), Bresil Street, ☎ 117700.
Traditional hotel near the business centre, government offices and embassies.
Rooms: 70, on request, ☎. Suites available.
Facilities: Restaurant, bars, pizzeria and snack bar. Roof garden. Tennis.
Services: TC, FC, S. Dr. on call.
Conference room – max. capacity 100.

Restaurants

Toledo, Khalil Mardam Bey Street, ☎ 333810; *Ali Baba*, Fardous Street, ☎ 119881; *Caves du Roi*, Ahmed Moureywed Street, ☎ 330093; *Abu Kamel*, 29 Ayyar Street, ☎ 115216.

Others include the *Al-Gursan* (Versailles), the *Al-Bustan* (Vendôme), the *Kurtuba* (Piccadilly), the *Chaumière* and the *Orient Club*.

Shopping

Best buys: copper and brassware, silk brocades, mother-of-pearl inlaid boxes.

Aleppo

References to Aleppo in ancient manuscripts date back to the third millennium B.C., and the city clearly equals Damascus in terms of its historic interest. The Citadel is one of the main attractions and Aleppo has many fine old mosques. It is also well known for its old houses with their characteristic courtyards and fountains.

Aleppo's importance as Syria's major town in the north will be strengthened by the various development projects in the area of the Euphrates basin.

Aleppo/Neirab Airport is 5km/3 miles from the city centre.

Hotels

BARON (1st class), Baron Street, ☎ 10880.
Traditional hotel near the business and shopping districts of Aleppo.
Rooms: 60 and 2 suites. ☎.
Facilities: Restaurant and bar. Car hire. Travel agencies nearby.
Services: TC, FC. Credit cards not accepted. S. Dr. on call.

RAMSIS (1st/2nd class), Baron Street, P.O. Box 5097, ☎ 16700.
The hotel is in the city centre close to all the main amenities.
Rooms: 45 in some, ☎.
Facilities: Restaurant, bar and lounge.
Services: TC, FC. Credit cards not accepted. S. Dr. on call.

Restaurants

Apart from the hotel restaurants, others in Aleppo include the *Bachour* and *Hagob* restaurants.

TUNISIA

Republic of Tunisia

Size: 164,107 sq.km/63,362 sq.miles.

Population: 6.07 million (1978).

Distribution: 47% in urban areas.

Density: 36 persons per sq.km/93 per sq.mile.

Population Growth Rate: 2.3% p.a.

Ethnic Composition: The majority of the population are Arabs and Berbers. The number of Europeans living in Tunisia has continued to decrease since the country's independence in 1956. Today the European community numbers around 40,000 (mainly French and Italian) and is concentrated in and around Tunis.

Capital: Tunis Pop. 944,000.

Major Towns: Sfax Pop. 475,000; Sousse Pop. 255,000; Bizerte Pop. 62,000; Kairouan Pop. 54,000.

Language: Arabic is the official language. French is widely used in education, commerce and administration. English is rarely understood.

Religion: Most of the population are Sunni Muslims. The European community is largely Roman Catholic and there are Protestant, Greek Orthodox and Jewish minorities.

Government: Tunisia has a presidential regime and executive power lies with the President who chooses his own Prime Minister and government ministers. The National Assembly is elected by direct universal suffrage every five years.

The Parti Socialiste Destourien (PSD) is Tunisia's sole political party.

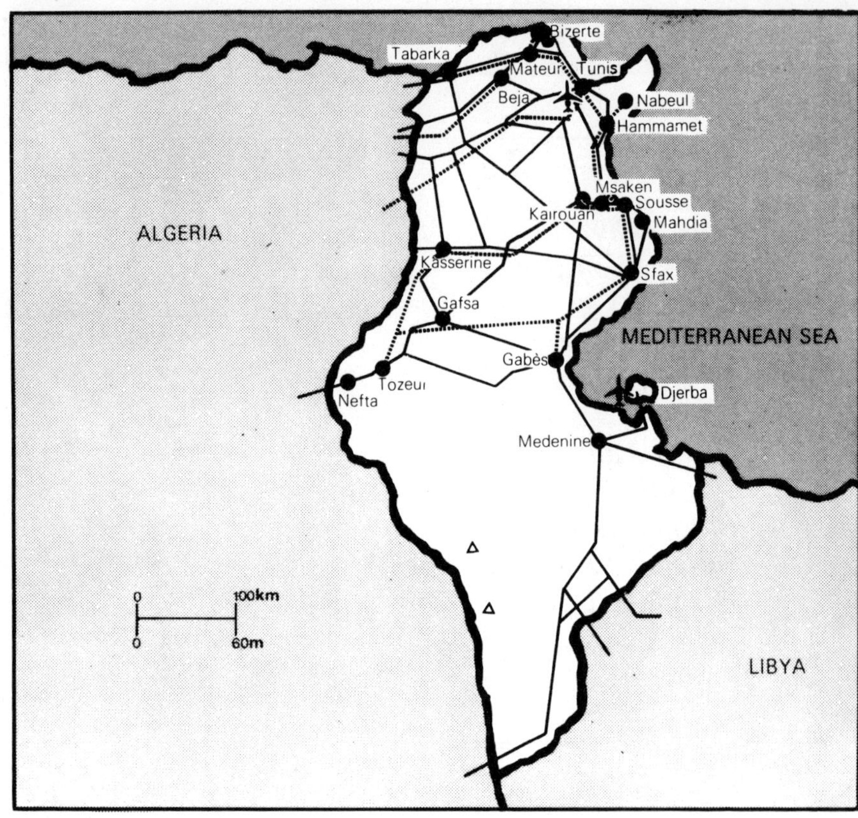

GEOGRAPHY

Tunisia is bordered by Algeria to the west, Libya to the southeast and by the Mediterranean to the north and east.

The country consists of three distinct physical regions. To the north are the mountains of the Tell Atlas (400–800m/1,320–2,640ft) and the Dorsale mountains near the Algerian border. The valley of the Medjerda lies between these two ranges and to the east are the fertile alluvial plains extending from Bizerte to Sfax. This is the principal cultivated area of Tunisia and the majority of the population live here where the country's chief cities have grown up.

South of the Dorsale range are the steppelands and expanse of salt lakes known as *chotts*. The chief one is the Chott el-Djerid which is surrounded by a number of oases and has now been partially developed for tourists. Further south lies the vast Sahara desert sector of Tunisia.

Climate

Northern and coastal Tunisia have a Mediterranean climate with temperatures ranging from 30°C/85°F to 37°C/100°F in summer, and average temperatures of

13°C/55°F in winter. Rainfall is concentrated in the winter months. Winter temperatures are generally cooler inland. Southern Tunisia has a desert climate and virtually no rainfall.

Agriculture

Approximately half of the population of Tunisia is dependent on agriculture for a livelihood, but the contribution of agriculture to the national income is declining.

Following independence, the Government introduced various co-operative schemes and the former European farms were nationalised. Much of the state-owned land has now reverted to private ownership and government involvement is largely in the form of credit schemes.

Olives are the main agricultural export, and Tunisia is the world's fourth-largest producer of olive oil.

A number of irrigation development schemes are being carried out in the north, partly financed by aid from West Germany and Canada in particular.

Main Crops: olives, wheat, barley, citrus fruits, dates, grapes, vegetables.

Mineral Resources: phosphates, iron ore, lead, zinc.

THE ECONOMY

Gross National Product (1976): US$4.5 billion.

Per Capita Income (1976): US$784.

Gross Domestic Product (1977): TD2,127 million.

Foreign Trade (1976): Total Imports US$1.4 billion; Total Exports US$814 million.

Main Trading Partners: Imports – France, Italy, West Germany, USA, UK. Exports – France, Italy, USA, West Germany, Greece, Brazil, Libya.

The Tunisian economy is primarily based on agriculture although its importance as a foreign-exchange earner has declined. Mining is the main industrial activity and the increase in the world price of phosphates, together with an increased demand for oil, has strengthened the economy considerably. Oil is Tunisia's principal export by value and the country has substantial oil and natural gas reserves.

Tunisia has been successful in attracting private investment and foreign aid – one of the main reasons for the former being the modest labour costs. This has enabled the implementation of ambitious economic development plans, particularly in the field of job creation which has been a major priority. A new focus on those manufacturing industries producing goods for export has also helped to alleviate the unemployment problem. Tourism plays an important role in the economy and has grown rapidly over the last decade.

Industry consists mainly of the processing of local raw materials with the State playing a dominant part in the major industries such as mining and the associated chemical industry. Phosphates production continues to increase and there has been recent growth in the textile and food-processing industries.

Major Industries: phosphates, chemicals and fertilisers, food processing, textiles, oil refining, cement and building materials, pulp and paper.

Main Commodities Traded: Imports – machinery and transport equipment, metal goods, sugar, wheat, industrial raw materials. Exports – petroleum, phosphates, olive oil, chemicals, wine.

Tunisia is a member of the OAU (Organisation of African Unity) and the Arab League.

HOW TO GET THERE

Air

Tunisia has three international airports – the principal one being Tunis-Carthage Airport 14km/9 miles from Tunis. The two other international airports are at Monastir and Djerba.

Major airlines serving Tunis-Carthage Airport are Aeroflot, Air France, Alitalia, British Airways, British Caledonian, KLM, Lufthansa, SAS, Sabena and Swissair with direct flights from Brussels, Frankfurt, London, Milan, Munich, Paris and Rome.

Tunis Air fly from French and other European cities, as well as from many Middle East capitals.

Flying times to Tunis: from London 2¾ hours; from New York 12 hours.

An airport tax of 1 dinar is payable on departure from Tunisia.

Sea

Regular passenger and car ferry services operate between Marseilles, Genoa, Naples, Palermo and Tunis. The main shipping lines involved are DFDS Seaways, the Tirrenia Line and the Société Nationale Maritime Corse Méditerranée (SNCM).

Rail

Tunis has rail links with Annaba and Constantine in Algeria via Souk Ahras.

Road

There is access to Tunisia by car from both Algeria and Libya. Motorists need an International Driving Licence, log book and insurance (international green card).

ENTRY REGULATIONS

Visas

Visas are required by nationals of all countries except: UK and holders of passports which bear on the cover United Kingdom of Great Britain and Northern Ireland, Jersey, Guernsey and its Dependencies, Hong Kong (1 month); also Barbados, Canada, Fiji, Ghana, Malaysia, Malta, Mauritius for a stay of up to 3 months except where otherwise stated. Also Algeria (unlimited stay), Austria, Belgium, Bulgaria (2 months), Chile, Denmark, Finland, France, West Germany (4 months), Greece (1 month), Guinea, Iceland, Iran, Republic of Ireland, Italy, Ivory Coast, Japan, South Korea (1 month), Kuwait, Liberia, Liechtenstein, Luxembourg, Mali, Mauritania, Monaco, Morocco (unlimited stay), Netherlands, Niger, Norway, Pakistan, Romania, San Marino, Senegal, Spain, Sweden, Switzerland, Turkey, USA (4 months) and Yugoslavia for a stay of up to 3 months except where otherwise stated.

All other nationals require visas obtainable from Tunisian embassies and consulates abroad.

Transit visas are issued for a stay of up to 7 days.

Evidence in a passport of a previous or planned visit to Israel may adversely affect the granting of a visa.

Health Regulations

Visitors are advised to be in possession of a valid certificate of vaccination against smallpox. Certificates of vaccination against smallpox, cholera and yellow fever are required if arriving from an infected area. TAB (typhoid and paratyphoid) inoculations are recommended.

Customs

Currency: The import and export of Tunisian currency is prohibited. There is no limit to the amount of foreign currency which may be taken into Tunisia.

It is advisable to exchange foreign currency and travellers' cheques in small amounts as it is often difficult to exchange back dinars and this will only be done on production of exchange slips from Tunisian banks. The amount of excess currency exchanged back into foreign currency must not exceed 30% of the foreign currency originally exchanged or 100 dinars, whichever is the greater.

Duty-free articles: Personal effects, 200 cigarettes or 50 cigars or 400g of tobacco, and 1 litre of alcohol. Samples of no commercial value and those deemed unusable. (Samples of commercial value are admitted duty-free on payment of a deposit or the provision of a bond equivalent to the normal duties and taxes. The deposit is refunded or the bond cancelled if the samples are re-exported within 6 months.)

PRACTICAL INFORMATION FOR THE VISITOR

1. Currency

Monetary Unit – Tunisian dinar (TD), divided into 1,000 millimes (m).
Notes – ½, 1, 5, 10 dinars.
Coins – 1, 2, 5, 10, 20, 50, 100, 500 millimes.

Banking Hours:

Winter	– 0800–1100	Monday to
	1400–1600	Friday
Summer	– 0730–1100	Monday to Friday

The Banque Centrale de Tunisie, 7 Place de la Monnaie, Tunis is the central bank of issue.

Principal Domestic Banks in Tunis:

Banque de Tunisie
2 Avenue de la France.
Société Tunisienne de Banque
1 Avenue Habib Thameur (correspondent of numerous foreign banks).
Union Internationale de Banque
65 Avenue Habib Bourguiba.

Foreign Banks in Tunis:

Arab Bank Ltd
21 rue al Djazira.
Chase Manhattan Bank
3 rue de Guinée, Place Jeanne d'Arc.

2. Electricity Supply

110V and 220V AC 50Hz.
Plugs: 2-pin.

3. Weights and Measures

The metric system is in use.

4. Media

Radiodiffusion Télévision Tunisienne broadcasts in Arabic, French and Italian. There is no commercial advertising on either radio or TV.

Newspapers:

There are five national daily newspapers in Tunisia: *L'Action* (PSD); *La Presse de Tunisie*; *Le Temps*; *Al Amal* (PSD); and *Al Sabah*.

There are a number of provincial daily newspapers as well as weekly and monthly journals. *Dialogue* and *Jeune Afrique* are the two main French-language weekly magazines.

5. Medical Care

The water supply in the main towns is drinkable, but mineral water is safer and readily available. Foreign visitors may suffer from stomach disorders, particularly during the hot summer months, and are advised to take suitable precautionary medicines.

6. Telephone, Telex and Postal Services

Telexes can be sent from the Central Post Office, rue Charles de Gaulle, Tunis, ☎ 245961, the Hilton Hotel in Tunis and from other large hotels.

The Central Post Office also has a 24-hour telegram service and *poste restante* facilities. There is a post office at Tunis-Carthage Airport.

7. Public Holidays

Fixed Holidays:

1 January	*New Year's Day*
18 January	*Anniversary of the National Revolution*
20 March	*Independence Day*
9 April	*Martyrs' Day*
1 May	*Labour Day*
1 June	*Fête de la Victoire*
2 June	*Fête de la Jeunesse*
25 July	*Republic Day*
3 August	*President's Birthday*
13 August	*Women's Day*
3 September	*Memorial Day*
15 October	*Evacuation Day*

Muslim Holidays:

These follow the Muslim calendar and occur 10–12 days earlier every year. The dates of the Muslim holidays are approximate as they depend upon sightings of the moon, and may differ by one or two days from those given below. 1981 dates are:

18 January	*Mouled* (Prophet's Birthday)
31 July –2 August	*Eid el Seghir* (end of *Ramadan*)
8–10 October	*Feast of the Sacrifice*
29 October	*Ras El Am El Hejir* Muslim New Year

Business travellers are advised to avoid visiting Tunisia during the month of *Ramadan*.

8. Time

GMT+1 (+2 May to September)

9. Internal Transport

Air

Tunis Air operates internal air services between Tunis and Monastir and Djerba. Unscheduled charter flights are operated by Tunisavia between Tunis and Sfax and other main towns.

Airline Offices in Tunis:

Aeroflot	☎ 249779/249773.
Air France	☎ 247922/255422.
British Caledonian	☎ 244261/246967.
KLM	☎ 242500.
Lufthansa	☎ 240714/241905.
PIA	☎ 245785/259189.
SAS	☎ 259800.
Swissair	☎ 242122.
Tunis Air	☎ 288100.

Rail

Most of the main towns are linked by railway services operated by the Société Nationale des Chemins de Fer Tunisiens.

Road

Self-drive cars are available for hire. An International Driving Licence is required. Traffic drives on the right-hand side of the road.

Car-Hire Firms in Tunis:

Avis, 90 Avenue de la Liberté, ☎ 282508/285734.

Europcar, 39 Avenue Kherredine Pacha, ☎ 287304.

Garage Excelsior, 53 Avenue de Paris, ☎ 245023.

Garage Majestic, 38 Avenue de Paris, ☎ 258228.

Hertz, 29 Avenue Habib Bourguiba, ☎ 248529.

Palace Garage, 15 Avenue de Madrid.

Long-distance taxis (*louages*) can be hired at reasonable rates for inter-town travel. These depart from fixed points in each town and the rates are fixed officially.

Within the towns an efficient form of travel is the bébé taxi – a small car operated as a taxi.

A radio taxi service is also in operation in Tunis: Société Radio Taxi, 39 Boulevard Bechir Sfar, ☎ 282866.

10. Tipping

Taxis – 100 millimes.

Porters – 100 millimes per bag.

Hotels/restaurants – 10% of the bill.

11. Social Customs

Although Tunisia is a Muslim country, social customs and practices are less restrictive than in the stricter Muslim states, and life in the capital, Tunis, is relatively informal. Most mosques in Tunisia are open to non-Muslims.

It is useful to take note of the forms of address used in government and business circles. Senior company officials should be addressed as simply *Monsieur* or *Monsieur* followed by their surname, while government ministers should be addressed as *Monsieur le Ministre*.

For further information, refer to page 12 under 'Muslim Social Customs'.

USEFUL ADDRESSES (GENERAL)

Embassies in Tunis

Canada: 2 Place Virgile, Notre-Dame de Tunis, B.P. 31 Belvédère, ☎ 286577.

France: Place de l'Indépendance, B.P. 689.

West Germany: 18 rue Felicien Challaye, B.P. 35, ☎ 281246.

Japan: 16 rue Djebel Aures, Notre-Dame, B.P. 1009, ☎ 285937/285960.

Netherlands: 24–26 Place de l'Afrique, ☎ 241481/ 241561.

Switzerland: 17 Avenue de France, B.P. 501, ☎ 245003.

UK: 5 Place de la Victoire, ☎ 245100/245324.

US: 144 Avenue de la Liberté, ☎ 282566.

Other addresses

Office National du Tourisme Tunisien, 1 Avenue Mohammed V, Tunis, ☎ 259217/8.

Ministry of Cultural Affairs and Information, Place du Gouvernement, Tunis.

Wagons-Lits Tourisme, 65 Avenue Habib Bourguiba, Tunis, ☎ 242673/247320.

American Express Authorised Representative: Tourafric, 52 Avenue Habib Bourguiba, Tunis, ☎ 245066.

BUSINESS INFORMATION

The import of consumer goods into Tunisia is restricted by import licensing and import substitution. However, the import of raw materials and semi-finished goods, together with agricultural and industrial equipment, has increased significantly in recent years, partly financed by foreign aid.

The Tunisian market is a small one, but with the reduction in the advantages given to French goods, it is becoming more competitive. Most sales are made by personal contact between the buyer and the seller, and both stockist and commission agents are also used.

Several government organisations have been established to undertake agency work and have a monopoly or near-monopoly in their particular sectors. Many large-scale purchases are made by these organisations which also deal with government contracts.

Import and Exchange Control Regulations

Import licences are required for all permitted imports and a few categories of goods may be imported only by state monopolies. Preferential quotas are available for certain imports from the EEC. Bilateral agreements provide for a number of products from France, Algeria, Morocco, Niger, Senegal and the Ivory Coast to enter at preferential rates of duty. The EEC/Tunisian Trade Agreement provides for preferential duty rates for some goods of EEC origin.

The possession of an import licence guarantees that the appropriate foreign currency will be available for payment. An *autorisation préalable* constitutes a right for foreign exchange and authorises the importer to make all payments specified in the contract.

Business Hours

Government Offices:
Winter –
0830–1300, 1500–1745 } Monday to Thursday
0830–1330 Friday and Saturday
Summer –
0730–1100 Monday to Saturday

Business Houses:
Winter –
0800–1200, 1430–1800 } Monday to Friday
0800–1200 Saturday
Summer –
0700–1300 Monday to Saturday

Business Events

The Tunis International Trade Fair has been held at irregular intervals since 1953. Further details can be obtained from: Foire Internationale de Tunis, Palais de la Foire, Avenue Mohammed V, Tunis.

BUSINESS SERVICES

Forwarding/Clearing Agents (including collection and/or despatch of samples)

Agence Africaine de Consignation et Commerce, 5 rue Champlain, Tunis.
Agence Bahri Said Ben Said, 16 bis Avenue des Nations-Unies, Tunis.
Compagnie Tunisienne d'Armement, 10 Avenue Farhat Hached, Tunis.
Lasry Brothers, 6 Avenue de Carthage, Tunis.
Société Générale de Surveillance, 8 rue Jean le Vacher, Tunis.
Socotu, 1 rue des Glacières, Tunis.
Tunisie-Maritime, 1 Avenue des Nations-Unies, Tunis.

USEFUL ADDRESSES (BUSINESS)

Chambre de Commerce de Tunis, 1 rue des Entrepreneurs, Tunis, ☎ 242872.

Chambre de Commerce du Centre, rue Chadly Khaznadar, Sousse.

Chambre de Commerce du Nord, 12 rue Ibn Khaldoun, Bizerte.

Chambre de Commerce du Sud, 21–23 rue Habib Thameur, Sfax.

Chambre Tuniso-Française de Commerce et d'Industrie, 14 rue de Vesoul, Tunis.

Agence de Promotion des Investissements (API), 18 Avenue Mohammed V, Tunis, ☎ 256022.

MAJOR CITY

Tunis

The most interesting part of Tunis for foreign visitors is the traditional *medina* with its narrow, winding alleys, *souks* and mosques. Entrance to the *medina* is through the gate known as Bab el-Bahar.

The *medina* contains a wealth of architectural delights: vaulted and ceramic-tiled courtyards or *zawias*, the eighteenth-century Palace of Dar Hussein, the ninth-century Great Mosque of Zitouna and the eleventh-century el-Ksar Mosque. The Museum of Islamic Art is open daily and contains some fine pieces of art.

The Punic capital of Carthage was founded in 815 B.C., but today is no more than a suburb of Tunis, and all that remains of the former Roman town are the Baths of Antonius and the port. An extensive collection of Roman art (and Punic and Islamic art) is housed in the Bardo Museum, about 5km/3 miles north of Tunis.

Tunis-Carthage Airport is 14km/9 miles from the centre of Tunis.

Hotels

The National Tourist Board grades hotels from 4 star deluxe, 4 star, etc., to 1 star.

AFRICA MERIDIEN (4 star deluxe), 50 Avenue Habib Bourguiba, ☎ 247477.
Modern hotel in the city centre, 15 minutes' drive from the airport.
Rooms: 168 ❄, ▥, ▲, ▭, ☎, ♨, ▣. Suites available.
Facilities: International restaurant, rooftop restaurant and bar, brasserie, bar, coffee shop. Shopping arcade. Cinema. Car hire. Golf, tennis, swimming, solarium.
Services: ▤ Access, Amex, Carte Blanche, Diners Club, Eurocard and Master Charge. **S**, ♿. Audio-visual equipment available. Dr. on call.
Conference room – max. capacity 500.

HILTON TUNIS (4 star deluxe), Avenue Salambo, B.P.1160, ☎ 282000.
Modern hotel in the Belvedere Park district of the city, 5 minutes from the city centre.
Rooms: 245 ❄, ▥, ▲, ▭, ♨, ▣. Suites available.
Facilities: Grill room, coffee shop, bars, dinner dancing. Swimming. Golf, tennis and riding privileges at nearby clubs. Car hire.
Services: **TC**, **FC**. ▤ Amex, Barclay Visa, Carte Blanche, Diners Club, Eurocard and Master Charge. **S**, ♿. Free transport to private beach and city centre. Audio-visual equipment available.
Conference room – max. capacity 450.
Banquet rooms – max. capacity 300.

INTERNATIONAL TUNISIA (4 star deluxe), 49 Avenue Habib Bourguiba, ☎ 254855/247854.
Modern hotel in the business centre of Tunis.
Rooms: 203 ❄, ▲, ▭.
Facilities: 2 restaurants, café, nightclub and bars. Conference and banquet facilities.
Services: ▤ Amex, Carte Blanche, Diners Club and Eurocard.

DU LAC (3 star), Avenue Habib Bourguiba, ☎ 258322.
Ultra-modern hotel in the city centre, 15 minutes from the airport.
Rooms: 200 ❄, ▥, ♨, ▣.
Facilities: Restaurant, bar and lounge. Golf, tennis and swimming. Ladies' and men's hairdressers.
Services: **TC**, **FC**. ▤ Amex, Diners Club and Eurocard. Dr. on call. **S**, ♿.

Restaurants

Apart from those restaurants in the larger hotels, others in Tunis are: *Chez Nous*, 5 rue de Marseille; *Chez Slah*, rue Pierre de Courbertin; *Hungaria*, 11 rue Bach Hamba; *Le Malouf*, rue de Yougoslavie (Tunisian); *M'Rabet*, Souk Ettrouk (Tunisian); *Le Palais*, Avenue de Carthage (Tunisian); *Strasbourg*, 100 rue de Yougoslavie (French).

Restaurants in the suburbs of Tunis: *Les Dunes*, Gammarth; *Le Pêcheur*, Gammarth (seafood); *Le Pirate*, Sidi Bou Said; *Neptune*, Carthage.

Nightclubs

The Hilton and Africa Hotels both have their own nightclubs. The *Café des Nattes* is a popular open-air nightclub at Sidi Bou Said. Several restaurants (including the *Palais*, *Malouf* and *M'Rabet*) have floor shows featuring belly-dancing.

Entertainment

The National Theatre in Tunis gives performances by local and visiting companies from November to May.

Opportunities for all watersports are very good and include skin-diving and deep-sea fishing. Horse racing takes place from October to May and there is camel riding at the beach resorts. There is a golf course at La Soukra (11km/7 miles from Tunis).

TURKEY

Republic of Turkey

Size: 766,640 sq.km/296,000 sq.miles.

Population: 42,130,000 (1978).

Distribution: 60% in rural areas.

Density: 53 persons per sq.km/138 per sq.mile.

Population Growth Rate: 2.5% p.a.

Ethnic Composition: The Kurds, who live mainly in the eastern part of Turkey, are the largest ethnic minority – over 4 million. There are also Arabic-speaking groups in the east, and Greek, Armenian, Circassian, Georgian and Jewish minorities – mainly in Istanbul.

Capital: Ankara Pop. 1,900,000.

Major Cities/Towns: Istanbul Pop 2,995,000; Izmir Pop. 900,000; Adana Pop. 500,000.

Language: Turkish is the mother tongue of over 90% of the population. English is the most widely used foreign language and many professional and technical workers speak French and/or German.

Religion: Almost 99% of the population are Muslims. There are small Christian and Jewish minorities, mainly in Istanbul and Izmir.

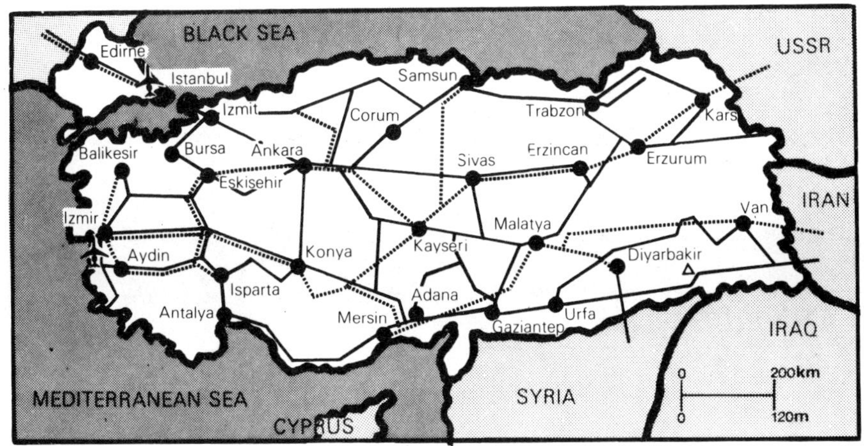

Government: Turkey was declared a republic in 1923 with the President as the Head of State. The Prime Minister is the head of the Government and is responsible to Parliament, which consists of a Senate and a National Assembly.

Turkey has several political parties of which the Republican People's Party and the Justice Party are the largest.

GEOGRAPHY

The greater part of Turkey lies in Asia (Anatolia) and is bordered by the Black Sea and the USSR to the north, by Iran to the east, and by Iraq, Syria and the Mediterranean to the south. European Turkey (Thrace) has borders with Greece and Bulgaria.

The country is predominantly mountainous and two mountain ranges – the Pontic in the north and the Taurus in the south – run from west to east across the country, enclosing the central Anatolian plateau. There are fertile plains along both the Black Sea and Mediterranean coasts of Turkey.

Climate

There is a sharp contrast in climate between the interior and the coastal areas. Winters inland are cold with snow and frost and average temperatures below freezing. Summers are hot and dry.

The Black Sea coast is mild and wet throughout much of the year, while the Aegean and Mediterranean coasts have mild, wet winters and hot, dry summers with high humidity in the southern coastal areas.

Agriculture

Over 60% of the labour force is engaged in agriculture and Turkey depends on agricultural surpluses for much of her export revenue. Many agricultural raw materials are used to supply Turkish industry. Considerable investment in agriculture is currently needed to maintain production growth and carry out irrigation and land improvement plans.

Main Crops: wheat, sugar beet, other cereals, olives, cotton, potatoes, fruits, nuts, tobacco.

Mineral Resources: coal, lignite, iron ore, chromite, copper and others.

THE ECONOMY

Gross National Product (1976): US$27.4 billion.

Per Capita Income (1976): US$681.

Gross Domestic Product (1977): TL807,000 million.

Foreign Trade (1976): Total Imports US$5.13 billion; Total Exports US$1.96 billion.

Main Trading Partners: Imports – West Germany, Iraq, USA, Italy, UK. Exports – West Germany, USA, Switzerland, Italy, USSR, UK.

The Turkish economy is a mixed one with private enterprise now accounting for nearly half the country's investment capital and approximately two-thirds of total industrial output.

Industrial development is aimed at providing consumer goods and reducing the level of industrial imports which has led to a considerable trade deficit in the past. This has been reduced by short-term borrowing and the devaluation of the Turkish lira. Development plans continue to suffer, however, from a lack of investment finance and foreign exchange. The economy has also suffered from a drop in workers' remittances following the sharp reduction in the number of Turkish workers recruited in Western Europe, and in West Germany in particular.

Industry is becoming more diversified and Turkey has a large steel industry as well as a variety of manufacturing industries. Through a policy of diversification, Turkey is aiming at self-sustained economic growth.

Major Industries: iron and steel, cotton textiles, cement, food processing, light engineering.

Main Commodities Traded: Imports – machinery, fuels, iron and steel. Exports – agricultural produce, minerals.

Turkey is a member of NATO, CENTO (Central Treaty Organisation) and the Organisation for Economic Co-operation and Development (OECD); also an associate member of the EEC.

HOW TO GET THERE

Air

Turkey has two international airports: Esenboğa which is 30km/19 miles from Ankara, and Yesilköy which is 24km/15 miles from Istanbul.

There are daily flights from London to Istanbul or Ankara by Turkish Airlines and British Airways, and from New York by Pan Am. Turkish Airlines also operate flights from Amsterdam, Athens, Brussels, Copenhagen, Frankfurt, Geneva, Milan, Munich, Paris, Rome, Vienna and Zurich.

Most major European airlines operate services to Turkey, but only Turkish Airlines connect several European countries directly with Izmir.

Flying times to Istanbul: from London 4 hours; from New York 15 hours; from Sydney 18 hours.

Sea

There are regular passenger services to Istanbul from Barcelona, Genoa, Marseilles and Naples, and from Venice to Izmir.

Rail

Scheduled rail services operate to Istanbul from Paris, Milan, Vienna and Munich.

Road

Turkey has road links with Greece, Bulgaria, Iran and Iraq.

ENTRY REGULATIONS

Visas

Nationals of the following countries do not require visas:
Australia, Bahamas, Barbados, Canada, Cyprus (only residents of the Turkish Federated area), Fiji, Gambia, Grenada, Guyana, Hong Kong, Jamaica, Kenya, Malta, Mauritius, New Zealand, Singapore, Trinidad and Tobago, Uganda and the UK (also British passport holders of Jersey, Guernsey, Antigua and Gibraltar) for a stay of up to 3 months.
Nationals of the following countries also do not require visas for a stay of up to 3 months except where otherwise stated:
Afghanistan (2 months), Austria, Belgium, Denmark, Finland, France, West Germany, Iceland, Iran, Republic of Ireland, Italy, Japan, South Korea, Liechtenstein, Luxembourg, Monaco, Morocco, Netherlands, Norway, Pakistan, Portugal (2 months), Romania (2 months), San Marino, Spain, Sweden, Switzerland, Tunisia, USA and Yugoslavia (2 months).

For a visit exceeding 3 months a residence permit must be obtained and visitors should notify the police of any change of address during their stay. Residence permits must be surrendered on departure from Turkey.

Business travellers should support their visa application with a letter from their firm giving full details of the business to be undertaken and confirming financial responsibility for the applicant.

Health Regulations

Visitors are not required to produce vaccination certificates unless arriving from an infected area. Cholera vaccinations are strongly recommended as there have been recent outbreaks of the disease in Eastern Turkey.

Customs

Currency: The import and export of Turkish currency is limited to 1,000 lira. Visitors bringing large amounts of foreign currency into Turkey which they may later wish to take out again (either part of or the whole amount) should obtain a written declaration or an endorsement in their passport from the Turkish authorities at the point of entry. Failure to do so could lead to confiscation of the currency on departure from Turkey. Bank exchange slips should also be retained as customs authorities may wish to see them as proof that local purchases being exported were bought with Turkish lira from authorised foreign exchange dealers.

Duty-free articles: Articles for personal use, 200 cigarettes or 50g of tobacco or 20 cigars, 1 litre of alcohol and 200g of tea.

Articles liable to duty: Samples of value may be imported duty-free provided a deposit for the amount of duty is paid and they are re-exported within 6 months. Samples and advertising matter are subject to duty at the same rate as commercial shipments of the goods represented.

Prohibited articles: The export of antiques without a licence is strictly prohibited.

PRACTICAL INFORMATION FOR THE VISITOR

1. Currency

Monetary Unit – Turkish lira (TL), divided into 100 kuruş.
Notes – 5, 10, 20, 50, 100, 500 lira.
Coins – 5, 10, 25, 50 kuruş and 1, 2½, 5 lira.

Travellers' cheques are widely accepted in Turkey and the Eurocheque system is in operation in banks in the main cities and towns.

Banking Hours:

0900–1200
1400–1730 Monday to Friday

The Central Bank of the Republic of Turkey is the bank of issue.

Turkey has about a dozen state banks including four development banks, and there are over forty commercial banks in operation.

Major Commercial Banks:

Türkiye Iş Bankasi
Galata Branch, Bankalar Street, Karakoy, Istanbul, ☎ 433000.
Ulus Square, Ankara, ☎ 110410.

Yapi ve Kredi Bankasi
Istiklal Caddesi 285, Beyoglu, Istanbul, ☎ 452030.
Kesiloy Branch, Atatürk Bulvari 93, Kesiloy Square, Ankara, ☎ 257620 (15 lines).

Akbank, TAS
Meclisi Mebusan Caddesi 65–69, Sindikli, Istanbul.
Istiklal Caddesi, Meymenet Han 417–419, Beyoglu, Istanbul.

Türk Diş Ticaret Bankasi
199–201 Cumhuriyet Caddesi, Harbiye, Istanbul.
19 Izmir Caddesi, Yenişehir, Ankara.

Osmanli Bankasi (Ottoman Bank)
Bankalar Caddesi, P.O. Box 297, Karaköy, Istanbul.

The four development banks are the State Investment Bank, the Industrial Development Bank, the Industrial Investment and Credit Bank and the State Tourism Bank. The Agricultural Bank is one of the largest financial institutions in Turkey.

2. Electricity Supply

110 or 220V AC (mainly 220V).
Plugs: 2 round pins.

3. Weights and Measures

The metric system is in use.

4. Media

Broadcasting is controlled by Turkish Radio and Television and advertising is accepted on both.

Newspapers (daily):

Milliyet; *Hurriyet*; *Gunaydin*; *Tercuman*; *Zafer* (Ankara).

Many daily newspapers are published in Turkey and the majority have a small, local circulation. Two English-language papers – the *Daily News* and *Outlook* (weekly) – are published in Ankara.

There is no trade press as such, but *Milliyet* has a page devoted to trade and economic news, and the British Chamber of Commerce of Turkey publishes a monthly trade journal.

5. Medical Care

Tap water is best avoided – all hotels and restaurants provide bottled water at a minimal cost. During the time of an epidemic, all water and milk should be boiled.

There have been recent outbreaks of cholera in Eastern Turkey but full publicity is always given to the existence of epidemic disease.

Istanbul Hospitals:

American Hospital ☎ 486030.
French Hospital ☎ 454070.
German Hospital ☎ 435500.

6. Telephone, Telex and Postal Services

International telephone calls can be made through the operator to most European countries and to the US. Public telephones are available and accept only tokens costing TL2.50, available at all post offices.
International telex facilities are available and there are public call offices at:
Main Post Office, Ulus Ankara (0900–1900 hours).
Main Post Office, Telegraf Gisesi, Sirkeci, Istanbul (open 24 hours).

7. Public Holidays

Fixed Holidays:

1 January	*New Year's Day*
23 April	*Independence Day*
1 May	*Spring Holiday*
19 May	*Sports Day*
27 May	*Constitution Day*
30 August	*Victory Day*
29 October	*Republic Day*

Muslim Holidays:

These follow the Muslim calendar and occur 10–12 days earlier every year. The dates of the Muslim holidays are approximate as they depend upon sightings of the moon, and may differ by one or two days from those given below.
1981 dates are:

31 July–2 August	*Seker Bayram* (end of *Ramadan*)
8–10 October	*Kurban Bayram* (Feast of the Sacrifice)

A public holiday which falls on a Sunday is not observed on an alternative day.

8. Time

GMT+2 (+3 in summer)

9. Internal Transport

Air

Turkish Airlines operates regular services between Istanbul, Ankara and Izmir.

Airline Offices:

Ankara

Aeroflot	☎ 170005.
Air France	☎ 253992/179702.
British Airways	☎ 178819/175988.
KLM	☎ 251519.
Lufthansa	☎ 253445/6.
Pan Am	☎ 253274/5.
PIA	☎ 170616.
Qantas	☎ 253274/5.
SAS	☎ 178600/255190.
Swissair	☎ 183152/4.
Turkish Airlines	☎ 440296.
TWA	☎ 182015.

Istanbul

Aeroflot	☎ 456202.
Air France	☎ 432424/9.
Air India	☎ 464017/471338.
British Airways	☎ 484235/8.
British Caledonian	☎ 478054/407644.
El Al	☎ 40192.
KLM	☎ 446204.
Lufthansa	☎ 465130/4.
Pan Am	☎ 474530.
PIA	☎ 404265.
Qantas	☎ 474530.
SAS	☎ 466075.
Swissair	☎ 484320.
Turkish Airlines	☎ 457055.
TWA	☎ 483610.

Sea

There are regular steamship services between Istanbul and the large coastal towns. The journey from Istanbul to Izmir takes 20–25 hours.

Rail

The Anadolu Express operates daily between Istanbul and Ankara (12 hours). Istanbul is also linked by rail with the coastal towns of Izmir, Mersin and Iskenderun.

Rail information (Istanbul):
☎ 360475 (Asian side)
☎ 270050 (European side)

Road

Self-drive cars are readily available in the cities and larger towns. An International Driving Licence is required for car hire. Traffic travels on the right-hand side of the road.

Car-Hire Firms:

Avis, Ankara, ☎ 254676.
Istanbul, ☎ 636542.
Hertz, Istanbul, ☎ 450756/448850.

There are two types of taxis available in the main cities – the ordinary type and the *dolmus* or shared taxi. *Dolmus* taxis are an economical way of travelling within a city and can be shared by as many as eight people. They usually operate along fixed routes and can be boarded anywhere en route. The *dolmus* system operates from Istanbul and Ankara to nearby towns.

Taxi meters in the ordinary taxis are unreliable and it is advisable to negotiate the fare before starting a journey.

10. Tipping

Taxis – no tip necessary, unless a taxi meter is in use when 10% of the fare is usual.

Porters – 5 lira per bag.

Hotels/restaurants – a service charge is included, but a tip of up to 10% can be given for special services.

11. Social Customs

Most Turks are Muslims, but over the last decade there has been a considerable amount of westernisation. It is common practice to shake hands on meeting someone. Unlike many of the Arab Muslim states, alcohol is not prohibited in Turkey.

For further information, refer to page number 12 under 'Muslim Social Customs'.

USEFUL ADDRESSES (GENERAL)

Embassies in Ankara

Australia: 83 Nenehatun Caddesi, Gazi Osman Pasa, ☎ 275318.

Canada: Nenehatun Caddesi No. 75, Gazi Osman Pasa, ☎ 275803.

France: Paris Caddesi No. 70, P.O. Box 403.

West Germany: Atatürk Bulvari 114, ☎ 189887/89.

Japan: Nenehatun Caddesi No. 66, Gazi Osman Pasa Mah, P.O. Box P.K. 31-Cankaya, ☎ 274324/5.

Netherlands: Sehit Ersan Caddesi 4, Cankaya, ☎ 274326/7.

Switzerland: Atatürk Bulvari No. 247, P.O. Box 25, ☎ 274316.

UK: Sehit Ersan Caddesi 46/A, Cankaya, ☎ 274310/5.

US: Atatürk Bulvari 110, ☎ 265470.

Other addresses in Ankara

American Express Authorised Representative: Turk Ekspres, Havacilik ve Turizm Ltd Sti, Sehit Adem Yavuz 12/B, Ankara, ☎ 252182/170576.

Tourist Information Office, Gazi Mustafa Kemal Bulvari 33, ☎ 173012.

Consulates in Istanbul

British Consulate-General, Tepebasi, Beyoglu, ☎ 447540.

Dutch Consulate, Istiklal Caddesi 393, Beyoglu, ☎ 495310/495311.

French Consulate, 8 Istiklal Caddesi (Taksim).

West German Consulate, Gümüssuyu Caddesi 16–18, ☎ 444997.

Japanese Consulate, Inonu Caddesi No. 24, Ayazpasa Taksim, ☎ 452533/452595.

Swiss Consulate, Husrev Gerede Caddesi 75/3, 2nd Floor, Tesvikiye-Istanbul, P.O. Box 122, ☎ 485070/71.

US Consulate, Mesrutiyet Caddesi, Tepebasi, ☎ 453220.

Other addresses in Istanbul

American Express Authorised Representative: Turk Ekspres Havacilik ve Turizm Ltd. Sti, Hilton Hotel, Beyoglu, P.O. Box 70, ☎ 483905/405640.

Tourist Information Office, Mesrutiyet Caddesi 57, Galatasaray, ☎ 456875.

Consulates in Izmir

British Consulate, Necatibey Bulvari 19/4, (PK 300), ☎ 45470/9.

Dutch Consulate, Cumhuriyet Meydani, Meydan Apartman 11/2, ☎ 132064.

West German Consulate, Atatürk Caddesi 260, ☎ 34916/32302.

US Consulate, Atatürk Caddesi 386, ☎ 132135/7.

Other addresses in Izmir

American Express Authorised Representative: Egetur Travel

Agency, Nato Arkasi, Cumhuriyet Caddesi, ☎ 37651/33088.

Tourist Information Office, Gazi Osman Pasa Bulvari 10/A, ☎ 142147.

Wagons-Lits Tourisme Authorised Representative: Key Tours Ltd, Atatürk Caddesi 212/1, ☎ 138150.

BUSINESS INFORMATION

The major priorities in recent Turkish development plans have been industrialisation, improvements to the country's infrastructure and the expansion of education, health facilities and other social services. However, a lack of investment finance together with attempts to reduce Turkey's import bill may result in the reduction of such improvement and development plans, and their fulfilment will depend largely on the amount of foreign aid forthcoming from the EEC countries and the United States in particular.

A large proportion of Western Europe's export trade with Turkey is done through local agents working mainly on a commission basis. Istanbul and Izmir are the chief markets for imported goods, while most government business is centred in Ankara. A large proportion of government business is done through the system of public tenders and a local representative or agent is essential for this purpose.

Import and Exchange Control Regulations

Imports are restricted by the import licensing and quota system. Most goods are subject to import licences, usually granted only to persons or firms in possession of an importer's certificate.

The issue of an import licence guarantees that the necessary foreign exchange will be made available.

Business Hours

Government Offices and Business Houses:

0830–1200
1300–1730 Monday to Friday

Business Events

An International Trade Fair is held annually at Izmir during late August–September. For further details contact: International Trade Fair of Izmir, 233 Mesyrutiyet Caddesi, Tepebasi, Beyoglu, Istanbul.

BUSINESS SERVICES

Translation

Türk Argüs Ajansi, PK 1025, Galata, Istanbul, ☎ 441634/498466.

Modern Tercüme Bürosu, Karanfil Sokak 49/2, Yenişehir, Ankara, ☎ 178122/181470.

Copies of Turkish legislation and government decrees in English may be obtained from these two firms. They will also arrange for documents to be translated provided due notice is given.

USEFUL ADDRESSES (BUSINESS)

Union of Chambers of Commerce, Industry and Commodity Exchanges of Turkey, 149 Atatürk Bulvari, Bakanliklar, Ankara.

Ankara Chamber of Commerce, Sehit Tegman Kalmaz Caddesi 20, Ankara.

Ankara Chamber of Industry, Izmir Caddesi 22/2, Ankara.

Istanbul Chamber of Commerce, Ragip Gumuspala Caddesi, Eminönü, Istanbul.

Izmir Chamber of Commerce, Atatürk Caddesi 126, Izmir.

British Chamber of Commerce of Turkey (Assn), Mesrutiyet Caddesi 34, P.O. Box 190, Karaköy, Istanbul, ☎ 490658.

MAJOR CITIES AND TOWNS

Ankara

Ankara became the capital of Turkey in 1923 and has subsequently developed into a modern, capital city with its large government buildings, wide avenues and spacious parks.

The Atatürk Mausoleum and the citadels of old Angora are both impressive sights to be found within the city. The Museum of Anatolian Civilisations is one of the city's more interesting features and contains some unusual and unique collections of Hittite art. There are also some ruins of Roman baths and an aqueduct and the Temple of Augustus in Ankara.

Esenboğa Airport is 30km/19 miles from the city centre.

Hotels

The Ministry of Tourism grades hotels into five categories: deluxe, 1st class to 4th class.

DEDEMAN (1st class), Buklam Sokak 1, Akay, ☎ 171100.
Modern, first-class hotel, 10 minutes from the city centre.
Rooms: 252.
Facilities: Restaurants, bar and nightclub. Swimming. Shopping arcade. Cinema.
Services: Amex and Diners Club. Conference and banquet facilities.

BÜYÜK ANKARA (deluxe), Atatürk Bulvari 183, ☎ 171106.
Deluxe hotel near the US Embassy, 10 minutes from the city centre.
Rooms: 210. 14 Suites.
Facilities: Restaurant, rooftop grill, bar and nightclub. Tea room. Beauty shop and barber's shop. Gift shop. Swimming. Banquet room.

KENT (1st class), Mithat Pasa Caddesi 4, ☎ 184220.
Modern, first-class hotel near the city centre and the Atatürk Bulvari.
Rooms: 120, on request. Suites available.
Facilities: Restaurant, bars, nightclub and tea room. Car hire.
Services: Amex and Diners Club. Dr. on call.
Conference room – max. capacity 300.
Banquet rooms – max. capacity 350.

MARMARA (deluxe), Atatürk Orman Ciftligi, ☎ 231361.
Deluxe hotel outside the city centre, overlooking the Atatürk farm.
Rooms: 51.

Facilities: Restaurants and nightclub. Private gardens. Swimming. Barber's shop and beauty salon. Car hire.
Services: **TC**, **FC**. ⊟ Diners Club. Banquet and conference rooms.

Restaurants

Altin Nal Lokantasi, Cinnah Caddesi 47; *Kristal Restoran*, Bayindir Sok 28/A; *Restoran R.V.*, Turan Emeksiz Sok 8; *Liman*, Izmir Caddesi 11 – lunch only (fish specialities); *Yakamoz*; *Hülya*; *Kazan*; *Kebapci Yesil Bursa* (kebabs); *Kebapci Bursa Iskender* (kebabs).

Nightclubs

Gar Gazinosu, Istasyou Meydani; *Kösk Gazinosu*, Gazi Mustafa Kemal Bulvari 71, Maltepe; *Yeni Sureyya Gazinosu*, Bestekar Sok 14, Kuckesaf. Also the *Angora*, *Babilon*, *Mon Amour* and *Tuna*.

Istanbul

Founded in 658 B.C., Istanbul became the capital of the Roman Empire under the name of Constantinople and later of the Ottoman Empire. The city is both extraordinarily beautiful and squalid, and has suffered at the expense of modernisation and development, although the old city remains relatively untouched and is divided from the modern city by the Golden Horn inlet.

The city abounds in old mosques giving it a somewhat exotic appearance. The sixteenth-century Suleymaniye Mosque contains a museum of Islamic art and the Mosque of Sultan Ahmed, better known as the Blue Mosque, is famous for its colourful interior tilework. In the centre stands the cathedral of St Sophia which was rebuilt in the sixth century by the Emperor Justinian. The gallery of the cathedral contains some beautiful mosaics.

The old palace of the sultans, now called the Topkapi Museum, lies on the eastern promontory of the walled town, jutting out into the water. From here the visitor will have a magnificent view of the Bosphorus, the Golden Horn and of Asia beyond.

Yesilköy Airport is 25km/15 miles from the city centre.

Hotels

CINAR (deluxe), Yesilköy Airport, ☎ 732910.
Modern, luxury hotel near the airport.
Rooms: 200 [bath], [heating], [air-conditioning], [telephone], [TV] on request, [radio], [room service]. Suites available.
Facilities: Restaurant, grill room and snack bar. Nightclub and discotheque. Golf and tennis nearby.
Services: **FC**. ⊟ Amex and Diners Club. Dr. on call.
Conference room – max. capacity 600.
Banquet rooms – max. capacity 500.

HILTON (deluxe), Cumhuriyet Caddesi, Harbiye, ☎ 467050.
Luxury hotel situated in spacious, landscaped gardens overlooking the Bosphorus and within walking distance of the city centre.
Rooms: 417 [bath], [air-conditioning], [telephone], [radio], [room service].
Facilities: Restaurant and rooftop rotisserie, cocktail lounge and bar. Casino. Tennis and swimming. Airline office and shops. Car hire.
Services: **TC**, **FC**. ⊟ Most major credit cards. [secretarial], [facilities for disabled]. Audio-visual equipment and translation bureau.
Conference room – max. capacity 550.

INTER-CONTINENTAL (deluxe), Taksim Square, ☎ 448850.
Modern, luxury hotel built on the highest point in the city with panoramic views over Istanbul and the Bosphorus.
Rooms: 432 [bath], [heating], [air-conditioning], [telephone], [TV] on request, [radio], [room service]. Suites available.
Facilities: Restaurant (Turkish cuisine), informal brasserie and rotisserie, rooftop nightclub and bars. Swimming, sauna and health club. Post office.

Beauty salon and barber's shop. Travel desk. Car hire.
Services: TC, FC. Access, Amex, Carte Blanche, Diners Club, Eurocard and Master Charge. S, . Dr. on call. Conference room – max. capacity 1,125.
Banquet rooms – max. capacity 600.

SHERATON (deluxe), Taksim Park, 489000.
Modern hotel overlooking the Bosphorus and close to the business and shopping districts of the city.
Rooms: 460 , , , , on request, , . Suites available.
Facilities: 2 restaurants and bars. Golf, tennis, swimming, sauna and horse riding. Car hire.
Services: TC, FC. Access, Amex, Bankamericard, Carte Blanche, Chargex, Diners Club, Eurocard and Master Charge. S, . Translation bureau and audio-visual equipment. Dr. on call.
Conference room – max. capacity 700.
Banquet rooms – max. capacity 500.

DIVAN (1st class), Cumhuriyet Caddesi 2, 464020.
Modern hotel centrally located near airline offices and the business centre of Istanbul.
Rooms: 100 , .
Facilities: Restaurant (international and Turkish cuisine), cocktail bar and American bar. Café.
Services: Amex, Carte Blanche and Diners Club.

PARK (1st class), Ayaz Pasa Avenue, Taksim, 450760/436150.
Modern hotel in attractive garden setting near the city centre.
Rooms: 215 .
Facilities: Restaurant, American bar and pavilion, tea room.
Services: Amex, Bankamericard, Carte Blanche, Diners Club, Eurocard and Master Charge. Airline bus from airport to hotel.

Restaurants

Abdullah, Emirgan Hills (seafood); *Liman Lokantasi*, Rihtim Caddesi, Karaköy, 441033 – lunch only (seafood); *Galata Tower*; *Pandeli*, Abacilar Caddesi 35, Zindan Kapi, 225534 – lunch only; *Konyali*, Sirkeci (local specialities); *Sürreyya*, Arnavutkoy (Russian); *Bogazici*, Yeniköj; *Canli Balik*, Mesa Burna Caddesi 4, Sariyer (seafood).

Nightclubs

The majority of nightclubs offer floorshows, variety acts and striptease. Apart from those in the larger hotels, others include:
Bebek Maksim Gazinosu, Cevdet Pasa Caddesi 350, Bebek; *Bebek Park*, Bebek; *Lunapark Gazinosu*, Vatan Caddesi 79, Aksaray; *Taslik Sark*, Macka Besiktas; *Kervansaray*, Cumhuriyet Caddesi 30; *Galata Tower*, Galata district; *Resat*, Istiklal Caddesi; *Taksim Belediye Gazinosu*, Taksim Square.

Entertainment

The Turkish State Opera and Ballet Company stage productions at the city theatre from October to June. Open-air concerts are given by the Istanbul Symphony Orchestra near the Hilton Hotel during the July festival. *Son et lumière* shows in front of the Blue Mosque can be seen throughout the summer (in English twice weekly).

Shopping

The Grand Bazaar is a fascinating sight for foreign visitors to Istanbul and houses more than four thousand stalls under one great roof. Fine craftwork and antiques are sold alongside modern, mass-produced consumer goods and every buyer is expected to bargain regardless of the price asked by the stallholder.

Some of the better buys here are leather coats and jackets, copper and brass goods, carpets and onyx jewellery.

Izmir

Izmir is Turkey's third largest city and the main export port. Much of the old town was destroyed by fire in 1922 when few buildings were spared with the exception of those houses built on the hillside surrounding the bay.

Some highlights of Izmir are the fortress of Kadifekale on Mount Pagos overlooking the Bay of Izmir, the Agora (ancient Greek market-place), the Archaeological Museum in the Kulturpark and the caravanserai (old inns).

Cigli Airport is 24km/15 miles from the city centre.

Hotels

BÜYÜK EFES (deluxe), ☎ 144300.
Modern hotel built in parkland facing the Gulf of Izmir and near the city centre.
Rooms: 300 [symbol], [symbol], [symbol], [symbol] on request, [symbol], [symbol]. 24 Suites.
Facilities: Restaurants, rooftop restaurant and bar, snack bar. Nightclub. Mini golf, tennis and swimming.
Services: TC, FC. [symbol] Amex and Diners Club. Dr. on call. [symbol], [symbol].
Conference room – max. capacity 350.
Banquet rooms – max. capacity 300.

KISMET (1st class), 1377 Sok 9, ☎ 144385.
First-class hotel in central location, 5 minutes' walk from the business district of Izmir.
Rooms: 68.
Facilities: Air-conditioned restaurant. American and Oriental bars. Roof garden.
Services: [symbol] Access, Amex, Diners Club, Eurocard, Master Charge.

Restaurants

Bergama, Atatürk Caddesi 190; *Yengec*, Atatürk Caddesi (seafood); *Abdullah*, Atatürk Caddesi; *Sato*; *Park*, Kulturpark.

Nightclubs

Kubana, Kulturpark; *Mehemet Ali*, Guzelyali; *Mogambo*, Kulturpark.

UNITED ARAB EMIRATES

Size: 85,300 sq.km/33,000 sq.miles. Abu Dhabi 67,600 sq.km/26,000 sq.miles; Dubai 3,900 sq.km/1,500 sq.miles; Sharjah 2,600 sq.km/1,000 sq.miles; Ras al Khaimah 1,690 sq.km/652 sq.miles; Fujairah 1,200 sq.km/463 sq.miles; Umm al Qawain 780 sq.km/300 sq.miles; Ajman 260 sq.km/100 sq.miles.

The Emirates of Dubai, Sharjah, Ras al Khaimah, Fujairah, Umm al Qawain and Ajman are collectively known as the Northern Emirates.

Population: 760,000 (1978 est.).
Abu Dhabi 235,700; Dubai 206,900; Sharjah 88,200; Ras al Khaimah 57,300; Fujairah 26,500; Ajman 21,600; Umm al Qawain 16,879.

Density: 7.6 persons per sq.km/19.8 per sq.mile.

Population Growth Rate: 19% p.a.

Ethnic Composition: The indigenous Arab population now forms a minority and Abu Dhabi has large numbers of Indians, Pakistanis and Northern Arabs. There are large numbers of expatriates from the UK and USA living in Abu Dhabi and Dubai, with smaller foreign communities in the other Emirates. More than 10,000 Europeans alone are at present resident in Abu Dhabi.

Capital: Abu Dhabi Pop. 210,000.

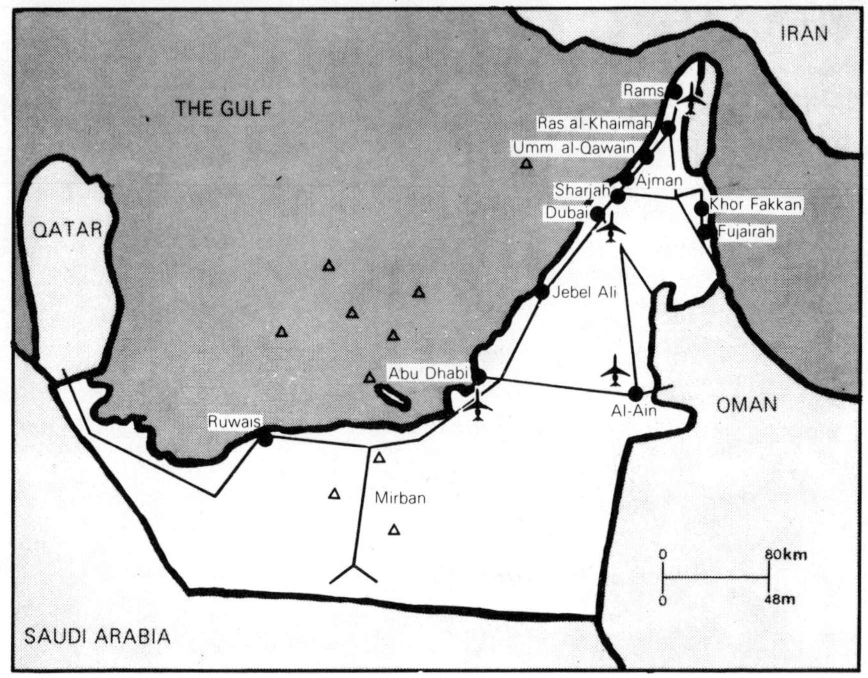

Major Towns: Dubai Pop. 200,000; Sharjah Pop. 75,000; Ras al Khaimah Pop. 55,000; Fujairah Pop. 25,000; Ajman Pop. 20,000; Umm al Qawain Pop. 15,000.

Language: Arabic is the official language but English is widely used in business circles.

Religion: Islam is the main religion and the majority of Arabs belong to the Sunni sect. There are Christian, Hindu and Parsee minorities.

Government: A Union Council of Ministers responsible to the Supreme Council has executive authority and implements Union laws. The headquarters of the various ministries are mainly in Abu Dhabi, with branches in the other Emirates.

GEOGRAPHY

The seven Emirates which form the UAE are located in the arid southern Gulf region and, with the exception of Fujairah, lie along the Trucial Gulf Coast. The coastline is characterised by small, natural creeks, sand bars and mud flats and it is here that the sea-trading communities were originally established (Dubai, Sharjah and Ras al Khaimah).

The UAE consists mainly of sand desert with scattered oases. Inland, narrow belts of silt and gravel are to be found between the sand areas and the Oman mountains.

Climate

The climate is hot and humid in summer with midday temperatures exceeding 48°C/118°F and humidity of 85% and above.

Winters are mild with temperatures ranging from 10°C/50°F to 20°C/68°F. The period from October to April is the best time to visit the region.

Agriculture

The harsh natural conditions and shortage of water make agricultural development difficult, but the Emirates are aiming to be self-sufficient in foodstuffs. Agricultural research and methods are advanced and include irrigation using a desalinated water supply and artificial environment vegetable production. There are large research and production centres at Sadiyat, Digdagga, Melaiha and Al Ain.

Main Crops: vegetables, fruit, dates, fodder crops.

Mineral Resources: oil, natural gas.

THE ECONOMY

Gross National Product (1976): US$6,700 million.

Per Capita Income (1976): US$9,571.

Foreign Trade (1976): Total Imports – US$3.33 billion; Total Exports – US$8.5 billion.

Main Trading Partners: Imports – Abu Dhabi: UK, USA, West Germany, Japan, France. Dubai: Japan, UK, USA, India, West Germany. Exports – Abu Dhabi: Qatar, Saudi Arabia, Kuwait, UK, Bahrain. Dubai: Saudi Arabia, Iran, Qatar, Oman.

Abu Dhabi

The economy of Abu Dhabi is based almost exclusively on oil and there are both on- and off-shore oilfields. The Abu Dhabi National Oil Company (ADNOC) is the Emirate agency for controlling the oil, gas and associated industries. Abu Dhabi has substantial gas reserves which have yet to be fully exploited. All these have now been formally nationalised.

The growth of Abu Dhabi followed the start of full-scale commercial oil production, and today Abu Dhabi has one of the highest per capita Gross National Products in the world. The 1970s witnessed a massive construction boom with the development of housing, social services, communications and public utilities at a rapid rate.

As the wealthiest of the Emirates, Abu Dhabi is able to make large grants and loans to the other Emirates and elsewhere in the Arab world.

Plans for the development of manufacturing industries in Abu Dhabi include steel, fertiliser and ethylene plants and the expansion of the building materials industry.

Dubai

Dubai is the main port and import centre for the UAE and Southern Gulf, and has a widespread re-export trade to the other Gulf States and the Indian sub-continent. Commercial oil production began in the mid-1960s and this provided a new source of wealth and allowed for the expansion of existing trading facilities. Dubai has the largest deepwater harbour in the Middle East (Port Rashid), and a multi-million pound dry dock complex and a trade and exhibition centre are both nearing completion.

Dubai has also developed as a leading financial centre with an abundance of banking, insurance and agency activities.

Industrialisation is in its infancy in Dubai and is progressing at a considerably slower pace than in Abu Dhabi. An aluminium-smelting complex is planned and also a steelworks and other associated industrial plants. Dubai has a number of light manufacturing industries – beverages, construction materials, bottling, etc.

The most recent producer of oil in the UAE is Sharjah where production began in 1973. This has given rise to some growth although on a much smaller scale than in Abu Dhabi or Dubai. To date, no oil has been discovered in the four smaller Northern Emirates. Ras al Khaimah has an important agricultural sector and exports vegetables to Dubai, Abu Dhabi and Oman. There are also important brick, asbestos and cement industries in Ras al Khaimah.

Major Industries: oil, gas, aluminium smelting, steel, various light manufacturing industries.

Main Commodities Traded:
Abu Dhabi: Imports – machinery and transport equipment, manufactured goods, foodstuffs, livestock. Exports – oil.
Dubai: Imports – machinery and transport equipment, manufactured goods, foodstuffs, livestock, mineral fuels, lubricants. Exports – oil, dried fish, dates, steel scrap.

Crude Oil Production (1976 est.):
Abu Dhabi 72 million tonnes; Dubai 15 million tonnes; Sharjah 1.9 million tonnes.

The United Arab Emirates are a member of the Organisation of Petroleum Exporting Countries (OPEC) and the Arab League.

HOW TO GET THERE

Air

Major airlines flying to Abu Dhabi, Dubai, Sharjah and Ras al Khaimah airports include Air India, Alia, British Airways, Egypt Air, Gulf Air, KLM, Kuwait Airways, Lufthansa, MEA, PIA, Sabena, Singapore Airlines and Swissair.

There are daily flights from Amsterdam, London and Paris to Dubai and several flights a week to Dubai from Brussels, Frankfurt, Rome and Zurich. A limited number of direct flights operate between North America and the UAE but most passengers travel via London or Amsterdam.

A daily service operates between Dubai and Bombay and Singapore, and there are regular flights from Bangkok, Dacca, Delhi, Kuala Lumpur, Manila, Hong Kong, Tokyo, Melbourne and Sydney.

There are no direct connections to Abu Dhabi from North America. Regular flights operate from Amsterdam, Brussels, Copenhagen, Frankfurt, London, Paris and Zurich. At least one flight a week connects Abu Dhabi with Bangkok, Manila, Singapore and Tokyo.

There is a weekly direct flight to Sharjah from Paris.

Gulf Air operates regular services between the major airports in the area.

Flying times to Abu Dhabi: from London 7½ hours; from New York 13½ hours.

Abu Dhabi Airport is 14km/9 miles from the town centre. Dubai Airport is 4km/2½ miles from the town centre.

ENTRY REGULATIONS

Visas

Flights between airports in the UAE are regarded as international. Visitors intending to fly between the different Emirates must be in possession of multi-entry visitors' visas where necessary.

UK citizens whose passports bear the endorsement 'Holder has the right of abode' are free to enter the UAE without having to obtain a visa in advance. On entry they will be given permission to stay for one month. This may be extended on application for up to a further two months.

Citizens of Bahrain, Kuwait, Oman, Qatar and Saudi Arabia require valid passports only. All other nationals require visas obtainable from UAE embassies abroad.

Business travellers should support their visa application with a letter in triplicate from their firm giving full details of the business to be undertaken and confirming financial responsibility for the applicant.

Evidence in a passport of a previous or planned visit to Israel may adversely affect the granting of a visa.

Travel and visa regulations are liable to change at short notice and intending visitors should keep themselves up to date with the latest requirements.

Further information may be obtained from: Ministry of the Interior, Department of Nationality, Passports and Residence, P.O. Box 228, Abu Dhabi, ☎ 41280, and Central Immigration Department, P.O. Box 4333, Dubai.

Health Regulations

An International Certificate of Vaccination against smallpox is required. Also cholera and/or yellow fever certificates of vaccination if arriving from an infected area. TAB (typhoid and paratyphoid) injections are recommended.

Customs

Currency: There are no restrictions on the amount of currency which may be taken into or out of the Emirates.

Duty-free articles: Visitors' personal effects are not liable to duty.

Articles liable to duty: Commercial samples of a value exceeding 500Dh are liable to the payment of duty in Abu Dhabi – this is refunded on re-export of the samples.

Import duty is not usually levied on samples imported into the Northern Emirates, but in the case of samples of a high value, e.g., jewellery, prior permission to import and arrangement for free entry must be sought from the Director of Customs.

Prohibited articles: Pornographic literature, narcotics.

PRACTICAL INFORMATION FOR THE VISITOR

1. Currency

Monetary Unit – dirham (Dh), divided into 100 fils. The dirham replaced the Bahraini dinar and the Qatari riyal in 1973.
Notes – 1, 5, 10, 50, 100 dirhams.
Coins – 1, 5, 10, 25, 50 fils and 1 dirham.
UAE currency is issued by the UAE Currency Board, P.O. Box 854, Abu Dhabi, ☎ 43728.

Banking Hours:
Abu Dhabi – 0800–1200 Saturday to Wednesday; 0800–1100 Thursday.
Northern Emirates – 0800–1200 Saturday to Thursday.

Some sixty licensed banks operate in the UAE – twelve overseas banking units are permitted to operate tax free. Most international and Arab banks have offices in the UAE.

Banks in Abu Dhabi:

Algemene Bank Nederland
P.O. Box 2720, ☎ 45400.
Arab Bank for Investment and Foreign Trade
Sheikh Khalifa Street, P.O. Box 2484, ☎ 42082.
Bank of Credit and Commerce International
Corniche Road, P.O. Box 2622, ☎ 44622.
Barclays Bank International
Corniche Road, P.O. Box 2734, ☎ 45313.
British Bank of the Middle East
Corniche Road, P.O. Box 242, ☎ 43080.
Chartered Bank Ltd
Corniche Road, P.O. Box 240, ☎ 43077.
Chase Manhattan Bank
P.O. Box 3491, ☎ 24288.
Commercial Bank of Dubai Ltd
Sheikh Khalifa Street, P.O. Box 2466, ☎ 45700.
First National Bank of Chicago
P.O. Box 2747, ☎ 45720.
Citibank
Lulu Street, P.O. Box 999, ☎ 41410.
Federal Commercial Bank
P.O. Box 2934, ☎ 24920/25290/3.
Grindlays Bank
Corniche Road, P.O. Box 241, ☎ 44770.
Khalij Commercial Bank
P.O. Box 2832, ☎ 45820.
National Bank of Abu Dhabi
Sheikh Khalifa Street, P.O. Box 4, ☎ 43262.
United Bank Ltd
Corniche Road, P.O. Box 237, ☎ 41397.

Banks in Dubai:

American Express International Banking Corporation
P.O. Box 3304, ☎ 223236.
Arab Bank
P.O. Box 1650, ☎ 221231.
Bank of Credit and Commerce International
P.O. Box 5032, ☎ 220281.
Barclays Bank International
P.O. Box 1891, ☎ 226158.
British Bank of the Middle East
P.O. Box 66, ☎ 432000.
Chartered Bank Ltd
P.O. Box 999, ☎ 431515.

Commercial Bank of Dubai
P.O. Box 1709, ☎ 227121.
Dubai Bank
P.O. Box 2545, ☎ 221201.
First National Bank of Chicago
P.O. Box 1655, ☎ 226161.
Citibank
P.O. Box 749, ☎ 432100.
Grindlays Bank
P.O. Box 4166, ☎ 226291.
Lloyds Bank International
P.O. Box 3766, ☎ 224151.
National Bank of Dubai
P.O. Box 777, ☎ 222241.
Royal Bank of Canada
P.O. Box 3614, ☎ 225536.
Union Bank of the Middle East
P.O. Box 2923, ☎ 35545.
UAE Development Bank
P.O. Box 5022, ☎ 229800.

2. Electricity Supply

Abu Dhabi – 240V AC 50Hz.

Northern Emirates – 220V AC 50Hz. Plugs: 3-pin flat (13 amp) or round (15 amp).

3. Weights and Measures

British and American standard weights are used as well as the metric system. Also some local weights and measures are occasionally used.

4. Media

Both Abu Dhabi and Dubai have colour television transmissions and commercial advertising is accepted. UAE Radio is based in Dubai and has programmes in English. It also accepts commercial advertising.

Newspapers and Periodicals:

Daily – *Al Ittihad* (Ministry of Information, Abu Dhabi), *Gulf News* (Dubai), *Khaleej Times* (English-language – Dubai), *Al Wahda* (Dubai), *Emirates News* (Abu Dhabi).
Weekly – *Akhbar Dubai, Gulf Weekly Mirror* (Bahrain), *Al Dhafra* (Abu Dhabi).
Monthly – *Akhbar Ras al Khaimah, Abu Dhabi Chamber of Commerce Review, Al Tijarah* (Sharjah Chamber of Commerce), *Akhbar al Petrol wa al-Sinad* (Ministry of Petroleum, Abu Dhabi), *Dubai Chamber of Commerce Review.*
Anglo-Arab Trade and *Middle East Trade* are published six times a year in Arabic in London.

5. Medical Care

Dubai has a modern, British-administered hospital (Al Maktoum) and there are Government hospitals in all the Emirates. There are a number of European and American doctors in practice as well as Western-trained Arab doctors.

Abu Dhabi:
Abu Dhabi General Hospital, off the Airport Road.
New General Hospital, near the Ramada Inn.
Corniche Hospital, Corniche – maternity and gynaecology.
The New Medical Centre, off Sheikh Zayed Street, ☎ 26535 – pharmacy and dental clinic.

Dubai:
Rashid Hospital, ☎ 471111.
Al-Maktoum Hospital, Deira,
☎ 221211.

Sharjah:
Al Qasimi, ☎ 354211.

Visitors are likely to suffer from prickly heat and mild stomach upsets and should take suitable medicines with them.

Dubai and Sharjah have piped sweet well water which is safe to drink but should be taken in moderation. The water supply in Abu Dhabi is provided by distillation plants.

6. Telephone, Telex and Postal Services

Automatic telephone systems connect the major towns in the UAE. Local calls within each town are free of charge. International communications are extensive and generally very efficient.

There are telegraph offices in the capital towns of all the Emirates, and Cable & Wireless Ltd have offices in Dubai and Fujairah.

International telex facilities are available in Abu Dhabi and Dubai. There is a public telex facility at the EMIRTEL office in Abu Dhabi.

The General Post Office in Abu Dhabi is on the Airport Road and there are also offices in Hamdan Street and in Khalidya off the Corniche. The Central Post Office in Dubai is on the Dubai side of the creek, ☎ 432900, with a branch on the Deira side, ☎ 221952. The post office in Sharjah is in Al-Roba Street. Post offices are usually open from 0800–1300 and 1600–1800 hours.

Useful Telephone Numbers:

	Abu Dhabi	Dubai
Fire	☎ 997	☎ 222222
Ambulance	☎ 998	—
Police	☎ 999	☎ 221111

7. Public Holidays

Fixed Holidays:

1 January	*New Year's Day*
6 August	*Accession of the Ruler of Abu Dhabi*
2 December	*UAE National Day*

Muslim Holidays:

These follow the Muslim calendar and occur 10–12 days earlier every year. The dates of the Muslim holidays are approximate as they depend upon sightings of the moon, and may differ by one or two days from those given below. 1981 dates are:

18 January	*Prophet's Birthday*
31 May	*Ascension of the Prophet*
31 July –2 August	*Eid el fitr* (end of *Ramadan*)
8–10 October	*Eid el Adha*
29 October	*Muslim New Year*

Friday is the weekly holiday. Saturday and Sunday are normal working days.

8. Time

GMT+4

9. Internal Transport

Air

Gulf Air operates a daily shuttle service between Abu Dhabi and Dubai (tickets can be purchased at the airport). Frequent flights connect Abu Dhabi with Sharjah and Ras al Khaimah. Small aircraft and helicopters may be chartered. It is important to remember that flights between the various Emirates are regarded as international.

Airline Offices:

Abu Dhabi

Air France	☎ 45743/4.
Air India	☎ 41197.
British Airways	☎ 41328.
Gulf Air	☎ 41662.
JAL	☎ 23333.
KLM	☎ 23280.
Lufthansa	☎ 29144/5.
MEA	☎ 41341.
Pan Am	☎ 41821.
SAS	☎ 41821/2.
Singapore Airlines	☎ 41328.
Swissair	☎ 45409.
TWA	☎ 45538.

Dubai

Air France	☎ 222522.
Air India	☎ 23717.
British Airways	☎ 222151.
Gulf Air	—
JAL	☎ 228353.
KLM	☎ 221533.
Lufthansa	☎ 221191.
MEA	☎ 21888.
Pan Am	☎ 436800.
SAS	☎ 28151.

Singapore Airlines	☎ 222151.
Swissair	☎ 285637.
TWA	☎ 222317.

Road
Road links in the UAE are good, and there are many car-hire firms. Visitors wishing to drive hired cars must obtain a temporary driving licence from the Traffic Police. A passport, two passport photos and a current driving licence must be produced to obtain this.

Car-Hire Firms:

Abu Dhabi

Avis	☎ 23760/1/2.
Abu Dhabi Car Sales & Rental Company	☎ 44351/41185.
Al Nabeel Quick Service	☎ 43370.
Mohammed Abdulla Al Sheibani & Sons National Co.	☎ 41610.
Emco Car Rent-a-Car	☎ 67701.

Dubai

Avis	☎ 665345/6.
Dubai Rent-a-Car	☎ 228886.
Gulf Rent-a-Car	☎ 225545.
National Rent-a-Car	☎ 224647.

Sharjah

Worldwide Rent-a-Car	☎ 355547.

Taxis are plentiful throughout the Emirates and can be hired on an hourly basis. Long-distance trips by taxi can be arranged. Air-conditioned taxis are more expensive.

It is advisable to agree upon all fares in advance.

Fares within Abu Dhabi and Dubai should cost around Dh3–5.

10. Tipping

Taxis – no tip.

Porters – Dh2 per bag.

Hotels – Abu Dhabi: Dh10 for one night's stay, Dh20 for a week's stay. Northern Emirates: service charge included in the bill.

Restaurants – Abu Dhabi: 10%. Northern Emirates: 10% service charge and 5% tax are added to the bill.

11. Social Customs

Customs and mores are more relaxed in the Emirates than in neighbouring Saudi Arabia. However, the majority of the population are Muslims and the foreign visitor should be aware of the religious practices and restrictions.

Non-Muslims can buy alcohol in hotel bars and restaurants, although in Abu Dhabi recently the authorities have tried to clamp down on drinking in restaurants.

Anyone wishing to purchase alcohol in the licensed shops in Dubai requires a special licence obtainable from the Dubai Police.

For further information, refer to page 12 under 'Muslim Social Customs'.

USEFUL ADDRESSES (GENERAL)

Embassies in Abu Dhabi

France: Khalifa Street, P.O. Box 4014, ☎ 43516/7.

West Germany: Derwish Bin Seery Building, Sheikh Hamdan Street, P.O. Box 2591, ☎ 43359.

Japan: Al-Otaiba Building, Corniche, P.O. Box 2430, ☎ 44696.

Netherlands: Sheikh Zayed Building, 1st Floor, Flat No. 2, Khalifa Street,

P.O. Box 6560, ☎ 21920.

Switzerland: Juma Assian Al-Mansoori Building, Sheikh Khalifa Street, P.O. Box 6116, ☎ 43636/43644.

UK: Khalid bin Al-Waleed Street, P.O. Box 248, ☎ 26600.

US: Sheikh Khalid Building, Corniche Road, P.O. Box 4009, ☎ 61534/5.

Other addresses in Abu Dhabi

Ministry of Information and Culture, P.O. Box 17, ☎ 26000.

Addresses in Dubai

Dutch Consulate, ABN, Kuwait Building, Binyas Street, P.O. Box 2567, Deira-Dubai, ☎ 225156/7/8.

UK Embassy, Tariq bin Zayed Street, P.O. Box 65, ☎ 431070.

US Consulate, Al Futtaim Building, Creek Road, Deira, P.O. Box 5343, ☎ 229003.

Ministry of Information and Culture, P.O. Box 5010, Deira, ☎ 225994.

Addresses in Sharjah

Ministry of Information and Culture, P.O. Box 155, ☎ 22010.

BUSINESS INFORMATION

The rapid growth of business activity in the UAE is reflected by the massive increase in imports over recent years and the large numbers of foreign banks which now operate in the Emirates, centred in Dubai. The main categories of imports are electrical equipment, luxury goods, vehicles, textiles and clothing, foodstuffs and oilfield equipment.

Foreign investment is generally welcomed, providing it is seen as contributing to the wider development of the UAE. Incentives such as tax holidays, exemption from customs duties on machinery and raw materials and a rent-free lease period are offered to foreign firms of this kind. In Sharjah, the attitude towards foreign businesses is a liberal one and land for construction together with low-cost utilities may be offered to the foreign investor.

It is advisable to appoint separate agents in Abu Dhabi and the Northern Emirates as commercial agencies in Abu Dhabi may only be held by firms with an Abu Dhabi trading licence. In Dubai, the Chamber of Commerce states that once an agency is held by a local agent, it may not be taken over by a foreigner.

Import and Exchange Control Regulations

No duty is charged on goods entering Dubai from any other Emirate or on goods imported into Abu Dhabi from or through Dubai or the other Emirates.

Prohibited items include pornographic literature and narcotics (except for scientific or medical purposes when an import licence is required).

Many foodstuffs and livestock are exempt from customs duties as are religious and educational books.

There is no exchange control in the UAE and transfers may be made freely to all parts of the world.

Business Hours

Government Offices:

Winter –	0800–1400	Saturday to Wednesday
	0800–1200	Thursday
Summer –	0700–1300	Saturday to Wednesday
	0700–1100	Thursday

Business Houses:

Abu Dhabi

Winter –	0800–1300 1530–1900	Saturday to Thursday
Summer –	0800–1300 1600–1930	Saturday to Thursday

Northern Emirates

Winter –	0900–1300 1600–2000 or 2100	Saturday to Thursday
Summer –	0900–1300 1630–2000 or 2100	Saturday to Thursday

Oil Companies:

Abu Dhabi

	0700–1400	Saturday to Wednesday
	0700–1300	Thursday

Northern Emirates

Winter –	0830–1300 1600–1800	Saturday to Thursday
Summer –	0830–1300	Saturday to Thursday

Friday is the weekly holiday; Saturday and Sunday are normal working days. Business visitors are advised to avoid visiting the UAE during the month of *Ramadan* which ends with a 3-day holiday – *Eid el Fitr*.

BUSINESS SERVICES

Accountants

Saba & Co, P.O. Box 202, Abu Dhabi, ☎ 41658.

Saba & Co, P.O. Box 1222, Dubai, ☎ 224297.

Talal Abu Ghazalah, P.O. Box 4295, Abu Dhabi, ☎ 43242.

Whinney Murray & Co, P.O. Box 1855, Dubai, ☎ 224201.

Consultants

Sir Alexander Gibb & Partners, P.O. Box 528, Abu Dhabi, ☎ 22652.

Costain Civil Engineers, P.O. Box 4742, Abu Dhabi, ☎ 43552.

Six Construct, P.O. Box 226, Abu Dhabi, ☎ 22579.

Sir William Halcrow & Partners, P.O. Box 360, Dubai, ☎ 282101/9.

Insurance

Abu Dhabi National Insurance Co, P.O. Box 839, Abu Dhabi, ☎ 43171.

Dubai Insurance Company, P.O. Box 3027, Dubai, ☎ 224911.

Arab Commercial Enterprises, P.O.

Box 585, Abu Dhabi, ☎ 41989/41993.

Arab Commercial Enterprises, P.O. Box 1100, Dubai, ☎ 221445/223354.

Shipping

Gray Mackenzie & Co, Corniche, P.O. Box 247, Abu Dhabi, ☎ 23131, and P.O. Box 70, Dubai, ☎ 221221.

Yusef bin-Ahmed Kanoo, Beniyas Street, P.O. Box 245, Abu Dhabi, ☎ 44444, and P.O. Box 290, Dubai, ☎ 432525.

National Shipping Gulf Agency, 6th Floor, Abdul Jahil Building, Sheikh Khalifa Street, P.O. Box 377, Abu Dhabi, ☎ 43008.

Gulf Shipping Company, P.O. Box 2578, Dubai, ☎ 431151.

USEFUL ADDRESSES (BUSINESS)

Ministry of Finance and Industry, P.O. Box 433, Abu Dhabi, and P.O. Box 1565, Dubai, ☎ 25579.

Ministry of the Economy and Trade, P.O. Box 901, Abu Dhabi, ☎ 62520.

Ministry of Petroleum and Mineral Resources, P.O. Box 9, Abu Dhabi, ☎ 61051.

Abu Dhabi Chamber of Commerce and Industry, P.O. Box 662, ☎ 41880/1.

Dubai Chamber of Commerce and Industry, P.O. Box 1457, ☎ 221327.

Sharjah Chamber of Commerce and Industry, P.O. Box 580, ☎ 22464.

Ras al Khaimah Chamber of Commerce, Industry and Agriculture, P.O. Box 87, ☎ 212348.

MAJOR CITIES AND TOWNS

Abu Dhabi

Most of the old city of Abu Dhabi has now been demolished to make way for the mass of commercial and government offices and other functional buildings needed for the modern metropolis of Abu Dhabi. The Old Palace behind the Corniche is virtually the only remaining old building from the city's past. Originally a fortified palace built around 1790, the Palace consisted of four walls with corner towers surrounding a courtyard, but much of this was destroyed by the present Sheikh's predecessor.

The residence of the present Sheikh is the Batin Palace, surrounded by blue and white walls – the Guest Palace nearby is encircled by red and white walls. One of Abu Dhabi's most impressive modern buildings is that of Sheikh Mohammed near the British Embassy, with its luxurious interior furnished in marble, bronze and suede. The Trade Centre is another spectacular piece of modern architecture and will eventually contain shops, showrooms, a cinema and a tropical decorative garden.

Abu Dhabi Airport is 14km/9 miles from the city centre.

Hotels

There is no official hotel rating system in the United Arab Emirates.

ABU DHABI HILTON, Corniche Avenue, P.O. Box 877, ☎ 61900.

Deluxe hotel facing the Gulf, 3km/2

miles from the town centre and 13km/8 miles from the airport.
Rooms: 186. Suites available.
Facilities: Restaurant (international and Oriental cuisine), coffee shop, bars, poolside snack bar, discotheque, private dining rooms. Tennis, swimming, sauna, bowling alley. Private beach. Golf nearby. Car hire.
Services: TC, FC. Amex, Bankamericard, Carte Blanche, Diners Club and Master Charge. S. Audio-visual aids. Dr. on call.
Conference rooms – max. capacity 500.

AL AIN PALACE, P.O. Box 33, 22377.
First-class hotel in the town centre.
Rooms: 90. 14 suites.
Facilities: 2 restaurants and bars, private dining rooms. Swimming and tennis.
Services: TC. No credit cards accepted. S. Dr. on call.
Conference room – max. capacity 100.

KHALIDIA PALACE, P.O. Box 4010, 67470.
Modern hotel built on the seafront.
Rooms: 124. Suites available.
Facilities: Restaurant, bar, nightclub, coffee shop. Swimming. Private beach. Conference facilities.

OMAR KHAYAM, P.O. Box 123, 22101/22370.
Modern hotel in the town centre.
Rooms: 170. 15 suites.
Facilities: Restaurant, bar and nightclub. Private dining rooms.
Services: No credit cards accepted.

RAMADA INN, P.O. Box 3118, 77260.
Modern hotel near the airport.
Rooms: 250.
Facilities: Restaurant and bar. Swimming. Barbecues. Conference facilities.
Services: TC, FC. Amex, Diners Club, Eurocard and Master Charge. S.

Restaurants

The Golden Falcon, Hamdan Street, 23943; *The Club*, 22788 – members and their guests only; *Mandarin*, Sheikh Zayed Street, 61361 – Chinese; *Capri*, off the Corniche, 61282 – French; *Golden Fish Restaurant*, Corniche, 61091 – Lebanese.

Nightclubs

The *Ewan Super Night Club*, Corniche, 41184 and the *Al-Tannur Night Club* (part of the Zakher Hotel) are popular nightspots in Abu Dhabi.

Entertainment

The Club in Abu Dhabi offers excellent facilities for all kinds of sporting activities and is also a lively social centre. Guests are admitted with a member. Facilities include a swimming pool, badminton court, squash and tennis courts and sailing. The *Tourist Club* is also open to overseas visitors and has tennis courts, a bowling alley and private beach.

There is a golf course near the camel-racing track and social evenings are held at *The Club* on a regular basis.

Shopping

Allied Enterprises, near the Old Fort, 43609 – glass, china and silverware; *Salam Studio & Stores*, off Umm al-Nas Street, 44643 – films and processing (5-day service); *Wong and Sons Trading*, Sheikh Zayed Street, 61362 – Chinese and Oriental goods; *Antique Shop*, off Sheikh Zayed Street – Arabian souvenirs and antiquities; *Art Shoppe*, Hamdan Street, 41596 arts, crafts and local paintings; *The Family Bookshop*, Sheikh Zayed Street, 45702 – large selection of English-language books.

Dubai

The development of Dubai over the past three decades has been quite spectacular. Only 20 years ago Dubai was a small settlement with no paved roads, running water or electricity, and most of the houses were simple two-storey buildings made from chunks of coral.

Today Dubai is important as a major trading port and, in addition, as an entrepôt for the Trucial States and Oman. The Emirate is also a major gold trading centre and has been a happy victim of the oil boom since 1969 when oil first flowed in Dubai.

Urban development has not remained confined to the town of Dubai itself. The suburb of Jumaira along the coast is a conglomeration of luxury villas mainly occupied by expatriates. The commercial complex on the Dubai side of the Creek includes the Hilton Hotel and the 39-storey International Trade and Exhibition Centre which is the tallest building in the Emirates.

Dubai Airport is 4km/2½ miles from the town centre.

Hotels

Ambassador, P.O. Box 3226, 431000.
Modern, first-class hotel near the city centre.
Rooms: 81. 18 suites.
Facilities: Restaurants, bars, nightclub. Private dining rooms. Swimming.
Services: TC, FC. Amex. Telex facilities.
Conference rooms – max. capacity 150.

Carlton Tower, P.O. Box 1955, 227111.
Luxury, modern hotel.
Rooms: 144. 18 suites.
Facilities: Restaurant (European and Oriental cuisine), bar and cocktail lounge, 24-hour coffee shop, disco club. Private dining rooms. Swimming.
Services: TC, FC. Amex.
Conference room – max. capacity 500.

Dubai Hilton, P.O. Box 927, Deira, 470000.
Part of Dubai International Centre and Exhibition Hall, the Dubai Hilton is at Deira, 5km/3 miles from the town centre and 8km/5 miles from the airport.
Rooms: 368.
Facilities: Restaurant, cocktail lounge and bar, 24-hour coffee shop. Swimming and sauna. Shops. Extensive meeting facilities available in the Trade Centre.
Services: TC, FC. Amex, Bankamericard, Carte Blanche, Diners Club, Eurocard and Master Charge.

Inter-Continental Dubai, P.O. Box 476, 227171.
Modern, deluxe hotel in its own grounds, 2 minutes from the town centre.
Rooms: 333. 39 suites.
Facilities: Rooftop restaurant, cocktail lounge and bars, 24-hour coffee shop, private dining rooms. Shopping arcade. Travel desk and car-hire service. Tennis and swimming.
Services: TC, FC. Amex, Bankamericard, Carte Blanche and Diners Club.
Conference room – max. capacity 600.
Banquet rooms – max. capacity 400.

Dubai Sheraton, P.O. Box 4250, 281111.
Luxurious modern hotel within walking distance of the commercial district of Dubai.
Rooms: 298. Suites available.
Facilities: Grill room, 24-hour coffee shop, poolside snack bar, nightclub. Bar. Swimming, tennis, sauna and health club. Shops. Beauty and barber shops. Car hire. Travel agency. Bank.
Services: TC, FC. Amex, Barclay Visa, Diners Club and Eurocard.
Conference and banquet rooms – max. capacity 800.

Restaurants

There are some excellent restaurants in the main hotels in Dubai. Others within the city include: *Bistro*, ☎ 225718 – French; *The Safari Club*, ☎ 225552 – international; *Mandarin*, ☎ 433272 – Chinese; *Golden Dragon*, ☎ 435517 – Chinese; *Chalet Suisse*, ☎ 222392 – international; *Sahara*, ☎ 221518 – international; *Pizza-Vino*, ☎ 224884 – pizzas only.

Entertainment

Dubai has many sports and social clubs which welcome foreign visitors as guests of a member, and may offer temporary membership. The *Dubai Country Club* is on the Aweer Road, about 20 minutes' drive north of the city, and has tennis, squash, badminton, golf, swimming and clay-pigeon shooting facilities. Other clubs in Dubai include the *Dubai Offshore Sailing Club*, ☎ 441616, *Polo Club*, ☎ 43631 and the *Darjeeling Club*, ☎ 222034 – cricket.

The *Al-Masr Club* is a large sporting complex which includes an ice rink, squash courts, bowling alley and soccer stadium.

Shopping

Arts and Gems, Deira, ☎ 224937 – gifts; *Khalid*, Deira, ☎ 222326 – jewellery and glass; *Wong & Son*, ☎ 433272 – Oriental and Chinese goods.

There are several *souks* in Dubai and these are best visited during the late afternoon when trade is at its busiest. The *Souk al-Theheb* (Gold *Souk*) will be of most interest to the foreign visitor as there are a number of antique stalls and many gold dealers, although their jewellery is not normally made locally.

Sharjah

The town of Sharjah is built along a creek, like Dubai, and used to be an important harbour for pearl boats. The creek was also used by traders transporting slaves from Africa to Arab ports.

Sharjah now relies on its oil supplies although production is low, putting the Emirate at the lower end of the Middle East oil league. Oil revenues and aid from the Federal Government have enabled the large-scale development of the town and the construction of new port facilities, an international airport, roads and large public buildings. Many major facilities have yet to be installed, however, and the reduction of federal aid together with the increasing attraction of Dubai for investors is likely to slow down the development of Sharjah in comparison with some of the other Emirates.

Sharjah Airport is 1½km/1 mile from the town centre.

Hotels

HOLIDAY INN OF SHARJAH, P.O. Box 5802, ☎ 357357.
Modern hotel built near the business centre of Sharjah.
Rooms: 270 ⛶, ⛶, ⛶, ⛶, ⛶, ⛶. 22 suites.
Facilities: Rooftop restaurant, bars and 24-hour coffee shop. Tennis and swimming. Shops. Car hire.
Services: **TC**, **FC**. ⊟ Amex, Bankamericard, Diners Club, Eurocard and Master Charge. **S**, ♂. Dr. on call.
Conference room – max. capacity 500.
Banquet room – max. capacity 750.

NOVOTEL SHARJAH BEACH, P.O. Box 6015, ☎ 356566.
Modern hotel near the town centre, located between Dubai and Sharjah Airports.
Rooms: 140 ⛶, ⛶, ⛶, ⛶, ⛶.
Facilities: Restaurant, bars and coffee shop. Swimming. Private beach and garden. Newsagent. Bus service into Dubai. Car hire.
Services: **TC**, **FC**. ⊟ Amex. **S**, ♂. Dr. on call.

Conference room – max. capacity 120.
Banquet rooms – max. capacity 70.

SHARJAH CARLTON, P.O. Box 1198, ☎ 23811.
Modern hotel on the seafront, close to the business centre of Sharjah.
Rooms: 175 [icons]. 16 suites.
Facilities: Restaurant and nightclub, bars and 24-hour coffee shop. Swimming and tennis. Shops.
Services: TC, FC. No credit cards accepted. [icons]. Dr. on call.
Conference room – max. capacity 120.
Banquet rooms – max. capacity 700.

Restaurants

The main restaurants in Sharjah are in the hotels and are open to non-residents. They include: *The Cellar*, Sands Motel, ☎ 356475 – international cuisine, live music; *Al Khaina*, Meridien Hotel, ☎ 356557 – Oriental; *Al-Tannur*, Summerland Motel, ☎ 354321 – Oriental/European cuisine; *Carlton Hotel Restaurant*, ☎ 23711 – international and Lebanese cuisine.

Nightclubs

La Belle Epoque, Meridien Hotel, ☎ 356557; *Al-Andaleeb*, Holiday Inn, ☎ 357357; *Beachcomber*, Carlton Hotel, ☎ 23711.

Entertainment

The *Sharjah International Club*, ☎ 357605, the *Marbella Club*, ☎ 357123 and *Sharjah Wanderers Club* all offer a variety of sporting and social activities, and temporary membership of these clubs is usually available to foreign visitors.

Shopping

The *souk* in Sharjah is regarded as one of the best in the Emirates where gold and silver articles are sold at very cheap rates. Gift and souvenir shops in Sharjah include *Jashanmal & Sons*, ☎ 22412; *Salman Poor Ahwazi*, ☎ 23389; and *Eastern Star Novelties*, ☎ 22190.

YEMEN ARAB REPUBLIC

Size: 195,000 sq.km/75,290 sq.miles.

Population: 7,080,000 (1978), of whom 1.5 million are working abroad.

Distribution: 11% in urban areas.

Density: 36 persons per sq.km/93 per sq.mile.

Population Growth Rate: 2.9% p.a.

Ethnic Composition: The population is predominantly Arab with some Negroid elements in the coastal area in particular.

Capital: Sana'a Pop. 140,000.

Major Towns: Hodeida Pop. 85,000; Taiz Pop. 80,000.

Language: Arabic is the official language. English is the most widely used foreign language, followed by Russian.

Religion: The population of the Yemen Arab Republic (YAR) is Muslim, being almost equally divided between the Zeidis (a Shia sect) in the north and the Shafei (a Sunni sect) in the south. There are a few minority groups including a small Jewish community in Sa'da.

Government: The Yemen Arab Republic was formed in 1962. Shortly after this a civil war broke out between the Royalist and Republican elements, ending in 1970 with victory for the Republicans who subsequently accepted the Royalists into their government.

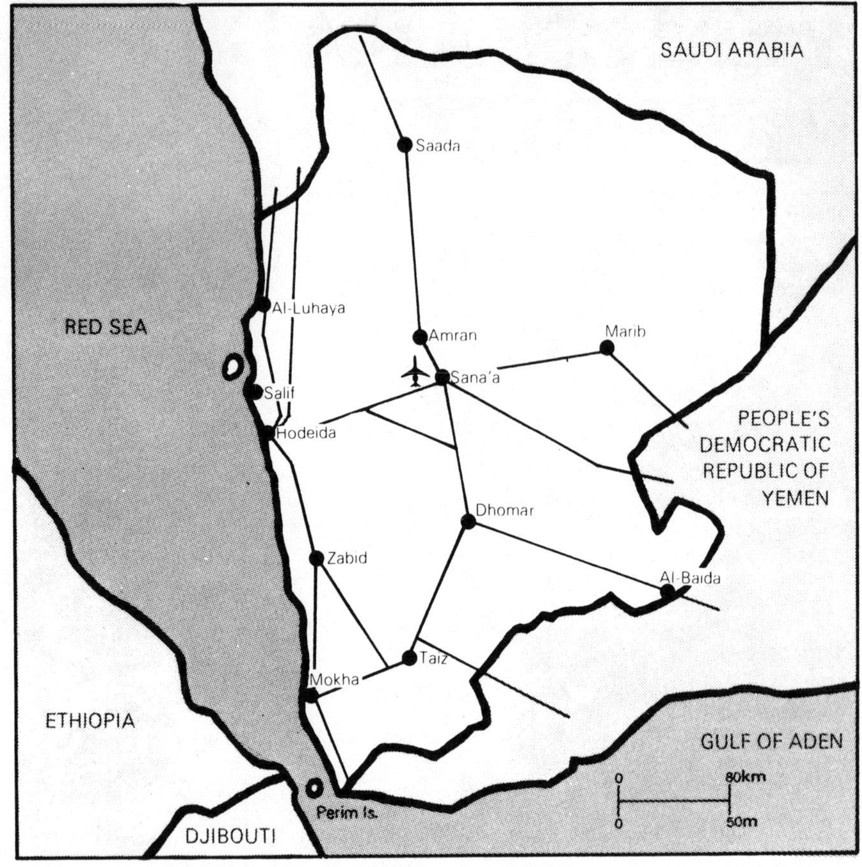

The President was overthrown during a military coup in 1974 and the Constitution and Consultative Assembly were dissolved. The present Government consists of a Military Command Council whose leader is the Head of State, and a Council of Ministers (mainly civilian) whose head is the Prime Minister.

All political organisations are banned in the YAR.

GEOGRAPHY

The Yemen Arab Republic is situated east of the Red Sea, to the north of the People's Democratic Republic of Yemen (formerly Aden Colony and Protectorates). It is bordered to the north and east by Saudi Arabia.

The country can be divided into three main regions: the wide coastal plain or Tihama (between 50 and 100km/31 and 62 miles wide) whose rivers and streams carry water only in the rainy season; the Highlands which rise from the Tihama to a maximum height of 3,660m/12,000ft – the fertile valleys and plains of this region have always been intensively cultivated; the Eastern Slopes which fall away from the mountains towards the Empty Quarter of the Arabian Peninsula, becoming increasingly arid towards the east.

Climate

The climate of the YAR varies according to altitude – the coastal plain is hot and humid for most of the year while the Highlands have warm summers with a higher rainfall and cold winters with occasional snow and frost. The annual rainfall is unpredictable and droughts are fairly common – the main rainy season is July to September.

Agriculture

The YAR is the most fertile country on the Arabian Peninsula and agriculture is the mainstay of the economy, providing more than 70% of the Gross National Product and approximately 90% of all exports.

Agricultural production fluctuates because of rainfall variations, and during the civil war it was adversely affected. However, production has increased during recent years with concentrated efforts to find new, reliable water sources and irrigation methods together with experimentation in new methods of farming and livestock breeding. A number of foreign firms are engaged in development projects such as dam building, pilot farms, livestock rearing, etc. There are large herds of sheep, goats, cattle and camels with a great potential for further expansion in this sector.

Main Crops: cereals (sorghum and millet), cotton, coffee, qat (a narcotic leaf), vegetables, fruit.

Mineral Resources: Salt is mined near Salif and there are known deposits of copper, coal, iron, lead, zinc and other minerals although no thorough surveys have been conducted.

THE ECONOMY

Gross National Product (1976): US$8 million.

Per Capita Income (1976): US$120.

Gross Domestic Product (1976): YR million 7,545.

Foreign Trade (1976): Total Imports US$272 million; Total Exports US$14 million.

Main Trading Partners: Imports – Japan, India, China, Australia, Saudi Arabia, Netherlands, UK, PDRY, West Germany. Exports – China, Japan, PDRY, Saudi Arabia, France.

Until 1970, the YAR was largely cut off from the outside world and despite the progress and development which has taken place over the last decade, much of the economy is still based on subsistence agriculture, livestock-rearing and fishing. Successive YAR governments have been acutely conscious of the backward nature of their economy and in their determination to speed up development have shown willingness to trade with any country and accept foreign aid wherever offered. To this end both foreign investment and visitors are welcome in the YAR.

In recent years aid has been forthcoming from individual countries as well as international agencies, and more recently from other States in the Arabian peninsula. The remittances and repatriation of funds by Yemeni workers abroad is an important economic factor and together with foreign aid these pay for about 90% of the YAR's imports.

Industry employs approximately 1% of the labour force and is still very underdeveloped. Traditional craft industries still dominate although these are suffering increasingly from competition by machine-made goods. An industrial estate at Sana'a has been established, with plans for factories processing local raw materials such as fish, vegetables and cotton seed. A Russian-built cement works is to be expanded and a textile branch has been established with Chinese aid and there are plans to develop this sector further.

High-quality salt is mined and exported at Salif, where the deepwater port has been improved. To date there has been no commercial exploitation of the YAR's other known mineral deposits. On-shore and off-shore oil exploration continues although no oil has been found yet. The main prospecting interests are West German, Japanese and American.

Major Industries: cotton textiles, foodstuffs, cement and building materials, aluminium and furniture.

Main Commodities Traded: Imports – foodstuffs, fuels, machinery, manufactured goods, chemicals. Exports – cotton, coffee, hides and skins, salt.

The Yemen Arab Republic is a member of the Arab League.

HOW TO GET THERE

Air

Sana'a has the main airport in the YAR while Taiz and Hodeida also have airports. Most direct flights to Sana'a are from neighbouring countries: Saudia fly daily from Jeddah; Ethiopian Airlines twice weekly from Addis Ababa and once weekly from Abu Dhabi/Bahrain; Kuwait Airlines once weekly from Kuwait; Syrian Arab Airlines twice weekly from Damascus; Sudan Airways once weekly from Khartoum; Somali Airways once weekly from Rome and from Mogadishu; Air Djibouti fly to Taiz daily from Djibouti and Aeroflot fly to Sana'a once weekly from Cairo.

Two direct flights a week from London to Sana'a are available, one by Syrian Arab Airlines and one by Ethiopian Airlines.

Flying times to Sana'a: from London 11 hours; from New York 16 hours.

Visitors to the YAR who travel via Jeddah in Saudi Arabia are warned that their luggage will be thoroughly searched at Jeddah Airport and any alcoholic liquor, together with any politically tendentious or pornographic literature, will be confiscated. A transit visa from a Saudi Arabian Embassy is required for an overnight stay in Jeddah.

An airport tax of YR10 is payable by all passengers leaving the YAR on international flights.

El-Rahaba Airport is 3km/2 miles from the centre of Sana'a.

ENTRY REGULATIONS

Visas

Visas are required by nationals of all countries except Egypt, Iraq, Libya and Syria.

Visa applications should be made to the nearest Yemeni Embassy or Consulate. Three passport-size photographs are required plus a letter from the applicant's firm stating the dates of entry and exit, the length of stay and full details of the business to be undertaken, together with the name and address of any contact(s) to be visited.

Visas are usually valid for 3 months and the length of stay is variable. Evidence in a passport of a previous or planned visit to Israel may adversely affect the granting of a visa.

Exit visas are also required and this can usually be arranged through hotel receptionists. Emergency entry and exit visas can usually be obtained at the airport for a cost of about YR10.

All visitors must register with the Security Department Office (Sana'a, Hodeida and Taiz) within 3 days of arrival in the YAR and exit visas can be obtained from the same office.

Health Regulations

An International Certificate of Vaccination against smallpox is required by all persons entering the YAR. All visitors should also be inoculated against cholera both for their own protection in the YAR and also for their onward travel, e.g., through Jeddah. The Saudi Arabian authorities may impose other health requirements at short notice on travellers from the YAR, and visitors should check with the airline office before departing for Jeddah.

Travellers from Africa to the YAR must be in possession of an International Yellow Fever Vaccination Certificate. Visitors are also advised to obtain TAB (typhoid and paratyphoid) injections before entering the YAR. All the necessary vaccinations can be obtained in Sana'a or Taiz.

Customs

Currency: There is no limit to the amount of foreign currency which may be imported or exported.

Duty-free articles: Personal effects including a reasonable number of cigarettes, but no alcohol, provided Customs officials are satisfied that they are not for sale. Samples of no commercial value.

Articles liable to duty: Commercial samples of value may be imported under payment of a deposit which will be refunded upon re-export of the samples.

Prohibited articles: Alcohol, raw cotton, salt.

PRACTICAL INFORMATION FOR THE VISITOR

1. Currency

Monetary Unit – Yemeni riyal (YR), divided into 100 fils.

Notes – 1, 5, 10, 20, 50, 100 Yemeni riyals.

Coins – 5, 10, 25, 50 fils and 1 riyal.

Travellers' cheques and most foreign

currencies can be easily changed into Yemeni currency at banks in the YAR. Some hotels will cash travellers' cheques. It is difficult to dispose of Yemeni riyals outside the YAR.

Banking Hours:
0800–1200 Saturday to Wednesday
0800–1130 Thursday

The Central Bank of Yemen issues and controls currency, authorises foreign exchange transactions and grants import licences.

Domestic Banks in the YAR:

Central Bank
Liberation (Tahrir) Square, P.O. Box 59 and 206, Sana'a, ☎ 5216/7.
Gamal Abdul Nasser Street, P.O. Box 4758, Taiz, ☎ 2151.

The only Yemeni-owned commercial bank is the Yemen Bank of Reconstruction and Development which has its head office in Sana'a (Tahrir Square, ☎ 2311/2314), and branches at Hodeida, Taiz and several other towns.

Major Foreign Commercial Banks:

Arab Bank of Jordan
Liberation (Tahrir) Square, P.O. Box 1301, Sana'a, ☎ 5558 (also at Hodeida).

Bank of Credit and Commerce International, SA
P.O. Box 160, Sana'a, ☎ 2168.

British Bank of the Middle East
Gamal Abdul Nasser Street, P.O. Box 4886, Taiz, ☎ 2671/2937/2973, and 26 September Street, P.O. Box 3932, Hodeida, ☎ 2728.

Citibank
Zubein Road, P.O. Box 2133, Sana'a, ☎ 5796.

United Bank of Pakistan
Ali Abdul Mughi Street, P.O. Box 1295, Sana'a, ☎ 5012/3.

The Habib Bank (Pakistan) has a branch at Hodeida, and the *Banque de l'Indochine* has branches in Taiz and Hodeida.

2. Electricity Supply

220V AC 50Hz.
Plugs: 2-pin (bayonet).

3. Weights and Measures

The metric system is used for import purposes while in the market places a wide variety of local and often inexplicable weights and measures are still used.

4. Media

Television broadcasting began in 1975 in Sana'a. There is no commercial radio station but the government-controlled Sana'a Radio now accepts advertising.

Newspapers (daily):

Al-Thawra (Sana'a) and *Al-Goumhouriya* (Taiz). Both these papers are in Arabic and are government-owned.

There is no trade press in the YAR but a number of official magazines are published by government departments. Foreign magazines and journals may be bought in the YAR and the leading Egyptian and Lebanese weeklies are on sale in the main towns.

5. Medical Care

Medical facilities in the YAR are poor and often very basic. Chemists in the main towns are normally well stocked but visitors in need of further treatment should seek the advice of their embassy in Sana'a.

The capital, Sana'a, stands at 2,133m/7,000ft above sea level and visitors with a history of heart or lung complaints should avoid undue exertion while staying there.

Malaria is endemic in the Tihama (coastal) region and travellers visiting this region should be equipped with preventative drugs. Bilharzia is widespread and standing water should be avoided.

Visitors should avoid drinking untreated water and are advised to take with them appropriate remedies for gastric upsets.

6. Telephone, Telex and Postal Services

International telephone services between the YAR and the United States, United Kingdom and other major countries are available from 0800 to 2030 hours local time.

Telex messages may be sent from telex booths at the offices of Cable and Wireless Ltd in Sana'a, Hodeida and Taiz (see below). A number of local businesses, airlines, banks, etc., also have telex facilities, and telex messages may be sent between the main towns of Sana'a, Hodeida and Taiz.

Cable and Wireless Ltd can be located at the following addresses:

Sana'a: Gamal Abdul Nasser Street, ☎ 2139.

Hodeida: Alamnie Building, 26 September Street.

Taiz: Hayel Saeed Building, Aqaba Street, ☎ 2976.

All mail to and from the YAR should be sent by air. Exporters to the YAR should advise (by letter) consignees in the YAR of the despatch of goods to them by parcel post.

General Post Office, Liberation (Tahrir) Square, Sana'a, ☎ 2313.

7. Public Holidays

Fixed Holidays:

13 June	*Corrective Movement Anniversary*
26 September	*Revolution Day*
14 October	*PDRY National Day*

Muslim Holidays:

These follow the Muslim calendar and occur 10–12 days earlier every year. The dates of the Muslim holidays are approximate as they depend upon sightings of the moon, and may differ by one or two days from those given below. 1981 dates are:

18 January	*Prophet's Birthday*
31 July –2 August	*Eid el Fitr* end of *Ramadan*)
8–10 October	*Eid el Adha*

Business travellers are advised to avoid visiting the YAR during the month of *Ramadan* which ends with the *Eid el Fitr* holiday.

8. Time

GMT+3

9. Internal Transport

Air

There are flights between Sana'a, Hodeida and Taiz but schedules are variable.

Airline Offices in Sana'a:

Aeroflot	☎ 476704.
Air France	☎ 5834.
British Airways	☎ 2422.
Lufthansa	☎ 5072.
Pan Am	☎ 6677.
SAS	☎ 5072/3955.
Swissair	☎ 6677/8.
TWA	☎ 5530.
Yemen Airways	☎ 6677.

Road

A bus service links the three main cities but the more common form of transport is taxi or shared taxi. The cost of a seat is subject to bargaining and it is advisable to fix the fare before starting the journey.

Within the main towns, taxis can be hired for a single journey or by the hour, while shared taxis operate along fixed routes.

Self-drive cars are available for hire.

Traffic travels on the right-hand side of the road. An International Driving Licence is required.

10. Tipping

Tipping in the YAR is entirely optional. In view of the low wages a tip of YR1 is customary for any single job or service.

11. Social Customs

In general, the Yemen Arab Republic is a Muslim country which is fairly traditional. Alcohol is strictly forbidden for all Muslims although the foreign community is permitted a limited amount. Many Yemeni men chew a mildly narcotic leaf called qat in the afternoon while discussing business.

For further information, refer to page 12 under 'Muslim Social Customs'.

USEFUL ADDRESSES (GENERAL)

Embassies in Sana'a

France: Jamal Abdel Nasser Street, P.O. Box 1286.

West Germany: Republican Palace Street, P.O. Box 41, ☎ 2818/2901.

Japan: Al-Tareeq Al-Da-Ery Al-Safiyah Al-Gharbiyah, P.O. Box 817, ☎ 7330.

Netherlands: House of Abdullah Sofaan, near Old Radio Station, P.O. Box 463, ☎ 6234.

UK: 11/13 Republican Palace Street (Qasr al Jumhuriya), P.O. Box 1287, ☎ 2684/5714/2477/5428.

US: Beit Al-Halali, P.O. Box 1088, ☎ 5826/2790.

Other addresses

British Council, Sinan Abu Luhum Building, Bir el Azeb, Sana'a, ☎ 5023.

Immigration Office, 26 September Street, Sana'a, ☎ 2669 and Moses Gate (Bab Musa), Taiz, ☎ 2548.

BUSINESS INFORMATION

There are five main sectors of the economy of the Yemen Arab Republic which are of interest to foreign suppliers and investors: the development of the infrastructure, light industry, agricultural industries, mining and tourism.

The Government places a strong emphasis on the development of transport and communications and the main projects are concerned with road construction, electrification, airline development and water and sewage works for the urban centres. Food processing is also given a high priority as well as the construction of fishmeal plants and the manufacture of farm machinery. The new Sana'a industrial estate offers possibilities for foreign investment and as the country's airline network extends there will be a further expansion of the tourist industry which remains relatively underdeveloped.

The Yemen Arab Republic's earlier isolation from world trade means that few European trading houses are established there. A number of firms which were well established in Aden before 1967 now have branches in the Yemen Arab Republic. There are many commission agents but few have the expertise to specialise in a particular line of business. As the YAR imports from a large number of foreign countries it is often necessary to share a good agent with one or more competitors. Firms importing on their own account usually have a head office and retail outlet in Hodeida (the principal port) with retail branches in Sana'a and Taiz.

Most private businesses are based in Hodeida and Taiz while state enterprises and all the ministries and government agencies have their head offices in the capital, Sana'a. Business visitors should allow half a day's travel between any of these centres.

Import and Exchange Control Regulations

Imports originating in certain specified countries are banned, as well as the import of raw cotton, salt and alcohol. Import licences for goods which are also produced locally are often difficult to obtain.

Import licences are required for items normally handled by state trading organisations such as petroleum products and pharmaceuticals, and for firearms and ammunition. Import licences for pharmaceuticals require a prior certificate from the Ministry of Health.

Exchange control approval is obtained from the Central Bank of Yemen for all imports on letter of credit and collection basis. This is usually done through one of the commercial banks.

Business Hours

Government Offices:
0900–1330 Saturday to Thursday (variable)

Business Houses:
0800–1230
1600–1900 Saturday to Thursday

BUSINESS SERVICES

Insurance

Arab Commercial Enterprises, P.O. Box 2073, Sana'a, ☎ 6677/8.

USEFUL ADDRESSES (BUSINESS)

Chamber of Commerce, Bab al Yemen, P.O. Box 195, Sana'a, ☎ 5917.

Central Planning Organisation, 26 September Street, Sana'a, ☎ 5331/2.

Customs Office, Sana'a (South) Old Airport Road, Sana'a, ☎ 2878.

United Nations Development Programme, Zubeiri Street, Sana'a, ☎ 2703.

Chamber of Commerce, 26 September Street, P.O. Box 4029, Taiz, ☎ 2097.

Chamber of Commerce, Tahrir (Liberation) Square, P.O. Box 3370, Hodeida, ☎ 2604.

MAJOR CITY

Sana'a

Sana'a, the capital of the Yemen Arab Republic, stands at a height of over 2,135m/7,000ft above sea level. A unique feature of the town is that its buildings, both old and new, are built in the traditional architectural style with white decorated exterior walls and ornate arched windows. This harmony extends from private dwellings to government and commercial offices. A fine and accessible example of Yemeni architecture is the former palace of Dar al Hamd which is now a hotel. The Rawdah Palace, some 8km/5 miles from the centre has also been converted into a hotel and gives visitors the opportunity to inspect the fine architectural work at close hand.

Sana'a has over forty mosques – the great mosque of Aroua dates back to the seventh century – but these are rarely open to non-Muslims. A visit to the main *souk* or market, the Bab al-Yaman, is worthwhile. The *souk* is packed with tiny stalls selling a variety of antiques, curios and jewellery and the best time to go is on a weekday in the late afternoon.

Two places of interest outside Sana'a itself are the gardens and orchards of Hadda (5km/3 miles) where tourist facilities have been built, and the ghost town of Kawkaban with its white stone palace standing at a height of nearly 3,000m/9,846ft above sea level.

El Rahaba Airport is 3km/2 miles from the centre of Sana'a.

Hotels

Hotel accommodation in the Yemen Arab Republic is very limited and the standards of the different hotels vary enormously. Visitors should book accommodation well in advance of their visit, and are advised to confirm their bookings at regular intervals.

The hotels listed below are those which are most frequently used by foreign business visitors.

Hamd Palace, P.O. Box 2187, ☎ 5365.

Mocha, P.O. Box 533, ☎ 2402 (centrally located).

Rawdah Palace, ☎ 9201 (8km/5 miles from the town centre).

Sam City Hotel, P.O. Box 520, ☎ 6251/4 (centrally located).

APPENDICES

METRIC MEASURES AND EQUIVALENTS

Length

1 millimetre (mm)		=0·0394in
1 centimetre (cm)	=10mm	=0·3937in
1 metre (m)	=1000mm	=1·0936 yards
1 kilometre (km)	=1000m	=0·6214 mile

Surface or area

1 sq cm (cm^2)	=100mm^2	=0·1550sq in
1 sq metre (m^2)	=10000cm^2	=1·1960sq yds
1 hectare (ha)	=10000m^2	=2·4711 acres
1 sq km (km^2)	=100 hectares	=0·3861sq mile

Capacity

1 cu cm (cm^3)		=0·0610cu in
1 cu decimetre (dm^3)	=1000cm^3	=0·0353cu ft
1 cu metre (m^3)	=1000dm^3	=1·3079cu yds
1 litre (l)	=1dm^3	=0·2642 US gal
1 litre (l)		=0·2200 Imp gal
1 hectolitre (hl)	=100 litres	=2·8378 US bus
1 hectolitre (hl)		=2·7497 Imp bus

Weight

1 milligramme (mg)		=0·0154 grain
1 gramme (g)	=1000mg	=0·0353oz
1 kilogramme (kg)	=1000g	=2·2046lb
1 tonne (t)	=1000kg	=1·1023 short tons
1 tonne (t)		=0·9842 long tons

IMPERIAL MEASURES AND EQUIVALENTS

Length

1 inch (in)		=2·5400cm
1 foot (ft)	=12in	=0·3048m
1 yard (yd)	=3ft	=0·9144m
1 mile	=1760yd	=1·6093km

Surface or area

1 sq inch		=6·4516cm^2
1 sq yard	=9sq ft	=0·8361m^2
1 acre	=4840sq yd	=4046·86m^2
1 sq mile	=640 acres	=259·0 hectares

Capacity

1 cu inch		=16·387cm^3
1 cu yard	=27cu ft	=0·7646m^3

US dry measures

1 pint	=0·9689 Imp pt	=0·5506 litres

US liquid measures

1 pint	=0·8327Imp pt	=0·4732 litres
1 gallon	=8 pints	=3·7853 litres

Imperial liquid measures

1 pint	=1·0321 US pt	=0·5683 litres
1 gallon	=8 pints	=4·5461 litres

Weight (Avoirdupois)

1 ounce (oz)	=437·5 grains	=28·350g
1 pound (lb)	=16oz	=0·4536kg
1 short cwt	=100lb	=45·359kg
1 long cwt	=112lb	=50·802kg
1 short ton	=2000lb	=0·9072 tonnes
1 long ton	=2240lb	=1·0161 tonnes

CONVERSION TABLES

Length

centimetres	No.	inches	metres	No.	yards
2.540	**1**	0.394	0.914	**1**	1.094
5.080	**2**	0.787	1.829	**2**	2.187
7.620	**3**	1.181	2.743	**3**	3.281
10.160	**4**	1.575	3.658	**4**	4.374
12.700	**5**	1.969	4.572	**5**	5.468
15.240	**6**	2.362	5.486	**6**	6.562
17.780	**7**	2.756	6.401	**7**	7.655
20.320	**8**	3.150	7.315	**8**	8.749
22.860	**9**	3.543	8.230	**9**	9.843
25.400	**10**	3.937	9.144	**10**	10.936
50.800	**20**	7.874	18.288	**20**	21.872
76.200	**30**	11.811	27.432	**30**	32.808
101.600	**40**	15.748	36.576	**40**	43.745
127.000	**50**	19.685	45.720	**50**	54.681
152.400	**60**	23.622	54.864	**60**	65.617
177.800	**70**	27.559	64.008	**70**	76.553
203.200	**80**	31.496	73.152	**80**	87.489
228.600	**90**	35.433	82.296	**90**	98.425
254.000	**100**	39.370	91.440	**100**	109.361

kilometres	No.	miles	kilometres	No.	miles
1.609	**1**	0.621	32.187	**20**	12.427
3.219	**2**	1.243	48.281	**30**	18.641
4.828	**3**	1.864	64.374	**40**	24.854
6.437	**4**	2.485	80.468	**50**	31.068
8.047	**5**	3.107	96.562	**60**	37.282
9.656	**6**	3.728	112.655	**70**	43.495
11.266	**7**	4.350	128.749	**80**	49.709
12.875	**8**	4.971	144.842	**90**	55.922
14.484	**9**	5.592	160.936	**100**	62.136
16.094	**10**	6.214			

Area

sq. kilometres	No.	sq. miles	sq. kilometres	No.	sq. miles
2.590	**1**	0.386	51.800	**20**	7.722
5.180	**2**	0.772	77.699	**30**	11.583
7.770	**3**	1.158	103.598	**40**	15.444
10.360	**4**	1.544	129.498	**50**	19.306
12.950	**5**	1.931	155.397	**60**	23.167
15.540	**6**	2.317	181.297	**70**	27.028
18.130	**7**	2.703	207.196	**80**	30.889
20.720	**8**	3.089	233.096	**90**	34.750
23.310	**9**	3.475	258.995	**100**	38.611
25.900	**10**	3.861			

hectares	No.	acres
0.41	**1**	2.47
0.81	**2**	4.94
1.21	**3**	7.41
1.62	**4**	9.88
2.02	**5**	12.36
2.43	**6**	14.83
2.83	**7**	17.30
3.24	**8**	19.77
3.64	**9**	22.24
4.05	**10**	24.71
8.09	**20**	49.42
12.14	**30**	74.13
16.19	**40**	98.84
20.23	**50**	123.60
24.28	**60**	148.30
28.33	**70**	173.00
32.38	**80**	197.70
36.42	**90**	222.40
40.47	**100**	247.10

Capacity

litres	No.	Imperial pints
0.568	**1**	1.760
1.136	**2**	3.520
1.705	**3**	5.279
2.273	**4**	7.039
2.841	**5**	8.799
3.409	**6**	10.559
3.978	**7**	12.319
4.546	**8**	14.078
5.114	**9**	15.838
5.682	**10**	17.598
11.365	**20**	35.196
17.047	**30**	52.794
22.730	**40**	70.392
28.412	**50**	87.990
34.094	**60**	105.588
39.777	**70**	123.186
45.459	**80**	140.784
51.142	**90**	158.382
56.824	**100**	175.980

litres	No.	Imperial gallons
4.546	**1**	0.220
9.092	**2**	0.440
13.638	**3**	0.660
18.184	**4**	0.880
22.730	**5**	1.100
27.276	**6**	1.320
31.822	**7**	1.540
36.368	**8**	1.760
40.914	**9**	1.980
45.460	**10**	2.200
90.919	**20**	4.399
136.379	**30**	6.599
181.838	**40**	8.799
227.298	**50**	10.999
272.758	**60**	13.198
318.217	**70**	15.398
363.677	**80**	17.598
409.136	**90**	19.797
454.596	**100**	21.997

US gallons	No.	litres
0.264	**1**	3.785
0.528	**2**	7.571
0.793	**3**	11.356
1.057	**4**	15.141
1.321	**5**	18.927
1.585	**6**	22.712
1.849	**7**	26.497
2.113	**8**	30.282
2.378	**9**	34.068
2.642	**10**	37.853
5.284	**20**	75.706
7.925	**30**	113.559
10.567	**40**	151.412
13.209	**50**	189.265
15.851	**60**	227.118
18.493	**70**	264.971
21.134	**80**	302.824
23.776	**90**	340.678
26.418	**100**	378.531

US gallons	No.	Imperial gallons	US gallons	No.	Imperial gallons
1.201	**1**	0.833	24.019	**20**	16.654
2.402	**2**	1.665	36.028	**30**	24.980
3.603	**3**	2.498	48.038	**40**	33.307
4.804	**4**	3.331	60.047	**50**	41.634
6.005	**5**	4.163	72.057	**60**	49.961
7.206	**6**	4.996	84.066	**70**	58.287
8.407	**7**	5.829	96.076	**80**	66.614
9.608	**8**	6.661	108.085	**90**	74.941
10.809	**9**	7.494	120.095	**100**	83.267
12.010	**10**	8.327			

Weight

kilogrammes	No.	pounds	tonnes	No.	long tons
0.454	**1**	2.205	1.016	**1**	0.984
0.907	**2**	4.409	2.032	**2**	1.968
1.361	**3**	6.614	3.048	**3**	2.953
1.814	**4**	8.818	4.064	**4**	3.937
2.268	**5**	11.023	5.080	**5**	4.921
2.722	**6**	13.228	6.096	**6**	5.905
3.175	**7**	15.432	7.112	**7**	6.889
3.629	**8**	17.637	8.128	**8**	7.874
4.082	**9**	19.842	9.144	**9**	8.858
4.536	**10**	22.046	10.161	**10**	9.842
9.072	**20**	44.092	20.321	**20**	19.684
13.608	**30**	66.139	30.482	**30**	29.526
18.144	**40**	88.185	40.642	**40**	39.368
22.680	**50**	110.231	50.803	**50**	49.211
27.216	**60**	132.277	60.963	**60**	59.053
31.751	**70**	154.324	71.124	**70**	68.895
36.287	**80**	176.370	81.284	**80**	78.737
40.823	**90**	198.416	91.445	**90**	88.579
45.359	**100**	220.462	101.605	**100**	98.421

Volume

cu. metres	No.	cu. yards	cu. metres	No.	cu. yards
0.765	**1**	1.308	7.646	**10**	13.080
1.529	**2**	2.616	15.291	**20**	26.159
2.294	**3**	3.924	22.937	**30**	39.239
3.058	**4**	5.232	30.582	**40**	52.318
3.823	**5**	6.540	38.228	**50**	65.398
4.587	**6**	7.848	45.873	**60**	78.477
5.352	**7**	9.156	53.519	**70**	91.557
6.116	**8**	10.464	61.164	**80**	104.636
6.881	**9**	11.772	68.810	**90**	117.716
			76.455	**100**	130.795

TEMPERATURES

°C	No.	°F	°C	No.	°F	°C	No.	°F
−17·8	**0**	+32·0	4·4	**40**	104·0	26·7	**80**	176·0
17·2	**1**	33·8	5·0	**41**	105·8	27·2	**81**	177·8
16·7	**2**	35·6	5·6	**42**	107·6	27·8	**82**	179·6
16·1	**3**	37·4	6·1	**43**	109·4	28·3	**83**	181·4
15·6	**4**	39·2	6·7	**44**	111·2	28·9	**84**	183·2
15·0	**5**	41·0	7·2	**45**	113·0	29·4	**85**	185·0
14·4	**6**	42·8	7·8	**46**	114·8	30·0	**86**	186·8
13·9	**7**	44·6	8·3	**47**	116·6	30·6	**87**	188·6
13·3	**8**	46·4	8·9	**48**	118·4	31·1	**88**	190·4
12·8	**9**	48·2	9·4	**49**	120·2	31·7	**89**	192·2
12·2	**10**	50·0	10·0	**50**	122·0	32·2	**90**	194·0
11·7	**11**	51·8	10·6	**51**	123·8	32·8	**91**	195·8
11·1	**12**	53·6	11·1	**52**	125·6	33·3	**92**	197·6
10·6	**13**	55·4	11·7	**53**	127·4	33·9	**93**	199·4
10·0	**14**	57·2	12·2	**54**	129·2	34·4	**94**	201·2
9·4	**15**	59·0	12·8	**55**	131·0	35·0	**95**	203·0
8·9	**16**	60·8	13·3	**56**	132·8	35·6	**96**	204·8
8·3	**17**	62·6	13·9	**57**	134·6	36·1	**97**	206·6
7·8	**18**	64·4	14·4	**58**	136·4	36·7	**98**	208·4
7·2	**19**	66·2	15·0	**59**	138·2	36·9	**98·4**	209·1
6·7	**20**	68·0	15·6	**60**	140·0	37·2	**99**	210·2
6·1	**21**	69·8	16·1	**61**	141·8	37·8	**100**	212·0
5·6	**22**	71·6	16·7	**62**	143·6	38·3	**101**	213·8
5·0	**23**	73·4	17·2	**63**	145·4	38·9	**102**	215·6
4·4	**24**	75·2	17·8	**64**	147·2	39·4	**103**	217·4
3·9	**25**	77·0	18·3	**65**	149·0	40·0	**104**	219·2
3·3	**26**	78·8	18·9	**66**	150·8	40·6	**105**	221·0
2·8	**27**	80·6	19·4	**67**	152·6	41·1	**106**	222·8
2·2	**28**	82·4	20·0	**68**	154·4	41·7	**107**	224·6
1·7	**29**	84·2	20·6	**69**	156·2	42·2	**108**	226·4
1·1	**30**	86·0	21·1	**70**	158·0	42·8	**109**	228·2
0·6	**31**	87·8	21·7	**71**	159·8	43·3	**110**	230·0
0·0	**32**	89·6	22·2	**72**	161·6	43·9	**111**	231·8
+0·6	**33**	91·4	22·8	**73**	163·4	44·4	**112**	233·6
1·1	**34**	93·2	23·3	**74**	165·2	65·6	**150**	302·0
1·7	**35**	95·0	23·9	**75**	167·0	93·3	**200**	392·0
2·2	**36**	96·8	24·4	**76**	168·8	100·0	**212**	413·6
2·8	**37**	98·6	25·0	**77**	170·6	121·1	**250**	482·0
3·3	**38**	100·4	25·6	**78**	172·4	537·8	**1000**	1832·0
3·9	**39**	102·2	26·1	**79**	174·2	1648·9	**3000**	5432·0

WORLD TIME ZONES

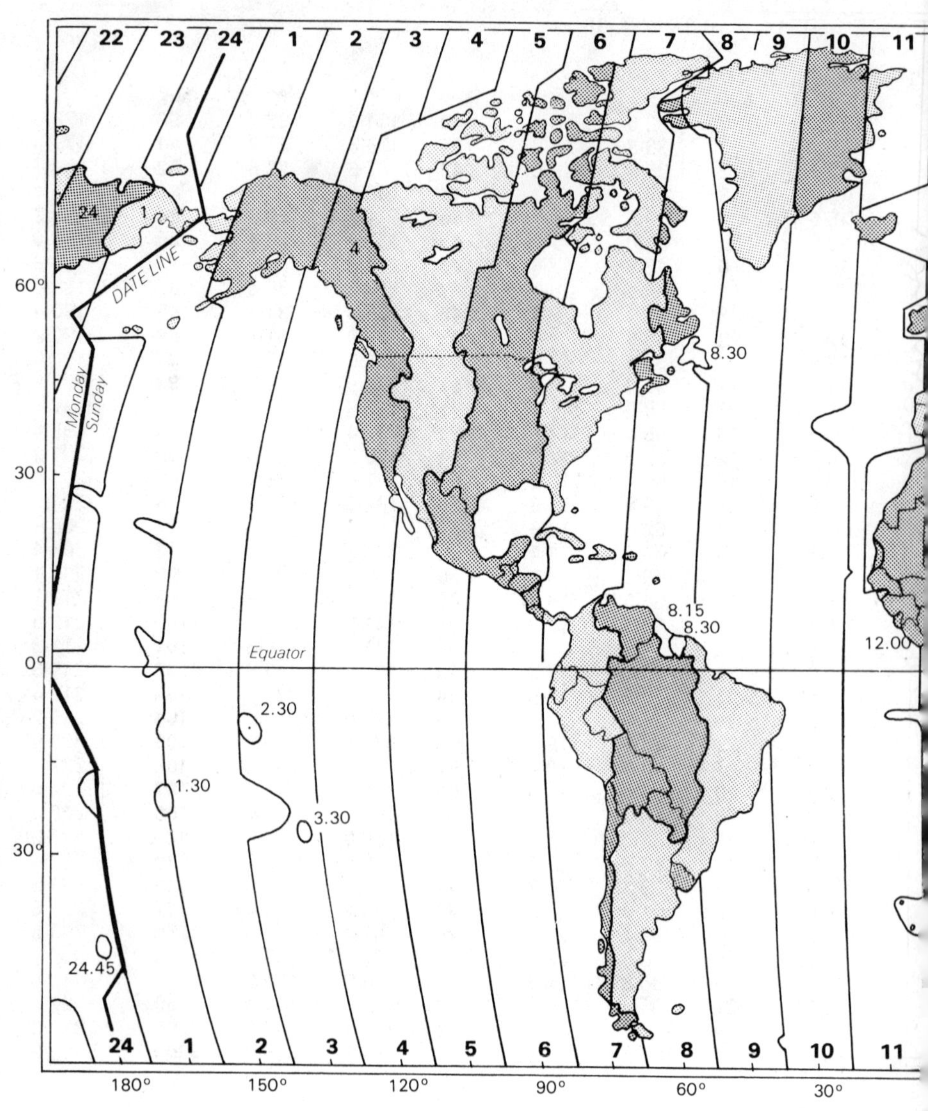

This map shows the Standard Times observed in the 24 time zones of the world as compared with 1200 hours (midday) Greenwich Mean Time. Daylight Saving Time, usually one hour ahead of local Standard Time, is not shown on this map.

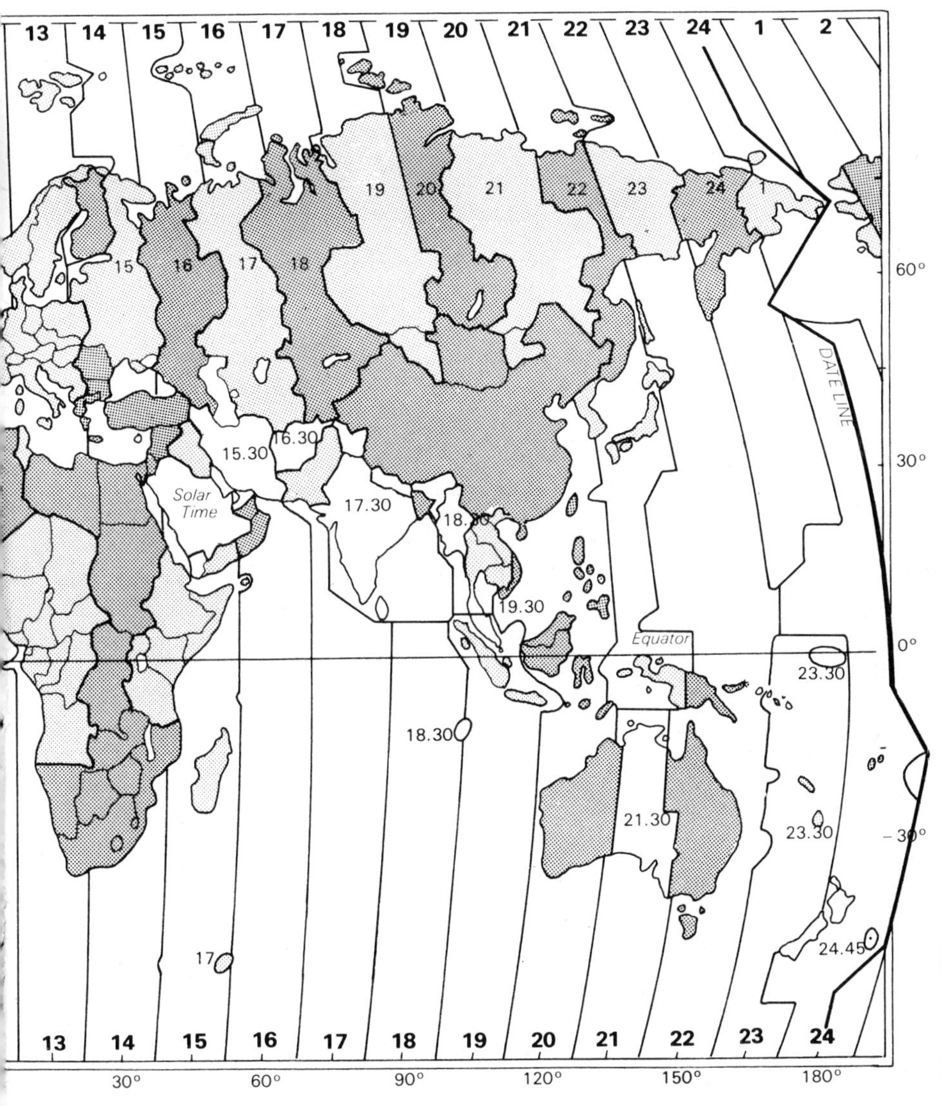

INDEX TO PLACES